DATE DUE

~~JY 28 99~~		
~~Mar 13~~		
DE 17 01		
~~DE 10 02~~		
~~DE 21 02~~		

DEMCO 38-296

SEX, PREFERENCE, AND FAMILY

SEX, PREFERENCE, AND FAMILY

ESSAYS ON LAW AND NATURE

Edited by

DAVID M. ESTLUND and
MARTHA C. NUSSBAUM

New York   Oxford

OXFORD UNIVERSITY PRESS

1997

Oxford University Press

Oxford   New York
Athens   Auckland   Bangkok   Bogotá   Bombay
Buenos Aires   Calcutta   Cape Town   Dar es Salaam   Delhi
Florence   Hong Kong   Istanbul   Karachi
Kuala Lumpur   Madras   Madrid   Melbourne
Mexico City   Nairobi   Paris   Singapore
Taipei   Tokyo   Toronto

and associated companies in
Berlin   Ibadan

Copyright © 1997 by Oxford University Press, Inc.

Published by Oxford University Press, Inc.
198 Madison Avenue, New York, New York 10016

Oxford is a registered trademark of Oxford University Press, Inc.

Library of Congress Cataloging-in-Publication Data
Sex, preference, and family: essays on law and nature
edited by David M. Estlund and Martha C. Nussbaum
p. cm.   Includes bibliographical references and index.
ISBN 0-19-509894-3
1. Persons (Law).   2. Sex and law.   3. Domestic relations.   4. Natural law.
I. Estlund, David M.   II. Nussbaum, Martha Craven, 1947–   III. Title: Laws and nature.
K625.L39   1996
346.01'5
[342.615]—DC20   95-49825

1 3 5 7 9 8 6 4 2

Printed in the United States of America
on acid-free paper

Preface

And Venus joined the bodies of lovers in the woods. For each woman was made receptive either by mutual desire or by the violent force and overwhelming sexual energy of the male, or by a price—acorns and arbute-berries, or choice pears.

LUCRETIUS, On The Nature of Things

Not only among animals domesticated and reared by us but also among the other species there are those which appear to have self-restraint. When the Egyptian crocodile . . . is inclined to copulate, he diverts the female to the bank and turns her over, it being natural to approach her when she is lying on her back. After copulating, he turns her over with his forearms. But when she senses the copulation and the impregnation, she becomes malicious in purpose and indicates that she desires copulation once more, displaying a harlot-like affection and assuming the usual position for copulation. So he immediately comes to ascertain, either by scent or by other means, whether the invitation is genuine or merely pretense. By nature he is alert to hidden things. When the intent of the action is truly established by their looking into each other's eyes, he claws her guts and consumes them, for they are tender. And unhindered by armored skin or hard and pointed spines, he tears her flesh apart. But enough about self-restraint.

PHILO, On Animals

"How do you mean, Hieron? Are you telling me that erotic passion for young men does not grow by nature in a ruler, as it does in other people? How is it then that you are in love with Dailochos?" "My erotic passion for Dailochos is for what human nature perhaps compels us to want from the beautiful, but I have a very strong desire to attain the object of my passion only with his love and consent."

XENOPHON, Hieron

We know that law and custom influence the shape of our lives in many ways. We are members of a legal and political order, and we participate in that order not only when we actively function as citizens but also when we enjoy the security and freedom from care that only a system of law can provide. And yet we frequently imagine that we are also inhabitants of a prelegal realm of "nature," which constrains and guides our choices in a multitude of ways. We imagine that we come into the world as bearers of a "human nature," which leads us to want certain things and to avoid others, and that this "nature," though it can be either encouraged or suppressed by laws and social forces, is not fundamentally shaped or altered by them. We are especially likely to think of "nature" and the "natural" when we think of the intimately personal and (at least apparently) private parts of our lives: our sexual desires and activities, our love and personal commitment, our membership in families. All of this is easily imagined as forming a prepolitical domain of the "natural" or "personal," which law may regulate, but does not help to create.

And yet this idea of a distinction between nature and law, between the personal and the political, is much more difficult to maintain than one might at first suppose. Consider the three quotations above, all from ancient philosophical sources, all lying close to the origins of the Western philosophical tradition. They use the nature/law distinction; and yet, in the process of elaborating it, they give us reason to call it into question. Lucretius tries to imagine a time when human beings existed outside of law and society "in the manner of the beasts." He indicates, not surprisingly, that even in this prelegal condition they would still desire and choose sexual activity—that this is part of the "nature" that law will later restrict, but not modify. Yet the detailed description he gives us is fascinating for the way in which it casts doubt on some aspects of the nature/law distinction. On the one hand, the account of prelegal human sexuality leaves out a huge amount of what has been thought of as the domain of the private and personal: the family, the male-dominated household, the subordination of women. All this Lucretius intuits as an artifact of custom and law, not something that can be coherently imagined without laws and institutions. He cannot imagine women in the state of nature agreeing to sex unless they get something out of it, whether a price or some sexual pleasure of their own—unless, of course, they are simply raped. In his view, the dependence and domestic submission of women is thoroughly unnatural and awaits the creation of complex forms of political life.[1] As he later shows, it is only the transition to settled agricultural life and the need for male protection of offspring that give rise to the patriarchal family in its current form.

On the other hand, Lucretius's perceptive account of human nature allegedly stripped bare of law seems to have difficulties of its own in getting down to a prelegal bedrock of animal-like human nature. Even Lucretius, who acknowledges the ubiquity of law in constituting what we now think of as nature and the natural, cannot imagine human beings having sex without imagining something like a market, in which women trade their sexual favors for "acorns and arbute-berries, or choice pears." Could this market in pears have existed without some quasi-legal regulation, however unwritten and informal? When we follow out the fantasy, we find ourselves asking how the bargaining process took place, how men detected fraudulent offers, how they dealt with someone who passed off a rotten pear as a choice pear, how women coordinated their bargaining strategies, and so forth. As a strong champion of the view that women have sexual pleasure,[2] Lucretius allows that the market mechanism may be supplemented by consensual unions (as well as by rape). But insofar as he introduces the fruit market, in a form that seems to cry out for structure and rule, he makes us wonder how effectively he has done away with law. (And are we even sure that the vestiges of law and rule had no effect at all on the structure of sexual desire itself, that women did not internalize the man's decisive command over arbute berries as part of what they found sexually desirable, that men did not start dreaming that a future mate might be a "one-pear woman" or a "five-pear woman"?) Maybe even in our hypothetical quasi-animal state our conduct is not as free from institutional regulation and shaping as we might at first suppose.

Philo appeals to the animal kingdom to show that male control over female sexuality is grounded in nature. When we look at the crocodile world, we find support for the idea that there is one natural position for intercourse (did the crocodiles get it from the missionaries or the missionaries from the crocodiles?[3]), that it is natural for males to initiate and control sexual activity, that reproduction is the one natural purpose for sex, that it is natural for females to be sexually rapacious and for males to keep them in line, by bloody means if necessary. But, of course, the reader finds in the very concocted nature of Philo's account of crocodiles many reasons to call the whole set of claims into question. It is clear that he has been none-too-neutral an observer or reporter of animal life and has projected onto the prepolitical domain, customs and laws of his own Jewish/Greek milieu. Because we stand at a distance from Philo, we can easily see this dynamic operating, when we might be inclined to miss it in the operations of biologists of our own era.[4] Again, what we see as nature and prelaw may actually be heavily shaped by laws, customs, and institutions.

Consider, finally, the passage from Xenophon, a conversation about erotic passion between the poet Simonides and the ruler Hieron, both men being treated by the philosopher Xenophon as high-minded, morally sensitive figures. The two men discuss human nature and its compulsions, and Hieron insists that his own strong premoral desire for the beautiful young man is suitably constrained by social morality: though he is extremely passionate about him, he will hold off until he has consent and (friendly) love. So far, so clear: sexual desire for a beautiful object is given in nature, and social morality, custom, and law simply constrain its expression in various ways. But consider Hieron's views about nature, which both his interlocutor and the author appear to find unremarkable.[5] The view is that human nature compels a man to want sex with beautiful young men. This desire, of course, is one that many societies, and a large part of our own, consider to be unnatural, indeed a salient case of the unnatural. The striking variation in ideas of what lies in "nature," behind the social and customary realm, does not exactly show us that there is no such realm or that it, too, is shaped by social and legal forces. But it does get us to raise those questions. If what Hieron and Xenophon think is most paradigmatically natural is what we frequently think of as paradigmatically unnatural in sex, maybe the whole idea of the "natural" deserves our critical scrutiny. Maybe there's more custom and law in nature than we usually think.

The papers in this volume reexamine the relationship between nature and law, the "personal" and the "political." Some make general arguments about the relationship between biology and society, examining the oft-heard idea that many forms of human interaction and desire are "socially constructed." Others focus on specific areas of human life that have frequently been thought to be "natural" rather than socially shaped and investigate them with these concepts in mind. Two such areas are sexuality—including sexual behavior, sexual orientation and object choice, and the role of pornography in shaping sexuality—and the family—frequently seen as a sphere of intimate personal love existing prior to and outside of the political domain. Many of the papers not only scrutinize the role of laws and institutions in shaping these aspects of our lives but also ask normative questions about how law should operate in order to address these parts of human life in the most appropriate way. They bring to the current legal-political debate the insights of a variety of disciplines—

above all, philosophy, political science, and legal theory, but also psychology, sociology, and anthropology.

Our four sections contain a good deal of overlapping discussion. The general treatments of sexuality and social construction in Sections I and II are closely connected to the concrete arguments about sexual preference and family presented in Sections III and IV. In some cases, the authors in the earlier section illustrate their theses using the family and sexual orientation as examples, and some authors in the later sections raise general theoretical questions about sex and social construction.

Our critical discussions of the papers are more extensive than the usual introduction; we have therefore placed them after the papers in the two groups.

The book grew out of a conference held at Brown University, on February 5 and 6, 1993. For financial assistance with that conference, the editors are grateful to the C. V. Starr Lectureships Fund, Departments of Philosophy and Political Science, the Pembroke Center, the Wayland Collegium, and the Provost and Dean of the Faculty, all at Brown. For other help with the conference, thanks to Victor Caston, James Dreier, Jane Sanchez, and Eleanor Thum. Finally, for his unflagging work preparing the excellent index, many thanks to Ross Davies.

Notes

1. For Rousseau's version of this story, see *Discourse on the Origin of Inequality*, in *First and Second Discourses*, trans. Roger D. and Judith R. Masters (New York: St. Martin's, 1964), pp. 135, 216. See also the good discussion in Susan Moller Okin, *Women in Western Political Thought* (Princeton: Princeton University Press, 1979), pp. 108 ff. Rousseau follows Lucretius's account when he holds that in the state of nature people lived nomadic lives without settled family structures and that sex would take place through chance encounters. Sex was just an animal appetite, readily satisfied by any willing partner. Children were raised by women alone, and males had no reason to care for their offspring.

2. See Book IV, and the discussion in Nussbaum, *The Therapy of Desire* (Princeton: Princeton University Press, 1994), ch. 5.

3. I owe this question to the late John J. Winkler, in his memorable discussion of the Philo passage in *The Constraints of Desire: The Anthropology of Sex and Gender in Greece* (New York: Routledge, 1990).

4. For a powerful argument that male primatologists have been guilty of similar projecting in their descriptions of the sexuality of primate species, see Sarah Hardy, also F. de Waal's account of the society of the bonoboes in "Bonobo Sex and Society," *Scientific American* (March 1995): 82–88.

5. See the discussion of this passage in Kenneth Dover, *Greek Homosexuality*, 2d ed. (Cambridge, Mass.: 2d ed., 1986), p. 61. The young man's love is *philia*, not *eros*. "Empathy, Polyandry, and the Myth of the Coy Female," in *Feminist Approaches to Science*, ed. R. Bleier (New York: Teacher's College Press, 1991), pp. 119–46.

Contents

Part IV Family

SEX, PREFERENCE, AND FAMILY

Part I

SEX, PREFERENCE,
AND FAMILY

1

The Social Construction
and Reconstruction of Care

Michele M. Moody-Adams

THE IMPORTANCE OF THE PUBLIC HOUSEHOLD

On a recent anniversary of the 1973 decision in *Roe v. Wade*, a fundamentalist Christian church in a small Midwestern city displayed the following message: "Thinking abortion? First visit our pastor. He cares." This message suggests a good deal of the ambiguity in contemporary debates, not only about abortion but also about "family values," by not saying for what, for whom, and in what form the pastor "cares." That ambiguity raises important questions about how care for children and families might be supplemented by agencies outside the domestic household—most notably, voluntary private assistance or the workings of what Daniel Bell has called the public household. The expansion of the public household—the management, through the political process, of state revenues and expenditures to provide for public needs and wants—is one of the most important twentieth-century developments in liberal democracies. Bell contends that this development challenges the traditional, dichotomous understanding of the mechanisms by which citizens of liberal democracies provide for their needs and wants since the public household has assumed an importance rivaling that of the domestic household on the one hand and the market economy on the other (Bell, 1976:220–27). This expansion has been accompanied by an enlargement of the liberal democratic conception of public goods (once confined to goods like national defense and public highways), which is now commonly understood to extend to complex schemes of benefits like unemployment insurance, social security, and a variety of income supports.

To be sure, there has been resistance to these developments. Some consider the revenues required to support such schemes to be inimical to liberty (Nozick, 1974). Others believe that some elements of these schemes encourage traits of character incompatible with the individual "initiative" that allegedly fuels socially beneficial economic activity in liberal societies. Yet such resistance has failed to discredit completely the expansion of the public household. Even where the notion of individual responsibility for well-being exercises an almost magical hold on the political imagination, it is still generally assumed that the provision of needs arising from certain misfortunes and, especially, from undeserved vulnerability is at least in part a common problem. Recent debates in public forums in the United States have finally taken seriously the *social* importance of each citizen's vulnerability to sickness and injury. Even vigorous opponents of health care reform have had to discuss the possibility that general access to health care might be a public good.

Yet the social task of caring for the vulnerable complicates the relationship between familiar liberal democratic mechanisms for the provision of needs and wants. Moreover, it does so in ways that profoundly unsettle central components of the self-conception of American liberal democracy. The American debate about health care, for instance, has largely been a debate about the appropriate boundaries between the market and the public household; solutions to the difficulties of those who are most vulnerable to the vicissitudes of the market (the uninsured working poor, the unemployed, and underinsured victims of catastrophic injury or illness) may challenge longstanding assumptions about the efficiency and fairness of American enterprise. In a similar manner, the extraordinary economic vulnerability of women and children—who currently make up the majority of the American poor—has generated scrutiny of the boundaries between the market and the domestic household (Sidel, 1992; Polakow, 1993). Such scrutiny exposes the myopic inattention to economic fact informing a potent American myth, according to which individual economic well-being simply requires self-reliant, self-sacrificing, "stable" two-parent families who "work hard and play by the rules." Contemporary social critics afflicted with this myopia assume that most of the vulnerability of women and children is due principally, if not entirely, to failures of individual responsibility. But such appeals ignore the process by which developments in the market, and in the law underwriting it, have transformed restrictions on "women's work" into questionable social policy. Occupational segregation, disparity in wages between men and women (often in the same occupations), and continued discrimination in employment are important instances of the flawed social policy that has resulted. Thus familiar debates about equal pay for equal work, family leave, and child care challenge the boundary between domestic goods and services, which cannot be "valued" since they are not exchanged on the market, and marketable goods and services, whose value is measured by relative price (Okin, 1989; Kemp, 1994).[1] The distress of women and children displaced by separation, divorce, and inadequate child-support policies—as well as by the structural decline in regional economies that threatens stable and unstable families alike—is likely to generate more vehement challenges to conventional boundaries between the domestic household and the market.

But many liberal democracies have recognized that the task of caring for their most vulnerable citizens— principally, of course, their children—requires a further rethinking of conventional boundaries. More precisely, they recognize the importance of accepting economic and moral continuities between the domestic household and the public household: important elements of care for *all* children must be treated as public goods, to be provided through judicious use of the mechanisms of the public household. To be sure, principles basic to liberal democracy give individual families the primary responsibility to provide for the material and psychological well-being of children, in a manner consistent both with personal liberty (especially as liberty is understood in America) and with the demands of socialization. Yet the many liberal societies that treat social investment in care for children as both a public *and* a private concern—through public support for day care, mandatory (often paid) child-care leave, family income support, and more—show that defensible visions of the liberal democratic family are compatible with reliance on the mechanisms of the public household. American social thinkers sometimes assume that such reliance is antithetical to the economically independent, morally self-reliant family allegedly central to American well-being; such thinkers contend, in effect, that the best social investment in children is the private investment of their individual families. But some historians of American family life have begun to challenge the accuracy of the assumptions underlying such claims. Thus, for instance, Stephanie Coontz compellingly argues that the family types commonly celebrated as ideals of American economic self-reliance—the nineteenth-century frontier family and the suburban family of the 1950s—may have been more heavily subsidized by government programs than any other families in American history (Coontz, 1992:68–92).

There will be resistance to Coontz's characterization of the initiatives that worked to support the relevant families as, in fact, government subsidies to families.[2] But that is surely what they were; resistance to the characterization no doubt rests on the curious—if influential—belief that such subsidies must carry some social stigma if they are not to be destructive of moral character. Nor should we be surprised by the widespread readiness to rely on such formal public mechanisms of social support for families in periods of rapid social, economic, and technological change. In periods of rapid change, continuity between the efforts of the domestic and public households is likely to be crucial to the stability of both. I do not wish to defend the terms on which this continuity was actually established in the periods covered in Coontz's study. Yet the success of families thus supported provides important lessons for contemporary liberal democracies, where internal stability is constantly challenged by scientific and technological change, periodic economic upheaval and long-term structural economic change, and the social consequences of internal migration and increased immigration. In such conditions, a collective resolve to use the mechanisms of the public household to strengthen domestic households will prove central to the stability of democratic institutions. Of course, some will object that, however well-intentioned, these mechanisms threaten the liberty and autonomy of families. On the other hand, as John Stuart Mill might have argued, the danger of internal dissolution posed by disaffected and poorly socialized children—a danger exacerbated by continued inaction of the public household—may prove as great a threat to personal liberty as external attack from a foreign power (Mill, 1859). When the public household is responsibly controlled by free and open exchange in the political process, it not only poses no threat to the liberty and autonomy of the family, it underwrites the successful performance of each individual family's caretaking tasks. Reasonable and defensible family policy simply must treat central aspects of care for every child as public goods at least as important as national defense and public highways.

THE FAMILY AS A SOCIAL INSTITUTION

I have claimed that domestic households in contemporary liberal democracies can properly provide for the material and psychological well-being of children only when the public household helps to create the kind of environment in which families can flourish. But this claim constitutes a serious challenge to the conception of caring for children that is central to contemporary American political culture. On that conception, the most reasonable and efficient form of social investment in children is *primarily* private investment by their individual families, and the mechanisms of the public household are to be used—if at all—as a last (and generally stigmatized) resort for families that are for some reason unable to make the necessary private investment. In challenging this view, I am attempting to enlarge the American conception of public goods so that it *explicitly* includes the protection of children against undeserved vulnerability and misfortune. Current American family policy is largely implicit in the complex legal regulations that govern divorce and custody cases, inheritance and tax law, the structure of employment and unemployment, as well as insurance and social security police (Glendon, 1987:135). But in order to fully express the social value of raising children to be happy and productive citizens, it is necessary to take seriously the undeserved vulnerability of children. This, in turn, demands an explicit and coherent family policy that represents a readiness to responsibly expand public investment in protecting every child against undeserved vulnerability.

My challenge appeals in part, as I have suggested, to the character of those social and economic institutions that are central to liberal democracy—and in particular, to their tendency to change rapidly. In this respect, my view is an important consequence of accepting that the family is indeed a basic *social* institution. Many failings of American social policy concerning children—most fundamentally, the lack of an explicit and coherent national family policy—follow from inattention to this basic fact. An appropriate understanding of this fact involves, first of all, a commitment to a version of the "social constructionist" thesis, in this instance, to the moderate claim that the family is partly, if not principally, a product of social conventions. But, second, this moderate social constructionism about the family implies that there are important economic, social, and moral continuities between families and the societies that contain them. Moreover, it accepts that changes in important elements of the social conventions governing families cannot help but affect the structure and stability of these families. To be sure, basic biological processes of parenthood have helped determine the general character of families. No defensible version of the social constructionist position can ignore this fact—although advances in the technological enhancement of reproduction, such as egg donation and embryo transfer, may eventually challenge our conventional understanding of biological parenthood (Moody-Adams, 1991:175, 180–81). Yet even the unmodified biology of parenthood does not infallibly determine a particular family form as more "natural" than any other. Thinkers like David Hume, who insist that the family is a "natural society" bound together by natural inclination, readily acknowledge that families are also structured all around by social artifice. Importantly, in Hume's view, the most important such artifices are the "rules of justice" that govern promise keeping, contracts, and property (Hume, 1739:484–526). But Hume also insisted that many components of the moral regulations that govern families—regulations defining the nature of incest or the requirement of "chastity and modesty in women"—were also the product of artifice and, hence, might vary or cease to exist in response to varying social circumstances (Hume, 1739:579–87; 1777:324–43).

It is in principle possible, of course, that "natural" phenomena beyond the biogenetic processes of parenthood are relevant to the structure of the family. Yet many of the most concerted attempts to establish particular instances of such phenomena have been remarkably unsuccessful. Thus, for instance, the alleged discovery of a powerful instinctual attachment of a newborn baby to its birth mother, and subsequent claims that this attachment is the primary social bond on which all other social relations must be based, have been shown to be radically underdetermined by all available evidence (Eyer, 1992). The more richly textured model of classical Freudian theory focuses on the internal psychological dynamics of a set of family dramas that are allegedly scripted by biology and instinct. But claims about the role of biology in structuring these dramas—and particularly about women's "maternal instincts"—are, once again, largely speculative and clearly underdetermined by available evidence (Chodorow, 1978). The questionable empirical credentials of these familiar attempts to challenge the social constructionist account of the family are important in this context for two main reasons. First, such claims are often invoked in arguments with far-reaching, and sometimes distressing, social implications. Until quite recently, for instance, mothers were often told that returning to work prior to a child's first birthday would irreparably damage the child's chances for successful socialization—whether or not the financial well-being of the family depended on the mother's earnings. In such cases, dangerously speculative conclusions have been used to make the responsibilities of caring for children even more difficult than they normally would have been. But second, and perhaps more important, all such speculations tend to encourage an excessive preoccupation with the internal dynamics of families (whether or not they are treated as natural in origin) at the expense of much-needed attention to the social and economic environments in which families must attempt to carry out their basic social functions.

This emphasis on internal dynamics is especially dangerous when it results in artificially narrow explanations of the complex difficulties experienced by families whose children must make choices in a social environment that families cannot always control. Even the most thoughtful social theorists can be tempted to offer such narrow explanations. For instance, everything from falling S.A.T. scores to the rise in violent crime has been all too easily attributed to a "breakdown in the traditional family structure."[3] Yet both of these phenomena are at least partly the result of a decline in the genuine social importance of two virtues once given at least lip service in public life: the worth attached to settling disputes peacefully and the worth attached to hard work. I cannot undertake here a careful assessment of research that purports to show otherwise, but it is surely folly to suggest that the widespread celebration of material possessions detached from the pursuit of honest work, the glorification of violence on television and in movies, and the ready availability of guns on the streets and in schools would have no significant effect on the choices that children make. Even with regard to choices likely to be made by adults, the influence of advertisements is clear; this was explicitly acknowledged in the late 1960s and early 1970s when the decision was finally made to ban cigarette advertising from television and radio. Equally important, social theorists have long noted the success of American advertising (as well as some television and movies) in appealing directly to the child, bypassing parental authority in order to shape the child as a consumer (Bell, 1976:67–70; Lasch, 1977, 1978; Coontz, 1992:171–78). The notion that the break-down of the traditional family structure is the principal cause of the vast social difficulties of contemporary American children simply masks a basic truth: certain kinds of changes in families are symptoms of still deeper social disruptions.

But appealing to family breakdown provides an equally impoverished account of the economic decline of a fairly large group of American children. The tendency to offer such an explanation, of course, reflects the notion—a commonplace of liberal philosophy—that the family is essentially a private buffer against the vicissitudes of the market. Yet families register the effects of economic decline and distress: the strain of continued membership in economically marginal positions, for instance, eventually takes a toll on the structure and well-being of families (Moody-Adams, 1992–93:257–58; cf. Rawls, 1971:440). To be fair, some contemporary theorists who favor the family-breakdown account are willing to acknowledge such facts. Barbara Dafoe Whitehead, for example, admits that economic forces "significantly affect marriage related behavior." Whitehead is particularly concerned that the loss of high-paying jobs for those without college degrees, and the virtual disappearance of stable jobs from urban neighborhoods, cannot but influence the willingness of young men living in urban neighborhoods to form lasting unions (Whitehead, 1993:71). Yet given the force of such considerations, it is surely beside the point to argue, as William Galston does, that "the best antipoverty program for children is a stable intact family" (Galston, 1991:284).[4] Recognizing the importance of structural economic changes need not prevent one from acknowledging the merits of arguments in favor of placing more obstacles in the way of divorce for parents with children (Galston, 1991; Whitehead, 1993; Glendon, 1987); the well-known economic vulnerability of women and children after divorce makes such arguments particularly compelling. However, to concentrate on reforming divorce law in order to make *individual* children less badly off ignores the underlying forces that tend to leave divorced women economically worse off than their former spouses—particularly in those cases where the male spouse has abandoned his family. Such efforts fail to confront the social and economic stresses that have led to higher divorce rates in the first place. Family policy addressed primarily to private investment in children overlooks the need to assist families in their search for the means necessary to make that private investment.

My conception thus challenges policy that focuses on private investment in children to the virtual exclusion of any widespread, nonstigmatized supporting investment by the public household. The weakness of such policy is underscored by its past failures, the most glaring evidence of which is the increasing child poverty in America. In the early 1990s, approximately one in five American children, and one in four under the age of six, lived in families with incomes below the poverty line. It is estimated, still further, that somewhere between eight and ten million American children lack health care insurance (Minow and Weissbourd, 1993; cf. Sidel, 1992).

There is no small irony in these developments: child poverty soared in the relative "boom" years of the 1980s (to a rate higher than any since the mid 1960s) and the rate of childhood poverty continued to grow while poverty levels for the other most vulnerable segment of the population—older people—declined (Minow and Weissbourd, 1993). Of course, it must be noted that an increasingly important cause of this poverty is the rise of single motherhood, especially an increase in the number of babies born to unwed mothers. But this trend is not confined, as some commentators would have it, to certain racial or ethnic groups. To be sure, the percentage of African-American babies born to single mothers has risen to approximately 66 percentage, but the percentage of white American babies born to single mothers has risen to somewhere between 22 and 25 percent (Polakow, 1993). The percentage of white babies born to single mothers in the mid-1990s thus approximates the rate of 27 percent that the Moynihan report in the 1960s took to indicate a "crisis in the black family" (Smothers, 1993). Moreover, although African Americans are indeed disproportionately poor, most poor children in America are not African American, but white (Sidel, 1992:210–20; Minow and Weissbourd 1993). This fact bears emphasis since one unfortunate cause of the relative inattention in the past decade to the problems of poor children was the common misperception that poverty is a problem confined to racial and ethnic minorities rather than a problem that confronts all Americans. Thus, though there is clearly a "crisis" of single motherhood in America generally—a crisis eventually likely to have profound effects on the economic well-being of all Americans—public political rhetoric has managed to obscure that truth for far too long.[5]

Of course, a number of contemporary social thinkers are tempted to attribute many of these developments to failures of individual responsibility—and no doubt some of the causes of these trends must surely be explained in this way. But even if every single case of a child born in poverty to an unmarried single mother could in fact be explained as a failure of responsible behavior on the part of the biological parents, there still would be good reason to marshal the mechanisms of the public household to protect every such child. There would be good reason to do so simply in virtue of each child's vulnerability. There is admittedly reason to discourage irresponsible behavior, but it must be considered whether worsening employment prospects for the poor of both sexes, along with the continuing occupational segregation and disparity in wages that afflict poor young women in particular, create a social and economic climate that discourages the poor's confidence in responsible forms of family life. More important, in the familiar cliché, no child asks to be born. Marshaling social resources in a coherent plan of social insurance to protect all children is the only defensible way of recognizing the social importance of their vulnerability.

THE SPECIAL VULNERABILITY OF CHILDREN

Any argument for such a plan of social insurance has to show at least two things. First, it must show the importance of the fact that the vulnerability of children—especially their economic vulnerability—is an ongoing function of the vulnerability of their parents. Of course, few social thinkers—if any—would deny the connection between the economic status of parents and that of their children, but in response to

conservative challenges, many such thinkers retreat to an American ideal of the economically independent, and thus morally self-reliant, family. Yet the persistent retreat to such notions continues to impoverish important debates about the domestic
realm. Second, a defense of social insurance must show that policies designed to
provide children with *positive* social insurance against vulnerability would more effectively protect them than many current policies that work only to punish parents
for any role in creating the conditions of their children's vulnerability. These latter
policies either ultimately punish the children themselves or pit the interests of parents (and potential parents, especially pregnant women) against those of the vulnerable beings they are being expected to care for. Any policy likely to have such results
is bound to fail at its stated goal of protecting children.

In order to understand the ways in which some contemporary debates miscon-
strue the vulnerability of children, I turn to some controversies bound up with the
issue of abortion and the appropriate social expression of care for the vulnerable. Let
me return to the position implicit in the message with which I began: "Thinking
abortion? First visit our pastor. He cares." It seems safe to assume, of course, that the
authors of this message care about preventing abortion; many of them would no
doubt contend that the *principal* object of their care is any developing fetus whose
existence might be ended by abortion. It is also important, however, that on occasion
expressions of this care might well lead to various kinds of social and even economic assistance—including temporary housing, prenatal medical care, counseling
about adoption, and so forth—intended to encourage the pregnant woman not to
have an abortion. As Glendon has noted, many opponents of abortion now believe
that the effort to deny or restrict abortions *should* be accompanied by efforts to provide such assistance (Glendon, 1987:53). Yet it remains an open—and important—
question whether any such assistance would be extended, for any substantial period
beyond the point of giving birth, to a woman who has refrained from having an abortion. Many who would voluntarily sacrifice *private* resources to provide temporary
assistance to pregnant women contemplating abortion would nonetheless resist the
notion that the public household ought to provide assistance to the mother and her
baby. Yet a growing number of contemporary thinkers—from scholars concerned
with applying the lessons gleaned from the comparative analysis of abortion law to
U.S. Catholic bishops concerned to defend a distinctive understanding of the biblical
conception of care—consider such resistance to be deeply problematic. My objective is neither to endorse nor reject any particular stand on abortion but to examine
the merits of some important objections to the manner in which debates about abortion are typically conducted.

Critics have argued that it is not possible to formulate and pursue a defensible
national policy on abortion—at least, if the principal aim of that policy is to express
genuine *care* for children—independent of some coherent national effort to reform
the legal and economic institutions that affect the ongoing well-being of mothers and
children. At the conclusion of a compelling and insightful comparative study of
abortion regulation in several nations, Glendon—who calls for according "increased
protection" to fetal life, though she seems to oppose a total ban on abortion—argues
that the United States may well be alone in assuming that reasonable abortion policy
can be pursued in isolation from debate about positive social insurance for children.

Glendon contends that the European experience in particular raises the question of "why pregnant women in the United States should be asked to make significant sacrifices (whether they abort or bear children), if absent fathers and the community as a whole are not asked to sacrifice too" (1987:53). The relevant community sacrifices would provide such benefits and services as the option to use publicly funded day care, economic support for mothers at the time of childbirth, income supplements to families with children, extensive public health services for children, and especially, a vigorous pursuit of child-support collection and even mandatory paternity actions (1987:53–59).

A similar connection between abortion policy and concern for the economic context of care for children is suggested by the U.S. bishops' pastoral letter on Catholic social teaching and the economy, *Economic Justice for All*. Of course, unlike Glendon's position, official Catholic doctrine involves a rejection of abortion. But the bishops—even more vehemently than Glendon—urged a substantial rethinking of the social and economic context of care for children: their letter calls, for instance, for a "new American experiment" that would form a "partnership for the public good" in service of children and families (Gannon, 1987:299 ff.). Of course, some influential critics have condemned the letter for its allegedly heretical attitude toward American free enterprise; Milton Friedman, for instance, chides the bishops for their lack of faith in the manner in which "free cooperation among individuals through a market can achieve coordination on a large scale" (in Gannon, 1987:100). Still others may object to the letter as an unwarranted interference of the church in public politics; the bishops certainly consider the letter as, at least in part, an attempt to give a correct construal of the biblical injunction to "love thy neighbor as thyself." But the letter also appeals to the decidedly secular moral notion of respect for the dignity of persons, and thus challenges the champion of the doctrine of free enterprise to establish that social and economic arrangements associated with that doctrine accord better with human dignity than do the policies recommended by their letter.

Perhaps most important is the way in which the U.S. bishops' challenge bears upon the fundamentalist Christian offer of care discussed above. Consider that a pregnant woman driven to rely on the private kindness of strangers (if only for a time) might well be the sort of person likely to remain in need—perhaps even dire economic need—for some time after the child is born. In such circumstances, as the bishops' challenge reminds us, an offer of temporary private assistance will prove insufficient to ensure care for a vulnerable child. The policies implicit in the position defended in *Economic Justice for All* thus resist the tendency to separate the vulnerability of a newborn infant from the ongoing vulnerability of its parent(s). In so doing, they also resist a tendency common in familiar debates about abortion: in the moral and legal tug-of-war between defenders of fetal rights and defenders of abortion rights, the interests and rights of the fetus are pitted against those of the pregnant woman.

This tendency was interestingly revealed by the curious "family policy" that emerged in the United States in the 1980s. The policy centered around the attempt to criminalize certain kinds of behavior during pregnancy under the label of "fetal abuse." Because the prosecution of these cases relied on the use of post-birth sanctions, the implications of this policy are even more central to advancing our understanding of the vulnerability of children: the policy concerned the behavior of women who—unlike women contemplating abortion—had decided to carry their pregnancies to term. One outspoken defender of the criminalization of fetal abuse, the legal theorist John Robertson, has argued that the policy "may turn out to be an effective tool for demonstrating society's attempt to protect children." Attaching criminal sanctions to certain kinds of prenatal conduct by means of post-birth sanctions, Robertson continues, is an important way of "meeting obligations to the unborn child" (Robertson, 1988:38; cf. 1989).

But there has been a marked lack of reflection about the circumstances under which these cases have been prosecuted. To begin with, in some of the most visible cases pregnant women were charged under statutes not originally intended to criminalize the conduct of women during pregnancy. Thus in a 1986 case in San Diego, California, a woman was charged with fetal abuse under a statute intended to enforce child support arrangements; the statute's definition of "child" had been extended to include fetuses in order that husbands who abandoned their pregnant wives could not lawfully refuse to pay a share of the relevant expenses.[6] Yet ironically, mothers and prospective mothers are regularly unable to collect much-needed child-support payments. Still further, the use of post-birth sanctions has meant that most of the cases have had little *explicit* relation to prenatal conduct. Thus in a 1987 Florida case, a woman who confessed to having ingested dangerous illegal drugs during pregnancy was charged (and later convicted) of having delivered drugs to a child in the moments after birth, just before the umbilical cord was severed (Losco, 1992:235). It is true that continued lack of consensus about the legal status of fetuses is a principal cause of reliance on so-called post-birth sanctions; Robertson, among others, contends that this reliance simply respects the existence of a woman's constitutional right to choose abortion. Yet it is unclear how this legal sleight-of-hand might have a genuine long-term influence in encouraging responsible care for children. Instead, the policy seems likely to encourage offending women to try to hide the harm they may do to their fetuses rather than to seek education and assistance in changing their bad habits. Ironically, the woman in the Florida case had actually sought treatment for her drug addiction prior to giving birth, but had been turned away from several existing drug treatment programs—indeed, the vast majority of drug treatment programs are simply not open to pregnant women (Losco, 1992:253–54). In view of this fact, along with the woeful scarcity of affordable prenatal care, the prosecution of pregnant women for harmful prenatal conduct may well prove to be counterproductive to protecting the interests of the child. As many critics have argued, the proliferation of such prosecutions is likely to dissuade pregnant women from seeking medical care and even to encourage them to withhold accurate information about their conduct (Paltrow, 1989).

Such policies are of a piece with social policy that in general seeks to use public power and the vast resources of the public household to legislate against certain behavior rather than to provide positive social support that might help prevent the behavior in the first place. I refer in particular to the contemporary American readiness to spend billions of dollars building more prisons rather than to try policies that embody a socially unstigmatized message of concern for the well-being and socialization of all children. This preference for such reactive policies is ultimately inimical to the stability of truly vital liberal democratic institutions. As Mill once urged, a society that lets "any considerable number of its members grow up . . . incapable of being acted upon by rational consideration of distant motives" has only itself to blame (1859:80). The current circumstances of contemporary American children make Mill's warning more compelling than ever.

THE LIMITS OF "PRIVATISM" AS FAMILY POLICY

The preference for reactive policies over more positive proposals reflects the fact that major demographic and economic changes since the 1970s have tended to concentrate income, political power, and social attention *away* from families with children. As Coontz has noted, in the 1950s almost 70 percent of the adult population of the United States had school-age children (Coontz, 1992:278); yet in the early 1990s, the percentage had dropped to as low as 28 percent. Coontz rightly argues that in such circumstances the tendency toward a "privatism" that appeals to the self-reliance of individual families is bound to make the formation of socially responsible family policy exceedingly difficult. Indeed, it encourages the view that the funding and maintenance of public facilities for children are, *de facto*, "minority" concerns. Thus the funding crises of large urban school systems are simply a symptom of even larger social problems. To be sure, the slow increase in birth rates may eventually mitigate the effects of these demographic changes. Yet political argument that continues to posit a sharp boundary between the moral and economic functions of private families on one hand and the mechanisms of the public household on the other is likely to impoverish debate and stifle the search for creative solutions to the problems of children.

But in one of the most striking ironies of recent political life, the public attention given to the child-care troubles of a series of relatively well-off families suggests the possibilities for a reawakening of widespread social concern for children. I refer to the heated debate that emerged during President Clinton's first efforts to nominate a woman candidate for Attorney General. Writing under the suggestive byline. "Public and Private," *New York Times* columnist Anna Quindlen reminded us of the dangers of being "single-minded and sure about the sins of Zoe Baird. The first woman chosen to be Attorney General was caught with her child care down . . ." (Quindlen, 1993). The nominee had, of course, hired undocumented immigrant workers to care for her children and in the process had run afoul of the legal requirement to pay Social Security taxes on their wages. Quindlen went on to quote a particularly poignant remark made by the former nominee: "Quite honestly, I was acting at that time really more as a mother than as someone who would be sitting here designated to be Attorney General." Such explanations, to be sure, tend to ignore the potentially exploitative character of the relationship between illegal immigrants and their employers. Moreover, there are vast differences between the child-care difficulties of an affluent corporate attorney and those of the less affluent families, especially of the working poor. Yet the debate over Zoe Baird's nomination revealed—as Quindlen rightly emphasizes—that the problems of child care continue to be viewed as "private female troubles." One can only hope that the publicity given to the problems of a few relatively affluent women will generate sustained reflection on the need for accessible and affordable day care for all.

Of course, if I am correct, the limits of privatism as family policy will be revealed in many domains beyond that of child care for working mothers. Access to affordable health care for children (as well as for the women who give birth to them), more aggressive support for family leave policies, even more aggressive divorce law and child-support regulation that would protect children from vulnerability are all examples of the kind of policies that would express collective public support for protecting the most vulnerable citizens. Some may object that virtues like self-sacrifice and deferred gratification will be neglected in a society that expresses this kind of public support for the needs of children. Yet there is little reason to presume that private virtues can flourish without widespread public support. Indeed this is one point on which popular debate about the importance of widespread moral support for "family values" acknowledges an important truth. What the debate too often fails to acknowledge is that the material well-being of children likewise depends on widespread public support.

Notes

1. Debates about how to provide appropriate legal remedies for victims of sexual harassment, and over the predicament of women who work outside the home and yet work the "second shift" at home, provide further challenges to these conventional boundaries. On the "second shift," see Hochshild, 1989.

2. According to Coontz, prairie farmers and other pioneer families "owed their existence to massive federal land grants, government funded military mobilizations . . . and state sponsored economic investment in these new lands" (1992:73). She contends further that much of the upward mobility of the 1950s suburban family was subsidized by government spending in a variety of forms. She argues that policies carried out under the auspices of the following agencies and under the terms of the following regulations provide important examples: the GI Bill, the National Defense Education Act, the FHA, as well as the Interstate Highway Commission, and more (1992:73–79).

3. A particularly thoughtful (if ultimately unsatisfying) discussion of this position is offered by Barbara Dafoe Whitehead, a research associate in the Institute for American Values, in her tantalizingly titled piece, "Dan Quayle Was Right" (Whitehead, 1993).

4. Ruth Shalit notes that the focus on family breakdown—especially on the admittedly shattering effects of divorce—encourages inattention to the very different problems affecting the least well-off members of American society (Shalit, 1993).

5. Anyone who needs to be convinced that excessive poverty in America affects the life prospects of all Americans need only consider some of the most pressing health care concerns. Treatment of the urgent health problems of the uninsured poor, who of necessity postpone preventive health care, eventually raise the cost of health care for all. I have tried to show that important arguments can be made for the *intrinsic* importance of trying to remedy childhood poverty. Yet it is important to note that it is possible to construct a series of arguments, analogous to this point about health care, capable of showing that excessive childhood poverty ultimately lowers the overall standard of living for all Americans.

6. The special importance of this point is discussed in "Maternal Rights and Wrongs" (*Harvard Law Review*, 1988).

References

Bell, Daniel. 1976. *The Cultural Contradictions of Capitalism*, New York: Basic Books.

Chodorow, Nancy. 1978. *The Reproduction of Mothering*. Berkeley: University of California Press.

Coontz, Stephanie. 1992. *The Way We Never Were: American Families and the Nostalgia Trap*. New York: Basic Books.

Eyer, Diane E. 1992. *Mother-Infant Bonding: A Scientific Fiction*. New Haven: Yale University Press.

Galston, William A. 1991. *Liberal Purposes: Goods, Virtues, and Diversity in the Liberal State*. Cambridge: Cambridge University Press.

Gannon, Thomas M., 1987. *The Catholic Challenge to the American Economy. Reflections on the U.S. Bishops' Pastoral Letter on Catholic Social Teaching and the U.S. Economy*. New York: Macmillian.

Glendon, Mary Ann. 1987. *Abortion and Divorce in Western Law: American Failures, European Challenges*. Cambridge: Harvard University Press.

Harvard Law Review. 1988. Maternal Rights and Fetal Wrongs: The Case Against the Criminalization of 'Fetal Abuse.' *Harvard Law Review* 101:994–1012.

Hochshild, Arlie, and Machung, Anne. 1989. *The Second Shift: Working Parents and the Revolution at Home*. New York: Viking Penguin, Inc.

Hume, David. [1777] 1975. *Enquiry Concerning the Principles of Morals*. Reprint edited by L.A. Selby-Biggge, 3d ed. revised by P. H. Nidditch. Oxford: Clarendon Press.

———. [1739–40] 1978. *A Treatise of Human Nature*. Reprint, edited by L.A. Selby-Bigge, 2d ed. revised by P. H. Nidditch. Oxford: Clarendon Press.

Kemp, Alice Abel. 1994. *Women's Work: Devalued and Degraded*. Englewood Cliffs, N.J.: Prentice Hall.

Lasch, Christopher. 1977. *Haven in a Heartless World. The Family Besieged*. New York: Basic Books.

———. 1978. *The Culture of Narcissism*. New York: W. W. Norton.

Losco, Joseph. 1992. Fetal Rights and Feminism. In *Feminist Jurisprudence*, edited by Leslie Friedman Goldstein:231–62. Lanham, Md.: Rowman and Littlefield.

Mill, John Stuart. [1859] 1978. *On Liberty*. Reprint. Indianapolis: Hackett Publishing.

Minow, Martha, and Richard Weissbourd. 1993. Social Movements for Children. *America's Childhood: Daedelus* 122:1–29.

Moody-Adams, Michele M. 1991. On Surrogacy: Morality, Markets, and Motherhood. *Public Affairs Quarterly*. 5:175–89.

———. 1992–93. Race, Class, and the Social Construction of Self-Respect. *Philosophical Forum* 24, 1–3:251–66.

Nozick, Robert. 1974. *Anarchy, State and Utopia*. New York: Basic Books.

Okin, Susan Moller. 1989. *Justice, Gender, and the Family*. New York: Basic Books.

Paltrow, Lynn. 1989. 'Fetal Abuse': Should We Recognize It as a Crime? No. *ABA Journal* 75 (August):39.

Polakow, Valerie. 1993. *Lives on the Edge: Single Mothers and Their Children in the Other America*. Chicago: University of Chicago Press.

Quindlen, Anna. 1993. The Sins of Zoe Baird. *New York Times*, Jan. 2.

Rawls, John. 1971. *A Theory of Justice*. Cambridge, Mass.: Harvard University Press.

Robertson, John. 1989. 'Fetal Abuse': Should We Recognize It as a Crime? Yes. *ABA Journal*. 75 (August):38.

———. 1989. Reconciling Offspring and Maternal Interests During Pregnancy. In *Repro-*

    ductive Laws for the 1990's, edited by N. Taub and S. Cohen: 259–74. Clifton, N.J.:
         Humana Press.

Shalit, Ruth. 1993. Family Mongers. *New Republic*, Aug. 16, 12–14.

Sidel, Ruth. 1992. *Women and Children Last. The Plight of Poor Women in Affluent America.*
         2d ed., revised. New York: Viking Penguin.

Smothers, Ronald. 1993. Tell It to Mom, Dad and the Authorities. *New York Times*, Nov. 14.

Whitehead, Barbara Dafoe. 1993. Dan Quayle Was Right. *Atlantic Monthly* 27 (April).

2

Constructing Love, Desire, and Care

Martha C. Nussbaum

According to an ancient Indian legend, wise men were once troubled about the power of sexuality in the life of the world. Blaming the situation on Siva, the erotic god, they cried out in irritation, "May his penis fall to the ground." Siva's penis promptly fell to the ground. Sexual intercourse and sexual desire were no longer. This was more than the wise men had bargained for, and they begged him to put his penis back on again. Siva said, "If gods and humans will worship my penis, I will put it back, not otherwise." They could not bring themselves to go that far, so they refused. As the legend tells it, the penis lay there in the snow, "frost-bitten, knobby, and sleekly black, glistening in the spring thaw . . . while Siva passed over the final ridge of grief and was lost to the world on the far side." With intercourse thus removed, the story continues, "there then ensued 3600 years of peace and quiet" in the world—and if Siva had only stayed away, this peace would be with us still.[1]

Here we have one of the earliest versions of the idea that human sexuality is not a brute necessity—given in the nature of things—but, rather, an artifact of social arrangements and agreements. What "the wise" decide to honor socially creates not only the social circumstances of sexual intercourse but also the possibility and the nature of sexual desire, and even the experience of the body considered as a subject of desire. When society refuses to honor Siva's eroticism, he inhabits his body differently: a part of it is gone, counts for nothing, lies there on the ground. And his experience of sexual exuberance shifts into an experience of helplessness and loss, as he goes over the final ridge of the world.

This state of "peace and quiet" for the world is portrayed as a remote and impossible condition, very unlike that of our current world. But what this means is that the current world is one in which various social arrangements of recognition, honor, and power create possibilities for the emergence and activity of desire, and its concrete experiential shape. According to another Indian story of similar antiquity, the very existence and biology of sexual intercourse were created by a combination of accident and agreement in the following way: Males, the story goes, used to have a penis—or something that in hindsight the story calls a penis—sticking out of their forehead, like an elephant's trunk. Since female genitals—or what in hindsight can be called genitals—were in the middle of the chest, it did not occur to them to put their organs together, nor did they feel any desire. (Note that what is really being said here is that male and female did not exist as such before the erotic experiment: we had a general human form with different types of surface ornamentation.[2]) Then the appendage on the "male" forehead got cut short one day by accident—reduced to four fingers' breadth, as the legend goes. (This part of the story usually causes consternation to male readers, who hold up their fingers in bewilderment, until it dawns on them that the males of ancient times were just different and a bit inferior.) Now the males didn't like the stump in the middle of their forehead, it was no longer so good as an ornament, so they asked Siva to move it to another place and find some other use for it. He put it between their legs, moved women's chest-decoration between their legs, and invented the experience of sexual desire and sexual intercourse so that these parts would have some useful function to perform.[3] (In most Indian stories of the creation of intercourse, it was not necessary for the birth of children, who were produced before that by other and sometimes better means, in particular by intense mental concentration.[4])

In this essay I shall investigate the philosophical basis for the thesis that human love, desire, and sexuality are "socially constructed." I want to look clearly at the philosophical arguments involved and at the bearing of historical and cross-cultural data on the arguments. I shall begin with the case of love and other related emotions since here the issues seem to me somewhat clearer than in the case of sexual desire, where biological arguments begin to complicate the issue. I shall then turn to sexual desire itself, and the related issues of sexual preference and gender structure, assessing the strength of the case that these phenomena too are socially constructed. This will involve looking at the status of the sexual body and the sexual organs themselves and asking whether even these are in some significant sense social and historical artifacts. I shall then draw on all of this material to look more briefly at the social construction of the family. My general thesis will be that, in many central respects, the sexual domain of human life—and its close relative, the domain of the family—are domains of symbolic cultural interpretation, shaped by historical and institutional forces, though within constraints imposed by biology; that cultural formations affect not just the theoretical explanation of desire but the very experience of desire, and of oneself as a desiring agent; that such considerable overlap as one does encounter among cultures in these areas can best be explained by the considerable overlap in the problems with which different human societies must grapple as they try to get on in the world;[5] that the feeling most human beings have that certain ways of doing things sexually are "natural" and necessary is often best explained not by biology but by the depth of social conditioning in the life of every human being, giving a sense of what is possible and impossible, what is an available role and what is not. Finally, I shall argue that recognizing the depth of interpretation in sexuality does not remove rational debate or force us into a rootless relativism; instead, it opens up a space for normative argument, political criticism, and reasoned change.

These claims will sound peculiar to some, excessively familiar to others. To those who find them overly familiar, coming from the large "cultural studies" literature that has investigated them for some time, I can only say that I believe this literature has not set out the philosophical arguments surrounding the issue as clearly as might be done—I shall try in that way to take the investigation further—nor has it connected questions about the constructedness of desire and sexuality to a study of the cultural construction of emotion, a comparison that I believe to be very illuminating.

EMOTIONS AND THEIR SOCIAL FORM

The thesis that emotions are socially constructed, in the form in which I shall defend it, rests on a cognitive view of emotion, which holds that perceptions and beliefs of a certain sort play a central role in emotional experience.[6] We shall see that a cognitive view, while necessary for the social-construction thesis, is not sufficient for it, and I shall add further arguments to get to that thesis, holding that human cognition in the relevant area is socially shaped. But we can best begin by articulating and defending the cognitive view itself. This view, in turn, can best be understood by beginning with its theoretical adversary, which is also the thesis most commonly held by opponents of social construction.[7]

The adversary claims that emotions such as grief, anger, fear, and love do not involve any form of cognitive interpretation of the world: they are just unthinking energies that push a person around. Like gusts of wind or the currents of the sea, they move—and move the person, but obtusely, without a vision of an object or beliefs about it. The view is frequently linked with the idea that emotions are "natural," "innate," or "bodily" rather than learned, for this seems to be the adversary's characteristic way of explaining how these unthinking forces got there and why most people seem to have them. The adversary's view has had a certain influence in behaviorist experimental psychology and also in popular talk and thought about the emotions.[8] But it never fared well in philosophy, where most major writers—in the Western tradition and in what is known to me of non-Western traditions[9]—have endorsed some form of cognitive analysis. And by now it has been thoroughly repudiated in anthropology, in psychoanalysis, and even in cognitive psychology, where, as one major theorist[10] ironically observes, the field has just managed to fight its way back to the position defended in Aristotle's *Rhetoric*. What are the reasons for this shift? If we see what has led to the current consensus about a cognitive analysis for emotion—which, as I have said, is a necessary, if not a sufficient, condition for a social-constructionist project—we will be in a better position to understand the arguments in favor of that project. We need an example: I shall take one from Euripides' tragedy, *The Trojan Women*.

Hecuba kneels in front of the shield of her dead son Hector.[11] On the shield is the dead body of her little grandson Astyanax. The victorious Greek commanders, fearing that this royal child might later cause them political trouble, have arranged for him to be thrown from the walls of the Trojan city. Hecuba pours out her grief in a speech of intense passion and lyrical beauty as she remembers how each bodily part that now lies dead used to be full of hope, and brightness, and humor, and love, as she sees how the face that once smiled at her is now just a mass of splintered bones and blood. She angrily denounces the Greeks for their cruelty and their cowardice.

She observes that human life is in general ferociously unstable, and all the most important things are beyond our control, without any firm foundation. What makes Hecuba's emotions here so different from the mindless currents hypothesized by the adversary?

First of all, Hecuba's emotions have an object: her grief is for the death of her grandson, and her anger is at his killers. They are *about* these objects in a way that a wind is not *about* the tree against which it strikes. Internal to the emotion itself is a focusing on the object, and the emotion contains a representation of the object, seeing it in the way in which the person interprets and sees it. Hecuba's grief sees Astyanax as both enormously important and as irrevocably cut off from her; her anger sees the Greeks as culpable wrongdoers[12] and their wrongdoing as bad and serious. This aboutness comes from her active ways of seeing and interpreting; it is not like being given a snapshot of the object, but requires looking at the object, so to speak, through her own interpretive window. This perception might contain an accurate vision of the object or it might not. It is what she thinks that matters: if it were not the Greeks but a suddenly invading Scythian army who had killed the boy, she would still be angry at the Greeks until she knew this—for in her view they are the agents of wrong.

This brings out a further point about these emotions: they embody not just ways of seeing but also beliefs, and Aristotle already stressed, they are highly responsive to a change in beliefs.[13] If Hecuba comes to believe that Scythian invaders, not Greeks, killed her grandson, her anger will change its object. If she finds out that Astyanax was not killed but fell from the walls by accident, she will not be angry at anyone and will grieve very differently. If she finds out that the body at her feet is not her grandson after all but a dummy dressed in her child's clothes,[14] she will stop grieving altogether.

And this brings me to one last point, in some ways the most important of all. Hecuba's emotions involve various beliefs, including beliefs about what events have and have not taken place and who caused them. But very prominent in the emotions are beliefs of a very particular sort, namely, beliefs about value, worth, and salience. It is because Hecuba has invested her grandson's life with tremendous importance that his death crushes her as it does and in a way that the death of a stranger would not do. Again, it is because his death is so salient in her life that her anger is so intense; the destruction of a drinking cup would not affect her in the same way. And these beliefs, too, may alter. The Greek Stoics, teaching the importance of self-sufficiency, claimed that they ought to alter, so that nothing outside one's own virtue would seem to have real importance. A good Stoic father, reports Cicero, responded to the news of his son's death with the words, "I was already aware that I had begotten a mortal."[15]

To show all this about how perceptions and beliefs figure in emotions does not by itself show that there is much social variation in emotional life, or that emotions are in any meaningful sense "socially constructed." It does establish that an emotional repertory is not innate but learned[16] and that it is in principle possible to alter emotions through altering the beliefs on which they rest.[17] But there might be some beliefs that would almost inevitably be formed by a living creature interacting with an uncertain world, beliefs so central to the creature's whole way of life that the idea of removing them or significantly changing them makes little sense. And this is to a large extent the way things seem to be with the emotions of nonhuman animals.[18] According to the best recent studies, the fear and anger and grief of animals cannot be explained without invoking the animal's own cognitive interpretation of the world, and this interpretation must contain patterns of salience or importance. As psychologists Richard Lazarus and Keith Oatley have put it in the two most acute recent studies of the topic, the emotions are the animal's way of taking in news of how things are going in the world with respect to its most cherished or most urgent projects and needs. These ways of responding must be learned since no creature comes into the world knowing what parts of the world are helpful and harmful to it in important ways. On the other hand, the emotional repertory is highly functional and crucial in guiding the animal's actions; it is therefore likely to be pretty uniform, given a type of creature and a general form of life. It would not be plausible, for example, that we should find a "higher animal"[19] who never experienced fear, for the belief that one's important projects are threatened is not only true for every mortal living creature at some times, but highly useful in prompting evasive behavior.[20]

To some extent, much the same seems to be true of human beings. Fear of death and bodily injury is ubiquitous in some form because the belief that these are important bad things is ubiquitous.[21] So, too, with grief at the deaths of loved ones, joy at their presence and safety, anger at the agents of willful damages to them or to oneself. Furthermore, the human body—whose states of pain, hunger, need for warmth and cold, and so on, are so prominent within the emotional life as occasions for fear, anger, joy, relief, and also love and gratitude—is itself ubiquitous. Although infants are from the beginning handled in accordance with cultural rules, there is much about them—their hungry neediness, the way their cognitive capacities develop over time, the shape of their bodies,[22] and the ways in which the body metabolizes nutrients—that is not itself a cultural construct and that gives emotional experience a common terrain and geography. On the other hand, within this generally shared framework there is a great deal of room, in the human case, for social shaping and variation. This variation takes four different forms:

1. *Rules for emotional expression and behavior vary.* Each society teaches rules for the proper expression of emotions such as grief, love, and anger. The public wailing and tearing of clothing and hair that seemed normal to ancient Greeks mourning the death of a loved one would cause a social scandal in contemporary England. The public displays of love and affection that are acceptable among Brown University undergraduates would have been regarded as morally hideous in nineteenth-century India. And, of course, most societies also have different rules internally for different types of social actors, dividing them along lines of age, gender, and social class.

2. *Normative judgments about an emotion vary.*

(a) *Judgments about the entire emotion type.* I have said that most societies contain some species of anger and grief and fear and love since it is hard to find a society that does not ascribe to objects outside oneself a salience or importance that leads to these emotions in certain circumstances. But not all societies take the same view about the value of these attachments to objects or the concomitant emotions. Let me focus here on anger. In a remarkable study of an Eskimo tribe, the Utku, anthropologist Jean Briggs[23] carefully showed that these people strongly disapprove of anger, viewing it as all right in children, who feel weak and dependent and therefore ascribe to slights and damages a considerable significance, but as totally defective in an adult, who ought to have a kind of proud self-mastery that would make all such damages seem trivial. (In effect, this society seems to realize quite a lot of what the ancient Greek and Roman Stoics taught and tried to practice.) The Utku admit that it is hard to get rid of attachments that give rise to anger, so they expect anger to occur. But they describe it always in pejorative language, as a socially pernicious force. Contrast the attitude to anger in ancient Rome. It seems that being a truly manly man in Rome of Seneca's time actually required getting extremely angry at all sorts of slights and damages, to oneself, one's property, one's family, one's honor and reputation. If one didn't get angry, one was being soft. Here I want to say not only that the behavior of angry people in these two cultures will be very different—the Utku trying to cover things up and looking shamefaced, the Roman proudly proclaiming his rage and his vindictive intentions—I want to say, too, that the *experience* of anger will differ. For an Utku, being angry will be hooked up to the experience of shame and a sense of diminished adulthood; one will feel infantilized by anger. The Roman, by contrast, will feel his anger accompanied by a feeling of manly self-assertion and full adulthood, and by a quasi-erotic excitement,[24] as he prepares to smash the adversary. In much the same way—to jump ahead to sexuality itself for a minute—one can expect the experience of sexual desire in a society that has deeply internalized the idea of original sin to be different from the experience of desire in a society that has no such teaching: the Augustinian Christian will feel desire itself tainted with shame and possibly even revulsion;[25] the ancient Greek has no such general shame to contend with.

(b) *Judgments internal to the emotion type.* Every society teaches norms about the proper objects and occasions for anger, fear, grief, and so forth. Once again, these norms exhibit considerable variation—both across societies and over time in a single society. In the United States, for example, the distinction between first degree murder and voluntary manslaughter is defined in accordance with normative judgments about the anger of a "reasonable man." The events that are taken to supply this man with "adequate provocation" evolve and change. In the nineteenth century, the paradigm triggering event was adultery, seen as an invasion of a man's property. Today, the "reasonable man" may be a woman, and her anger may be about domestic violence.[26]

3. *The taxonomy of recognized emotions varies.* This grows directly out of my last point: we can say that the anger experienced by the Utku is not precisely the same emotion as the anger experienced by the Roman, given its different links to shame and childishness. And, in general, we find that the precise description of the emotion taxonomy of any society yields subtle variations from that of any other. The fact that Roman taxonomies recognize numerous varieties and subspecies of retributive anger, subtly differentiated according to the type of re-

venge sought, the length of time one spends planning one's revenge, and the type of slight that occasioned the anger is not separable from the fact that the Romans are enthusiastic cultivators of this emotional plant and love to observe its every nuance. One assumes that as a result of this cultivation Romans felt their anger differently, just as a cultivated wine taster tastes wine differently.[27] One can even find emotion categories that are important for one culture but don't occur at all in another, given the differences in patterns and circumstances of life. I spend part of every summer in Finland, and the Finns have repeatedly described to me an emotion connected with the experience of being alone in the forest; it combines awe, the sense of one's own insignificance, a terror of death. It is said to be expressed by certain passages in Sibelius's music. I had never had precisely that emotion, though by now, by taking on the form of life (and being anyway a devotee of long solitary walks in the forest), I am beginning to see what it is all about.

4. *Individual histories vary, and emotions bear traces of their history.* Human emotions are unlike most other animal emotions in that the present object is often not alone: it bears the trace of loved or feared or hated objects from one's past, and the past lends the present some of its wonder or terror. This history is all along culturally mediated; even infants are handled from the beginning in accordance with cultural scenarios. But there is much variation with the general cultural pattern.

Let me now put all this together, focusing on the case of erotic love. It is not surprising to find that more or less all known societies have some emotion or other that might roughly be called erotic love—a kind of intense attachment to an object connected with sexual feeling. But it is obvious to any devotee of love poetry and love stories that this allegedly single emotion turns up in remarkably different forms in different times and places, forms that do not all share a common core or essence, although they may exhibit many complicated interrelationships. In fact, we find here all four of the types of variation I have identified. First, and most obviously, norms of expression and behavior for lovers very enormously across cultures and within a culture in connection with differences in age, gender, and social status. Normative judgments on the emotion also vary: the ancient Greeks seem on the whole, to have considered *eros* a fearful and terrible sort of bondage and constraint; very much the same picture is implicit in my Indian story; we modern Americans tend to adopt a more rosy view.[28] Here, as with anger, the normative judgment can be expected to enter into the experience itself: the ancient Greek feels bound and made passive by *eros*; the ancient Indian male both wishes and doesn't wish to get rid of his penis; by contrast, a modern American romantic will be likely to feel love as beautiful and uplifting.[29] Third, the emotion taxonomy itself exhibits cultural variation. Plato perceptively defined his culture's erotic emotion as a longing for possession of an object one views as good.[30] In that sense, it has nothing about mutuality or reciprocity built into its definition, and we can also see that it is closely bound up with jealous wishes to immobilize the object.[31] Contemporary American conceptions of love place a heavy stress on reciprocity. This means that we really are dealing with subtly different emotions: Plato and John Updike are not describing the same passion. What we have to get rid of here is the idea that there is some one *thing* beneath the surface that is simply being described in different language. For the language itself reproduces (even as it represents) the structure of a pattern of life; these forms, and the experiences of the agents who inhabit them, have obvious similarities but also some very important differences.[32] Finally, of course, all this is made vastly more complicated by each person's early history, as intense attachments to parents—themselves impregnated with cultural information—are worked out in individual ways and color the perception of future objects. Norms internal to the emotion vary as well. The characteristics the ancient Greeks found lovable are not exactly the same ones that the courtly lover prizes, and there is much reason to think of this difference as explained by changing social norms.

Is this "ontological relativity"[33] in emotion a special case within our metaphysics of experience, or is it simply one example of a phenomenon that is ubiquitous in the human use of categories to interpret the world? The tribe whom Quine famously imagined see a rabbit passing by and exclaim, "Gavagai!" The external observer, Quine plausibly argues, will be unable to be certain what ontology underlies this utterance. Even after extensive observations, she will not be able to decide whether the utterance is best interpreted as referring to a "rabbit," to a "rabbit-stage," a "rabbit-part," or even the abstract "Rabbithood." And, like differences in the emotional categories, such ontological differences presumably do color experience at a deep level. What this shows is that ultimately the social constructionist must engage in exacting metaphysical, and also epistemological, analysis, investigating the twin Quinean claims of the indeterminacy of translation and the underdetermination of theory by empirical evidence.[34] She must take a position in the subtle debates among philosophers such as Quine, Hilary Putnam, Nelson Goodman, and Donald Davidson and come to grips, in particular, with Davidson's argument that the ascription of rationality to a human being from another culture entails a shared conceptual framework. I am obviously not going to solve all of these problems in this paper, and I must simply sketch here the direction in which I would wish to take the argument. On the one hand, I would agree with Quine, Putnam, and Goodman that our basic theories of the world exhibit variation of the sort social constructionists find in the areas of emotion and desire. There are multiple theories that are adequate to the data, and these theories employ, in many cases, different basic categories that cut up the world in different ways. On the other hand, I would argue that the area of emotion and desire has particular features that set it apart from our categorizing practices in general. These features point in opposing directions. The evolutionary adaptive significance of emotion and of sexual desire pushes us toward greater commonality of categorization than will be likely to hold in areas that are not so urgently connected with survival; but the close connection of these areas to issues of political power leads them to become a scene of cultural manipulation and conflict to a greater degree than may be the case elsewhere. This will often lead in the direction of greater diversity in categorization. Understanding the emotion and desire categories in any given society will be a matter of understanding the extremely complex interplay between these two dimensions of our categorical activity.

To return, now, to my thesis and to the example of erotic love: what I have said shows that there is considerable relativity in erotic emotion, as in emotion generally.

It does not make a case for cultural relativism in the normative sense, that is, for the view that there are no criteria of adjudication by which we can assess these different patterns, asking which are conducive to human flourishing and which are not. Cultural variation, here as elsewhere, means that it will be difficult to ask and answer normative questions; no language we use will be free of particularity, and there will be many consequent dangers of false translation, of blindness, and of either excessive romanticization of the strange or excessive chauvinism toward the familiar.[35] But there is no reason why these dangers should be taken to defeat the project of normative analysis.[36] We may judge, as the Stoics did, that the value judgments on which the Romans based their conceptions of anger are wrong, that they ascribe too much importance to honor and reputation; we may judge that the negative attitude to sexuality embodied in the Augustinian conception of original sin is without a sound foundation and is an impediment to human flourishing. We may ask ourselves what forms of erotic love are and are not compatible with our other commitments, to justice, to equality, to productive work, to other loves and friendships.

In all these cases, judgment does not lead directly to change. To change beliefs in matters of this depth and importance cannot be a matter of a one-shot argument, but, if at all, of a life's patient effort. As Seneca said of anger, "Slow is the resistance to evils that are continuous and prolific."[37] But this does not mean that change is impossible, that an ironic distance is our only option. First, no cultural scheme is as monolithic and as universally constraining as the social-constructionist story sometimes suggests. In every society there is room to maneuver, room for individuals to wink knowingly at the rules, to play games with the rules, even to improvise mutual love in a situation of distance and hierarchy. (This aspect of the issue has been beautifully treated in some fundamental work on women and men in Greece by the late John J. Winkler.[38]) Second, individuals within societies, and societies themselves, do change, however slowly. One might consider the related case of racist beliefs: one does not change these overnight in oneself or in another simply as a result of becoming convinced by an ethical argument. On the other hand, once one is convinced, one can go to work on oneself and, I believe, to a significant extent transform oneself— first conduct, then, gradually, the inner world. And at the same time, of course, if one is involved in educating the next generation, one goes to work on them—and, at the same time, on the political and social institutions that shape their experience[39]—with greater optimism. This sort of patient effort forms the core of morality.[40] And the payoff for the position that emotions are not given in nature but are socially constructed is that emotions become a part of the domain of moral effort, so construed.[41]

THE CONSTRUCTION OF DESIRE

This may be all very well for complex emotions such as anger, grief, and even love. But why should we think it true of sexual desire? For surely sexual desire is rooted in our biology, in our animal nature itself. So it must surely be a precultural given, in which the cognitive interpretations engendered by social learning play little role.[42]

So one might think. And although the old behaviorist program of reducing every emotion to a single bodily response collapsed long ago in the cases of fear and joy and anger—when it was discovered, to the great surprise of psychologists, that the beliefs people had about the situation they are in affect their identification of their emotional state[43]—it is still alive, in its own peculiar way, in the case of sexual desire. I refer here to the heroic attempts of psychologist James Weinrich to define sexual desire in terms of genital blood volume, as measured by an ingenious machine called a penile plethysmograph.[44] (Weinrich notes that the vaginal plethysmography is still under development, so there are "few results for women.") If we begin by asking ourselves what is wrong with this elegantly simple device, we can begin to make progress on our problem. The plethysmograph, a metal measuring device, is attached to the man's penis. If the man proves at all able to have an erection with this device around him, it measures changes in penile blood volume. That is precisely all it measures. It is perfectly culture neutral. It brings in nothing about belief or interpretation to mess things up. If we can see why it is not a good measure of sexual desire, we can begin to see where there is room, in sexual desire, for culture to enter in.

Sexual desire does have, it is true, a "drive" component, much like hunger or thirst.[45] It is not terribly clear that the plesthymograph is a good measure of the bodily need for sexual gratification, or even of immediate sexual arousal; but let me pass over the arguments on that question.[46] What is evident is that the blood volume change measured by the plethysmograph cannot possibly be either necessary or sufficient for (male) sexual desire. Not necessary because it is possible to desire to have intercourse without having an erection: Weinrich cheerfully defines away the whole phenomenon of impotence. (And can't one have desire without even the wish for genital arousal?) Not sufficient because even Weinrich would probably not count as instances of sexual desire erections that occur outside of sexual contexts: when a person is waking up in the morning, for example, or when he is being put to death by hanging. What this brings out is that sexual desire is a complicated intentional phenomenon, as well as a drive—a "pull" as well as a "push." Desire, like grief and anger, is *about* an object and *for* an object. And it doesn't just take a snapshot of the object, it attends to the object, interprets its object *as desirable*. Desire, in short, is in good part "in the head."

Here, of course, is where culture and cultural variation play a major role. Society shapes a great deal, if not all, of what is found erotically desirable and social forms are themselves eroticized.[47] We see this quickly in the tremendous variety of what is found erotically appealing in different societies and, of course, by different individuals in different societies: different attributes of bodily shape,[48] of demeanor and gesture, of clothing, of sexual behavior itself. Social constructions of an attractive sexual object vary enormously, and with these, the social meaning of sexual arousal and interaction themselves.[49] To give just one very obvious example, in many societies—including, clearly, the ancient Indian culture depicted in my penis-worship story—female submissiveness and male power have become eroticized in such a way that the meaning of male-female sexual interaction itself is, at least in part, that it is an exercise of domination. This is a major theme in the work of Catharine MacKinnon and Andrea Dworkin;[50] and while I would take issue with the claim that all male-female intercourse must have this feature, I would not deny that intercourse between what many societies construct as male and what many societies construct as female has this feature—nor that sexual intercourse is, in crucial respects, a meeting of socially constructed fantasies and role enactments more than it is of uninterpreted bodies.

The difference of my argument from MacKinnon's can be best clarified by referring once again to the work of the late John J. Winkler, with whom MacKinnon collaborated at Yale to create grievance procedures for sexual harassment. Winkler's work on sexuality stresses repeatedly, and I think correctly, that even when hierarchical and oppressive social codes are in place, actors have a certain room to negotiate and to create their own possibilities within these codes, using the resources of their own individual histories, even thumbing their nose at the code in the very process of paying lip service to it. He uses this approach, for example, to argue that men and women in ancient Greece could find ways of expressing a mutual recognition of equality, even when the cultural language made it impossible to describe such equality except through the resources of poetic metaphor.[51] He used it in his life to show how a gay man in America might succeed in constructing a life whose terms were not those dictated by those who hate and marginalize gays, the life of a particular person capable of love and joy.

Such claims can only be made good by the detailed analysis of variety and negotiability within a particular culture; I shall not be able to do that here, either for ancient Greece or for contemporary America. But many such studies have shown that, even in the most rigid of cultures, one finds internal plurality, dissension, and a certain flexibility for improvisation.[52] (And indeed it is difficult to know how the process of social change in which MacKinnon is a leading participant could take place, if women and men were all as completely imprisoned by cultural stereotypes as the view sometimes seems to suggest.) One may grant, as I do, that institutional change is a necessary condition for lasting or effective behavioral and attitudinal changes, without granting that prior to such large-scale changes there is no room in individual lives for change or variety of perception.

Let me illustrate my general claim about sexuality, however, by taking one complex example involving both male-female and male-male relations to investigate the related claim that homosexuality is itself a cultural construct.[53]

Let us consider, then, the life of a young male in Athens of the fifth century B.C. Let us call this young man Glaukon, after the young Athenian gentleman who is one of the participants in Plato's *Republic*.[54] Glaukon will not be one of Winkler's resourceful real-life actors, but, rather, a collection of prevalent social norms, although we can assume that these norms impinge to at least a large degree on his behavior and experience. Glaukon grows up in a culture in which being a real adult man is defined largely in terms of honor and status in the community. Assuming the status of an adult citizen entails a certain attitude toward the needs of the body. Glaukon learns as he grows up that a real man has strong bodily desires, including sexual desire and the desires for food and drink; he exercises them, but is not mastered by them. Sexual desire is not specially problematic or an occasion of shame;[55] it is problematic in just the way other strong appetites are. (Already here we see a big difference in experience from the experience of bodily desire in a Christian culture.) What is crucial about sexual desire is, first, that Glaukon should not pursue it in a way that distracts him from his other pursuits or wastes his fortune; and, second, that it should be exercised solely in the act of penetration, by entering a suitably receptive body. The crucial opposition Glaukon learns is that of activity and passivity: he knows that it is a good thing—indeed an exciting and a desirable thing—to be the active penetrator, a shameful and terrible thing to be the passive penetratee.[56] One sphere in which he will exercise his active dominance will be marriage, in order to produce children for the city. But he will not expect much from marriage, either in the way of companionship or in the way of sexual artistry and know how: an uneducated sixteen-year-old girl who is never permitted to go out of the house[57] may well not completely occupy his imagination. On the other hand, trips to both male and female prostitutes are considered a good thing, so long as he doesn't spend too much money; and it doesn't make too much difference which sort he goes to, so long as it is clear that he goes there to penetrate.[58] Finally, given that he is urban and well off, his most intense erotic relationships are likely to be with young males, the *eromenoi*, beloveds, for whom he is the *erastes*, lover. These young males are future citizens, so he is not to dishonor them by anal penetration; on the other hand, intercrural intercourse (intercourse in which he achieves orgasm by thrusting between the boy's tightly clenched thighs[59] is all right. And if he is seen to be an intense lover of males, his friends will not judge that he has a "homosexual preference" and dislikes sex with women: on the contrary, they will infer that he is a sexually greedy fellow, and they will run to guard their wives.[60]

Glaukon's world, compared to our own, exhibits with respect to sexual desire all the four types of difference I identified when I talked about emotion. He learns different norms of sexual behavior, and he learns different normative judgments about the rightness and wrongness of various sorts of sexual activity and about the sexual attractiveness of different types of partners. He has an individual history of a distinctive sort. And, most important, the very taxonomy of types of sexual desire exhibits variation from our own: Glaukon does not conceive of, and therefore in a significant sense does not feel the desire for, males qua males, females qua females, any more than most modern Americans feel a generalized desire to penetrate, regardless of the gender of the object.

Is Glaukon a homosexual? This is a peculiar question. For unless we suppose that there is buried inside him somewhere a thing called a preference, rather like an extra bodily organ, we can find no reason at all, in his behavior or in his statements, for saying that he has a stable disposition toward partners of one gender rather than another. He sees partners as receptive bodies of various sorts: in a sense women are a species of a class to which anally penetrable male prostitutes also belong, and the citizen boy escapes belonging only by his conventionally ordained anal chastity.[61] On the one hand, he certainly does not have a steady inclination toward males rather than toward females—he likes young men for the conversation they afford, but he likes sex with women also. On the other hand, he is also not the "opportunistic homosexual" of Richard Posner's book and paper,[62] for he has ready access to women of various educational levels and sexual abilities and does not opt for boys simply out of frustration.[63] The way his desire sees the world, it is a scene for the enactment of various strategies of possession and penetration: that is his role, and it is the possibility of it that excites him.

Ancient Greece, in short, does not divide its sexual actors according to the concept of a stable inner "preference" for objects of a particular gender. In that sense, it lacks the very experience of homosexuality in its modern sense.[64] And this affects the way we cast our normative political arguments. The libertarian ideal articulated in Richard Posner's *Sex and Reason* is that our society contains various sexual kinds, some of them "normal" and some of them not so "normal," but that no moral or legal judgment should be passed on the less normal. We should protect liberty of sexual activity, except where compelling arguments show grave harm to others. But the social constructionist holds that this way of seeing things doesn't drive the criticism deep enough: it does not problematize the so-called normal, doesn't recognize the extent to which the contemporary heterosexual male—like the homosexual male—is the inhabitant of a social role that might have been otherwise.[65] Both are in that sense "unnatural actors."[66] And as Cass Sunstein argues in chapter 10 of this volume, the heterosexual may well have the more morally problematic role in this social drama since his role includes the domination of women. Seeing things this way is likely to move on from the combination of complacence about self and slightly condescending tolerance of the other so frequently encountered in liberal rhetoric to a more radical critical scrutiny of society's sexual drama as a whole.

THE SOCIAL MEANING OF THE BODY

But isn't this all given in the body? And don't bodies come by nature in different kinds? Even if we grant that nobody has shown that "homosexual" bodies are in any biological way different from "straight" bodies, surely we at least have a naturally given division between men and women. Surely this counts for something and provides a "natural" basis for social role divisions.

Yes and no. I want to insist that the body is not simply a cultural sign—as some culture theorists tend to suggest it is.[67] Questions of life and death, of good and bad nutritional status, of fitness and strength, of good and ill health, are not simply matters of cultural advertising, though, of course, experiences that are culturally shaped may influence them in many ways. And in the domain of sexuality the same is also true; there is much that is independent of cultural representation. The fact that individuals begin to feel sexual desire at a certain age, for example, or that sexual desire fluctuates with fatigue or changing health status—all these things appear to be rooted in the body independently of culture, though at every point they interact with culturally shaped factors in highly complex ways.

On the other hand, culture does enter in, even here. It used to be common to distinguish "sex"—the biological category—from "gender—a socially constructed category—and to think of one's sex as "given," one's gender as a socially learned role. But matters are actually not quite so simple. Bodily parts are not self-interpreting. As any woman knows who grew up during the change from the fifties to the sixties in America, and from Marilyn Monroe as norm of the woman to Twiggy, the meaning of breasts and legs is not given in nature: what is made of it by social advertising makes all the difference.[68] It is not so different with the so-called sexual organs. Things really are very much the way they are in my Indian story: there are these different decorations, but so much depends on what parents and other social actors make of them, what uses they ascribe to them, what metaphors they use about them, what roles and experiences they attach to them. No less a biologist than Charles Darwin, at the conclusion of a lengthy study of sexual dimorphism in plants and animals, expressed the limits of strictly biological knowledge on this topic when he wrote that we "do not even in the least know" what the significance of dimorphic reproduction is, as opposed to a process of parthenogenesis: "the whole subject is as yet hidden in darkness."[69]

What we do know a lot about, by contrast, is the insistent way in which parents classify children on the basis of their external genitalia, forcing a binary choice even when the genitalia themselves do not clearly announce their affiliation.[70] What we do know a lot about is the way in which this genital identification leads to pervasive differences in the shaping and interpretation of behavior. (Anne Fausto-Sterling has shown, for example, that the same emotional behavior on the part of infants is differently labelled in accordance with the sex announced to the observer: so-called boys are called angry, so-called girls frightened, though the cries they utter are the same.[71])

Genital organs, in short, do not interpret themselves; they do not announce to their bearers what they are and what is salient about them. On the other hand, they are the objects of cultural interpretation and representation from the time an infant is born; they figure in human experience only as mediated through many representations, and these representations interact in many ways with other representations of gender. Historical inquiry has shown that there is, here again, tremendous latitude for differences of reading, even in the apparently neutral domain of science.[72] Historian Thomas Laqueur concludes that the whole question whether there are in a morphologically salient sense two sexes, to be contrasted with one another, or a single sex, whose members vary be degree, is a question to which Western science has given sharply varying answers, even over a rather short period of history.[73] And modern biological research has recently lent the social constructionist strong support here, stressing the extent to which human (unlike most animal) sexuality is plastic, not subject to rigid genetic or hormonal patterning but determined by the learning and symbolic areas of the brain.[74] In short, gender is inextricable from sex: as soon as we are aware of the bodily parts that are signs of sex, we are aware of them *as* signs.[75] And this means that they are already within the domain of cultural interpretation and variation. My second Indian story can't even fully imagine a time when a penis was not a penis, just an unnamed decorative object, when men and women were not men and women, just differently decorated humans. The social significance of genital differences seems to be there already, lurking in the wings, awaiting the invention of genitals.

In short, the body, like emotion and desire, is in a sense "there," but in many ways that matter it is a sphere of experience and interpretation, a social artifact.

This does not mean that there is no biological basis for differences in sexual desire and attraction. The thesis of social construction is good at explaining how societies come to have the sexual categories they do. It is also good at showing how deeply such social patterning enters into the experience of each and every member of society from early infancy on, informing not just reflection, but also the very experience of desire and of oneself as desiring. It is far less adequate as an account of how particular social actors come to inhabit the categories they do inhabit. With the male and the female, we can see how parental recognition of differences in external genitalia leads from the start to differences in experience that end up producing a "man" or a "woman." This does not mean that no biological factors are relevant to explaining gender differences; but it does mean, as Fausto-Sterling has shown, that it will in practice be next to impossible to separate these from the pervasive influences of cultural patterning and that a healthy dose of skepticism about all naturalist claims is therefore warranted. In the case of sexual orientation, skepticism of a similar sort still seems warranted, given the thin and a *prioristic* character of much of the biological work that has been done.[76] But the fact that, of two infants whose external genital appearance does not differ in any way, one turns out a "homosexual" and the other a "heterosexual" still seems inadequately explained by social construction all by itself: the two may be in exactly the same stratum of society and may have had very similar experiences. The feeling of determination and constraint that is such a common feature of self-reports concerning homosexuality in our society suggests that either biological factors or very early individual experiences, or both, need to be invoked to complete the picture. But social construction will lead us to ask the right skeptical questions about premature claims in these areas as research evolves and will also show the researcher how complicated the conceptual terrain of her explanadum actually is—that the experiential category one is led to inhabit, by whatever combination of causal factors, is not, in many crucial respects, a transcultural and transhistorical category.

CONSTRUCTING CARE AND PARENTHOOD

I have said little here about the family. I hope it is clear by now that—given the role of culture in constructing what it is to be male, what it is to be female, what it is to desire, and even what it is to have a body—much follows from this about the social origins of that structure we naively refer to as "*the* family." But really showing this is the easy task, for even the most cursory excursion into comparative anthropology and social history makes plain that the "nuclear" family unit headed by a heterosexual couple, dwelling in its own private little house, and committed to intimate concern for one another and for the well-being of children is so far from being "natural" that it has hardly ever existed outside of Western Europe and North America after the Protestant Reformation.[77] Children are cared for by many different social arrangements: extended kinship structures, same-gender groupings, village cooperation. Indeed, what it is to *be* a parent, and what it is to *be* a child, varies enormously with respect to the type and length of care thought good and its social meaning.

The year 1994 was the United Nations's declared International Year of the Family. And no clearer evidence of my thesis can be found than the interagency documents that attempted to formulate a definition of "family" to serve as the basis of that year. At first there was an attempt made to treat the family as a "natural unit of socialization" and to offer some definition of its structure. But it quickly became obvious that any simple definition was parochial—leaving out many cultural variants, including a single-parent households, lesbian and gay families, and many more traditional forms of polygamous or multiadult bonding that the deliberators wished to include. Even a disjunctive definition proved ridiculous since it would have to be both cumbersomely lengthy and open-ended. So the parties settled on no definition at all, using the term "families" without restrictive specification and stating only, "As basic units of society, families and their well-being are germane to all our organizations."[78]

But instead of going into this matter more deeply at this time,[79] I shall return, in concluding, to ancient Athens and to a passage from Aristotle's school about the socially constructed meaning of the term "offspring." It was brought to my attention by my own offspring, who has what any social constructionist needs to have, a sense of humor, and who has been charmed, as I am, by its grace and its intellectual profundity.

In the *Problemata*, a work of questions and answers compiled by students in Aristotle's school, a bright pupil asks the following question: Why is it that when a human child is born from one's semen one calls it one's "offspring" (*ekgonon*), but when one's semen falls on the ground and a worm comes out of it (Aristotelians believed in spontaneous generation) one does not call it one's "offspring"? The answer comes back, it would be very strange to do so because it seems foreign and unnatural.[80]

Now even if we are not believers in the spontaneous generation of animals from waste products, and even if we have never asked ourselves that particular haunting question, we may see that it does in fact get at an issue of some depth, one that is debated right now in controversies about surrogacy and stepparenthood, family unity and dissolution, the claims of biological versus adoptive parents: the issue, that is, of what really is salient in our practices of naming some creatures "our offspring" and others not, what we think a parent is and does, what we think a real child is and does.[81] For from Aristotle's biological point of view the worm is just as physically continuous with the semen as the human child is,[82] and what he, or his student, is really getting at is that being a parent of offspring is a cultural and social matter, a matter of recognition and responsibility, not of mere bodily continuity.

The only way to ask this question well is the way Aristotle actually asks it in his ethical writings—holistically, in the context of a larger inquiry into what it is for a human being to flourish.[83] For only when we have a conception, however vague and general, of what the important activities in a human life are, and what support they need in order to develop, can we even begin to say what role that care of various sorts by other human beings does and does not play in getting young human beings to those goals. Only then can we imagine fruitfully the various different ways in which the care that we want may be instantiated in a society such as ours, with our resources and our history. Only then, as well, can we even begin to ask what material support is required for the kind of care we want and think good, and to take the necessary measures to make such support available to those capable of giving care. My own hunch, which I shall not try to defend here, is that children do need intimate and stable care from a small number of adults who are persistently devoted to the child's well-being, know the child's particularity, and provide the child with a materially secure and emotionally stable environment.[84] These conditions can obviously be met, and have throughout history been met, by quite a number of different configurations of caring adults, so there is no reason to think our options confined to the nuclear family in its traditional romanticized form. But what is equally clear is that none of them will be adequately met by adults, single or in couples or groups, who are afflicted by severe economic burdens that make it impossible for them to have stable and flourishing and physically healthy lives themselves, much less to create such a context for their children.

What I hope to have shown in this paper is that the role of society goes very deep, in matters that our tradition has tended to define as outside society, as "private" and "natural." This can feel like a source of constraint as we come to see to what extent we are artifacts, even in our apparently most internal and intimate lives. On the other hand, and this is what I want to emphasize, it can also feel like a source of freedom since we can see that many ways of experiencing the body, the emotions, and the care of children that might have seemed given and inevitable are actually made by us and can therefore be otherwise. This freedom, as I have said, is not limitless. For social construction does not deny that biology imposes constraints on the lives both of groups and of individuals, though it encourages a healthy skepticism about research that too quickly discovers a root in "nature" for the social status quo. Even where a social origin for a distinction is agreed, freedom to change does not follow unproblematically: it is difficult to change anything that is as deeply rooted in many people's very ways of seeing the world as is, for example, the perception that sexual relations between men and women are a way of exerting domination over women. With sex as with race: the only changes are likely to be hard-won, slow, and incremental, occurring in individual minds and in the possibilities that these create for the education of the next generation. Such changes are unlikely to take place without broader institutional and legal changes. Nor is it easy even to get agreement on the proper direction for change, for what we are saying is that there is no Archimedean point given from outside us, that the constraints come not from on high but from our own ethical convictions and choices, our commitments to justice and equality, our sense of what human flourishing is and should be. Belief in "nature" and the divine may be confining, but at least it gets us off the hook without having to make a respectable argument, without having to evaluate the values with which tradition has presented us.[85] The freedom of social construction is a freedom to follow good human arguments, which may lead to the conclusion that tradition is in many ways stupid and oppressive and bad. And that freedom imposes responsibilities that are all too easy to evade.

In Plato's *Republic*, Socrates, discussing the radical changes he proposes in the structure of the family and the role of women, remarks to the young Glaukon that people usually do not pursue such discussions very far because they stop with the agreements people have made over the ages and think that these agreements are sufficient. "They do this," answers Glaukon, "out of laziness." "Laziness, however," replies Socrates, "is a quality that the guardians of our laws can afford to do without." "You have made a good point there," answers Glaukon.

Notes

I am most grateful to David Estlund, Lawrence Lessig, Richard Posner, and Cass Sunstein for their extremely helpful comments on an earlier draft.

1. Cited from Wendy Doniger O'Flaherty, *Siva: The Erotic Ascetic* (Oxford: Oxford University Press, 1973), 294–95; Doniger in turn cites the story from David Stacton, *Kaliyuga: A Quarrel with the Gods* (London, 1975), 108. In some versions of the story the "wise men" are not humans but gods; as often in Hindu myth, the two worlds are contiguous and continuous.

2. The story is obviously not consistent on this point: it uses the later organ names, betray-

ing how difficult it is, in a society divided into two kinds, to imagine a state of things prior to the division. In this sense it is very close to the anomalies in Protagoras' account of the creation of species in Plato's *Protagoras*—in which the distinction between horses and birds predates the giving of hoofs to the former and wings to the latter, and in which the distinction between "rational" humans and "irrational beasts" precedes the invention and gift of rationality.

3. Doniger O'Flaherty, *Siva*, 112, cited from V. Elwin, *Myths of Middle India* (Oxford: Oxford University Press, 1949), 258.

4. See Doniger O'Flaherty, esp. 105 ff. It is striking that when Siva is involved in the intercourse-creation story, "he" must at first assume the form of an androgyne, and create the two sexes out of two parts or aspects of himself; see p. 112. Sexual dimorphism is thus imagined as a mysterious and somewhat arbitrary splitting of what was one, and capable of parthenogenetic reproduction. (These stories bear a striking resemblance to the story of sexual difference in Aristophanes' speech in Plato's *Symposium*.)

5. These problems include having a body of a certain type that demands a certain sort and quantity of nutrition; in that way biological commonality does shape the experience of emotion and desire—see p. 19.

6. The material in this section is presented much more fully, and with more complete references to relevant philosophical and anthropological studies, in my *Upheavals of Thought: A Theory of the Emotions*, Gifford Lectures 1993, University of Edinburgh, and forthcoming, Cambridge University Press.

7. The argument in what follows is closely related to the argument of Gifford Lecture 1. See also the related account of ancient Greek Stoic views, in my *The Therapy of Desire: Theory and Practice in Hellenistic Ethics* (Princeton: Princeton University Press, 1994), ch. 10.

8. There is much confusion here between two importantly distinct claims: (1) the claim that emotions are "irrational" in the sense of "noncognitive," and (2) the claim that they are "irrational" in a normative sense, meaning "ill-suited to guide us when we wish to think well." One might, of course, hold 2 without 1; and indeed most of the major philosophical holders of 2—such as Plato, the ancient Greek and Roman Stoics, Spinoza, and Kant—were all defenders of some type of cognitive view of emotion. They just thought that the cognitions in question were inaccurate because they ascribed too much importance to aspects of the world outside ourselves that we don't control.

9. In the Gifford Lectures I discuss related views from Chinese and Indian traditions.

10. Richard Lazarus, *Emotion and Adaptation* (New York: Oxford University Press, 1991).

11. Euripides, *The Trojan Women*, 1158–1207.

12. Hecuba's criticism focuses on the gratuitous exercise of overwhelming power to crush a helpless small child who could have been rendered politically ineffectual by less brutal means—in particular, by sending him off into exile with his mother. Hecuba sees in the Greek action a sign of cowardice and weakness, not of political good sense.

13. This does not mean that a person who has a certain emotion—and therefore the beliefs that go with that—could not also have contradictory beliefs about the same matter. For example, if I am trying to become a good Stoic, I may find myself grieving at the death of a loved one (and having the beliefs about the badness of that event and the importance of the person that this grief entails) while also believing that the Stoics are correct—these things have no real importance. What my view says about these cases is that they are instances of internal conflict, in which the conflict has the form of a debate about what is really true, not the form of a noncognitive struggle between forces.

14. An intermediate case would be one in which she discovered that it was a real child but not her grandchild. Here she would presumably have some emotion, although not of this intensity. I discuss this problematic unevenness in the emotions in several of the Gifford Lectures.

15. Cicero, *Tusculan Disputations*, III.30.

16. I am assuming here that the relevant beliefs and other cognitive representations are not innate, but learned. This has in fact been experimentally confirmed in some very interesting work by Martin Seligman on animal learning; see below, notes 18–20.

17. Here I have only argued that beliefs are necessary for emotions—and necessary as constituent parts of what a given emotion is. (One cannot say what grief is without mentioning the typical beliefs that differentiate grief from anger and fear and pity.) I do not argue here for the thesis that cognitions of a certain type are sufficient conditions for the emotion. But in fact I am prepared to argue for that thesis, and I do argue for it in Gifford Lecture 1. Indeed, I argue (though with some qualification) that the emotion is identical with a cognition of this sort.

18. I discuss this in Gifford Lecture 2. The works on which I most prominently rely in constructing my account are Martin Seligman, *Helplessness* (New York: W.H. Freeman, 1975); Lazarus, *Emotion and Adaptation*; Keith Oatley, *Best-Laid Schemes* (Cambridge: Cambridge University Press, 1992); also Nico Frijda, *The Emotions* (Cambridge: Cambridge University Press, 1986). Of particular importance for my purposes here is the work of James Averill, which combines cognitive-psychological analysis with an analysis of socially constructed role playing: see "Grief: Its Nature and Significance," *Psychological Bulletin* 70 (1968): 721–48, and *Anger and Aggression: An Essay on Emotion* (New York: Springer, 1982). Within philosophy, an excellent and rigorous account of the cognitive dimensions of emotion, with an analysis of their adaptive significance in the lives of animals generally, is in Ronald de Sousa, *The Rationality of Emotion* (Cambridge, Mass.: MIT Press, 1987).

It should be noted that a good deal of the psychological literature implicitly commits itself to mental "representationalism"—that is, to the view that the way in which the world impinges on animals is through mental representations that they produce and that then have causal properties. Since the psychologists who use this language do not offer arguments in favor of representationalism or against other ways of understanding the animal/world relation, and since I myself have grave doubts about the adequacy of representationalism as a view of mind, I shall simply speak here of the animal's "interpretation" of the world, remaining neutral concerning the mental mode of the interpreting. The psychologists' basic argument is untouched by this change, and one may note that more philosophically trained psychologists such as Lazarus and Oatley do not use representationalist language.

19. How far "down" do emotions go? Experimental evidence suggests that it is not possible to give adequate explanations of the behavior even of rats without positing cognitive representations of the sort involved in fear; see Seligman, *Helplessness*. And Darwin long ago discovered remarkable cognitive complexity in the activities of worms—see James Rachels, *Created From Animals* (New York: Oxford University Press, 1990). But Darwin also argued convincingly that evasive behavior in some insects could be explained without invoking cognitive interpretations, and the issue clearly needs to be resolved by prolonged inspection of the behavior of each species.

20. My cognitive position is perfectly compatible with the thesis that emotions have evolved as they have *because* of their adaptive value (I stress this thesis in Gifford Lecture 2). Evolutionary biologists who offer functional accounts of emotion do not presently hold that such accounts require us to believe that emotions are "hardwired" rather than learned in interaction with other animals. The best philosophical investigation of this issue is in de Sousa, *Rationality of Emotion*. And see also Oatley, *Best-Laid Schemes*; Lazarus, *Emotion and Adaptation*; and Seligman, *Helplessness*. Because emotions can be shown to require cognitive interpretations that must be learned, can—as Seligman shows with painstaking experimental work—be disrupted by a disruption of ordinary learning processes, they occupy a different status from that of reflex activities such as sneezing.

21. This does not mean that individuals could not be taught to lose that fear—either through religious belief, becoming so hardened to risk that it no longer seems terrible, or losing the love of life. But no known society is, as a whole, totally without that fear.

22. Although, as we shall shortly see, cultural manipulation of bodily shape begins very early in life.

23. Jean Briggs, *Never in Anger* (Cambridge, Mass.: Harvard University Press, 1970); for a related anthropological study, see Catherine Lutz, *Unnatural Emotions* (Chicago: University of Chicago Press, 1988).

24. On those close connections between erotic excitement and anger in Roman life, see chapters 11 and 13 of Nussbaum, *Therapy of Desire*. A full study of this phenomenon would include a study of Roman erotic language—very different from Greek erotic language in the role played by invective, enemy smashing, and humiliation—and a study of the sexual activities reported in Roman biography—in which assertions of power over one's male enemies are very frequently linked with sexual arousal. Here one may note that the Penthouse magazine film of Suetonius' life of Caligula, which looked obscene to many American eyes, looked evasive and prettified to a student of ancient Rome since consensual sexual activity between adults was again and again substituted for the exercise of vindictive sexual humiliation and mutilation against powerless inferiors (usually male). There is not a really good account of Roman sexuality corresponding to Dover's work on Greece, but for a start, see J. Adam, *The Latin Sexual Vocabulary*. For related observations about the role of cruelty in the "social construction" of Roman parenthood, see Richard Saller's excellent studies of the Roman family, including "Pietas, Obligation and Authority in the Roman Family," *Festschrift Karl Christ* (Darmstadt: Wissenschattliche Buchgesellschaft, 1988): 393–410.)

25. For a wonderful literary embodiment of this idea, see Samuel Beckett's *Molloy* trilogy; I discuss its emotion taxonomy in "Narrative Emotions," in Nussbaum, *Love's Knowledge* (New York: Oxford University Press, 1990). Consider, for example, the following passage:

> The idea of punishment came to his mind, addicted it is true to that chimera and probably impressed by the posture of the body and the fingers clenched as though in torment. And without knowing exactly what his sin was he felt full well that living was not a sufficient atonement for it or that this atonement was in itself a sin, calling for more atonement, and so on, as if there could be anything but life, for the living. And no doubt he would have wondered it if was really necessary to be guilty in order to be punished but for the memory, more and more galling, of his having consented to live in his mother, then to leave her. And this again he could not see as his true sin, but as yet another atonement which had miscarried and, far from cleansing him of his sin, plunged him in it deeper than before. And truth to tell the ideas of guilt and punishment were confused together in his mind, as those of cause and effect so often are in the minds of those who continue to think. And it was often in fear and trembling that he suffered, saying, This will cost me dear . . . (Beckett, *Molloy* [New York: Grove Press, 1955], pp. 239–40)

Here we see a specifically Irish-Christian taxonomy of emotions, in which desire, guilt, fear, disgust, self-hatred, and the desire for atonement are all interwoven in a characteristic way.

26. See D. Kahan and M. Nussbaum, "Two Conceptions of Emotion in Criminal Law," *Columbia Law Review* 96 (1996): 270–374.

27. It is not simply that they give names to emotions that we experience but don't bother to name. A longer study of the example would show, I think, that the zealous interest in and pride concerning anger that emerges in this taxonomic activity also enters into the experience of the emotion, tinging it with a manly pride and a self-conscious classificatory zeal that would be no part of the Utku experience.

28. See John J. Winkler, *The Constraints of Desire: The Anthropology of Sex and Gender in Greece* (New York: Routledge, 1990).

29. I am not claiming that this is universally true: for our culture, where *eros* is concerned, stands at the confluence of quite a few different traditions, prominently including the Christian and the Romantic, both of which have darker understandings of *eros*.

30. Plato, *Symposium*, 199E ff. On the close relationship of this definition to popular understandings, see Winkler, *Constraints of Desire*. Plato's primary departure from tradition is in holding that *eros* is all along really directed toward an object—the form of the *kalon*—that is immortal and unchanging; popular accounts take it for granted that the object is a human being and that the goal of *eros* is intercourse with that human being.

31. Lucretius describes a closely related cultural pattern in which fusion with a divine or quasi-divine object is the goal; see Nussbaum, "Beyond Obsession and Disgust: Lucretius's Genealogy of Love," *Apeiron* 22 (1989): 1–59.

32. All this could be pursued further by discussing Wittgenstein's ideas of "family resemblance" and his views about the connections between meanings and forms of life.

33. I take this term from W. V. O. Quine, "Ontological Relativity," in *Ontological Relativity and Other Essays* (New York: Columbia University Press, 1969).

34. On the importance of metaphysics and epistemology for feminist inquiries in these areas, see Charlotte Wit, "Feminist Metaphysics," and Louise Antony, "Quine as Feminist," in *A Mind of One's Own: Feminist Essays on Reason and Objectivity*, ed. Antony and Witt (Boulder: Westview Press, 1993).

35. See the excellent discussion of these pitfalls in Lee Yearley, *Mencius and Aquinas: Comparing Virtues and Theories of Courage* (Albany: State University of New York Press, 1990).

36. See Nussbaum, "Non-Relative Virtues," in Nussbaum and Sen, *The Quality of Life* (Oxford: Clarendon Press, 1993), 242–69.

37. Seneca, *On Anger*, II.10.

38. See John J. Winkler, *Constraints of Desire*, esp. "Penelope's Cunning and Homer's" and "The Laughter of the Oppressed."

39. For the social constructionist, change that does not include structural, institutional, and legal change is likely to be ineffective and short-lived. It is my view that social and institutional meanings have no agency and reality on their own, apart from their role in the judgments and actions of individuals. But there is no doubt that social change may often occur at an institutional level before many of the agents in question have themselves been changed. Thus laws might be made that have implications for the structure of racist emotion even by people who themselves still experience such emotions at one level of their personalities—because they decide, for whatever reason, that it is best for things to be this way. The institutional meanings themselves will gradually alter the meanings to which individuals attach themselves. Seneca's proposals for judicial institutions have a similar character. People who note in themselves a tendency to vindicate anger and who, as a result of reflection, deplore those tendencies may commit themselves to judicial institutions embodying mercy in their structure and meaning. This is expected not to suppress, but to transform the motives for revenge.

40. See Iris Murdoch, *The Sovereignty of Good* (London: Routledge, 1970).

41. See Seneca, *On Anger*, esp. I.5. It is important to qualify this optimistic claim in three ways, for constraints of two different sorts may make the success (or the complete success) of such a project impossible: (1) It may turn out that the experience in question does indeed have a biological component that cannot itself be altered by change of thought; I shall discuss this further below. (2) It may turn out that the structure of human life makes it impossible not to have experiences that engender the emotion—unless one withdraws one's cares from the world in such a radical way as to lose all motives for action. This is, I think, Seneca's final po-

sition about anger. (3) The roots of the emotion may lie so deep in infancy, and may so permeate the personality, that change will not know where to locate its target or, if it does, may find the costs of alteration too high.

42. Note that the "argument" here assumes an erroneous view of animal psychology, in which cognitive interpretation plays no important role. On this, see Seligman, *Helplessness*; Lazarus, *Emotion and Adaptation*; Oatley, *Best-Laid Schemes*.

43. I am thinking here of the famous Schachter-Singer experiments, which I discuss in detail in Gifford Lecture 2; S. Schachter and J. E. Singer, "Cognitive, Social, and Physiological Determinants of Emotional State," *Psychological Review* 69 (1982): 379–99. Subjects were injected with adrenalin while being given different views about their situation—whether they were being threatened or insulted or amused. Their identification of fear and anger and joy followed the beliefs.

44. See James Weinrich "Toward a Sociobiological Theory of the Emotions," in *Emotion: Theory, Research, and Experience*, ed. R. Plutehih and H. Kellerman (New York: Academic Press, 1980), 13–38; discussed in detail in Gifford Lecture 2.

45. I do not mean to grant here that hunger and thirst are *only* "drives," lacking in all intentional or interpretive content. I mean only that they do arise "from behind," so to speak, from the state the body is in, whether or not there is any suitable object on the scene, even in fantasy, though of course the presence of an object may alter both intensity and experience, and cultural beliefs about suitable objects may play a large role here as well.

46. Briefly put, they include the observation that one may have frequent erections without any sexual feeling or pleasure, and, indeed, with a diminished capacity for sexual feeling: this is a common side effect, for example, of some medications. On the other hand, one may have intense sexual feeling and orgasm without erection, or at least without a full erection, so that even the claim of necessity seems unsuccessful. Weinrich's way of phrasing his claims has other difficulties: for example, it appears that he is committed to the view that a man with a larger penile blood volume is more aroused (and more desirous) than a man with a smaller blood volume and, thus, that penis size is a measure of the capacity for arousal and desire.

47. See the good statement of this point in Sherry B. Ortner and Harriet Whitehead, *Sexual Meanings: The Cultural Construction of Gender and Sexuality* (Cambridge: Cambridge University Press, 1981).

48. See Ann Hollander, *Seeing Through Clothes* (New York: Viking, 1978). The slender female figure that is considered desirable in contemporary America would be regarded as altogether without sexual interest in many parts of the world, past and present. And stories abound about siblings of different figure types whose erotic fortunes are reversed by a change of geographical location. A valuable recent study of the American body norm, in all of its cultural contradictions, is Susan Bordo, *Unbearable Weight* (Berkeley: University of California Press, 1993). Through analysis of advertisements and other cultural signs, Bordo argues that the American female learns to eroticize incompatibles: on the one hand, susceptibility to the seductive lure of consumer commodities of many sorts, but foods above all; on the other hand, iron control over the body, manifested in an ideal form with no "wiggles." She argues cogently that bulimia is the cultural expression of these contradictions.

49. Some wonderful material on this is in Ortner and Whitehead, *Sexual Meanings*; see also Jane Collier and Sylvia Yanagisako, *Gender and Kinship: Essays Toward a Unified Analysis* (Stanford: Stanford University Press, 1987). For ancient Greece, see the essays in *Before Sexuality*, ed. D. Halperin, J. Winkler, and F. Zeitlin (Princeton: Princeton University Press, 1990).

50. MacKinnon, especially *Feminism Unmodified: Discourses on Life and Law* (Cambridge, Mass.: Harvard University Press, 1987); Dworkin, especially *Intercourse* (New York 1987).

51. Winkler, "Penelope's Cunning and Homer's," delivered as a Charles Alexander Robinson Lecture at Brown University and published in *Constraints of Desire*.

52. See, for example, Brigg's subtle account of variations in children's responses to the Utku cultural norms and similar material in Lutz, *Unnatural Emotions*. On the general issue of internal plurality and contestation, see, among others, Seyla Benhabib, "Cultural Complexity, Moral Interdependence, and The Global Biological Community," in *Women, Culture, and Development*, ed. Nussbaum and Glover. (Oxford: Clarendon Press, 1995). Amartya Sen and I have argued the point for India in "Internal Criticism and Indian Rationalist Traditions," in *Relativism*, ed. M. Krausz (Notre Dame: Notre Dame University Press, 1988). And see now Sen's "India and the West," *New Republic*, June 7, 1993, 27–33.

53. This claim is associated above all with the work of Michel Foucault, especially *The Use of Pleasure: The History of Sexuality*, Vol. 2, trans. Robert Hurley (New York: Pantheon, 1984); it has also, for Greece, been very well discussed by David M. Halperin in *One Hundred Years of Homosexuality and Other Essays on Greek Love* (New York: Routledge, 1990). The best historical account of Greek sexual customs is K. J. Dover, *Greek Homosexuality*, 2d ed. (Cambridge, Mass: Harvard University Press, 1978, 1989).

54. Glaukon is also Plato's own half-brother.

55. Although the other bodily appetites are contrasted with the desire *to be penetrated* in respect of shamefulness; see Ps.-Aristotle, *Problemata*, IV.27.

56. See Winkler, "Laying Down the Law: The Oversight of Men's Sexual Behavior in Classical Athens," in *Constraints of Desire*: "The concept of a *kinaidos* was of a man socially deviant in his entire being, principally observable in behavior that flagrantly violated or contravened the dominant social definition of masculinity." For a fascinating attempt to explain how such a creature could ever be produced, see Ps.-Aristotle, *Problemata* IV.27, brilliantly analyzed by Winkler in the above article. After a lengthy appeal to innate biological difference supported by a theory that the ducts that in most men run to the penis run, in some, to the anus by mistake, the author throws up his hands and says, "Besides, in some people habit is a second nature." The contemporary search for a biological explanation of homosexuality sometimes seems as a prioristic and as inconclusive as this fourth-century B.C. work.

57. There may be occasional exceptions for religious festivals, and possibly the theater (as a religious occasion). But on the whole even the complex operations of a woman who manages her husband's estate—like the young wife described in Xenophon's *Oeconomicus*—are carried on indoors. Xenophon's advice to her is to get some exercise dusting the pots and pans so that her complexion will glow without makeup.

58. See Halperin, "The Democratic Body," in *One Hundred Years*. The evidence makes it clear that prostitutes were available at a price within any man's means. The story is told that the existence of low-price public brothels was the idea of Solon the lawgiver himself, in order to reinforce the idea of democratic equality by guaranteeing to all citizens regardless of means a way of exercising manly domination in matters of pleasure.

59. For the visual evidence on this point, with many reproductions, see Dover. It is worthy of note that the apparently obvious alternative of oral sex is disdained in Greek culture, in both male-female and male-male relationships. The activity is considered "unclean," and the performer of either fellatio or cunnilingus is thought to be humiliated by the act. Artemidoros, the A.D. second-century dream interpreter, explains at length that dreams of oral sex are always ill-omened—unless the dreamer is a person who "makes his living by his mouth," such as "trumpet players, rhetoricians, sophists, and the like." In that case, the dream is a happy sign of the profitable exercise of one's chosen profession. I discuss this and other aspects of Artemidoros' account in "The *Oedipus Rex* and the Ancient Unconscious," in *Freud and Forbidden Knowledge* ed. P. Rudnytsky (New York: New York University Press, 1993). Ancient India also had a strong taboo against oral sex: the permissive *Kama Sutra* is sternly negative.

60. On this see the evidence in the title essay of Halperin, *One Hundred Years*.

61. On the boy's lack of sexual arousal, see Dover *Greek Homosexuality*, on the artistic evidence, which displays cultural norms if not invariable cultural practices.

62. Richard Posner, *Sex and Reason* (Cambridge, Mass.: Harvard University Press, 1992). I have reviewed Posner's book in "Venus in Robes," *New Republic*, April 20, 1992, and in "'Only Grey Matter'? Richard Posner's Cost-Benefit Analysis of Sex," *University of Chicago Law Review* 59 (1992): 1689–1734.

63. The most recent version of Posner's paper in Chapter 8 of this volume, "The Economic Approach to Homosexuality," makes a more complicated and, I think, much more plausible argument. Given, Posner says, that relationships with women could rarely involve companionship and friendship, the male formed relations of that sort with other males, and then felt in some cases the desire to "cement" that companionship with sex. I think that this represents a marked departure from the book's analysis of opportunistic homosexuality since it represents the desire for sex with the young male as arising not from frustrated desire for (unavailable) women but from the boy's own attractiveness in other respects, and thus recognizes the intentional and interpretive character of sexual desire to a far greater degree than Posner's book usually does. On the other hand, it seems to me still to recognize the role of culture too little. The Greek male did not just find himself desiring to make love with a male friend; in fact, the entire culture saturated his experience with images proclaiming the beauty of young males, as well as their suitability for friendship. And the relationship thus constructed was different in all sorts of ways from Posner's image of "companionate marriage" (in its asymmetry and nonmutuality, for example, and its intense focus on a particular sort of bodily beauty), while Posner's analysis tends to assimilate the two.

64. Compare to both the Greek and the modern cases the case of the Navajo "berdache," discussed in Harriet Whitehead, "The Bow and the Burden Strap: A New Look at Institutionalized Homosexuality in Native North America," in Ortner and Whitehead, *Sexual Meanings*, 80–115, and also in Walter Williams, *The Spirit and the Flesh: Sexual Diversity in American Indian Culture* (Boston: Beacon Press, 1988). This male who shows a preference for female work (especially basket weaving) gets classified as socially female *on that account*, and for this reason, is steered into wearing female dress. "She" will become the wife of some male, usually one too poor to pay the usual bride-price. Whereas Christian missionaries who encountered this custom recoiled in horror, seeing "sodomy" and "unnatural activity" before their eyes, the Navajo clearly regard the intercourse of such a couple as male-female intercourse—albeit of a peculiar sort—since the berdache has been previously classified as female. And occupational classification is the central definiens on which sexual role follows; there is no reason to see the berdache as having an antecedent preference for sex with males. To read the evidence this way is to impose our sexual categories a priori.

65. This does not mean that there is no biological element involved in explaining how, given the society one is in, one gets assigned to this sexual category rather than that; see below, "The Social Meaning of the Body."

66. See William Eskridge's excellent "A Social Constructionist Critique of Posner's *Sex and Reason*: Steps Toward a Gaylegal Agenda," *Yale Law Journal* 102 (1992): 333–86. It should be noted that, although Posner's libertarianism traces its origins to J. S. Mill, Posner on the whole does not follow Mill in his radical criticism of current preferences in matters of gender, which Mill holds to be distorted and highly irrational (see *The Subjection of Women* ed. S. M. Okin (Indianapolis: Hachett, 1988).

67. This, I think, is the main defect of Bordo's imaginative analysis. For example, she criticizes those who call extremely obese people self-destructive, saying that such people are in the grip of cultural images of thinness, although extreme obesity is linked to various causes of death in a causal chain that does not run through cultural perceptions—although, of course,

the cultural discrimination experienced by obese people may make their health worse in a variety of ways. Again, she treats exercise as simply a matter of sculpting one's bodily "signifier," without recognizing that a person who is fitter and stronger can actually do certain things that she couldn't do before, say, lift a heavy object without damaging herself. The fact that lifting weight has a certain effect on the muscles and on their ability to perform certain tasks appears to be independent of the muscles' cultural symbolism.

68. For much more along these lines, see Hollander, *Seeing Through Clothes*. It is instructive to note that the first Miss America (in the 1920s) had a bust measurement of 28 inches. To take another case in point, the most cursory reading of classical Indian poetry reveals an eroticization of fleshy thighs (so fleshy that they make it hard to walk) that strikes contemporary American readers as peculiar and even a bit disgusting, rather like a praise of decaying food. Again, see Bordo's *Unbearable Weight* for the current American norm.

69. Charles Darwin, "On the Two Forms, or Dimorphic Condition, in the Species of *Primula*, and on Their Remarkable Sexual Relations," in *The Collected Papers of Charles Darwin: Volume Two* (Chicago: University of Chicago Press, 1977), 61.

70. See Judith Butler, *Gender Trouble: Feminism and the Subversion of Identity* (New York: Routledge, 1990); M. Foucault, *Herculine Barbin, Being the Recently Discovered Memoirs of a Nineteenth-Century Hermaphrodite*, trans. Richard McDongall (New York: Pantheon, 1980).

71. Fausto-Sterling, *Myths of Gender*, 2d ed. (New York: Basic Books, 1985, 1992).

72. Here my argument connects with a broader set of issues in contemporary metaphysics concerning the "interest relativity" of all categorization in science and elsewhere. I cannot defend a general position in this complex debate here, but the position I would wish to defend is close to that of Hilary Putnam, who argues that all distinctions are in a significant sense made by human beings and relative to human interests—but that there are many constraints on the ways in which this can be done, and some categorizations are therefore superior to others. In the area of emotion and sexuality, however, I think we see considerably more variation of schematization than we do in many of the areas investigated by Putnam, given the intensity of the political interests in the outcome. This does not mean that we cannot still argue cogently that some categorizations are better than others; it does mean that it will be a long and difficult process.

73. Thomas Laqueur, *Making Sex: Body and Gender from the Greeks to Freud* (Cambridge, Mass.: Harvard University Press, 1990). Laqueur's treatment of the ancient Greek evidence does not seem to me very satisfactory, but the later chapters, which deal with his real period of expertise, appear convincing.

74. This research also stresses that insofar as hormones govern sexual arousal the operative hormone is the same for "men" and for "women," it is androgen. For a good summary of recent research, see Salvatore Cucchiari, "The Origins of Gender Hierarchy," in Ortner and Whitehead, *Sexual Meanings*, 31–79. Among the studies whose results are discussed are John Money, "Psychosexual Differentiation," in *Sex Research: New Developments*, ed. John Money (New York: Holt, Rinehart, and Winston, 1965), 3–23; Money and Patricia Tucker, *Sexual Signatures: On Being a Man or a Woman* (Boston: Little, Brown, 1975); Frank A. Beach, "Evolutionary Changes in the Physiological Control of Mating Behavior in Mammals," *Psychological Review* 54 (1947): 346–55; Saul Rosenzweig, "Human Sexual Autonomy as an Evolutionary Attainment, Anticipating Proceptive Sex Choice and Idiodynamic Bisexuality," in *Contemporary Sexual Behavior: Critical Issues for the 70's*, ed. J. Zubin and J. Money (Baltimore: Johns Hopkins University Press, 1973), 189–229. And for a brilliant and persistent account of the misreading of biological evidence on the question of sex difference, see Anne Fausto-Sterling, *Myths of Gender*.

75. See Cucchiari, "Gender Hierarchy" 45: "We perceive vaginas and penises not merely

as biological features but apperceive them as meaningful signs representing gender categories
. . . Nothing about the morphology of genitalia necessitates this point of view. "In effect, Cucchiari seems to be taking the point of view defended by Susan Okin in *Justice, Gender, and the
Family* (New York: Basic Books, 1989): it is perfectly conceivable that these signs of difference could be viewed as having as little social significance as differences in eye color, or differences between left-handed and right-handed people, have in our society. That is, the distinction of sex would still be relevant to the choices and responses of individuals, but
large-scale social divisions would not be built around it.

76. On LeVay's work (Simon LeVay, "Difference in Hypothalamic Structure Between Heterosexual and Homosexual Men," *Brain Research* 253 [1991]: 1034–37), see, among other
criticisms, Fausto-Sterling's in the new second edition of her book (1992), pp. 223–59.
Among the difficulties: LeVay's sample was extremely small; it consisted of people with
AIDS, whose capacity for causing massive brain changes is well known but not understood in
detail; the sample contained no lesbians; it did not discriminate concerning preferred sexual
acts and sexual roles, thus making any mapping of the U.S. situation onto ancient Greece and
many other cultures altogether impossible.

77. See Charles Taylor, *Sources of the Self: The Making of the Modern Identity* (Cambridge, Mass.: Harvard University Press, 1989). For comparative data, see Ortner and Whitehead, *Sexual Meanings*; Collier and Yanagisako, *Gender and Kinship*; and many others. Of
course, many societies do have separate dwelling places for groupings that are in some sense
"nuclear." But the peculiar Western emphasis on the moral worth of the intimate bonds of the
family and on the privacy of the dwelling place as scene for this intimate moral bonding is virtually unique. The ancient Greek household, for example, would have set very little store on
privacy in the relevant sense; and the husband would have had very little contact with the children, and more or less no social intimacy with the wife.

78. "Interagency Statement on the International Year of the Family, 1994," jointly issued
by the concerned organizations and specialized agencies of the United Nations system.

79. It will be the subject of a paper that Richard Posner and I are writing together for
Women, Equality, and Reproduction, ed. J. Glover, M. Nussbaum, and C. Sunstein, for the
WIDER series.

80. "Aristotle," *Problemata*, IV.13, 878A.

81. For another fascinating Greek example on this issue, see the dialogue between father
and son about father beating in Aristophanes' *Clouds*; I discuss this in "Sophistry About Conventions" in *Love's Knowledge* (New York: Oxford University Press, 1990).

82. This is so because he denies that the maternal matter makes any contribution to reproduction beyond that of keeping the growing creature warm.

83. I have discussed his views on this topic in *The Fragility of Goodness* (Cambridge:
Cambridge University Press, 1986), ch. 12. And see also Nancy Sherman, *The Fabric of Character* (Oxford: Clarendon Press, 1989).

84. In Gifford Lecture 3, I examine psychoanalytic developmental accounts of childhood
and conclude that this, and nothing more specific, is what they really show. Especially significant, but also culturally narrow, is the work of John Bowlby—*Attachment*, (New York: Basic
Books, 2d ed. 1982); *Separation* (1973); and *Loss* (1980)—which move far too rapidly from
the conclusion I make here to a narrower conclusion about the role of the mother and the nuclear family. One difficulty in Bowlby's research is that the only children in nonnuclear families he observed had some other source of stress. Some were children removed from their families by World War II bombing raids, some were bereaved children, some were in day care
because their parents were poor and had to work. Bowlby never considered the obvious fact
that most "normal" ruling class English men and women rarely saw their parents in infancy,
and yet (by his lights, at any rate) emerged psychologically healthy as a result of the activity of

their nannies and other servants. And his own research with primates shows that, though a close attachment figure is crucial to psychological health, that figure can take many forms: it may be a primate of another species, or a human, or even a cuddly stuffed animal that dispenses food.

85. Consider, for example, the way appeals to the Judaeo-Christian tradition functions in the majority and concurring opinions in Bowers v. Hardwick, 478 U.S. 186, 106 S. Ct. 2841 (1986), as debate stoppers.

3

Sexual Orientation and Gender: Dichotomizing Differences

Susan Moller Okin

Laws in the United States, as in many other countries, have had a significant impact on both the differential treatment of men and women, and the differential treatment of heterosexuals and of gay men and lesbians. Because of many changes during the last twenty-five years, explicit legal discrimination on the grounds of sex is now considerably less extensive than is legal discrimination on the grounds of sexual orientation. But there are still many ways in which social, economic, and political structures and expectations, as well as some laws, privilege men over women, as well as heterosexual over homosexual persons. These are two of the many dimensions along which persons in our society are not afforded equal treatment—in which their different bodies or desires are made to affect considerably the ways in which and the extent to which they are able to be effective citizens and to lead personally fulfilling lives. The issue to be addressed here is not the privileging of heterosexual men *per se*, but the relationship between the two aspects of it—between sexism and heterosexism. Specifically, I argue that both the dichotomizing of masculine and feminine attributes, and the privileging of the former, are closely related to the stigmatization of homosexuality. Consequently, to the extent that a theory or social policy aims at reducing gender—by which I mean the social salience and institutionalization of sexual difference—it is also likely to reduce heterosexism.[1]

In *Justice, Gender, and the Family*, I have argued for the greater justice of a future society *free from gender*—one in which, as I put it: "[i]n its social structures and practices, one's sex is of no more social relevance than one's eye color or the length of one's toes. . . ."[2] One point of criticism of the book has come up a number of times: its supposed heterosexist bias.[3] As I shall argue here, rather than being biased *against* homosexual or other non-traditional relationships or families, my arguments taken as a whole are indeed conducive to more, rather than less, acceptance and endorsement of such relationships. For the kinds of changes that would enable women to become equal with men would also lead to greater equality between homosexuals and heterosexuals.

I shall start by explaining further what I mean by a "gender-free" society. It would result from the diminution and eventual disappearance of sex roles, of expectations that persons of different sexes think, act, dress, and adorn themselves, feel, or react in ways supposedly representative of or proper to their sex. In such a society, no assumptions would be made about "male" and "female" roles, and men and women would participate in more or less equal numbers in every sphere of life, from infant care to different kinds of paid work to high-level politics. This would bring with it many benefits: women and children, who now suffer many of the injustices of gender, would enjoy greater socio-economic equality with men; equality of opportunity would be enhanced-both for women and for the increasing numbers of children of both sexes who are economically dependent on women alone; and the environment of early childhood would be far more conducive to the development of that "sense of justice" that citizens need to acquire in order to want to preserve social justice.[4]

Many people, including some feminists, oppose reducing the salience of sexual difference to a minimum because, among other reasons, they think this would make life boring. They envisage, it seems, a gender-free world as one inhabited by a species of persons who, despite still having male or female genitals and a few other physical characteristics typical of females and males, would all be the same: a world of hermaphroditic-looking beings with none of the differences amongst them that we now tend to associate with femininity or masculinity. However just this vision might be, such interpreters declaim it for being monotonous and repressive.

This is certainly not the only imaginable vision of a gender-free society, however, and it is certainly not one that I either endorse or expect might ever come about. Human beings are too varied and too creative for this to happen. The gender-free society that I envision would not be boring; rather, it would be filled with diversity. Its people would vary in innumerable respects, including those we now associate with masculinity and femininity. The difference between it and our present society is that the different personal characteristics, appearances, capacities would not be distributed—or be expected to be distributed—along the lines of sex. Most men would be—and would be expected to be—as capable of nurturance as most women; and some women and men might not be nurturant at all. Some women and some men would be more aggressive than others—but no one would blame women for the degree of assertiveness that they now laud in men. Rather, they would judge the appropriateness of aggressive or assertive behavior in accordance with the circumstances, not the sex of the agent. Similarly with interests, talents, and personal styles.

There can be little doubt that such a society would be liberating to many people—to those who do not like being stereotyped by sex, especially to those who find themselves punished for not fitting into prevailing gender stereotypes, for being, for example, effeminate men or pushy or emasculating women. It would be advantageous to a great number of other women, too, to the extent that they still suffer from the distorted judgments that find what is "good" and "appropriate" in a man, but not in a woman, to be very similar to what is regarded as good and appropriate in a human being.[5] The diminished salience of gender would also, I think, be very freeing for those who consider themselves to have been born in the "wrong-sexed" body—many of whom now go through the trials and rigors of physical transformation. Quite possibly many would still choose this course of action, though the psychological traumas of adjustment would be far less in a gender-free society. But quite possibly many transsexuals might live quite happily without surgical or hormonal treatment, if the sex of their "birth bodies" was not regarded as of much importance for the kinds of persons they wanted to be.

Now let us turn to our central focus—a further benefit that would accrue from the freeing of society from gender. It would contribute significantly, I contend, to diminishing the still significant stigmatization of homosexuality. This further benefit, I claim, may well in turn reinforce the diminution of sex roles and sex role expectations: some men and women may currently be deterred from crossing sex role boundaries—in particular, entering occupations or doing tasks thought typically feminine or masculine, respectively—because of the fear of being thought homosexual. The destigmatizing of homosexuality would significantly decrease this cost.

At one level, it seems immediately obvious that, to the extent that society became more gender-free, homosexuality would be seen as less of an aberration. If a person's sex were of almost no social or legal significance, then the sex of whomever a person was sexually attracted to or developed an intimate relationship with would be, *ipso facto*, similarly lacking in social salience.[6] if a person's sex were of greatly diminished social and legal significance, then it would also be seen as of little matter whether a child who had two parents had two parents of the same sex or of different sexes. In another respect, however, the point is more complex and less obvious. It requires that we try to understand the perception of homosexuality and homosexuals as threats to what is otherwise seen as a clear distinction between men and women. Exploring this requires delving into both ancient and current connections between the prevailing drive to dichotomize sexual difference and the opposition to homosexual relationships.

To bring this introductory section to an end, I should mention what I think is an important corollary to my main argument. This corollary, which I shall discuss at the end of the paper, is that there are reasons to think that homosexual families can serve as a model, in some respects, for heterosexual families that aim to shed their gendered divisions of labor and their often-associated maldistributions of opportunity and power.[7]

DICHOTOMIZING SEXUAL DIFFERENCE

The need—compulsion, it might well be called—to separate out human beings into two sexes and the salience that has then been attributed to this assignment have almost certainly not been constant in their intensity, from one historical period or culture to another. They seem, however, to have existed to a significant extent throughout recorded human history. Thomas Laqueur has recently argued that the emphasis on sexual difference is a relatively recent phenomenon, arguing that up until the latter eighteenth century women's and men's genitalia, internal reproductive organs, and sexuality in general were not seen as so different as they have come to be constructed over the last two centuries.[8] However, while seen as typologically similar to men, women were seen as deformed or inverted versions of this type, which was held to justify their different sociopolitical status. The difference between these modes of categorization may be of great interest to the historian of biology but, sociopolitically, it is immaterial whether women are excluded and controlled by men because they are regarded as in some sense similar, but are still *differentiated* as clearly inferior, or because they are regarded as typologically different.

Even confining one's reference point to political philosophy, it is easy to come up with some striking examples of the seemingly enduring compulsion to dichotomize persons by sex. Hegel, discussing the "opposing natures" of the sexes, concludes that "[t]he difference between men and women is like that between animals and plants. . ."[9] Rousseau first writes that "in everything not connected with sex, woman is man. She has the same organs, the same needs, the same faculties. . ." However, he rapidly concludes, within the space of two paragraphs, that virtually everything is connected with sex, so that "[a] perfect woman and a perfect man ought not to resemble each other in mind any more than in looks. . ."[10]

One of the most curious examples of the determination to assign distinct sexual identities—even to insects—comes from Aristotle, who is fond of both anthropomorphizing animals and, conversely, drawing lessons for humans from the behavior of other animals. (In a way, he was the first sociobiologist.) In *The Generation of Animals*, where he gives many very detailed and often remarkably accurate accounts of sexual reproduction (though far from accurate in the case of humans), Aristotle is totally confused by the sexuality and reproduction of bees, which he alludes to as "peculiar" and "a great puzzle." The main problem is that he cannot figure out the sex of any of the types of bees, since they do not fit any of his stereotypes about gender. He is sure (it seems, because they are few in number, larger, and do not labor) that those we know as queen bees are male; thus, he calls them "kings" or "leaders." And he is less sure, though equally misled in his reasoning, about those we call drones and workers. It cannot be, he argues, that the workers are female and the drones male, since workers have stings and drones do not, and "[n]ature does not assign defensive weapons to any female creature. . . ." However, "[n]or is the converse view reasonable," since worker bees take care of their young, and "no male creatures make a habit of taking care of their young." Finally, he finds it impossible to accept the explanation that some of the worker bees may be female and some male, since, he says, "in all kinds of animals the male and the female are different." Aristotle is therefore stumped (as by little else) in trying to assign sexes to bees, and therefore in figuring out how they reproduce.[11] Clearly, he would have been far less misled if he had not assumed dichotomous stereotypes about the sexes.

But we need not dwell further on Aristotle's unusual inaccuracies to convince ourselves that great amounts of human concentration have been expended in emphasizing differences between the sexes. Even now, when gender is in some respects less salient than previously, what is the first question people usually ask, when told that a new baby has been born? Studies, as well as our everyday observations, tell us that adults handle and talk to babies differently right from the start, depending on what sex they are told the child is. And how many of us are not intrigued, or even made uncomfortable, by not being able to assign a sex to someone we meet or even casually pass by? How many are not thrown somewhat off balance by the challenge to our dichotomous expectations posed by the phenomenon of transsexualism? As Anne Fausto-Sterling has argued persuasively, studies that purport to discover differences between the sexes are far more likely to receive public attention and affirmation than those that discover similarities.[12] At various levels of consciousness, most people want to be assured that a clear dichotomy between the sexes is a fact of human life. Moreover, "*vive la différence*" has long been a great rationalization for *inequality* between the sexes, and has played a large part in the exclusion of women, until recently, from even the most basic formal rights of democratic citizenship.

Virginia Woolf's novel *Orlando* is a wonderful spoof on this phenomenon. Orlando is born, male and aristocratic, in the sixteenth century, then magically and instantaneously becomes a woman, at the age of thirty, some time in the seventeenth century, and lives on "in the prime of life," at least until 1928, when she has reached the age of thirty-six, and the book ends. Not surprisingly, this fascinating tale is dedicated to, and in some respects modelled after, Woolf's bisexual intimate friend, Vita Sackville-West. At least as I read it, the book's main point is to combat the dichotomization of sexual difference. For Orlando's personal identity does not change when her change of sex suddenly occurs. Woolf writes: "Orlando had become a woman—there is no denying it. But in every other respect, Orlando remained precisely as he had been. The change of sex, though it altered their future, did nothing whatever to alter their identity."[13]

Gradually, however, what we now refer to as "social constructions of gender" begin to impinge on Orlando's identity. Having been both man and woman, she begins to see what is absurd, and what appealing, about men from a woman's point of view, and vice versa. She discovers that virtually all of the allegedly significant and "natural" differences between the sexes result from the different rights and privileges that accrue to each, to the different behavioral expectations of each, the different ways they are addressed and treated and often, to their different modes of dress. Not surprisingly, she finds the nineteenth century the most trying time for women—with fifteen to twenty children expected of them, and twenty yards of fabric in their skirts. No wonder that, at this point in the story, she takes to living her life partly as a woman and partly, by cross-dressing several times in the course of a typical day, as a man.

Not only does Orlando live a full and exciting life in this manner; having learned both roles, she also assumes each with great ease. As Woolf writes:

> She had, it seems, no difficulty in sustaining the different parts, for her sex changed far more frequently than those who have worn only one set of clothing can conceive; nor can there be any doubt that she reaped a twofold harvest by this device; the pleasures of life were increased and its experiences multiplied. From the probity of breeches she turned to the seductiveness of petticoats and enjoyed the love of both sexes equally.[14]

Blessed with the social capacity to be both, Orlando succeeded, through periods when the sexes were extremely differentiated by society and its customs and laws, in living a much fuller life than either a man or a woman could have done.

These strong views—of gender as almost totally socially constructed, and of the creative individual as able to span the supposed dichotomy of sexual difference, were s/he to find some socially acceptable way of doing so—are consistent with other works of Woolf. In *A Room of One's Own*, she imagines the dire fate that would have befallen Shakespeare's sister, if she instead had been endowed with Shakespeare's genius but confined by society to living as a woman. In *Three Guineas*, she argues that the root of almost all the differences between men and women of the English educated classes is that the former are the educated, travelled, insiders, and the latter are the unprivileged outsiders.[15] Woolf's views, of course, are very unusual—shared only by some, but by no means all feminists. The far greater tendencies throughout history have been both to dichotomize sexual differences and to explain them as natural, not socially constructed.

DICHOTOMIZING SEXUAL DIFFERENCE AND HOSTILITY TO HOMOSEXUALITY

What does dichotomizing sexual difference have to do with hostility toward and discrimination against homosexuality? The ancient Greeks seem, at first, to provide a counter-example to any attempt to link the two. For they are famous (or infamous, depending on one's point of view) for tolerating, even celebrating, homosexuality, but their views about and treatment of women seem to undercut the case that this tolerance has anything to do with the extent to which a culture draws strict dichotomies along sex lines. However, the example of the Greeks does not undercut my claim. For, first, approved Greek homoeroticism was almost entirely between adult men and boys, who were frequently thought of as feminine or as playing the sexual role of women.[16] And, second, Plato (whom Kenneth Dover says is one of the five most important sources of material on Greek male homosexuality) celebrated sublimated, intellectualized male/male love far more than he celebrated it (or even approved of it) on any physical plane.[17]

Moreover, comparing Plato's dialogues yields at least a hint of the connection between attitudes about gender and tolerance of homosexuality. In the Republic, where Plato minimizes the differences between the sexes amongst the guardians, admitting women to eligibility for philosophic rulership, he does not oppose all physical expression of homosexual impulses (between men, at least; he doesn't mention them between women).[18] However, in the Laws, despite his increasing conviction that women had great untapped potential, he reinstates the private family and more traditional roles for women. At the same time, he also prohibits homosexual activity by men or women, indeed condemning it as "an outrage on nature."[19] He is clearly concerned that homoerotic relations will draw the citizens' attention away both from their families and from procreation, as well as diminishing their physical fitness. It is also noteworthy that he condemns the one whom he regards as the "seduced" partner of a homosexual male couple as "the impersonator of the female."[20] Thus even in the writings of Plato, one of the most famous celebrants of certain aspects of homoeroticism between men, the "passive" partner is stigmatized as behaving like a woman, and the degree to which sexual difference is seen as dichotomous is correlated with attitudes about homosexuality.

It is not difficult to show that homosexuality still evokes similar anxieties about sexual difference and gender roles in the minds of many people. It is most obvious in the literature of the conservative right but, as I shall show, it is much more widely shared as well. Social conservatives often state that homosexuality is a threat to "the family." What exactly does this mean, though? Is the specter that looms large in the minds of the traditionalist right, and seems to be accepted by many others also, the likelihood that increasing the option of homosexual relationships would result in many people's opting out of heterosexual families? Sometimes, yes, as in the statement by Patrick Robertson in the summer of 1992 that "feminists" were enjoining women to leave their families and become lesbians. Antifeminist activist Anita Bryant has made this same linkage: feminism/homosexuality/"family breakdown." In such charges that both feminism and homosexuality are "anti-family," "the family" undeniably means (at the very least) "the heterosexual family." For in fact, gay men and lesbians who do not wish to marry, or to stay married—since legal marriage in the United States is restricted to heterosexuals—are not necessarily "anti-family" at all. As Kath Weston's recent book, *Families We Choose*, demonstrates, many gay men and lesbians are very concerned both to maintain ties with their families of origin, and to form new families of various kinds.[21] What often stops many from doing the former is the immense degree of hostility and rejection they experience from their "blood families." And what prevents them from officially doing the latter is far less often the lack of desire to be part of a family than the fact that the laws in all of our states prohibit homosexual marriage and in most states place many other formidable obstacles in the way of gay and lesbian family formation, especially gay and lesbian parenthood. Thus it seems that most gay men and lesbians are not anti-family, but anti a legal and social definition of family that excludes and stigmatizes them.

However, even stronger than the conservative fear that homosexuality threatens "the family" seems to be the idea that it poses a more diffuse threat to the whole dichotomization of sex that forms the rationale for gender inequality. So it is not just the heterosexual family that is seen as under threat, but the traditional, gendered family, and the other gendered institutions that reinforce it. Evidence that this latter fear is actually the more powerful force behind hostility to homosexuals can be found in both sociological research and legal cases.[22]

A number of sociological studies have established significant correlations between expectations about "appropriate" sex role behavior (or sex stereotyping) and negative attitudes about homosexuality. In some cases these correlations are quite significant even when such factors as "sexual guilt" and "liberal/conservative" attitudes about sexuality have been controlled for.[23] To quote a summary of some of this research: "persons who hold strong beliefs in a masculine-feminine sex-role dichotomy may condemn or reject homosexuals in order to reduce . . . sex role confusion . . . that they experience when confronted by persons whose behavior is perceived as incongruent with traditional sex role norms."[24] A comparison between the attitudes of Canadian and Brazilian college students suggests that this correlation is more pronounced in more than in less "macho" cultures.[25] In publishing the results of a study in 1983, Alan Taylor states that "[f]or several years evidence has been available to suggest that sex role evaluations are a major predictor of attitudes toward homosexuals. . . . Those who value traditional sex roles devalue homosexuals because they perceive them to be role deviants, and those who do not value the roles so highly do not care."[26] Moreover, this study goes on to establish much more clearly than previous ones that "the necessary mediating belief, that is, *that homosexuals be-have like the opposite sex*, is alive and well."[27]

At the same time, there is also a growing body of research that contradicts this "mediating belief" that gay males are effeminate and lesbians masculine in both appearance and manner, showing instead that "it is not the case, as most of the . . . respondents believe, that most homosexuals behave like the opposite sex."[28] It is not surprising, then, that hostility to gay men and lesbians is also correlated with social distance from and corresponding lack of knowledge about them. The fact that a large percentage of the population of the United States claims not to know anyone who is gay or lesbian tends to confirm that their expectations of the appearances, traits, and behavior of homosexuals must be rather far from much of the reality. For in most cases, given estimates that perhaps 10 percent of men are gay and 4 percent of women lesbian, respondents are likely to know homosexuals but not to know that they know them, given the stereotypes they have in mind.[29]

Unfortunately, this highly erroneous stereotyping of and attitude toward homosexuals seems to affect the thinking of a great number of legislators and judges just as much as that of the general population. According to a number of legal scholars, such mistaken stereotypes and corresponding negative attitudes are reflected in what has been said in the course of legislative debate and the opinions of courts, over a wide range of decisions concerning homosexuality. Let us now look at one well-known case, and then at what some legal scholars have discerned from it and other bases.

The majority's opinion in the 1986 Supreme Court case, *Bowers v. Hardwick*, makes little attempt to disguise the connection between gender dichotomization and hostility to homosexuality. First, as has often been noted, the Georgia statute whose constitutionality was being challenged criminalized sodomy (including oral and anal sex) for all adults, regardless of sex or sexual orientation. It was not the plaintiff, but the courts, as has been pointed out by a number of commentators much troubled by the decision, that made homosexuality the issue, with the Supreme Court's declining to rule on the constitutionality of the statute as a whole.[30] Indeed, early in Justice White's opinion, he announces that the issue is "[w]hether the Federal Constitution confers a fundamental right upon homosexuals to engage in sodomy."[31] He also argues that previous privacy cases, such as *Griswold, Eisenstadt, Loving, Roe*, and so on had to do with marriage, the family, and procreation, and that "homosexual activity" has "no connection" to any of these three categories.[32] As Jed Rubenfeld has argued, this "eviscerat[es] . . . privacy's principles.[33] For the previous cases are also very much concerned with sex and sexuality, as has been pointed out, although they had not established any constitutional right regarding sexual matters *per se*.[34]

In addition, there is in such rhetoric, as I have already suggested, a serious "catch-22" for gay men and lesbians. They themselves, their activities and their lifestyles are accused of being "anti-marriage" and "anti-family." But of course, it is largely because both marriage and "the family" are so frequently, officially and exclusively defined as heterosexual that homosexuality can in any way be regarded as opposed to these institutions. And it is only because of this definition that homosexual activity can be seen as having "no relationship" to marriage, the family, and procreation.

Justice White also argued that no fundamental right undermining the statute's constitutionality could be found either "deeply rooted in this nation's history and tradition" or implicit in the concept of "ordered liberty." He was able, strictly speaking, to separate out the question of homosexual sodomy, since a lower court had dismissed the case of the heterosexual couple who had joined the suit with Michael Hardwick. However, there seems to be something distinctly discriminatory about denying that the liberty exercised by a homosexual couple who chose to practice oral sex is protected by the constitution, while avoiding (to put the best interpretation on it) the issue of the constitutional protection of the same liberty if exercised by a heterosexual couple. Does there not seem to be something distinctly related to gender, some need to preserve the dichotomy of the sexes and their proper roles—including their roles in sexual activity—inherent in this conception of ordered liberty? Perhaps it might better be called "gendered liberty" or "the liberty of a gendered order."

When the Court, in *Eisenstadt*, extended the right of privacy from families or married couples to individuals, the majority opinion stated (in what can reasonably be regarded, however much one might approve of the move, as something of a leap from precedent) that "[i]f the right of privacy means anything, it is the right of the *individual*, married or single, to be free from unwarranted intrusion into matters so fundamentally affecting a person as the distinction whether to bear or beget a child."[35] Very soon after, in *Roe*, the majority of seven agreed that this individual right of privacy was "broad enough to encompass a woman's decision whether or not to terminate her pregnancy."[36] Once these precedents were established, surely in *Hardwick* (especially since here, as Richard Posner has pointed out, no actual or potential third party interests were involved),[37] the right of privacy regarding "matters . . . fundamentally affecting a person" might have been held to encompass the types of consensual sexual behavior between adults that were criminalized by the Georgia statute. But instead, Justice White characterized Hardwick's claim to sexual privacy as "at best, facetious," yet made no attempt to show that consensual adult sodomy is harmful.

Justice Burger's concurring opinion is even more offensive; he characterizes homosexual sodomy as "heinous," calling on Blackstone's characterization of it as "a crime not fit to be named" and even as "an offense of deeper malignity than rape." What can explain such dismissive treatment—in Justice Burger's case insulting both to gay men and all women?

Some have read the abrupt truncation of the right of privacy that occurred in the *Hardwick* decision as a fairly straightforward shift from liberalism to conservatism—partly due to changes in the composition of the court, partly to a change of view on the part of Justice Burger.[38] This is undoubtedly part of the explanation. But as I have indicated, there is an equally important explanation, which is also quite credible in the light of the sociological studies about hostility to homosexuality examined above, and which helps better to explain why it was in *this* case, handled as it was so as to focus exclusively on homosexual sodomy, that the Court chose to truncate the right of privacy. It is that a major determining factor in *Hardwick* was the perceived threat posed by homosexuality to otherwise supposedly clear distinctions between the sexes, and thence to the whole structure of gender.

This view is endorsed by a number of those who have examined the case. In an early analysis of *Hardwick* that also takes account of other relevant cases and of the history of hostility to homosexuality, Sylvia Law finds the key to such hostility and disapproval in the fact that:

[h]omosexual relationships challenge dichotomous concepts of gender. These relationships challenge the notion that social traits, such as dominance and nurturance, are naturally linked to one sex or the other. Moreover, those involved in homosexual relations implicitly reject the social institutions of family, economic and political life that are premised on gender inequality and differentiation.[39]

Law points out that the state of Georgia based its case against Hardwick firmly on the claims that "[h]omosexual sodomy is anathema of [*sic*] the basic units of our society—marriage and the family," and that "to artificially withdraw the public's expression of its disdain for this conduct does not uplift sodomy but rather demotes these sacred institutions to merely alternative lifestyles."[40] The only two *amicus curiae* briefs filed in support of Georgia's case argued similarly, one stating that if private consensual homosexual activity is protected, "the very foundations of this society . . . i.e. monogamous marriage and the family unit . . . will be shaken."[41] There is an ironic similarity between this belief and the argument of radical feminist Adrienne Rich that heterosexuality is compulsory and hides the extent of homosexuality (especially female) that would be likely without its strong sanctions.[42] It is ironic because—despite the similarity of the arguments about the compulsory character of heterosexuality—the positions taken on the issues are diametrically opposed, Rich's being that all institutions privileging heterosexuality should be done away with. Law also points out the paradox that conservatives opposed to allowing homosexuality argue both that the patriarchal gendered family is "natural" and that it is "vulnerable," needing to be privileged in order to survive.[43]

In a 1990 analysis of the right to privacy, centered on *Hardwick*, Jed Rubenfeld comes to conclusions very similar to Law's. Noting that, given the impracticality of celibacy for most people, "the prohibition against homosexual sex channels individuals' sexual desires into *reproductive* outlets," he asserts that

it is difficult to separate our society's inculcation of a heterosexual identity from the simultaneous inculcation of a dichotomized complementarity of roles to be borne by men and women. Homosexual couples by necessity throw into question the allocation of specific functions—whether professional, personal, or emotional— between the sexes. It is this aspect of the ban on homosexuality—its central role in the maintenance of institutionalized sexual identities and normalized reproductive relations—that have made its *affirmative* or formative consequences, as well as the reaction against these consequences, so powerful a force in modern society.[44]

In a monograph entitled *Sexual Orientation and the Law*, the editors of the *Harvard Law Review*, deeply critical of the decision in Hardwick, concur closely with the above analyses. Pointing out that since "the physical acts themselves—anal and oral sex—are the same whether between a man and a woman or two persons of the same sex; the difference is in the cultural significance attached to the gender of the participants."[45] Thus, they argue, same-sex sodomy statutes are sex discriminatory just as anti-miscegenation statutes were race discriminatory:

Not only do these statutes classify based on gender, but the classification also reinforces stereotypical sex roles, and therefore may not [by the Court's own reasoning
in other cases] be sustained as a "benign" classification. The prohibition of same-
sex sodomy reinforces a dichotomous view of gender in which differences between
men and women are so significant that same-sex sexual conduct violates the roles
assigned to each gender through cultural indoctrination.[46]

This analysis is highly plausible. Not only a large percentage of the general public but some of our most powerful judges, it appears, are strongly prejudiced against
homosexuality *because* they interpret it as violating the supposed dichotomy of sex,
and "natural" gender norms. Though this may not be their only reason for opposition, it is beyond any doubt a crucial one. But if this is so, then surely movement towards a society in which sexual difference is far less salient than now—a gender free
society—is very likely to diminish hostility toward and discrimination against gay
men and lesbians.

GAY AND LESBIAN FAMILIES AS A MODEL

I shall argue, finally, that, rather than constituting the grave threat to "the family" that
many courts, legislatures, and purveyors of public opinion have considered them, in
some important respects homosexual relationships can serve as a model, at a time at
which forms of family are undergoing rapid change. Again in opposition to the attitudes of most public authorities and much of public opinion, I contend that—from
what modest evidence is available so far—homosexual couples may provide a particularly good model of parenthood. In arguing this, I first need to point out, quickly,
why some obvious points that might lead one to conclude the reverse are not valid. It
has sometimes been claimed a child is more likely to develop a gay or lesbian sexual
orientation, if raised by a gay or lesbian couple. Leaving aside the question of
whether this would constitute a problem, even if it were true, numerous studies have
now indicated that it is not.[47] Second, it might be claimed that homosexual relationships are less long-lasting than heterosexual ones, and therefore more potentially
disruptive for children. Though this seems, on average, to be true at present, it might
not be true if lesbians and gay men could legally marry, and it might be even less true
of those committed to raising children. It should also be noted that so far, given the
difficulties confronted by such couples in becoming parents (whether by gaining
custody, adopting, or using alternative insemination or some form of surrogate motherhood), lesbians and gay men are far more likely than heterosexuals to have only really *wanted* children. Finally, of course, whether any particular parent is a good parent depends on an enormous range of factors. Thus, I certainly make no claims about
what makes up the totality of good parenting.

The reason gay and lesbian families may be, at least in one important respect, a
model to be followed, is that they are far less likely than heterosexual families to
practice anything resembling a gendered division of labor. In their detailed study,
American Couples, of thousands of couples, married and unmarried heterosexual,
gay, and lesbian, Philip Blumstein and Pepper Schwartz found considerable disparities in the ways the various types of couples thought about their sharing of responsi-

bilities. Not only past and present family law but also traditional expectations about gendered marriage influence greatly the attitudes, expectations, and behavior of married couples. By contrast the absence of sexual difference and therefore of expectations based on gender, and the absence of the institution of marriage, allow gay and lesbian couples far more freedom in organizing their lives together—and more opportunity to do so in an egalitarian manner. Many of the married respondents (about a third of the husbands and a quarter of the wives) still enthusiastically endorsed the traditional male/female separation of wage work from household work, and nearly two-thirds did not think that a wife should be employed while children are small. This is strikingly different from the attitudes of the homosexual households, of which all but about 1 percent eschewed the homemaker/provider division of roles, avoiding the terminology even when one partner is temporarily not working for wages, and is doing more of the housework. Blumstein and Schwartz conclude, about this aspect of the various types of relationship): "First, while the heterosexual model offers more stability and certainty, it inhibits change, innovation, and choice regarding roles and tasks. Second, the heterosexual model, which provides so much efficiency, is predicated on the man's being the dominant partner."[48]

Thus, inequality seems likely to be built into the heterosexual model. But what about the argument for its supposed greater "efficiency."[49] First, there seems to be no indication that gay and lesbian couples (especially the latter, who avoid earning/non-earning divisions of labor more than any other type of couple) live inefficiently. Second, even if the division of labor between the sexes were currently more efficient (especially from the point of view of some men, and for that decreasing percentage of the population who can afford it), it may be so only because so many aspects of our social institutions from the disparate hours and vacation times of workplaces and schools to the scarcity of affordable high-quality day care—make the equal sharing of earned and unearned work within families so difficult. The efficiency claim simply assumes these other, highly gendered, aspects of our society, which rely so heavily on the availability of women's unpaid labor.

Evidence that gay and lesbian couples (especially the latter) divide the paid and unpaid work of their families much more equally than heterosexual (especially married) ones, is further borne out by comparing even more recent studies of each type. Arlie Hochschild's *The Second Shift* presents evidence that even when wives are full-time members of the labor force, they still almost invariably do the vast majority of unpaid family work.[50] While some of the couples Hochschild studied were somewhat more egalitarian in this respect than others, her most discouraging account is of a wife who did even more of the family work than most in the study, *because* her greater success at work, reflected in her high earnings, was perceived as already sufficiently threatening to her husband. Expecting him to share the housework more equally, apparently, was therefore regarded as an intolerable threat to the marriage.

By contrast, Kath Weston's study of forty gay men and forty lesbian women, *Families We Choose*, found almost none of the division of labor that people have long associated with gender. Only four of her interviewees were either supporting or being financially supported by a lover, and each regarded this as temporary. (One, for example, was waiting for a green card). Typically, the participants in the study described a "50/50" responsibility for household work as prevailing in their relationships, and many regarded the equitable division of paid and unpaid labor as "one index of an egalitarian relationship." Interestingly, even the lesbian couples who identified themselves as butch/fem did not allocate tasks and responsibilities along gendered lines, and amongst those who bore children, it was not necessarily the fem-identified partner who was the biological mother.

Weston's study is not very helpful on the question of equal parenting, since only nine of her eighty respondents had children. But another recent, small study of lesbian couples who have borne children through artificial insemination found a high degree of equal parenting.[51] While the biological mothers took time off work or worked part-time during the first year, by the time the children were about fourteen months old, in all five cases, the "other mother" was doing 60 percent of the child care. "*All five?*" I can imagine a skeptical reader thinking; "What can one possibly learn from a study of five pairs of lesbian parents?" My response is to ask: out of all the hundreds of heterosexual parents you know and have known, can you think of five cases in which the father was doing 60 percent of the care during the child's second year of life?

There is considerable evidence, then, that gay and lesbian relationships involve far less economic dependence and far more equal divisions of labor than do heterosexual ones, especially marriages. But what is the significance of this? Its significance comes from the fact that, for a number of reasons, the division of labor that prevails between the sexes is a matter of social injustice. It often leads to the economic, psychological, or even physical vulnerability of women and children. It contributes much to women's inequality of opportunity and actual inequality of power and influence in society at large. And it means that the typical, gender-structured family is far from the best kind of environment in which children can learn—from the first adult interactions they observe—to develop the sense of justice that they need in order to be good citizens of a democratic society.[52] If these claims are right—and they have encountered little reasoned resistance so far—then it seems quite reasonable to suggest that, far from being a threat to "family values," gay and lesbian family relationships may provide, in important respects, a very good model for heterosexual families to follow.

Notes

I would like to thank Joshua Cohen, Richard Mohr, Nancy Rosenblum, Cass Sunstein, and Mark Tunick for their helpful comments on an earlier version of this chapter. It appeared in a slightly different form in a special issue of *Hypatia* on the family and feminist theory, vol. II, no. 1 (Winter 1996): 30–48.

1. Since I wrote this paper, I have become aware of several other arguments for the close connection between sexism and heterosexism. See, e.g., Suzanne Pharr, *Homophobia: A Weapon of Sexism* (Little Rock, Ark.: Chardon Press, 1988), which focuses mainly on sexism and anti-lesbianism; Andrew Koppelman, "The Miscegenation Analogy: Sodomy Law as Sex Discrimination," *Yale Law Journal* 98 (1988): 145; and Cass Sunstein, "Homosexuality and the Constitution," this volume, pp. 208–26.

2. Susan Moller Okin, *Justice, Gender, and the Family* (New York: Basic Books, 1989), p. 171.

3. See Joshua Cohen, "Okin on Justice, Gender, and the Family," *Canadian Journal of*

Philosophy 22 (1992): 263–86, at 281; Martha Fineman, Review of *Justice, Gender, and the Family, Ethics* 102, 3 (1991): 647–49; Will Kymlicka, "Rethinking the Family," *Philosophy and Public Affairs* 20, 1 (1991): 77–97, esp. 83–85. Fineman even asserts that the book fails to go beyond a "rather traditional view of the family (p. 649)," which is far from what I thought I was doing. There are, admittedly, a few carelessly worded passages in the book that give some credence to the charge of heterosexist bias because they speak of the desirability of children's being reared equally by mothers and fathers (e.g., pp. 100, 107, 176). I regret the lack of care taken in such passages, which were meant to apply only in the context of two-parent heterosexual families. However, in the Introduction to the book and from time to time throughout I make it clear that I acknowledge the many different forms—two-parent, single-parent, heterosexual, gay and lesbian—that families now take. Since I don't think that either I am or the book is biased against homosexual individuals or families, I have given much thought to this criticism.

4. These points are argued in *Justice, Gender, and the Family*, esp. chs. 1 and 8.

5. Sandra L. Bem and Daryl J. Bem, "Homogenizing the American Woman." Originally published in D. J. Bem, *Beliefs, Attitudes, and Human Affairs* (Monterey, Calif.: Brooks/Cole, 1970). Reprinted in Alison Jaggar and Paula Rothenberg Struhl, *Feminist Frameworks* (New York: McGraw-Hill, 1978), at p. 15. See also I. K. Broverman et al., "Sex-Role Stereotypes and Clinical Judgments of Mental Health," *Journal of Consulting and Clinical Psychology* 34 (1970): 1–7.

6. Note that I say social salience. I am not claiming that, in a gender-free society, the sex of a person's partners and potential partners would be of no importance to that person, or that all would be bisexual. The claim is, rather, that the sex of a person's sexual partner or partners would be of no significance to others.

7. The relative equality of homosexual couples, though mentioned briefly in my book, has not been noticed by those who have read the book as heterosexist. See *Justice, Gender, and the Family*, p. 140.

8. Thomas Laqueur, *Making Sex* (Cambridge, Mass.: Harvard University Press, 1990).

9. The *Philosophy of Right*, trans. T. M. Knox (Oxford: Oxford University Press, 1952), paragraph 166 and addition 107 (pp. 115 and 263). The terminology "the *opposite* sex" is, of course still both very prevalent and very revealing.

10. Jean-Jacques Rousseau, *Emile*, trans. Allan Bloom (New York: Basic Books, 1979), pp. 357–58.

11. Aristotle, *The Generation of Animals*, trans. A. L. Peck (Cambridge, Mass.: Loeb Classical Library, Harvard University Press, 1953), III: 759a–60b.

12. Anne Fausto-Sterling, *Myths of Gender: Biological Theories about Women and Men* (New York: Basic Books, 1985). See also Fausto-Sterling's Op-Ed article, *New York Times*, Mar. 12, 1993.

13. Virginia Woolf, *Orlando: A Biography* (New York: Harcourt Brace Jovanovich, 1928, 1956), p. 138. Note that, for these few lines, Woolf uses the plural "their," before switching from "he" to "she."

14. Ibid., pp. 220–21.

15. *A Room of One's Own* (New York: Harcourt Brace, 1929, 1957); *Three Guineas* (New York: Harcourt Brace, 1938, 1966).

16. Kenneth Dover, *Greek Homosexuality*, updated ed.: (Cambridge, Mass.: Harvard University Press, 1978, 1989), p. 9.

17. Dover, *Greek Homosexuality*, esp. pp. 153–70. This perspective is especially apparent in the *Symposium*, where the aims of the man/boy relationship are the enlightenment of the latter and the achievement of aesthetic revelation and intellectual truth. In the *Phaedrus*, occasional physical "lapses" are permitted, when physical desire proves too strong.

18. Socrates says of the guardian who has "proved best and earned a good reputation" in battle, that "as long as they are on that campaign no one whom he wants to kiss be permitted to refuse, so that if a man happens to love someone, either male or female, he would be more than eager to win the rewards of valor (V, 468c)." In Book III, at 403b, he proposes that a lover should "not go further" with "his boy" than kissing and touching him "as though he were a son." *The Republic of Plato*, trans. Allan Bloom (New York: Basic Books, 1968).

19. *Laws*, 636c (Huntington and Cairns translation).

20. *Laws*, 836e.

21. Kath Weston, *Families We Choose: Lesbians, Gays, Kinship* (New York: Columbia University Press, 1991).

22. See, e.g., Koppelman, "The Miscegenation Analogy," esp. pp. 158–60.

23. See, e.g., J. E. Krulewitz and J. E. Nash, "Effects of Sex Role Attitudes and Similarity on Men's Rejection of Male Homosexuals," *Journal of Personality and Social Psychology* 38, 1 (1980): 67–74; M. R. Laner and R. H. Laner, "Personal Style or Sexual Preference? Why Gay Men Are Disliked," *International Review of Modern Sociology* 9 (1979): 215–28, and "Sexual Preference or Personal Style? Why Lesbians Are Disliked," *Journal of Homosexuality* 5 (1980): 339–56; A. P. MacDonald and R. G. Games, "Some Characteristics of Those Who Hold Positive and Negative Attitudes Towards Homosexuals," *Journal of Homosexuality* 1 (1974): 9–27; F. A. Minnegerode, "Attitudes Toward Homosexuality; Feminist Attitudes and Sexual Conservatism," *Sex Roles* 2 (1976): 347–52; S. F. Morin and E. M. Garfinkle, "Male Homophobia," *Journal of Social Issues* 34, 1 (1978): 29–47; M. D. Storms, "Attitudes Toward Homosexuality and Femininity in Men," *Journal of Homosexuality* 3 (1978): 257–63; A. Taylor, "Conceptions of Masculinity and Femininity as a Basis for Stereotypes of Male and Female Homosexuals," *Journal of Homosexuality* 9 (1983): 37–53.

24. Krulewitz and Nash, "Rejection of Male Homosexuals," pp. 67–68.

25. J. Dunbar, M. Brown, and S. Vuorinen, "Attitudes Toward Homosexuality Among Brazilian and Canadian College Students," *Journal of Social Psychology* 90 (1973): 173–83.

26. Taylor, "Conceptions of Masculinity and Femininity," p. 50.

27. Taylor, pp. 50–51.

28. Taylor, p. 51, citing A. P. Bell and M. S. Weinberg, *Homosexualities: A Study of Diversities Amongst Men and Women* (London: Mitchell Beazley, 1978); R. Masters and V. Johnson, *Homosexuality in Perspective* (Boston: Little, Brown, 1978), and M. S. Weinberg and M. S. Williams, *Male Homosexuals: Their Problems and Adaptions* [rev. ed.] (New York: Penguin, 1975).

29. As John Hart Ely asks: Shouldn't the fact that "most of us must . . . interact with homosexuals quite frequently . . . serve substantially to neutralize our prejudices [and stereotyping]?" He suggests that the reason this doesn't have the effect it might is because people often don't know that a person they work with (for example) is gay. Thus "[o]ur stereotypes— whether to the effect that male homosexuals are effeminate, females "butch": that they are untrustworthy, unusually menacing to children, or whatever—are likely to remain fixed, given our obliviousness to the fact that the people around us may be counterexamples." *Democracy and Distrust* (Cambridge, Mass.: Harvard University Press, 1980), pp. 162–63. Perhaps one of the very few good outcomes of the tragic AIDS epidemic is that gay men and lesbians have tended to "come out" much more in the 1980s, so that Ely's conclusion is probably a lot less true now than when written.

30. For example, Richard Posner, *Sex and Reason* (Cambridge, Mass.: Harvard University Press, 1992), pp. 341–50 passim; Jed Rubenfeld, "The Right of Privacy," *Harvard Law Review* 102 (1989): 737; Cass Sunstein, "Sexual Orientation and the Constitution," *University of Chicago Law Review* 55 (1988): 1161, at 1166–69.

31. Bowers v. Hardwick, 478 U.S. 186, 106 S. Ct. 2841 (1986) at 2843.

32. Bowers v. Hardwick at 2844. Griswold v. Connecticut, 381 U.S. 479, 85 S. Ct. 1678 (1965); Eisenstadt v. Baird, 405 U.S. 438, 92 S. Ct. 1029 (1972); Loving v. Virginia, 388 U.S. 1, 87 S. Ct. 1817 (1967); Roe v. Wade, 410 U.S. 113 (1973), 93 S. Ct. 705 (1973).

33. Rubenfeld, "The Right of Privacy," at 748.

34. Posner, *Sex and Reason*, p. 342; Rubenfeld, "The Right of Privacy," at 744.

35. Eisenstadt v. Baird, 405 U.S. 483, 92 S. Ct. 1029 (1972).

36. Roe v. Wade, 410 U.S. 113 (1973).

37. Posner, *Sex and Reason*, p. 344.

38. Posner, *Sex and Reason*; Anne B. Goldstein, Comment: "History, Homosexuality, and Political Values: Searching for the Hidden Determinants of *Bowers v. Hardwick*," *Yale Law Journal* 97: 1009. See also Norman Vieira, "*Hardwick* and the Right of Privacy," *University of Chicago Law Review* 55 (1988): 1181, at 1186.

39. Sylvia Law, "Homosexuality and the Social Meaning of Gender," *Wisconsin Law Review* 2 (1988): 187, at 196.

40. Ibid., at 219.

41. Ibid., at p. 219 n. 150.

42. Adrienne Rich, "Compulsory Heterosexuality and Lesbian Existence," *SIGNS* 5, no. 4 (1980): 631–60.

43. Law, "Homosexuality and the Social Meaning of Gender," at 220.

44. Rubenfeld, "The Right of Privacy," at 800.

45. The Editors of the *Harvard Law Review, Sexual Orientation and the Law* (Cambridge, Mass.: Harvard University Press, 1989). The authors point out that, in *Hardwick*, Georgia "justified its facially neutral statute based on its 'interest in prosecuting homosexual activity'" (p. 21 n. 90, quoting Hardwick 478 U.S. 186, at 203 n. 2).

46. Ibid., pp. 17–18. On the miscegenation parallel, see also Koppelman, "The Miscegenation Analogy," and Sunstein, "Homosexuality and the Constitution."

47. For example, Mary B. Harris and Pauline H. Turner, "Gay and Lesbian Parents," *Journal of Homosexuality* 12, 2 (1985–86): 101–13. See also the discussion in Posner, *Sex and Reason*, pp. 418–19 and sources cited there in fn.16.

48. P. Blumstein and P. Schwartz, *American Couples* (New York: Morrow, 1983), p. 324. Some of the discussion here is paraphrased from chapter 7 of my *Justice, Gender, and the Family*, esp. pp. 140–41, 149.

49. On this see also, for example, Gary Becker, *A Treatise on the Family* (Cambridge, Mass.: Harvard University Press, 1981), and Talcott Parsons and Robert F. Bales, *Family, Socialization and Interaction Process* (Glencoe, Il.: Free Press, 1955).

50. Arlie Hochschild, *The Second Shift: Working Parents and the Revolution at Home* (New York: Viking Penguin, 1989).

51. Barbara M. McCandlish, "Against All Odds: Lesbian Mother Family Dynamics," in *Gay and Lesbian Parents*, ed. Frederick W. Bozett (New York: Prager, 1987).

52. I defend these claims at far greater length in Okin, *Justice, Gender, and the Family*, especially chapter 7.

Part II

SEX

4

Democratic Sex: Reynolds v. U.S., Sexual Relations, and Community

Nancy L. Rosenblum

> Sexual love is not naturally restricted to the pairs . . . the secret history of the human heart will bear out the assertion that it is capable of loving any number of times and any number of persons, and that the more it loves the more it can love. . . . The law of marriage 'worketh wrath.'
>
> JOHN HUMPHREY NOYES, *History of American Socialisms*

Democratic theory provides a distinctive vantage point on sexuality, one that rivals more familiar standpoints, such as popular morality and moral philosophy, religion, and the legal right to privacy. "Democratic sex" in my title is shorthand for the view that appropriately ordered intimate relations reinforce democracy. Preoccupied with the formative effects of sexuality on character and community, an increasing number of contemporary political theorists approach the legal regulation of sexual conduct and relations from the point of view of their congruence with democratic principles. Of course, religiously inspired accounts of the public interest in intimate relations have greater practical political force today, but they do not occupy the field alone. Democratic considerations, too, give sexuality a political face.

The idea that sexual relations support or subvert political order challenges familiar liberal "privacy" approaches to sexuality, as I show below in "Liberal Privacy versus Democratic Community," the first section of this essay but it is nothing new. Utopianism has always made congruence between sexual and social life imperative, and in the next section, "Sex and Utopia," I survey the widespread utopian assumption that sexual relations are the key to harmony.[1] Moreover, the philosophical connection between sexuality and communal ideals came to life in experimental communities in the United States: sexual arrangements provided the organizing principle of these elective communities, the focus of their internal governance and sanctions, and unorthodox sexual relations were one cause of conflict between these communities and political authority. That is why utopianism is doubly useful for any discussion of law and sexuality. Designed for complementarity between sexual and social order, these communities throw the idea of congruence into sharp relief. And incongruity between these groups' singular sexual practices and democratic norms was used to justify government intervention and legislation dictating "democratic sex." *Reynolds v. U.S.* provides a concrete focus for thinking about sexual relations, community, and democratic rationales for legal regulation. As I show in the third section, "Undemocratic Polygamy," the Supreme Court's decision to uphold the criminalization of Mormon polygamy reflected more than moral aversion to what was seen as the subjection of women to unbridled male lust. Its interest comes from the fact that the court denied polygamy protection under the free exercise clause of the First Amendment on grounds that the practice was theocratic and patriarchal, intolerably incongruent with democracy. American communitarianism, and the *Reynolds* case in particular, invite contemporary democratic theorists to move from conceptual discussions of law and sexuality to the political question of how far we are justified in going beyond liberal privacy in the direction of congruence between sex and political community.

LIBERAL PRIVACY VERSUS
DEMOCRATIC COMMUNITY

Two approaches dominate thinking about sexuality and political life in contemporary liberal-democratic thought, each appealing to one half of this marriage of political ideologies. The privacy model attaches to the liberal side of the union. It argues that sexual practices and relations should be left alone. The constitutional basis of official hands-off is not my subject; suffice it to say the privacy position need not rest on a doctrinal right to privacy, which extends with certainty only to decision making about reproduction and not to sexual freedom generally. Nothing in the privacy position suggests that sexuality is trivial or sexual relations inconsequential for social and political life, either. The fundamental idea is simply that where sexual arrangements between adults are voluntary they ought to be beyond the reach of government control, and that sexual categories should not be the basis for advantages or disadvantages in the distribution of public rights and benefits.

This suggests sex-blind counterpart to color blindness, appropriately so, since compounding every liberal objection to regulating intimate relations and to sex-based distributions is the apprehension that public intervention is often guided by prejudice.[2] *Bowers v. Hardwick* attacked homosexual not heterosexual sodomy, and avowed lesbians and homosexuals excluded from military service and employment or confronted with unique obstacles to child custody and adoption are collectively assigned an unequal and denigrated civil status.[3] From the start, religious matching in adoption was inspired by nativist and anti-Catholic animus rather than "the best interest of the child," and echoes of "Saving the Children for Protestantism" can be heard in disputes about sexual orientation and parenting today.

Parallels to race and equal protection may be useful in alerting us to legal discrimination and stigmatization, but they are liable to invoke group identity, which advocates of the privacy approach do not. Whether sexual practices and the relations

that flow from them are seen as the expression of eminently variable personal preference, unalterable desire, or (for agnostics on the subject of origin and mutability)
best regarded simply as a matter of consent among adults, they do not point to membership in a social identity group, to group rights, or to communal autonomy. On the
privacy view, "gay community" is a useful shorthand for solidarity for the purposes
of political advocacy, but it presumes nothing about the primacy of sexual orientation for the political identity of individual gay men and women and nothing about
belonging to an actual "gay community," whose distinctive neighborhoods, norms,
culture, and social relations are structured around sexual practices and erotic ties.
This bears mentioning because attempts to sort out the legitimate sphere of privacy
in sexual affairs have not always been premised on liberal individualism. Liberal
pluralism has a place in thinking about sexual freedom as well. Indeed, autonomy for
subcommunities organized around unconventional sexual practices has sometimes
eclipsed individual rights to privacy, and American legal history tells a story of official tolerance and accommodation of sexually organized communities on one side,
and rejection of these communities' claims for independent political and law-making
authority on the other.

Liberal justifications for sexual privacy vary, of course. The principal argument
today underscores individualism and assigns sexual intimacy a privileged status
because it is integral to personality. The idea is that sexual orientation, practices, and
relations are fundamental to both personhood generally and the development and
expression of individuality.[4] If this rarely leads, as it logically might, to the view that
government should not only respect liberty but positively facilitate erotic self-
definition and expression through sex-friendly public policies (mandating sexually
pluralistic environments, for example), it is because mistrust of government is also at
work.

This second and, to my mind, decisive justification for constraining government
is a version of elementary liberal limits on public authority, which become most urgent when police power is exercised most intrusively. Where scrutiny, supervision,
punishment, or protection depend on information about and intervention in intimate
aspects of people's lives, often in private spaces, the likelihood of official arbitrari-
ness and abuse increases.

A related justification has it that regulating sexuality and sexual relations
amounts not only to a negative restriction on liberty but also to a positive imposition
of privileged social roles. Officially sanctioned norms and government incentives
channel individuals into particular types of partnerships or parenting with unantici-
pated and long-lasting consequences for them personally and individually. On this
view, the sheer power of government to critically alter people's lives is a reason to secure liberty, whether or not sexual conduct is viewed as fundamental to identity. This
seems to have been what the Supreme Court had in mind in *Eisenstadt v. Baird*: "If
the right to privacy means anything it is the right of the individual, married or single,
to be free from unwarranted governmental intrusion into matters so fundamentally
affecting a person as the decision to bear or beget a child."[5]

The boundary implicit in the liberal privacy argument constrains movement in
just one direction, from government to sexual relations. Nothing in this position
promises that, left alone, sexual relations are without consequences for liberal

democracy, that these consequences are benign, or that policies informed by considerations of privacy will cultivate liberal attitudes toward sexuality or anything else. Foucauldians, for example, applaud erotic "limit experiences" as a form of resistance to the discipline of every social order including liberal and liberated ones. Advocates of the privacy approach to sexuality do not deny that public order may be vulnerable to sexual subversion, but they regard it as a justifiable risk of liberty, like freedom of speech.

Unwillingness to make the public effects of intimate life determinative is precisely the problem with the privacy position according to proponents of the second view, which appeals to the democratic half of the liberal-democratic union. These political theorists view sexual conduct and relations as central to political culture and as appropriate subjects of public concern. To this extent, democratic theorists mirror traditional moralists, often religious and often antiliberal, in defending state regulation of sexual mores and the authoritative definition and enforcement of permissible sexual conduct and intimate and family bonds. But unlike most religious advocates of state regulation of sex, some democratic theorists are willing to consider an unconventional range of sexual practices and relations as potential supports for democratic community. If one case for overturning *Bowers* and legalizing same-sex marriage rests on privacy and its justifications, this one is based on the argument that official recognition of the right to engage in lesbian and homosexual sex and marriage is a public good.

Thus, Michael Sandel argues that the Supreme Court's justification for the right to privacy granted in *Griswold v. Connecticut* was not a liberal defense of voluntarism and sexual choice but a reaffirmation of the state's interest in protecting the social institution of marriage. Homosexual marriage, he continues, participates in the virtues of this morally beneficial institution. It reinvigorates failing public norms of monogamy, loyalty, and mutual care. Like other familial relationships, it is a resource for cultivating the disposition to cooperation rather than competition without which democratic community is unthinkable.[6] In the same spirit, democratic theorists argue that public policies such as social benefits to same-sex or unwed partners provide unorthodox sexual relationships with a workable legal framework for property, child rearing, and so on.

The impulse behind this position may be grimly instrumental: "Perhaps something like marriage will have to be recognized for homosexual couples, not because they need it for their happiness (though they may), but because society needs it to avoid the insecurity and instability generated by the existence in its midst of a permanent and influential subculture outside the law."[7] Like the communitarians of a more radical disposition I discuss below, democratic theorists may prescribe innovations in the sexual relations that are permitted or encouraged as a response to perceived moral disorder and degradation: promiscuity, irresponsibility, and other vices of arrant libertinism.

Not all democratic theorists try to assimilate unorthodox sexual relations to conventional ones in the spirit of remediation. Some are avowedly radical, even utopian, in their claims. With a view to transforming democratic society into a progressively more egalitarian order, they advocate congruence among formative associations, public and private.[8] Just as participatory democrats traditionally looked to worker control in industry to instill a sense of political efficacy in worker-citizens, these democratic theorists look to specific sexual arrangements to cultivate democratic virtues. Susan Okin, for example, recognizes that "most gay men and lesbians are not anti-family, but anti a legal and social definition of family that excludes and stigmatizes them." She goes beyond condoning the legalization of homosexual marriage and argues that the distinctive characteristics of gay and lesbian marriage and parenting are exemplary. Because they reject or diminish rigid gender roles, same-sex relations are more egalitarian and come closer to embodying democratic norms of compassionate adult marriage, equal parenting, and a fair division of paid and unpaid domestic labor than heterosexual relations. Intimate relations, especially families, are schools of justice, on this view. The compelling reason for accommodating nontraditional sexual arrangements is their potential for democratic education.[9]

Advocates of "democratic sex" are seldom specific about who interprets the way the reciprocal relation between sex and democracy works and where it fails. They do not agree about who should make and enforce public policy in this area; they are not all majoritarians insistent on judicial restraint and favoring a free hand for legislated sex, for example. Democratic theorists are seldom explicit about how far they would go in the direction of publicly prescribing and enforcing democratic sex. Convinced that the structures of intimacy affect our life chances, moral dispositions, and capacities for democratic citizenship, still they do not call for outlawing the dominance and servility characteristic of sadomasochistic sex, or any other practice. Defining families as schools of justice has not produced a throwback to the colonial directive that individuals must live in families, or that families must be organized democratically. They have not addressed Laurence Tribe's rhetorical question about the prohibition of polygamy in *Reynolds:* If monogamous marriage as a support of democracy was at stake, why not order the marriage of priests and nuns?[10] The legal and policy implications of this approach are elusive, but appreciation for "democratic sex" as a bulwark of democracy is clear.

Democratic sex does not refer to the egalitarian distribution of opportunity for sexual pleasure then. Of the two approaches, liberal privacy theorists are more concerned than their counterparts with freedom for diverse sexual relations and chances for gratification. Democratic sex refers instead to sexual relations organized to constitute democratic character and support democratic justice. Approaching sexuality in terms of congruence with democratic community turns liberal privacy on its head.

SEX AND UTOPIA

If we step back from contemporary arguments, it is liberal privacy that seems extraordinary and preoccupation with the sexual basis of the just community that seems matter of fact. Nowhere is this clearer than in the theory and practice of utopianism. Until very recently, utopianism has been an acknowledged component of political philosophy generally, of course, and utopias since *The Republic* and *The Laws* have had eroticism at their heart.[11] Perfectionism's roots go all the way down. Academic studies of utopia typically focus on programs of education and the division of labor as bases of harmony, but it is hard to ignore the fact that in both literary utopias and actual experimental communities sex is key. Sexual concerns are the mainstay of

every jeremiad against existing social order: like most millenarians, Mormons pointed to adultery, fornication, whoredom, abortion, infanticide, and hypocrisy as signs
that America was sodom. And in response to perceived social disorder, utopian communities reorder sexual relations. Sometimes that means magnifying sexuality, as in
Joseph Smith's conviction that male sexuality was naturally polygamous and must
be freed from the unnatural sexual influence women hold over men under
monogamy. Other times it means diminishing desire and withdrawal from sexual involvement as in monasticism, celibacy, or eunuchism. Either way, it is a commonplace that sexual order reinforces communal ideals. The prohibition of romantic love
and monogamous marriage in many communities, for example, was intended to de-
flect members from exclusive proprietary relations and allow them to focus affection
and energy on the whole. The marriage bond and parenting, John Humphrey Noyes
argued, renders the world "a wilderness of self-hood," and "complex marriage" in
Oneida was really supervised promiscuity, a test of love for one's fellows and fitness
for communal life.[12]

Besides mirroring and reinforcing communal order, sexuality may provide
utopia with its basic organizing principle. Utopianism is based on the idea of congruence, but the defining notion of sexuality varies. Two examples demonstrate vividly
that if "democratic sex" was the organizing principle of some groups, "undemocratic
sex" defined others.

Consider first Charles Fourier. Designated a "utopian socialist" by Engels and
secured a place in the history of communism, Fourier was a ferocious critic of commercial society, whose writings inspired dozens of communitarian experiments in
the United States. At the top of his list of horrors, however, was neither private
property nor economic injustice but sexual repression with its attendant anxiety
and cruelty. The ordering of the phalanx in *Nouveau Monde Amoreux* is purely erotic. Fourier thought that sexual inclinations, always multiple and never simple, were
a natural given, and his taxonomy identified 810 erotic types. When these types
are brought together in community, their "manias" can be scientifically combined
in a regime of "passional equilibrium." The result of a division of labor based on
the "laws of passional attraction" is efficiency and remarkable abundance. Even
drudgery and dirty work are pleasurable if sadists were butchers and little hordes of
children—presumably in the anal stage of development—picked up the garbage
from the streets. Fourier's warning against "erotic Jacobinism" and his appreciation
of the multiplicity and nuances of the passions should be heeded in any discussion of
sexuality and community. It challenges not only rigidly dichotomous traditional gender stereotypes, now increasingly discredited, but also the unimaginatively restrictive categories of sexuality that are presently offered in their place. Fourier's list of
"penchants"— for repetition or alternation, orgies, fidelity or intrigue, fetishism and
flagellation, luxury and specific aesthetic delights, and passionate attraction to members of both sexes—is a cautionary reminder that heterosexual and homosexual is
not all there is to sexuality, and may be no more accurate as an account of sexual differences or useful for organizing sexual relations and creating legal classes than the
category male/female.

In Fourier's utopia, the promise of a guaranteed "sexual minimum" was as important as material satisfaction, and the phalanxes were designed to insure "sexual

philanthropy" for the elderly, poor, and those with bizarre desires. The distribution of pleasure was just. But the edifice on which sexual relations rested was not egalitarian. Appreciation of every desire and commitment to universal gratification do not eliminate sexual and social superiority or produce democratic sex. Fourier was an erotic elitist. He abhorred monogamy: never tiring of one another's company is evidence of the lowest passionate type, and in his hierarchy the "butterfly" with the greatest capacity for a variety of pleasures is superior. There was sexual officialdom in utopia, too. A system of sincerity had to be instituted if the laws of passionate attraction were to have effect; after all, matches and work assignments tend to harmony only if members confess their cravings. The system was managed by a female elite that elicited confidences and used confessions to arrange for each person's labor and love.[13]

On the other side, one of the best documented examples of communally organized "democratic sex" was the New York community Oneida, founded and led by Noyes from 1838 to 1881. Noyes prescribed "angelic mingling," counted sexual love a sacrament, and described genital love as a fine art purer and more aesthetic than singing. Because individuals are not equally attractive a perfect democracy of love may be impossible, but equality between the sexes can be guaranteed, and the main thrust of Oneida's system of "complex marriage" was egalitarian. Women are the chief sufferers from sexual convention, Noyes observed. Reliance on a man leads to pusillanimity, slavery, fear, fawning, and flattery; woman's sole ambition is "to settle down into a chattel and a convenience."[14] As a corrective, neither authority nor work followed gender lines; women worked in the machine shop and men knit at meetings. Women were as free to accept or decline and to initiate sexual proposals as men in this community of approximately two hundred that exchanged partners roughly twice a week.[15] The key to equality, as Noyes understood it, is the separation of "amative" sex from procreation and parenthood. The paramount function of the sexual organs is social affection not reproduction, and Noyes called the "propagative part of the sexual relation . . . its expensive part." It is a drain on the life of man, a waste of women's constitution, a burdensome care. Oneida was organized around sexual variety, practiced a form of continence called "stirpiculture," and controlled reproduction; its practices conformed less to what was then called free love than to scrupulously regulated democratic sex.[16]

What political conditions permitted the proliferation of utopias here, with their commitment to congruence between sexuality and society? And why was the response of state and federal governments sometimes accommodating and sometimes interventionist? Noyes summed up the attraction America had for Robert Owen and every other utopian: "a comparatively unperverted people, liberal institutions and cheap lands of the West."[17] Religious toleration was a *sine qua non*, and religiously inspired communities, often the work of "American originals" like the Church of Latter-day Saints, coexisted alongside socialist experiments like Brook Farm; social missions like Nashoba, which was dedicated to educating slaves for freedom; and secular communities based on ideals of friendship and love.[18] Besides religious freedom, experimental communities were beneficiaries of two other quintessential liberal institutions: voluntary association and freedom of contract. Political ideology invited communitarianism as well. Even the most exotic experiments can be seen as attempts to make good on the American promise of self-made identity unencumbered by inheritance, and elected rather than found community. Nathaniel Hawthorne was not alone in thinking that—despite the repudiation of aristocratic titles and hereditary privileges, social diversity, and mobility—revolutionary America had become a "Custom House." Communitarian joiners resisted; they threw off the grip of family and social place and entered by explicit consent into contractual arrangements regarding property, governance, status, sexual relations, and domestic order. Here was the social contract and Tom Paine's "revolution in every generation" made real. This was a classic result of liberalism: legal freedom generating pluralism, including the proliferation of communities whose internal lives are neither liberal nor democratic.

Most utopias have been short-lived; Noyes opened his *History of American Socialisms* by acknowledging that he was creating a record of failures: "all died young, and most of them before they were two years old." (The exception was the Shakers, founded by the "female Jesus" Ann Lee; the group's two-hundred-year history is remarkable when we recall that it was a celibate society that survived through adoption and conversion.) Extraordinary and short-lived, still, not even separatist communities bent on detachment from public affairs were self-sufficient. All were active, visible, and frequently visited. They were certainly publicized locally, often nationally, and much discussed. Lawsuits between the community and disaffected members as well as legal clashes between the group as a whole and political authorities were popular spectacles and occasions for thinking about the relation between sexuality and democratic society. In reviewing the jury selected to hear the *Reynolds* case, Chief Justice Waite remarked that while it was possible to form a fair-minded jury, it was impossible to find one ignorant and without some opinion of the issues raised by the legal prohibition of polygamy: "in these days of newspaper enterprise and universal education, every case of public interest is almost as a matter of necessity brought to the attention of all the intelligent people in the vicinity."[19] These cases inevitably raised the political question of the state's interest in regulating sexual practices—not only in a Devlinesque move to enforce popular moral opinion but also with a view to cultivating and defending democratic principles.

Separatists like the Oneida Perfectionists saw their communities as private enclaves set off from "the world." But when Noyes adopted Thoreau's abolitionist rhetoric and vowed to dissolve the union between himself and the state, he did not have a theory of a politically autonomous self-governing community in mind. Noyes took pains to distinguish Oneida from Mormon communities on this score; the Perfectionists do not defy civil authority, do not drill soldiers, do not try to increase their numbers by sending evangelists to proselytize abroad. In fact, Noyes was perfectly happy to rely on the courts' protection when it came to upholding Oneida's agreements against claims by disaffected members: "We only ask you not to help the rascals, after signing our contract, to break it." His point about independence was simply that state courts ought to refrain from intervening to regulate Oneida's internal arrangements concerning sex and property.

And for the most part, state governments not only tolerated these sexually nonconformist communities but enforced the contractual arrangements on which their survival depended. Carol Weisbrod's legal history demonstrates that "the legislatures did not force the utopias to reimburse seceders; they did not refuse the communities permission to raise children . . .; and they did not, even in the case of Oneida, move to close down the communities." When an ex-Shaker demanded wages for his years of work in the community, arguing that the Shaker covenant was "contrary to the genius and principles of free government, and therefore void," the court responded that "one of the blessings of a free government is, that under its mild influences, the citizens are at liberty to pursue that mode of life and species of employment best suited to their inclination and habits."[20] Conflict with state and federal authority, one historian suggests, was "determined more by the relative vigor and effectiveness of their proselytizing than by the extent to which their actual beliefs clashed with mainstream American attitudes."[21]

For some elective communities saw themselves not as private enclaves but as alternative political orders. They aimed not only at instituting their peculiar sexual arrangements and enforcing them by internal self-government and sanctions but also at political authority and territorial control. Not content with toleration and accommodation by the state, they wanted to make their sexual regulations general law. The Mormons epitomized congruence between the organization of sexual relations and communal life, and they projected their vision of congruence outward. They were committed by doctrine and in practice to congruence among sexual relations, marriage, ecclesiastical organization, and political authority. As I will show in the case of *Reynolds v. U.S.,* the federal government's legal intervention in the Mormon community was driven not only by aversion to religious heterodoxy and moral deviance but also by the determination to prohibit "undemocratic sex, with its presumed threat to democratic character and political community. In this case, the State's interest in democratic sex overrode liberal toleration of religious practices and accommodation of communal life. Nowhere is the power of the idea of congruence clearer, both for forming unorthodox subcommunities and for justifying state action against them in defense of democratic society.

UNDEMOCRATIC POLYGAMY

The history of Joseph Smith's vision commanding him to introduce polygamy and of how Brigham Young made it an integral part of Mormon communal organization is still being written.[22] The number of Joseph Smith's own wives (27? 55?) "sealed" to him in time and for eternity is uncertain, as are his motives in asking to marry the wives of other Mormon leaders (was this an imitation of God's test of Abraham?). In any case, the numbers attest to his seriousness. Mormon historians insist that practicing polygamists both before its legal prohibition and underground afterward were a small proportion (roughly 15 to 20% percent) of the faithful, and they emphasize that Mormons voted overwhelmingly in favor of the proposed state constitution that outlawed polygamy in the 1880.[23] But this is better understood as a capitulation to federal measures excluding Mormon voters from the polls and confiscating church property than a rejection of the practice, which has never been officially disavowed.

Like contemporary arguments in favor of same-sex marriage, public justifications of plural marriage tend to be soberly utilitarian. Polygamy, we read, was a practical way of providing marriage and motherhood to "deserving" women who would otherwise be condemned to spinsterhood. (At no time in Utah history did the total number of women outnumber men, but this rationale has long life: polygamy was considered a sound response to the devastation of the Thirty Years' War, Mormon polygamy was justified as a response to the million men lost in the Civil War, and polygamy had its secular supporters again after World War I.[24]) Plural marriage was also said to maximize the number of children in a frontier community that needed "additional manpower" and to provide company and support for wives left behind while their husbands were away proselytizing. Finally, along with conversion and the extraordinary ongoing business of baptizing the souls of all the world's dead, polygamy aimed at increasing the population of the church. Of course there was also this justification offered by Herbert Kimball who had forty-three wives: "a man who has but one wife and is inclined to that doctrine, soon begins to wither and dry up, while a man who goes into plurality looks fresh, young, and sprightly."[25]

The one compelling instrumental purpose of polygamy was group cohesion. Both a glory and a stigma, plural marriage was "the pragmatic instrument through which Smith hoped to create a new people." After Joseph Smith's death, "from the president down through the apostles and the Presiding Bishopric during the period, no general authority was monogamist," and plural marriage was an effective device for assuring irrevocable commitment.[26] The bonds of the faithful to one another and the church were stronger, and apostasy less likely, in the face of persecution and the consequences of leaving the community, especially for women and illegitimate children.

Unless polygamy is seen as an article of faith, however, its connection with un-democratic politics will remain unclear and the conflict between Mormon sexual practices and federal law will almost certainly be misunderstood. The remarkable doctrine of preexistence is one element: the souls of all the unborn await embodiment, ideally as children of Mormons, and given the immensity of this task, men must take more than one wife: "Blessed is the man whose quiver is full of them." Joseph Smith's revelation of 1831 instructing missionaries to Missouri to "take unto you wives of the Lamanites and Nephites that their posterity may become white, de-lightsome and just" can be explained by the doctrine that Native Americans are the (fallen) biological descendants of biblical Hebrews and have a special relation to the Mormons, themselves direct descendants of Abraham.[27] Most important, polygamy was inseparable from the revelation of the possibility of human divinity: "God him-self was once as we are now, and is an exalted man. . . . And you have got to learn how to be gods yourselves, and to be kings and priests to God, the same as all the gods have done before you."[28] The essential element of progression toward divinity is the sacredness of sexuality.[29] The reason for creating a "family kingdom" was not just to engage in creation by analogy to God (that is, by analogy to the conviction of God's sexual creation of man), or to mirror through patriarchy God's "control over the elementas," but for Mormon men to become coeternal with God.[30] "As man is God once was: as God is man may become." Male sexuality is part of divinity. Either bodies participate in faith, or the Kingdom of God is thwarted. These articles of faith were translated into political imperatives when Joseph Smith prophesied the restoration of the power of God not in another life or time but now, in a Kingdom of God ruled by Mormon priests. Harold Bloom calls the public pronouncement of polygamy "the most courageous act of spiritual defiance in all of American history," but the defiance was far from purely spiritual.[31] The thought was never to exist as just another tolerated minority. The Mormon Kingdom of God was an actual order of government, an alternative to democratic society. America's destiny was to be the Mormon Kingdom; Smith crowned himself its king and declared himself a candidate for the presidency in 1844.

The dramatic background to antipolygamy legislation in the United States includes Mormon persecution and exodus, but also Mormon political resistance and attempts at political control. It begins after the move from Missouri, with the formation of Joseph Smith's private militia in Nauvoo, where the church hoped to enact laws, maintain its own judiciary, establish its own army, and show only nominal subordination to the state of Illinois, as stated in the Nauvoo city charter. The year after Smith's death, war broke out between Mormons and non-Mormons, which the governor could not suppress, and led to the migration west. An autonomous Mormon state of Deseret was established in 1849, and the Saints drew up an ambitious map for a western empire in the Great Salt Lake basin of Utah that was to have encompassed parts of what is now California, Oregon, Arizona, New Mexico, Colorado, and Wyoming and all of Nevada and Utah.[32] The federal government rejected Mormon application for U.S. statehood and extended its jurisdiction to Utah territory in 1850, but Brigham Young, the first governor, continued to rule the territory as a theocracy.

There was little territorial organization apart from the church's system. Ecclesiastical wards were organized in each settlement with bishops responsible for the affairs of members under their jurisdiction. These ecclesiastical units initiated large-scale economic enterprises, including agriculture, mining, transportation, manufacturing, and irrigation canals, with a view to an economically independent Mormon state that discouraged trade with Gentiles. Utah had to accept federal appointees for judges, but the Mormons effectively bypassed them when the legislature authorized itself to appoint a probate judge in each county with jurisdiction in all cases of divorce, alimony, guardianship, and property distributions.[33] In order to give the church flexibility in dealing with converts who wanted to be separated from unbelieving spouses, these judges granted wives both in the territory and outside permission to divorce their husbands in any case where "the parties cannot live in peace and union together." Consistent with their view that civil marriage had little significance, the children of polygamous wives were permitted to inherit property though their parents were not married under civil law, and the courts upheld a variety of living and support arrangements for polygamous households.[34] Alienation from civil law and institutions is plain. "At least until the end of the Civil War," a Mormon historian observes, "many Mormons assumed that the federal government would dissolve in anarchy or become subordinate to the kingdom of God. . . ."[35] The publication of Smith's revelations concerning the duty of plural marriage in 1852 is often said to have caused the invasion of Utah by federal troops five years later to put down "disloyalty" to the United States. But this overlooks the fact that the publicization of plural marriage was just one aspect of Brigham Young's announcement of the Mormon political kingdom of God ruled by the Court of Fifty, including his design for a scorched-earth policy in the event of federal challenge.

Congress outlawed bigamy in 1862, but the Civil War diverted attention from the issue for more than a decade until the end of Reconstruction. In 1879 in *Reynolds v. U.S*, the U.S. Supreme Court upheld the Morrill antibigamy act, which criminalized plural marriage in the territories, and confirmed the conviction of Brigham Young's secretary, George Reynolds.[36] Although Chief Justice Waite recognized polygamy as a religious tenet ("the practice of polygamy was directly enjoined upon male members. . . by the Almighty God in a revelation to Joseph Smith. . . that the failing or refusing to practice polygamy. . . would be punished, and that the penalty for such failure and refusal would be damnation in the life to come"), he went on to reject Reynolds's claim that the institution was protected by the First Amendment, invoking Jefferson's "wall of separation" and insisting that the right of free exercise extended to belief not action. In short, Waite argued against constitutionally required exemptions from general laws within the legitimate power of Congress; to grant an exemption "would be to make the professed doctrines of religious belief superior to the law of the land, and in effect to permit every citizen to become a law unto himself. Government could exist only in name under such circumstances."[37]

The Mormon defense in *Reynolds* was that federal marriage laws prohibiting polygamy amounted to government establishment of religion. (A decision in a later Mormon case opposing polygamy as contrary to "the spirit of Christianity" supports the claim that religious favoritism was one element in the Court's decision.[38] The New Testament forbids polygamy, the Mormons argued, but a majority of the inhabitants of Utah Territory do not recognize its binding force. The Decalogue does not prohibit the practice. Their claim, however, did not stop at religious exemption for themselves from the civil law of marriage. Instead, the Mormons claimed a federal right to political authority in the territory, including authority to write domestic law: "We are therefore led to the assertion that as to the People of this Territory, the supposed offense is a creature of positive enactment. Had Congress a right to fasten this burden upon them?"[39] The Mormons argued for self-rule by Saints elected as state legislators and to territorial courts, including lawmaking authority over sexual relations and marriage, property, and an array of other social institutions, in Utah.

Against this claim, Justice Waite held that it fell within the power of Congress to regulate marriage in the territories. And he reaffirmed the secular purpose of the law: "Marriage while from its very nature a sacred obligation is nevertheless in most civilized nations a civil contract, and usually regulated by law." The prohibition of polygamy was a valid secular purpose within federal power. The heart of the case, then, was the state's civil interest in preserving monogamy. The importance the *Reynolds* opinion holds for us is that the interest the state advanced was the prohibition of polygamy as undemocratic: "According as monogamous or polygamous marriages are allowed, do we find the principles on which the Government of the People, to a greater or less extent, rests." Polygamy was not only the most vulnerable aspect of Mormon community but the core doctrine and practical support of a theocratic state within the state. Plural marriage rested on a theory of male sexuality as the key to apotheosis, and to social order, which explains Mormon insistence on congruence among sexuality, family structure, and ecclesiastical and political community. In this sense the *Reynolds* decision can be said to be hostile to polygamy as a tenet of Mormon religion, and the church was right to see the three decades of attack on antipolygamy as an attack on their community as a whole. But the reasons had more to do with political ideology than heterodoxy: the state was concerned that church authorities could exploit democratic institutions to gain political authority, which they exercised on behalf of faith.

Contemporary interpreters of *Reynolds* insist that the decision was a thinly disguised enforcement of popular moral abhorrence, and they discount the connection between antipolygamy laws and guarantees of republican government. Certainly, moral denunciation was part of the background of the case and is evident in the ruling: polygamy has always been "odious among the northern and western nations of Europe"; from the earliest history of England it was treated as an "offense against society"; the offence was enacted in all the American colonies, Justice Waite wrote. Polygamy was widely thought to breed "vice, incest, forced marriages, sexual slavery, degenerate children, and unbridled male lust."[40] Antipolygamy novels (similar to anti-Catholic and nativist writings) depicted polygamists as violent sadists; scenes of torture were the specialty of this literature.[41] Racial revulsion was mixed with moral aversion: until Mormonism, it was said, polygamy was exclusively a feature of the life of Asiatic and African people and the Mormon practice was called the "new Mohammedanism."[42] From the point of view of traditional morals, Mormons were only one of several social forces undermining sexual conventions. At the same time that polygamy was legally prohibited, mainstream organized religions tried unsuccessfully to attack looser divorce laws and remarriage, which was referred to as "serial" polygamy. (As late as 1946 in a case involving the Mann Act, Justice Douglas insisted that polygamous households were a notorious example of promiscuity and were immoral.)

The *Reynolds* Court, however, did not rest its decision on popular moral aversion, secular or religious. A review of jury selection claimed much of the Court's attention, and Justice Waite judged that the lower court had correctly screened for "passions or prejudice." The Supreme Court's concerns were political. The Mormons were not a tiny separatist community claiming toleration and free exercise exemption from laws. Their goal was statehood (clerical not secular), an expanding empire within the United States, and ultimately Mormon priesthood as the ideal and practice of the nation as a whole. Justice Waite justified the civil law of marriage by insisting that polygamy was "inconsistent with the peace and safety of the state." There was the problem of recurrent vigilantism threatening the peace, political resistance by Mormons, and the possibility of civil war. Justice Bradley summed up these concerns some years later in another case involving the Mormon church, pointing to "the past history of the sect, to their defiance of government authorities, to their attempt to establish an independent community, to their efforts to drive from the territory all who were not connected with them in communion and sympathy."[43]

Overriding the immediate problem of disorder, however, was the need to guarantee republicanism. During the debates over antipolygamy legislation, one congressman declared, "The government of Utah today has no semblance to republican government." President Hayes wrote at the time: "Laws must be enacted which will take from the Mormon Church its temporal power. Mormonism as a sectarian idea is nothing, but as a system of government it is our duty to deal with it as an enemy of our institutions and its supporters and leaders as criminals." This was the thing "that grinds the feelings of American citizens," he continued, not the "social, immoral or polygamic features" of Mormonism "but the hostile, treasonable and the mutinous."[44]

From the start, elections were the chief occasion for disorder. Anti-Mormons in the early Missouri settlements in the 1830s advised that "it requires no gift of prophecy to tell that the day is not far distant when the civil government of the county will be in their hands."[45] The power of a homogeneous religious majority frequently excites unrest among politically vulnerable minorities, but here the complaint was about actual day-to-day church authority over civilian affairs by elected Saints. From the start, the church's control of voting and its exercise of political authority was the source of dissension among Mormons as well. Arrested in 1844 on charges arising from his order to destroy the press of a dissenting Mormon group that challenged his authority to regulate marriage, Joseph Smith was awaiting trial in a Carthage jail when he was lynched by a Gentile mob. As one Saint declared, "the very principle of . . . ecclesiastical authority in temporal affairs I conceive to be couched in an attempt to set up a kind of petty government, controlled and dictated by ecclesiastical influence, in the midst of this national and state government. . . . I believe that principle never did fail to produce anarchy and confusion."[46]

The story of Mormon women's suffrage points up preoccupation with the consequences for democracy of undemocratic sex. Enfranchised in 1870, women in Utah were among the first in the United States to vote, and had the backing of Susan B. Anthony and Elizabeth Cady Stanton, who lobbied against proposed federal antipolygamy legislation.[47] The Congressional bill enfranchising women in all the territories was passed in part with the thought that downtrodden Mormon women would use their political rights to overturn polygamy. Since Utah's non-Mormons opposed female suffrage, passing the suffrage bill would have been impossible without the active support of the Mormon leadership, and to the surprise of federal officials the Utah legislature implemented it. They made it plain that public participation by women was an extension of domestic relations. As voters, women's main political activity was defense of plural marriage, and they voted solidly for the Mormon candidate in the elections of 1872. So female suffrage exacerbated fears that patriarchal polygamy would subvert secular democracy: "I have often seen one solitary man driving into the city a whole wagon load of women of all ages and sizes. They were going to the polls and their vote would be one."[48] In 1887, Eastern feminists joined with other antipolygamy groups to repeal the franchise of Mormon women.

Reynolds was accompanied by other measures reflecting democratic concerns. The Morrill Act outlawing polygamy also restricted the amount of property the church could acquire in an attempt to limit territorial expansion and control. Later, federal legislation was passed granting district courts exclusive jurisdiction in criminal and civil cases and abolishing territorial marshals and the attorney general. The Edmunds-Tucker Act in 1882 denied polygamists the right to vote, sit on juries, and hold public office. It also abolished female suffrage in Utah. In 1887 these political disabilities were extended to anyone refusing to take an antipolygamy test oath; in context, this was not only a demand to repudiate plural marriage but also an indirect imperative to accept separation of church and state and religious pluralism. Other blatantly punitive measures were added to these expressly political ones. The

Edmunds-Tucker Act allowed wives to testify against their husbands, and it disinherited illegitimate children. It annulled the corporate charter of the church and declared its property forfeit.

"Faced with a situation in which the Church could not own land or effectively conduct its affairs; in which most of the leaders of the Church were disenfranchised, in prison, or in hiding; and in which no legislative or judicial recourse remains," the president of the church announced a counterrrevelation inspiring Mormons to halt the teaching of plural marriage and submit to the law (at the same time he placed responsibility for ending the practice on state persecution). Still, the Mormon challenge to democratic institutions remained a concern. Only after the manifesto abandoning plural marriage and prior to the admission to Utah to statehood in 1896 did the church disband its political arm, the People's Party, and allow members to affiliate with national parties and to become politically independent. In 1907 the First Presidency publicly again assured that "[T]he Church of Jesus Christ of Latter-day Saints holds to the doctrine of the separation of church and state . . . and the absolute independence of the individual in the performance of political duties."[49]

The Court's second argument touches closely on contemporary thinking about democratic sex. Justice Waite argued that the federal government had an interest in enforcing the civil law of marriage against Mormon free exercise claims because "polygamy leads to the patriarchal principle." This case against polygamy as antidemocratic appears independent of concern about the political rule of Saints. Private patriarchy is permissible in all sorts of secondary associations, of course, explicitly so in the case of churches. The Church of Latter Day Saints is hardly alone in restricting offices to men, though the exclusion may be particularly galling to women since its priesthood is not an elect but open to any male over the age of sixteen. Why was patriarchal polygamy singled out as fatally incongruent with democracy?

For feminists, official indifference toward the civil standing of women under the terms of conventional marriage proves the disingenuousness of the *Reynolds* court's avowed intention to protect Mormon wives from patriarchal authority. After all, this Mormon prescription—"The order of heaven places man in the front ran. . . . Woman follows under the protection of his counsels and the superior strength of his arm"—is not appreciably different from those used to rationalize traditional marriage.[50] The conviction that male and female sexuality are different, dictate different capacities, and prescribe differentiated social roles (in particular women's primary function as reproducers) is not peculiar to polygamy. Clearly, the Court was not concerned with the equality of women within or outside of marriage, but that is no reason to discount the Court's preoccupation with patriarchy. The focus was on what was thought to be the extraordinary character and consequences of polygamous patriarchy. The standard civil marital contract may have been patriarchal, but the sexual relations and internal life of Mormon marriage was viewed as different in kind and degree, and these sinister differences were judged decisive. The patriarchal principle, the Court wrote, "fetters the people to stationary despotism." Polygamy was associated with harems; women were viewed as subjugated to sanctified male lust; polygamy was called sexual slavery and polygamy and slaver were the "twin relics" of barbarism. Of course, Noyes described all marriage as slavery, and John Stuart Mill wrote that the law of marriage was "the only actual bondage known to our law."[51] Finally, however, in the face of chattel slavery, American courts rightly rejected attempts to identify the condition of women in polygamous relations with the great contradiction at the heart of American democracy—involuntary servitudes.[52]

The matter of voluntary servitude remained: the exploitation and degradation of women in plural marriage out of necessity or religious devotion. Justice Waite even drew an analogy to Hindu women throwing themselves on their husbands' funeral pyres. The difficulty women had leaving polygamous sexual relationships and the Mormon church was of particular concern. In addition to the usual constraints on women, including poverty and civil disabilities, Mormon women faced public ignominy and the illegitimate status of their children. The *Reynolds* jury was instructed to consider "the innocent victims of this delusion," pure-minded women and innocent children.[53]

In retrospect, there is little evidence that Mormon women were coerced into polygamy, though documents show that they often submitted reluctantly as a matter of religious duty. And if subsequent wives consented, there is some reason to doubt whether the first wife in a plural marriage agreed to it; after all, in the context of church sanctions she had little argument against what may have seemed like authorized adultery, little recourse against her husband's decision, and no escape. The story of Joseph Smith's first wife Emma's disbelief in his revelation, her futile resistance to his other marriages, and her public opposition to polygamy after his death bears this out. In an interview with Brigham Young in 1859, Horace Greeley asked whether the system of the church was acceptable to the majority of its women? Young replied, "They could not be more averse to it than I was when it was first revealed to us as the Divine will. I think they generally accept it, as I do, as the will of God."[54]

Arguing before the Supreme Court in defense of plural marriage, George Tichnor Curtis conceded that Mormon polygamy entailed a self-described "patriarchal family system," but he challenged the assumption that Mormon women suffered degradation and needed to be saved by a regulatory state. "Unless we meet the Mormon women of Utah half way, and recognize who and what they are, we cannot accomplish anything useful." Curtis reminded the Court that many of these women were from New England by birth; they were people of intelligence, educated in the public and private schools of our older States. He urged the Court to lay aside the idea that they must be treated "as if they were a set of degraded beings, bearing a yoke under which they bend, and from which it is our duty to emancipate them by any and every means."[55]

Unwilling to take claims about women's degradation at face value, historians have attempted to draw up balance sheets of the advantages and disadvantages of Mormon polygamy for wives. We know that women in plural marriages comprised a female elite insofar as plural marriage was dominated by church leaders. As we would expect, there is also considerable evidence of jealousy and material hardship resulting from the difficulty of apportioning time, money, and affection among wives and often among households (to say nothing of the burden of a fugitive life underground after the legal prohibition). The most in-depth study has not been able to determine whether wives participated in these decisions.[56] Revisionist historians also stress the relative independence of wives in polygamous relations.[57] Their husbands' absence on missionary work and sheer exigency broke down gender roles, the argument goes. Mormon women worked, entered professions in large numbers, and were engaged in financial management. Much of this can be seen a practical consequence of economic conditions in frontier Utah, however, and women's "activities" (strictly speaking, their labor) increased during periods when the community was attempting economic self-sufficiency and home industry was crucial. Lastly, despite the fact that some plural wives were sisters, the solace of companionship may be more a wishful account of Mormon "sisterhood" than real; most polygamous husbands kept separate households; their wives were separated between communities and even states.

If polygamy was not despotic, did not conform to any definition of slavery, and was not necessarily degrading in practice, it was patriarchal. There was no intention as with Shaker celibacy to free women for full participation in community life and no parallel to Oneida's commitment to democratic sex. The effect of patriarchy on women and children is not the only possible democratic consideration, however. When Mill invoked despotism to characterize the civil law of marriage, he was as troubled by its effects on patriarchal husbands as on subservient wives. He described the sense of superiority men feel as "Sultan-like." In any patriarchal marriage, he observed, the relation of the superior to the dependent nurses "the violent, the sulky, the undisguisedly selfish side of character . . . wilfulness, overbearingness, unbounded self-indulgence." Inequality, supported by law, discourages marriage as "a school of sympathy, tenderness, and loving forgetfulness of self."[58] Variations on this theme underly the opening to congruence between sex and society in democratic theory today.

DEMOCRATIC SEX

The decline of Mormon polygamy paralleled the decline of Mormon nationalism.[59] Instead of autonomy, Mormons have sought accommodation, and they have been successful in advancing legal claims to exempt their practices from a range of general public regulations. In the 1987 case *Corporation of the Presiding Bishop of the Church of Latter-day Saints v. Amos,* the Supreme Court granted the church an exemption from Title VII, the federal law prohibiting discrimination in employments.[60] The Court permitted the community to discriminate on the basis of religion in hiring and firing despite the fact that the job at issue was purely secular (a janitor in a Mormon-run gymnasium open to the public) and that the community's viability was not at issue (in contrast to solicitude for the survival of the Old Order Amish community, which influenced the justices' decision in *Wisconsin v. Yoder).* To the extent that Mormons see themselves as one of many groups in a religiously pluralist society and as subordinate to secular political order, the reinstitution of polygamy as a tenet of faith would have a different valence. Disconnected from theocracy and political patriarchy, recast as a religious practice, what would privacy and democratic approaches recommend? What about secular polygamy?

The array of liberal arguments that might be marshaled on behalf of legalizing polygamy is straightforward. Plural marriage based on religious faith could be constitutionally upheld on free exercise grounds; the state's interest in preserving monogamy is arguably insufficient to justify the abridgement of this First Amendment right once it does not threaten civil order. For its part, secular polygamy could arguably be upheld as part of expanded statutory recognition for marriages based on a variety of sexual arrangements, entered into by consent.[61] These could be freely contractual on a libertarian model, or their terms (suitably adjusted) could be set by the state as the law of civil marriage has always done. Justifications for polygamy based on privacy would not differ from those for homosexual marriage outlined in "Liberal Privacy Versus Democratic Community," assuming that there was no violation of equal protection and marriages involving a wife and multiple husbands were permissible. It is impossible to predict whether the liberalization of laws regulating intimate relations along the privacy model would flush out polygamous relations. After all, the propensity for variety and group sex may not incline to institutionalization.

One reason for reviewing American communitarianism is to point up something privacy arguments ignore: liberalism's historical friendliness, in principal and practice, to pluralism. Religious liberty, broad freedom of association (not strictly interpreted as an adjunct of political speech), and contract law (which has never been in the exclusive service of property negotiations between egotistical individuals) combine with liberal reluctance to assign government the function of character formation. The result has been proliferation of various forms of communal life, and collectively sanctioned undemocratic sex. Contemporary liberal political thought is committed to thinking in terms of an individual right to privacy. Still, it is useful to keep in mind that the privatization of association, life that liberalism has traditionally protected may be a facilitating condition for the values most often at stake for theorists of privacy: individual autonomy, personality, self-expression, and choice.

In contrast, from the point of view of democratic theorists preoccupied with reinforcing failing supports for democratic community, the case for legalizing polygamy is less clear. Is polygamy more like the homosexual unions that Michael Sandel thinks channel sexuality into institutions that cultivate loyalty and mutual care? Or more like organized promiscuity, an extreme affirmation of voluntarism and sexual choice? Polygamy's moral valence is indeterminate. Democratic theorists who want intimate relations to function as schools of justice face a similar problem. If it is conceivable that monogamous marriage and same-sex partnerships can be reformed along egalitarian lines, why not polygamy? Is patriarchy endemic?

The historical picture of polygamy as an accompaniment of political despotism and patriarchal culture is not entirely of a piece if images of the high status of women in Tahiti and among Native American Indians are added (though anthropological study would have to ascertain whether the apparent status of women in these cultures conformed to actuality). Despite rare exceptions, patriarchy has been the dominant form of polygamy. It has never had its basis in reciprocity or friendship, not even ideally. Its justification has never been the expansiveness of affection or cooperation. It has rested on ideological or spiritual accounts of male authority and female subjection, on status associated with numbers of wives, and of course on beliefs about male sexual power (or the need to temper women's sexual power) and male entitlements.[62] It is doubtful that the known doctrinal supports for polygamy could be rehabilitated and made congruent with democratic sex.[63]

Of course, what may be true for traditionally polygamous cultures may not hold for voluntary arrangements today. Still, as a psychological matter we could expect polygamous relations to be more likely to foster favoritism than cooperation, jockeying for standing than equality. On the basis of Mormon records, it is plausible to think that multiple households would loosen fathers' (or mothers') ties to their children, or at least make participation in child rearing more difficult. Logically, however, internally democratic polygamous relations are conceivable. There is no reason why egalitarian norms of property distribution, parenting, and the division of domestic and market labor recommended by democratic theorists could not be adjusted for plural marriage. In fact, polygamous households are more like little communities than monogamous ones—the possibilities for cooperation among adult members is greater, and so is the potential for educating children in democratic virtues. Polygamy could be as subversive of dichotomous gender roles and inegalitarian domestic practices as the lesbian and homosexual relations Susan Okin describes, especially so in the case of a wife with several, or many, husbands. From the point of view of democratic congruence, rightly ordered group sex and domestic life might be positively prescribed!

The critical challenges *Reynolds* poses for democratic theory have to do with religion and communal life. From the standpoint of a democratic theory of congruence, it would seem that for polygamy (or any other sexual arrangement) to cultivate democratic virtues, its foundation would have to be secular. Strict complementarily of principle as well as conduct would seem to be required if intimate relations are to serve as schools of justice. *Reynolds* raises the question whether democratic sex is necessarily hostile to anything but civil religion. If so, in the absence of a privileged private sphere, what place is there for undemocratic belief and association?

In the same vein, the relation between democratic theory and communitarianism needs clarification. Because democratic theorists typically look to the cultivation of public democratic norms and habits as a corrective for arrant liberal individualism, the question of pluralism is pushed into the background. Reynolds brings it to the fore. We want to know not only what sexual practices and relations individuals can engage in consonant with democracy, but also the limits of communitarianism. From the point of view of democratic sex, is democracy reinforced if quasi-autonomous subcommunities generate loyalty and cooperation among their members? Would that be true only if their authority structure and organizing principles are democratic? Are groups and communities with egalitarian structures doing democratic work if they are separatists turned away from public affairs? Or if internal equality and cooperation is not based on democratic principles but on others? In short, must congruence between democratic society and secondary institutions reach all the way down?

As *Reynolds* shows, congruence turns out to have associations that democratic theorists have only begun to touch on. The question, of course, is what a democratic approach portends, not only for the exotic case of polygamy but for the legal framework of sexual relations generally. Up to now, the idea of congruence is often invoked in discussions of democracy and sexuality but seldom unequivocally applied. Will democratic theorists make the strong case for legal regulation of sexuality and intimate relations on behalf of democratic sex that the *Reynolds* Court made in 1879? What does the logic of congruence require?

Notes

1. At their height, utopian communities were massed in New York State during the first half of the nineteenth century and expanded west, appearing again in New England and California in the 1960s and 1970s. For discussions of modern communitarianism, see Steven Tipton, *Getting Saved from the Sixties: Moral Meaning in Conversion and Cultural Change* (Berkeley: University of California Press, 1983); Rosabeth Moss Kanter, *Commitment and Community* (Cambridge, Mass.: Harvard University Press, 1971); Francis Fitzgerald, *Cities on a Hill* (New York: Simon and Schuster, 1981).

2. Moreover, just as color blindness makes race an unacceptable reason for social and political inequality without attempting to suppress distinctive racial attributes, the irrelevance of sexuality and conformity to gender stereotypes, say, does not prescribe androgyny, a norm that would be oppressive not only for classically feminine women and masculine men but also for drag queens at the Crown and Anchor Hotel in Provincetown.

3. 478 U.S. 186 (1986). Criminalizing sexually intimate relations has consequences for property and inheritance rights, social security, pensions, work-related health benefits, and so on. For the thesis that the condemnation of homosexuality serves to preserve and reinforce the social meaning attached to gender, or "heterosexism," see Sylvia Law, "Homosexuality and the Social Meaning of Gender," *Wisconsin Law Review* 187 (1988).

4. Justice Blackmun's dissent in *Bowers* is an example: "We protect those rights not because they contribute . . . to the general public welfare, but because they form so central a part of an individual's life," 489 U.S. 747, 772.

5. 405 U.S. 438 (1972). For this "antitotalitarian" argument, see Jeb Rubenfeld, "The Right of Privacy," 102 *Harvard Law Review* 737 (1989).

6. Michael Sandel, "Symposium: Law, Community, and Moral Reasoning: Moral Argument and Liberal Toleration: Abortion and Homosexuality," 77 *Calif. Law Review* 521 (May 1989): 526. His optimism is unaccountable; why not expect a replication of heterosexual problems and weakened norms: gay divorce, property disputes, and custody battles?

7. Thomas C. Gray, "Eros, Civilization, and the Burger Court," 43 *Law and Contemporary Problems* 83 (Summer 1980): 97.

8. For a full discussion, see Nancy L. Rosenblum, "Democratic Character and Community: The Logic of Congruence?" *Journal of Political Philosophy* 2, 1 (1994): 67–97.

9. Susan Okin, "Sexual Orientation and Gender: Dichotomizing Differences" in this volume, pp. 44–59.

10. Laurence Tribe, *American Constitutional Law* (New York: Foundation Press, 1978), p. 854.

11. For a discussion of Greek utopianism see Doyne Dawson, *Cities of the Gods: Communist Utopias in Greek Thought* (Oxford: Oxford University Press, 1992).

12. John Humphrey Noyes, *History of American Socialisms*, p. 145. Kanter finds that "[a]ll but one of the successful nineteenth-century groups practiced either celibacy or free love at some time in their history," p. 87.

13. A branch of contemporary moral theory focuses on the operation of sincerity and empathy in ordering communal relations, and one way to assess these philosophical claims is to examine instances where caring scrutiny actually operated as a communal norm—Oneida's "mutual criticism," for example. Mutual criticism was inseparable from the sexual organization of the community; by eliminating marriage, Noyes intended to eliminate the barriers to sincerity created by spousal loyalty and exclusive affection. For a discussion, see Nancy L. Rosenblum, "Romantic Communitarianism," see Nancy L. Rosenblum, "Romantic Communitarianism," in *The Liberalism/Communitarianism Debate*, ed. C. F. Delaney (New York: Rowman and Littlefield, 1994).

14. Noyes cited in Alan Estlake, *The Oneida Community* (London: George Redway, 1900), p. 89. The author was a member of the community.

15. The estimate is Lawrence Foster's, *Religion and Sexuality* (New York: Oxford University Press, 1981), p. 235.

16. The novel aspects of this deserve mention, to name a few. Noyes's technique for "male continence"; "stirpiculture"; eugenics unconnected to race; "ascending fellowship," which encouraged sexual pairings between young people and elders. For a discussion of sexual practices, see Richard DeMaria, *Communal Love at Oneida* (New York: Mellen Press, 1978). Oneida gave up "complex marriage" only in part in response to the fear of hostile legislation; the history suggests that internal dissatisfaction was at least as important. The community was transformed into a joint stock company in 1881 and continues as a manufacturing enterprise.

17. Noyes, *American Socialisms*, p. 61.

18. Hawthorne's account of Brook Farm in *Blithedale Romance* describes how perfectionism and sexual tension were intertwined and mutually responsible for what he saw as the community's perfectly predictable failure. See Nancy L. Rosenblum, "Romantic Communitarianism." The sexually charged and insufficiently nurturing heroine Zenobia, modeled after Margaret Fuller, is the only character to come off well at Hawthorne's hands.

19. Reynolds v. U.S., 98 U.S. 145.

20. Carol Weisbrod, *The Boundaries of Utopia* (New York: Pantheon, 1980), pp. 77–79; 119; 54; citing the 1826 Maine case, *Waite v. Merrill*, p. 130. The book's focus is litigation between utopian communities and former members.

21. Foster, *Religion and Sexuality*, p. 240.

22. The system was not part of Smith's original revelation; it was not publicly acknowledged during his lifetime and was officially denied by Utah Mormons until 1852. An excellent detailed account is Foster's.

23. For a summary of the Mormon apologetic literature and of rewriting the history in terms of Turner's frontier thesis, see Klaus J. Hansen, *Mormonism and the American Experience* (Chicago: University of Chicago Press, 1981).

24. Cited in Foster, *Religion and Sexuality*, p. 210. A moral variation of the demographic argument had it that there were not enough "goodmen" for the number of deserving wives, Jessie Embry, *Mormon Polygamous Families* (Salt Lake City: University of Utah Press, 1987), p. 48.

25. Cited in Embry, *Mormon Polygamous Families*, p. 8. For the inconclusive evidence as to whether polygamy increased births, see ch. 3.

26. Lawrence Foster, cited in Bloom, *The American Religion* (New York: Simon and Schuster, 1992), p. 125; Bloom, p. 204.

27. America is not the New World, on this view, but the scene of antediluvian history, and the Garden will be recreated in its original setting. See Leonard J. Arrington and Davis Bitton, *The Mormon Experience: A History of the Latter-day Saints* (New York: Knopf, 1979), p. 1975. A later version emphasized Mormon genealogical ties to Adam, the eternal patriarch of the human race, cf. Rex Eugene Cooper, *Promises Made to the Fathers: Mormon Covenant Organization* (Salt Lake City: University of Utah Press, 1990), p. 162.

Mormon theology of descent and race also discouraged active proselytizing of blacks and, once they were converted, prohibited their entering the priesthood. That was changed with a revelation announced in 1978 that annulled the exclusion of black men from ordination and allows the church to be, at least as regards men, universal. Hansen argues that Mormon racism was tied to its nationalist ambitions, much as American Nationalism has been supported by racial identity, p. 188.

28. *History of the Church*, 6:305–306, cited in Cooper, *Promises Made*, p. 103.

29. "Abraham received concubines and they bore him children; and it was accounted unto

him for righteousness, because they were given unto him, and he abode in my law; as Isaac also and Jacob did none other things than that which they were commanded, they have entered into their exaltation, according to the promises, and sit upon thrones, and are not angels but are gods." Section 37 of the *Doctrine and Covenants*, cited by Bloom, *American Religion*, p. 104.

30. Brigham Young, cited in Hansen, *Mormonism*, p. 168. The logical step was taken by Smith's plural wife Eliza Snow, who wrote a hymn to Heavenly Mother; worship of Heavenly Mother lies behind the recent excommunication of Mormon feminists.

31. Bloom, *American Religion*, p. 108.

32. Cited in Weisbrod, *Boundaries of Utopia*, p. 17.

33. "[W]ith power to exercise original jurisdiction both civil and criminal, and as well in Chancery as at Common law." Utah Territory Legislative Assembly 1851: 43, cited in Cooper, *Promises Made*, p. 185.

34. Foster, *Religion and Sexuality*, p. 217.

35. Cited in Cooper, *Promises Made*, p. 185.

36. There were several subsequent cases. *Murphy v. Ramsey* (1885) upheld an act of Congress excluding polygamists from voting or holding office; *Davis v. Beason* (1890) upheld an Idaho Territory law that limited the right to vote to those who would swear not only that they were not practicing polygamists but also that they did not support the practice or belong to any group that teaches, advises, counsels, or encourages its members, devotees, or any other person to commit the crime of bigamy or polygamy. In 1946 in *Cleveland v. U.S.*, the Court interpreted the Mann Act to extend to Mormons who continued to practice polygamy.

37. Reynolds, 98 United States 145. A similar position has been taken by the contemporary Supreme Court in religious accommodation cases, where a valid secular purpose not directed at religion overrides free exercise claims.

38. Corporation of the Church of Jesus Christ of the Latter Day Saints v. United States, 136 U.S. 1 (1889).

39. Reynolds 98 U.S. 145. The unorthodoxy of historic Mormonism is unmistakable. It is not surprising that popular and judicial judgment would have it that plural marriage is "unchristian," the interesting thing is that Mormonism itself is deemed Christian, something Harold Bloom denies: "they are not even monotheists, and they take Jesus only as another name for the God of this world," p. 91.

40. Cited in Weisbrod, *Boundaries of Utopia*, p. 21.

41. Foster, *Religion and Sexuality*, p. 221.

42. See "Family, Church, and State: An Essay on Constitutionalism and Religious Authority," 26 *Journal of Family Law* 741 (1987–88): 758.

43. Cited in Weisbrod, *Boundaries of Utopia*, p. 26.

44. Cited in Hansen, *Mormonism*, p. 144. J. H. Beadle, a Catholic critic, writing in 1870, cited in Weisbrod, *Boundaries of Utopia*, p. 26.

45. Cited in Cooper, *Promises Made*, p. 94.

46. Oliver Cowdery, cited in Hansen, *Mormonism*, p. 137.

47. For a discussion of acceptance of Mormon women by the radical National Woman Suffrage Association but not the American Woman Suffrage Association, see Jill Mulvay Derr, "Strength in Our Union": The Making of Mormon Sisterhood," in *Sisters in Spirit: Mormon Women in Historical and Cultural Perspective*, ed. Maureen Beecher and Lavina Anderson (Urbana: University of Illinois Press, 1987), pp. 181–82.

48. Cited in Weisbrod, *Boundaries of Utopia*, p. 24.

49. Cited in Cooper, *Promises Made*, 198. Feminist concern continues but here the Mormons are hardly unique. Mormon women's participation in the International Women's Year in 1977 was highlighted by their uniform vote against the national platform supporting the ERA (which also included support for abortion and rights for homosexuals), and in a much publi-

cized case in 1979, Mormon feminist Sonia Johnson challenged the church's opposition to the ERA and was excommunicated (church authorities denied that her political opinions rather than her opposition to church leadership and divine revelation was the cause). See Hansen, *Mormonism*, p. 216.

50. Cited in Cooper, *Promises Made*, p. 131.

51. Published in 1869, *The Subjection of Women* (Indianapolis: Hackett, 1988), pp. 29, 86.

52. There is a partisan political account of the federal pressure on Mormons in this connection. President Buchanan felt called on to send an expedition to Utah because the Democrats were in need of an issue to compete with the Republican opposition to barbarism—antipolygamy was their answer to antislavery. Lincoln proposed to leave the Mormons alone as too knotty a problem. Hansen, pp. 142–44. Rhetorically, parallels to slavery were common, as among northern workers ("wage slavery") and feminists ("the subjection of women").

53. Reynolds, 98 U.S. 145.

54. Cited in Arrington and Britton, *Mormon Experience*, p. 185. The most important source for the positive and negative images of polygamy was Montesquieu's *Persian Letters*.

55. Cited in Weisbrod, *Boundaries of Utopia*, p. 23.

56. See Embry, *Mormon Polygamous Families*, p. 87.

57. For a history of the chief women's organization, the Relief Society, and its vulnerability to the direction of the priesthood, see Derr, "Strength is Our Union," p. 163. On the attempt to restrict other affiliations by making Mormon women's associations all-encompassing, see pp. 185–89.

58. *Subjection of Women*, p. 40; pp. 38–39, 87.

59. If polygamy was a source of group identity crucial to the Mormon bid for independence and patriarchal political rule, it is unlikely to reappear so long as the church sets aside its theocratic ambitions. Hansen argues, convincingly, that the abandonment of polygamy was part of the abdication of the idea of a kingdom of God, the result of cultural as well as political forces, Hansen, *Mormonism*, pp. 198–201. Bloom offers a more skeptical account of the degree of Mormon assimilation.

60. See Nancy L. Rosenblum, "The Moral Uses of Pluralism: Freedom of Association and Liberal Virtue, Illustrated with Cases on Religious Exemption and Accommodation," *Working Paper, University Center for the Study of Human Values*, Princeton University, 1993.

61. That is the parallel to the decision in Loving v. Virginia, 388 U.S. 1, 12 (1967), invalidating laws against interracial marriage, pronouncing freedom to marry "one of the vital personal rights essential to the orderly pursuit of happiness."

62. John Cairncross points out that after the First World War, the French were the chief apologists for polygamy, which was deeply rooted in the belief that man is entitled to several woman, *After Polygamy Was Made a Sin* (London: Routledge & K. Paul, 1974), p. 212.

63. Sociological studies maintain that patriarchal authority has not declined among Mormons as much as in the rest of American culture, cited in Marybeth Raynes, "Mormon Marriages in an American Context," in Beecher and Anderson, *Sisters in Spirit*, p. 235.

5

Sexuality and Liberty: Making Room for Nature and Tradition?

Stephen Macedo

INTRODUCTION: TOWARD A MORE JUDGMENTAL LIBERALISM

The obvious question provoked by my title is: why make room for nature and tradition? Such talk, a liberal might assert, is the stuff of intellectual reaction, and we have had more than enough of that over the last few years, no more so than in the realms of sexuality and family life. The aim of this essay, however, is to argue that liberals would do well to reclaim certain traditional moral resources and certain insights about sexuality from their captivity in the domain of intellectual and political reaction. That domain is nowadays defined by a particular aversion to the ideals of equality and liberation that came to the fore in the 1960s. Reclaiming these resources requires liberals to acknowledge that the conservative critics of the 1960s are not all wrong. Conservatives are right, for example, to argue that decent, elevated forms of human sexuality require a self-restraint and moderation that are undermined by simplistic celebrations of liberation from inherited constraints, celebrations that ignore the potentially tyrannical nature of sexual passion.

Liberals should acknowledge that conservatives are not all wrong, but they should not abandon liberalism. My aim here is to defend a judgmental liberalism. This would be a political program that acknowledges, first and foremost, the great good of a broad range of individual freedoms, and the basic justice of fairly extending fundamental rights and opportunities to all. Such a stance would abhor the narrowminded prejudice and demagoguery that underlies some right-wing talk of "family values," it would applaud the great gains made by women in the 1960s, and it would insist that more needs to be done to insure that gays and lesbians enjoy the same public opportunities and privileges as others in society.

Such commitments as these are the core of liberalism, and a judgmental liberalism would affirm them all. It would not, however, be untroubled by other aspects of the legacy of the 1960s, especially the ideal of sexual liberation and the resistance to making value judgments about people's personal lives.[1] Such a liberalism would be prepared to consider the possibility that gains made in social justice may be attended by an impoverishment in other aspects of our moral imaginations, including our thinking about sexuality. Liberals can and should do better than the non-judgmental, "lifestyles" liberalism whose hallmark is an insistence that public policy must be neutral on questions concerning the good life. The truest friends of liberty and equality, I will argue, are those prepared to learn from the critics of these ideals.

Too many liberals, especially in recent decades, have been content to defend only the most central parts of the liberal agenda: the concern with liberty, equal rights, and perhaps distributive justice. Too many have mistaken the most basic aspects of liberal public morality for the whole of it. A more judgmental liberalism would insist that the protection of a robust and fair-minded array of basic rights leaves ample room for moral judgments distinguishing better and worse ways of using our freedom, and for public policies that gently encourage the better ways. It is this conception of liberalism that I want to explore below, especially as it pertains to our sexual lives.

NONJUDGMENTALISM AND ITS PITFALLS

We can begin by considering a couple of examples of the morally thin liberalism I want to eschew, and then move on to a more adequate view. The first example comes from Supreme Court discourse, the justly celebrated opinion of Justice Blackmun in the well-known 1986 Supreme Court decision in *Bowers v. Hardwick*.[2] Michael Hardwick a gay man, unsuccessfully challenged the constitutionality of a Georgia statute making consensual sodomy a criminal offense. Hardwick claimed that the statute should have been interpreted as running afoul of his constitutional right to privacy. Over twenty years earlier, the Supreme Court announced a right to privacy implicit in the broad guarantees of the Constitution and held that this right was sufficient to overturn a Connecticut law making it a crime for married couples to use contraceptives.[3] Later the Court extended the protections of the privacy right to the reading of pornography at home, to unmarried couples using contraceptives, and to a woman's right to have an abortion, among other things.[4]

In *Bowers* a majority of the Supreme Court denied that constitutionally protected privacy rights extend to the intimate acts of homosexuals in their bedrooms. Justice White's majority opinion asserted that the Constitution's privacy rights are limited to sexual activities connected with "family, marriage, and procreation." This narrow construction struck many as odd since it is hard to see the connection between this triad of traditional values and protected activities such as reading pornography and contraceptive use by unmarried people. Even so, White argued that homosexual activity is outside the protected sphere because it has no connection with the values advanced by previously acknowledged privacy rights.

The resolution of *Bowers* turns on how broadly the right to privacy is construed and that, in turn, depends partly on how we construe the values underlying accepted instances of the right. According to dissenting Justice Blackmun, previous privacy rights cases should be understood as resting on much broader values than those identified by the majority. While Blackmun's conclusion seems exactly right, however, his account of the values at stake in the cases is, in crucial respects, rather thin.[5] He said that freedom in our intimate associations with others provides the "ability independently to define one's identity." Likewise, the decision of whether to have a child is protected because "parenthood alters so dramatically an individuals self-definition." Sexual intimacy in general deserves protection because

> [t]he fact that individuals define themselves in a significant way through their intimate sexual relationships with others suggests, in a Nation as diverse as ours, that there may be many "right" ways of conducting those relationships, and that much of the richness of a relationship will come from the freedom an individual has to choose the form and nature of these intensely personal bonds.[6]

One problem with Blackmun's argument is that the grounds he offers for gay and lesbian privacy rights are so morally insubstantial. We have not said much to recommend protection for an activity when we point out doing so would help individuals to define their identities, or that the activity is freely chosen. Individuals have many ways of defining their identities that are valueless or worse: drug-taking, prostitution, irresponsibly promiscuous sexual conduct, and so on. Mere choice and self-definition are thin grounds on which to argue for the recognition of a new and highly controversial constitutional right.

More morally substantial grounds were available to Blackmun, and they should have been tapped. The case for acknowledging Michael Hardwick's constitutional right would have been greatly strengthened if it had been shown that doing so would provide the opportunity for gays and lesbians not simply to define themselves or make choices but to pursue the same sorts of basic goods, such as love and intimate friendship, that are so central to heterosexual lives.[7]

Now, of course, I am not proposing that individuals should only have rights to make good choices and lead good lives. The goodness or intrinsic value of an activity is not the only reason to protect it. We may believe that individuals have a general right to freedom with respect to self-regarding acts that do not harm others. Or we may simply not trust the government to draw distinctions of value in the larger realm of which a valueless activity is a part. Some forms of pornography are protected partly because we do not trust government officials to draw justifiable distinctions among valuable and valueless forms of expression and because, in particular, we think that public officials may use their discretion here to censor political opinions they oppose. So we protect a broad and overinclusive class of expressions for the sake of limiting government's discretion and insuring ample space for valuable expression. There are also reasonable disagreements about whether certain activities are good.

The question of whether an activity is part of a good life is different from the question of whether it should be protected from political meddling, therefore, and all I mean to suggest at the moment is the weakness of Blackmun's way of ascribing value to homosexual acts. Liberals have every reason to be suspicious of government and tolerant of a range of ways of defining the good life. Nevertheless, richer accounts of the good life will sometimes have their uses. In *Bowers* such an account could have been used to establish a stronger analogy between the privacy rights of heterosexuals and those claimed by homosexuals. Protecting the sexual privacy of gays and lesbians could be defended as a way of making possible the pursuit of love, friendship, and other goods essential to happy and fulfilled lives, but Blackmun never quite made this case.

Before proceeding on to consider how a better moral foundation might be constructed for extending basic rights to gays and lesbians, let us turn to another effort to protect oppressed groups that, like Blackmun's, proceeds on a too insubstantial moral basis. Iris Marion Young's *Justice and the Politics of Difference* defends the notion that groups—especially oppressed groups—have group-specific perspectives not easily appreciated by outsiders, and she asserts that such differences should be attended to and preserved in public policy: "A conception of justice which challenges institutionalized domination and oppression should offer a vision of a heterogeneous public that acknowledges and affirms group differences."[8]

Young attacks such notions as moral universality, impartiality, human nature, and other traditional moral categories because they all deny the basic significance of group-based differences. She criticizes those who inject conceptions of the good life into politics because doing so is at odds with freedom and plurality. Young's aspiration is to deploy a conception of justice that does not "devalue or exclude any particular culture or way of life."[9] She seems to want a normative view that is nonjudgmental.

The problem with Young's account—as with so many other progressive moral theories built around the uncritical celebration of "diversity" or "difference"—is her reluctance to acknowledge that not all groups are good and not all of their perspectives should be affirmed in politics. We need criteria for distinguishing good and bad groups—groups worthy of solicitude and those that are not—but the broad and unqualified embrace of diversity allows for no such criteria.

This is not to say that Young or other proponents of diversity and difference really embrace an "anything goes" attitude toward group life. Young speaks only on behalf of warm and fuzzy forms of diversity that fit nicely within the progressive paradigm of special concern: gays and lesbians, blacks and native people, women, the disabled, and so on. All of these groups—as she describes them—are fluid, dynamic, open, and strongly characterized by accepting, nonjudgmental attitudes toward outsiders. Young simply ignores less appealing (especially right-wing) forms of diversity, including religious fundamentalists, Nazis, and racists, all of whom surely regard themselves as oppressed and marginalized groups.

Indiscriminate talk of difference, diversity, and inclusion seems to blind many postmodernists, such as Young, to the need to specify and defend criteria for distinguishing groups worthy of special support from those who are not. No one is for an indiscriminate embrace of difference, and being "inclusive" is not necessarily a virtue. We should be as inclusive as we have good reason to be.

The nonjudgmental stance, in any case, is more a matter of appearance than reality. Implicit within Young's very selectiveness are substantive if tacit and undefended criteria of moral goodness. She defends an ideal of "city life" that "embodies four virtues that represent heterogeneity rather than unity: social differentiation without exclusion, variety, eroticism, and publicity."[10] I do not wish to challenge merits of this ideal of life, only to note its distinctiveness. One does not have to be Amish to see that it is an ideal by no means lacking in moral substance, a social ideal that (like any other) is far from equally hospitable to all group-based perspectives.

The nonjudgmental stance gets us nowhere. In Young's hands it fails to furnish grounds for distinguishing valuable and valueless group-based claims, and so effectively leaves valuable group-based claims undefended. It seems to stand for a broad-minded inclusiveness and acceptance of difference, but it fails to either delimit or justify such attitudes. As soon as one fleshes out the implicit criteria for inclusion, one discovers a substantial but undefended conception of human flourishing. Such criteria are inescapable. They should be articulated and defended.

There is no escape from moral substance, as Blackmun's opinion and Young's book in their separate ways illustrate.[11] We cannot adequately defend privacy rights for gays and lesbians or greater concern for marginalized groups without a substantial account of the values that underlie rights and other protections. Liberals need, in particular, an account of the valuable forms of sexuality.

GAY RIGHTS, NATURAL LAW, AND THE HUMAN GOOD

We can approach the question of homosexual privacy once again by asking: why, on reflection, is heterosexual intimate privacy valuable, and are those values sufficiently present in homosexual relationships to justify protection for them? A more adequate analysis of sexual morality and privacy will result if we take seriously the genuine goods embodied in heterosexual intimate relationships, and then explore the analogies between heterosexual and homosexual relations.

I would like to begin by exploring the account of human sexual relations offered by certain contemporary proponents of natural law. While natural law arguments are typically quite inhospitable grounds for gay rights, I will try to show that for at least one prominent version of natural law, the exclusion of homosexuals rests on a mistake. Far from supporting the moral case against homosexual conduct and the political case against homosexual rights, natural law arguments properly understood help show that homosexual relations at their best embody many of the same profound human goods as heterosexual relations.

John Finnis (a prominent contemporary natural lawyer on whose arguments I will focus) begins by distinguishing what he takes to be a valueless form of sexuality. He argues that masturbation forgoes opportunities to participate in real human goods by using the body as a mere instrument of pleasure: it involves only fantasy rather than real friendship, play, knowledge, and other goods embodied in genuine intimate relations with others.[12] Masturbation is not alone in being valueless for Finnis, indeed, all non-procreative, recreational sex amounts to the mere instrumentalization of bodies for mutual use and pleasure, all are the moral equivalent of mutual masturbation: simultaneous individual gratifications with no shared good in common.[13] On these grounds, Finnis condemns extramarital sex and contracepted sex within marriage just as strongly as homosexual activity.

For Finnis, sexual acts have real value only when they are open to new life (uncontracepted) and within stable, permanent, heterosexual marriage):. heterosexual marriage is uniquely capable of making sex more than the mere use of bodies for pleasure.[14] Such relationships are uniquely capable of embodying truly common goods. Child rearing is obviously an important feature of the good of such relationships: a shared project replete with challenges and rewards, which is never fully attained, and so, a powerful inducement to stable mutual commitments. In all this, Finnis suggests that only when sexual activity takes place within a monogamous marriage and in a way that is open to new life is this urgent and troublesome desire integrated with higher emotional and rational capacities. Only when sex is confined to monogamous heterosexual marriage can one achieve a kind of harmony among one's higher plans and purposes, one's capacities for love and friendship, and one's sexual drive.

Though the foregoing is but a sketch of Finnis's argument, it will be clear that there are a number of problems here.[15] Finnis is not, however, all wrong. He is right to argue that we can distinguish better and worse forms of sexual relationship. He does not wholly mischaracterize the goods involved in rearing children in stable marriage relationships: those goods are real and profound, and Finnis's characterization of them is valuable.

And yet, I see no reason to accept Finnis's contention that extramarital sex, homosexuality, and indeed contracepted sex in a marriage relationship are all essentially variations on masturbation. According to Finnis, sexual activity participates in human goods only when it occurs within a permanent, monogamous heterosexual marriage and is open to the "unitive" good of procreation.

Finnis's narrow view of valuable sexual activity falls on several counts. He fails to offer any reasonable grounds for altogether denying that homosexual activity can have value. Consider his claim that

> whatever the generous hopes and dreams of *giving* of with which some same-sex partners surround their sexual acts, those acts cannot express or do more than is expressed or done if two strangers engage in such activity to give each other pleasure, or a prostitute pleasures a client to give him pleasure in return for money, or (say) a man masturbates to give himself a fantasy of more human relationships after a gruelling day on the assembly line.[16]

Is it even remotely plausible that all homosexual acts—including the most loving sexual acts within long-term monogamous relationships—embody nothing more than a quick trip to a prostitute?

Oddly, Finnis and his allies allow that sex can be part of the marital good for sterile heterosexual couples: married sterile heterosexuals may still be "open" to the great good of new life, they do nothing to choose against procreation, and so their sexual acts can still actualize their marital good, which includes their friendship and mutual commitment and deep lifelong love. The choice of gays and lesbians "to activate their reproductive organs," on the other hand, "cannot be an actualizing and experiencing of the *marital* good—as marital intercourse (intercourse between spouses in a marital way) can, even between spouses who *happen* to be sterile—it can do no more than provide each partner with an individual gratification."[17] Homosexual sex not only forgoes opportunities to participate in real goods, it positively undermines the goods that homosexual friends may share in their nonsexual relations: goodwill and affection can be expressed far more intelligibly and effectively by acts such as conversation, mutually beneficial help in work, or domestic task.

Just why sterile heterosexual couples and homosexuals should be treated differently is never adequately explained.[18] Today's "new natural lawyers" admit that homosexuality like sterility is an unchosen condition. They deny that the morally decisive thing is the presence or absence of the right sorts of sexual organs. Why, then, cannot loving sex between committed gay couples also be a good? Finnis and the other new natural lawyers have yet to justify this apparent double standard or to explain why sex as part of a committed, lifelong relationship is good for infertile heterosexuals but not for gays and lesbians.

The broader weakness in Finnis's position is that it is hard to see why sexual pleasure should be regarded as a good only when sex is uncontracepted and within traditional heterosexual marriage. Even masturbation may not be as totally valueless as Finnis insists: for single people, people whose spouses have medical problems, and others, masturbation may be one reasonable way to cope with sexual deprivation. Overindulgence, of course, can be a distraction from valuable activities and perhaps harmful in other respects. But the bad and the harm would seem to be in the overindulgence, not in the pleasurable acts themselves.

Masturbation may be a borderline case, and Finnis could be right were he simply to suggest that in many cases it will be a distraction from, rather than a component of, the good of most people. Nevertheless, it is very hard to see how one can morally proscribe—on public secular grounds—all contracepted sexual acts between loving couples, all homosexual acts, and so on. Finnis may be right, therefore, to emphasize the great goods of stable heterosexual marriage and all that goes with it at its best, but quite wrong to think that it is the only form of valuable sexual activity.

Finnis's natural law view of human sexuality has obvious and profound difficulties. How can it, therefore, help us step beyond the impoverished, nonjudgmental style of moral analysis described above? I believe that we should, at the very least, take to heart the view that there is no need to reduce the goods at stake in our intimate relations to self-expression, self-definition, and choice. There is no need to deny, as Blackmun seems to do, that the family as such embodies many goods worth promoting, or that the long-term loving commitment of two people is a profoundly valuable thing.

The case for extended privacy rights is strengthened, I believe, by recognizing that homosexual relationships embody many of the same real goods as heterosexual ones: friendship, love, and mutual help and caring stretching over a whole lifetime. All of these goods and more are promoted through homosexual as well as heterosexual relationships, and this is the moral core of the case for extending privacy rights. Obviously, many homosexual relationships will, like heterosexual ones, break down for a variety of reasons, often perfectly innocent ones. But the ideal of a commitment to share one another's successes and triumphs and trials and failures over a complete lifetime seems to me as noble an ideal for gays and lesbians as for straight people. Social welfare and the good of individuals may speak in favor of encouraging sexual fidelity within long-term relationships.

Sexual activity is an important part of the shared good of homosexuals as well as heterosexuals. It may be a sense of the difficulty of keeping sexual passions under control, however, that leads some to sympathize with the hard line taken by natural lawyers such as Finnis and to insist that all but a very narrow range of sexual expression is morally valueless. But how many people are prepared to join Finnis and his natural law allies in condemning all extramarital heterosexual sex, divorce, and contracepted sex in marriage? As David Boaz has pointed out, too many conservatives take the easy road of expressing their moral outrage about contemporary sexual mores by condemning homosexuality while remaining virtually silent about the much greater and more widespread harm done to "traditional family values" and many children by divorce and single parenting (especially teenage single parenting).[19]

We should take a broader view than Finnis does of the valuable forms of sexuality, but that does not mean we should jettison the very effort to think critically about what has value in the sexual realm. Wherever we draw the line, we need to draw it somewhere and to defend where we draw it. We should certainly draw the moral circle to include homosexuality but certain forms of sexual expression will be excluded—such as rampant forms of uncommitted promiscuity—which would seem a sure path to personal unhappiness as well as a variety of social pathologies.

We can reject the puritanical prescriptions of conservative moralists such as Finnis while acknowledging that sexual desire can be a problem. There is something to the observation of Plato, Aristotle, and others that the relative intensity of the "animal pleasures" means that most people will by nature tend toward overdoing rather than underdoing with respect not only to sex but food—at least absent efforts at self-control and a well-developed character. Some will, indeed, experience their sexuality as a tyrannical passion. Efforts at self-control and character development—crucial to a healthy and happy life—benefit greatly from social support. In these ways we can see that the conservatives are on to something that too many liberals—in their fear of being perceived as "judgmental"—fail to acknowledge.

RECONCILING GAY RIGHTS AND "FAMILY VALUES"

Holding that the right to intimate privacy extends to lesbians and gays does not mean that society can say or do nothing to shape and elevate the kinds of relationships that people have. Defending liberal rights—including privacy rights for gays and lesbians—does not require that we embrace a nonjudgmental stance with respect to the ways that people use their rights.[20] A judgmental liberalism would defend a broad range of freedoms while insisting that people need not simply options but channels encouraging them to favor better over worse ways of life. If incentives to form relatively stable commitments are good for straight people, then they may be good for gays and lesbians as well.

The most important thing for gays and lesbians to demand from society is the decriminalization of homosexual activity and the right, as Justice Blackmun emphasized, to "be let alone" by society. Also important, however, is the demand that homosexuals enjoy the same privileges and opportunities as others in society. As Andrew Sullivan puts it:

Society has good reason to extend legal advantages to heterosexuals who choose the formal sanction of marriage over simply living together. They make a deeper commitment to one another and to society; in exchange, society extends certain benefits to them. Marriage provides an anchor, if an arbitrary and weak one, in the chaos of sex and relationships to which we are all prone. It provides a mechanism for emotional stability, economic security, and the healthy rearing of the next generation. We rig the law in its favor not because we disparage all forms of relationship other than the nuclear family, but because we recognize that not to promote marriage would be to ask too much of human virtue.[21]

The central claim here is that encouraging people to make deeper and more stable commitments than they might otherwise do will be good for them and for society, and that seems reasonable.

Why are more stable commitments good for individuals? It is not, obviously, simply because deeper mutual commitments between people are always better; excessively deep commitments with no possibility of "exit" might lead to debilitating forms of dependency and oppression. Given certain background configurations of social norms—in a society of Muslim fundamentalists, for example—the best thing might be to encourage more unstable and critical forms of commitment.[22] The argument for encouraging more stable forms of commitment in our context is partly circumstantial: in the sex-riddled, divorce-prone culture of contemporary America, most of us do not err mainly on the side of excessively stable personal commitments.

Providing incentives for people to get and stay married is good for heterosexuals and for gays as well. Married men (much evidence suggests) live longer, have lower rates of homicide, suicide, accidents, and mental illness than unmarried ones; as James Q. Wilson reports, "crime rates are lower for married than unmarried males and incomes are higher."[23] The argument for marriage claims that more stable commitments promote public as well as private welfare. Most obviously, children seem to benefit from being nurtured by stable, two-parent families, and so child rearing within marriage promotes a good society.[24] There may be other public reasons to encourage childless people to get and stay married: stable relationships based on deep commitments may help encourage responsible conduct, planning for the future, and concern for others.

Gay and lesbian domestic partnerships and marriage offer ways of addressing the ambivalence about the sixties that I expressed at the beginning of this essay. By endorsing gay marriage, we give something to both sides of the "sixties question." We allow that the traditionalists were not all wrong: we have legitimate public reasons to favor certain institutions that help order, stabilize, and elevate sexual relations. But we offer these inducements from a posture of fundamental equality of respect: we offer them to everyone, not only to heterosexuals. We provide everyone with the resources that everyone needs to help to stabilize and elevate their sexual relationships and, so, to achieve the benefits that traditionalists rightly claim for marriage.

The "progay, profamily" policy advocated by increasing numbers of gay social commentators will not make everyone happy.[25] Some of those who want to emphasize the distinctiveness of "queer" culture and values will charge that the stance I have defended rests on a hegemonic desire to impose the interests and habits of the "straight" world on gays and lesbians. There is, however, no reason for us to accept this blanket compartmentalization of the moral world (just another tired version of moral relativism) into homosexual and heterosexual realms with wholly different standards applying in each. The wrongness of lying, cheating, and stealing having nothing to do with one's sexual orientation. Promiscuity is a tempting option for many men and women of all varieties, an option that is nevertheless detrimental to the long-term well-being of most.

This is not to say that there may not be some moral standards that apply to homosexuals but not heterosexuals. The fact that it is impossible for conception to result from gay sex is certainly morally relevant to the question of who has an obligation to use condoms (relevant but often not decisive given the risks of disease transmission). In any case, the question of which moral standards apply to homosexuals cannot be answered wholesale but must be taken up one moral standard at a time. The case for extending certain "bourgeois" norms and institutions to groups not traditionally included in bourgeois culture rests on the claim (which I have supported here, albeit inadequately) that those aspects of bourgeois culture (suitably amended perhaps) are good for those of us who have been regarded as outsiders in certain respects.

I do indeed favor the preservation and extension of bourgeois virtues, which are as much a matter of controversy in the gay world as in the straight. In *After the Ball*, gay writers Marshall Kirk and Hunter Madsen argue for a new gay ethos organized in part around what they call a "Self-Policing Code" of conduct.[26] Kirk and Madsen argue that today's gay lifestyle is "unworkable . . . , [it] diminish[es] the quality of gay life, and make[s] us look bad to straights . . . [because this lifestyle is] devoid of the values that straight society, with such good reason, respects." The social code they propose would be enforced through gay social censure undertaken by the gay victims of "gay misbehavior" and any gay bystanders. Consider some elements of this three-part code:

Rules for Relations With Straights
I Won't Have Sex in Public Places.
I Won't Make Passes at Straight Acquaintances, or at Strangers Who
Might Not Be Gay.
Wherever Possible and Sensible, I Will Come Out-Gracefully.
I Won't Talk Gay Sex and Gay Raunch in Public.
If I'm a Transvestite, However Glamorous, I'll Graciously Decline Invitations to
Model Lingerie for "Oprah" or "Donahue."

Rules for Relations With Other Gays
I Won't Lie.
I Won't Cheat on My Lover—With Someone Else's.
Tested or Otherwise, I'll Practice Safe Sex.
I Will Not Speak Scornfully or Cruelly of Another's Age,
Looks, Clothing, or Social Class . . .
When Forced To Reject a Suitor, I Will Do So Firmly But Kindly.

I'll Drop My Search for Mr. Right and Settle for What's Realistic.
I Won't Reenact Straight Oppression by Name-calling and
Shouting Down Gays Whose Opinions Don't Square with Mine.

Rules For Relations With Yourself
I'll Stop Trying To Be Eighteen Forever and Act My Age.
I'll Live for Something Meaningful Beyond Myself.
I Will Not Condone Sexual Practices I Think Harmful to Individuals or the
Community Just Because They're Homosexual.
I'll Start Making Some Value Judgments.

These rules of conduct seem to me to be eminently sensible, if far from complete. Not all gays and lesbians will agree, of course, nor will people in general. Mark Blasius charges that these strictures represent "the desire to conform to existing heterosexist norms rather than to create lesbian and gay criteria for existence."[27] It is extremely hard for me to see why Blasius calls "heterosexist" a set of rules that seem to me nothing more than basic parameters of common decency. The important question, which Blasius seems to ignore, is whether norms such as those proposed by Kirk and Madsen promote the good of homosexuals. Invoking stereotypes—even progressive stereotypes—about heterosexual and homosexual behavior will not help us answer this question. How, in any case, do we tell whether it is better to conform to some (suitably revised) traditional standards or to create new ones, until we are told what the new standards are (which Blasius does not do)?

An emphasis on group-based authenticity or "difference" should not lead us—gay or straight—to abandon traditional standards where these promote good forms of life. A radical rejectionism with respect to all that we inherit from the past is only another way of remaining a slave to the past. The people most sadly in thrall to "heterosexist" oppression may be those who refuse to acknowledge the justifiability of any of the "normal" moral standards.

We were right in the sixties to extend the bounds of toleration and freedom, but wrong (insofar as we did) to embrace the nonjudgmental attitude of liberation, authenticity, and expressive individualism. Having accepted broad rights and principles of freedom, we may still use public power in gentle ways—by providing tax benefits for married couples, for example—to encourage preferable forms of life.

In deciding which forms of life are preferable, liberals should be committed to public criticism and debate: the aim will not be to promote "traditional" values so much as values that withstand the test of critical scrutiny. Our aim should be neither blindly to uphold a tradition nor blindly to tear it down, but rather to regard it critically and to make sure that its benefits are available to all who have a reasonable claim on them.

Against my position, liberationists such as Young and Blasius might argue that political reliance on conceptions of the human good will always be perceived by some to be exclusionary and oppressive. If the objections are reasonable they should be attended to, and courts should be sensitive to claims of minority exclusion. But there will always be some people who object to any social policy, no matter how well it is justified. It should be remembered, therefore, that I am not proposing that anyone should be coerced to marry, or prevented by the law from engaging in forms of sexual behavior that are simply degrading or perverse but involve no harm to others. I endorse the liberal insistence that rights come first, but I also insist that rights are not the whole of public morality. Within the bounds of broad rights and liberties, a judgmental liberalism has room for some public policies that gently and unobtrusively promote better over worse ways of life, and that elevate and stabilize our sexual lives.

MORAL JUDGMENT AND DISCRIMINATION

One still might worry that the more judgmental stance I have proposed is liable to be perverted, and that instead of the relatively inclusive account I have given, homosexuality as such may be regarded as a "suboptimal" orientation. Once one begins thinking in terms of better and worse forms of sexuality, the argument could go, it might become legitimate to discourage homosexuality as such—not among those who are ineluctably committed to it, but among children and others whose sexual preferences are uncertain or divided or otherwise capable of being shaped (in a heterosexual or homosexual direction) by publicly created incentives.[28]

We could just dismiss this question on the ground that people are obviously heterosexual or homosexual by nature, but the question of nature versus nurture, here as elsewhere, is far from being settled conclusively. So let me ask: Do we have any reason to think it is better to be gay or straight? Is there any reason for public policy to offer gentle inducements or incentives for those who are sexual fence-sitters—as we might call them (and supposing they exist—to tend in a heterosexual direction?

One way to think about this would be to imagine ourselves in a kind of original position and ask what we would want to be if we had the power of determining our sexual preference (the power to be born again, but not in the usual sense). Of course, in a world full of prejudice, one would have reason to prefer heterosexuality. Given that prejudice is deeply rooted and difficult fully to eradicate, one has reason to wish to be heterosexual, but that tells us about the world rather than about the intrinsic disadvantages—if any—of homosexuality. So imagine that all prejudice has been washed away, and more, that marriage and adoption are equally available to gays and straights. Child rearing is, then, available to all, as is artificial insemination and surrogate motherhood. Now we can think more clearly about the intrinsic advantages and disadvantages of homosexuality.

One thing not available to homosexuals is the shared biological tie with children, and this is an important good, a unique form of relatedness to another being that is unavailable to homosexuals by nature, not simply as the consequence of prejudice or unequal treatment by other people. Of course, given time, technology is liable to advance to the point where an equal genetic contribution could be made by same-sex couples, at that point, is there any disadvantage to being homosexual? Finnis suggests that the technologically intrusive process of such forms of artificial procreation is tainted by the mastery and domination that technology represents.

Such attitudes may be a reflection of the novelty of such procedures, or of romanticism: do parents care less for a child delivered by Caesarean section? or for a child who is the product of an egg that was fertilized in a test tube?

I can imagine one other possible reason, from the perspective of our original position, for preferring to be heterosexual. It may be that the widespread dogma—so prevalent in progressive circles—that gender differences between men and women are socially constructed is false. Here again the issue is far from settled, but a variety of suggestive evidence is available supporting the notion of natural gender-based differences in personality and moral disposition: men tend to be more aggressive, hierarchical, and egotistical, women care more about comity and maintaining ongoing relationships.[29] Men are more promiscuous and are more easily and continuously aroused sexually than women, women place more emphasis on dependability in a mate.[30] There may be natural differences between the "typical" male and female moral personalities, therefore, and these differences may be complimentary in an important sense.

Of course, the male and female "types" would be mere tendencies and would represent imperfect generalizations: not all women are caring and not all men are roaming, rule-oriented creatures (witness Margaret Thatcher and Mister Rogers). Even so, if there are generalizable more or less "natural" differences among men and women, and if the men-types and women-types are complimentary, then it may be that people have a much greater chance of finding a complimentary partner if they are heterosexual. And that is not all. Same-sex relationships and subcultures may be prone to peculiar pathologies, which are related to the hyperconcentration of particular gender-based characteristics. Some gay men have themselves suggested that some unfortunate characteristics of the gay subculture—narcissism, an intense preoccupation with youth and appearances, a "cruisy superficiality," and a tendency toward unstable romantic involvements—are the consequence of an all-male erotic environment.[31] Posner may be right to conclude, therefore, that "even in a tolerant society the male homosexuals lot is likely to be a less happy one on average than that of his heterosexual counterpart."[32]

There may be reasons, aside from prejudice and convention, for encouraging those children who could "go either way" to prefer heterosexuality. Admittedly, these reasons are highly speculative and subject to dispute; the growth of our knowledge in this area may or may not support these speculations. No matter, even if there is something to the natural difference thesis and to the complementarity thesis, such claims do not settle any political questions.

Speculative reasons for thinking that heterosexuality has possible advantages may be inappropriate grounds for public policy. As things stand, homosexuals have reasonable and basic objections to a policy of encouraging heterosexuality among those who are capable of "going either way." Given the long history and present reality of widespread prejudice and discrimination, homosexuals would reasonably view such a policy of encouragement as an assault on their basic right to equality of political respect. Prejudice and discrimination would be exacerbated, moreover, by policies favoring heterosexuality. In anything like our current climate, it is impossible to see how such a policy of encouragement for young waverers could avoid doing great damage to homosexuals—most especially perhaps to those children who really are homosexual—all for the sake of wholly speculative benefits.

Our culture already sends innumerable signals that heterosexuality is "normal" and to be preferred. All of our cultural presumptions already tilt in the direction of heterosexuality. Given all this, those who now advocate a policy of encouragement seem to give little or no weight to the good of homosexuals and those children who are destined to become homosexual.

It does not, on the other hand, seem to me that offering public inducements to marriage over nonmarriage plays into antigay prejudice, so long as marriage is available to all. Public encouragement for stable marriage ties for all do not express a lack of equal concern for gays or lesbians, or any other "discrete and insular" minority, and it does not rest on a public judgment that homosexuality is intrinsically inferior.

MIDDLE GROUND IN THE CULTURE WARS

Jonathan Rauch rightly urges conservatives to embrace "the genuine universality of family values" by eschewing antigay rhetoric in favor of accepting all who "play by the rules of monogamy, fidelity, and responsibility . . . without regard to sexual orientation."[33] A progay, profamily policy provides conservatives with an opportunity to rise above the small-mindedness and prejudice that sometimes dogs talk about family values. Rather than treating gays and lesbians indiscriminately as the moral scapegoats for far more general social problems, such a policy would oppose irresponsible behavior as such and reward all of those prepared to form stable, committed relationships.

The point of extending marriage, I should emphasize, is to broaden but not to water down society's support for marriage and long-term interpersonal commitment. Indeed, as things currently stand, the debate about "domestic partnerships" is strangely confused. As Boaz and Rauch point out, a progay, profamily policy would not support the progressive proposal that benefits associated with marriage should be made available to both heterosexual and homosexual domestic partners. If heterosexual domestic partners want the benefits of marriage, they have the option of marrying. There is nothing wrong with society's making the conferral of marriage benefits contingent on couples' willingness to make a deep commitment to one another.

Gays and lesbians do not have the option of solemnizing their mutual commitments in marriage, and so to promote homosexual domestic partnerships, as opposed to heterosexual ones, is profamily. Whereas heterosexual domestic partnerships give some of the benefits of marriage without the commitment, recognizing domestic partnerships for gays and lesbians is a way of encouraging the sort of serious interpersonal commitment and responsible conduct that marriage rewards among heterosexuals.

My proposals with respect to sexuality are but one part of a more judgmental liberalism, which represents a middle ground in the wide-ranging moral clashes that some have called "culture wars." There may be, as Plato recognized, something about democratic egalitarian principles that push us toward the nonjudgmental stance. If we are, after all, the moral equals of one another, who are you to judge me, and who am I to pass judgment on you? The democratic danger, Plato suggested, is that affirming the fundamental moral and political equality of persons could lead to a more sweeping and radical form of equality, in which all pleasures and desires are respected equally.[34]

Many conservatives are acute enough to recognize this danger, but they also often sell short the genuine gains made by liberalism. We do better to embrace a reasonably judgmental version of liberalism, I believe; one that embraces equality of concern and respect for persons, but without extending the egalitarian principle to all of the choices that people make, or all of the objects of their desires and temptations.

We have good reason not to pursue the democratic principle of equality to its ultimate extreme—and that indeed is one of the dangers implicit in the legacy of the 1960s. Far better, with Plato and indeed Tocqueville, to recognize that equality pushed to an extreme is self-destructive.[35] Far better, with Tocqueville and Socrates, to acknowledge that the best friends of democracy and equality are those who recognizes their shortcomings.

Notes

1. My posture is not unlike that of William A. Galston in *Liberal Purposes* (Cambridge: Cambridge University Press, 1991), who also walks a middle ground between "liberationists" and "traditionalists."

2. 106 S. Ct. 2841 (1986).

3. Griswold v. Connecticut, 381 U.S. 479 (1965).

4. Stanley v. Georgia, 394 U.S. 557 (1969); Eisenstadt v. Baird, 405 U.S. 438 (1972); Roe v. Wade, 410 U.S. 113 (1973).

5. I should say that there is more to Blackmun's argument than the aspects I describe, and I am not the first one to criticize his opinion in this way, see Michael J. Sandel's, "Moral Argument and Liberal Toleration: Abortion and Homosexuality," *California Law Review* 77 (1989): 521–38.

6. Blackmun, dissenting opinion in *Bowers*.

7. I am indebted for conversations on these themes with Peter de Marneffe.

8. Iris Marion Young, *Justice and the Politics of Difference* (Princeton: Princeton University Press, 1990), p. 10.

9. Ibid., p. 36.

10. Ibid., p. 13, and see ch. 8, "City Life and Difference."

11. As Ronald Dworkin pointed out in another context, see "The Forum of Principle," in *A Matter of Principle* (Cambridge, Mass.: Harvard University Press, 1985).

12. John Finnis, "Personal Integrity, Sexual Morality, and Responsible Personhood," *Anthropos* 1 (1985): 43–55.

13. John M. Finnis, "Law, Morality, and 'Sexual Orientation,'" *Notre Dame University Law Review*, 69 (1994): 1–29, 19; for Germain Grisez's more elaborate but closely parallel account, see *The Way of the Lord Jesus*, vol. 2: *Living a Christian Life* (Quincy, Ill.: Franciscan Press, 1993), pp. 553–752.

14. Finnis, "Law, Morality, and 'Sexual Orientation,'" pp. 16–21.

15. I have written a much more elaborate commentary on and critique of Finnis's position in "Against the Old Sexual Morality of the New Natural Law: A Critique of John Finnis," in

Liberalism, Modernity, and Natural Law, ed. Robert George and Christopher Wolfe (Oxford: Oxford University Press, forthcoming), and "Homosexuality and the Conservative Mind," *Georgetown Law Journal* 84 (1995): 261–300, and the critical replies that follow, Robert P. George and Gerard V. Bradley, "Marriage and the Liberal Imagination," ibid.: 301–20; "Questions of Principle, Not Predictions: A Reply to Macedo," ibid. Hadley Avres, 321–27; and my "Reply to Critics," ibid.: 329–37.

16. Finnis, "Law, Morality, and 'Sexual Orientation,'" p. 19, emphasis in original.

17. Ibid., emphasis in original.

18. I pursue all of this at greater length in "Against the Old Sexual Morality."

19. David Boaz, "Don't Forget the Kids," *New York Times*, Sept. 10, 1994, which points out that conservative publications such as the *American Spectator* and the *National Review* run many more articles on homosexuality than on parenthood, teenage pregnancy, or divorce. See also James Q. Wilson's *The Moral Sense* (New York: Free Press, 1993), which describes evidence that seems to show that "the presence of a decent father helps a male child learn to control aggression, his absence impedes it," p. 178.

20. Contrary to what some critics of liberalism seem to believe, see, e.g., Michael Sandel's "Judgmental Toleration: Religion, Group Defamation, and Gay Rights," forthcoming in George and Woolf, *Liberalism*.

21. Andrew Sullivan, "Here Comes the Groom," *New Republic*, Aug. 28, 1989, pp. 20–22.

22. If rates of spouse abuse are very high, and if this goes unreported in many cases, this, too, is a powerful argument in favor of more critical and less stable commitments in those cases.

23. See the evidence and argument in Wilson's *Moral Sense*, p. 178.

24. Ibid., pp. 176–78.

25. I borrow this phrase from Jonathan Rauch's "A Pro-Gay, Pro-Family Policy," *Wall Street Journal*, Nov. 29, 1994. See also the pieces by Boaz and Sullivan cited above, notes 19 and 21; Bruce Bawer's important *A Place at the Table: The Gay Individual in American Society* (New York: Poseidon Press, 1993); and Stephen H. Miller's provocative "Culture Watch" column in *New York Native*, along with his "Who Stole the Gay Movement?" in *Christopher Street* no. 218 (Oct. 1994), pp. 16–19.

26. *After the Ball: How America Will Conquer its Fear and Hatred of Gays in the 90's* (New York: Plume, 1990), p. 360.

27. Mark Blasius, "An Ethos of Lesbian and Gay Existence," *Political Theory* 20 (1992): 642–71.

28. As has been proposed by E. L. Patullo, "Straight Talk About Gays," *Commentary* 94, 6 (Dec. 1992): 21–24.

29. See Carol Gilligan's *In A Different Voice* (Cambridge, Mass.: Harvard University Press, 1982), which provides an account of the differing moral perspectives of men and women without positing a basis for these in nature; Wilson provides a survey of evidence suggesting that the differences may have a physiological basis, *Moral Sense*, pp. 179–90.

30. Wilson, *Moral Sense*, pp. 179–90; and Posner, *Sex and Reason*, (Cambridge, Mass.: Harvard University Press, 1992), pp. 300–309.

31. Kirk and Madsen, *After the Ball*, pp. 316–23 and *passim*.

32. Posner, *Sex and Reason*, pp. 307–308.

33. Rauch, "Pro-Gay, Pro-Family Policy."

34. See the account of the decline of regimes in Book VIII of *The Republic* of Plato, trans. Allan Bloom (New York: Basic Books, 1968).

35. Plato does not issue this warning as a friendly critic, but Alexis de Tocqueville does, see *Democracy in America*, ed. J. P. Mayer, trans. George Lawrence (New York: Harper Perennial, 1988).

6

Pornography Left and Right

Catharine A. MacKinnon

A Review of Richard A. Posner, *Sex and Reason* (Cambridge, Mass.: Harvard University Press, 1992), and Edward de Grazia, *Girls Lean Back Everywhere: The Law of Obscenity and the Assault on Genius* (New York: Random House, 1992).

In a telling convergence between left and right, Rush Limbaugh, a conservative commentator, recently said that I say "all sex is rape," repeating a lie that *Playboy*, a glossy men's sex magazine with liberal politics and literary pretensions, has been pushing for years.[1] This is a lie, rather than a mistake, on the assumption that they both read my work, which may be giving them too much.[2] That those whose politics conventionally divide them are united on this point reveals the common nerve struck by questioning the presumptive equality of men and women in sex.

With issues other than sexuality, it has been possible to ask whether sex equality has been achieved without being slandered. In other areas of social life, poverty, physical coercion, socialization to passivity, and sexual abuse from cradle to grave are not seen to support freedom, consent, and choice. But to argue that these same forces may create something other than equality in sexual relations is to call forth in escalating litany of increasingly defamatory names.[3]

To say that I—and others who analyze sexual abuse as part of gender inequality—say all sex is rape is a political libel, a false statement of fact that destroys repute in a community in which sex is the secular religion. Focusing an amorphous, visceral misogyny in sound-bite, spit-out, get-her form, it targets hatred by harnessing the fantasy that men are deprived of sex and are about to be deprived of more sex. Sexual energy is thus mobilized and displaced onto those who would supposedly deprive men of sex as men are supposedly deprived of rape. For allegedly *saying* this, or what is said to amount to this, women are vilified, shunned, unemployed, unpublished, scorned, trivialized, stigmatized, marginalized, threatened, ignored, personally hated by people we have never met, and unread. All this for what we *do* say:

sexuality occurs in a context of gender inequality, a fact no hate propagandist has yet tried to rebut.

The line between those who wield this libel and those against whom it is wielded cuts across left and right. It divides those who want to maintain and advance under male supremacy from those who want to end it. It draws a line of sexual politics.

The same line divides the real sides in the pornography debate. Much of the left and right together, prominently including liberals, civil libertarians, and libertarians, occupy the pro-pornography side. On the other side are those for whom sexual abuse is real and matters, those who oppose inequality based on sex even in sexual relations. This alignment was visible, for example, in the sudden unity between the Moral Majority and some liberals in support of the U.S. obscenity approach to pornography,[4] a remarkable (if wholly unremarked) left-right consensus occasioned by the law Andrea Dworkin and I conceived to recognize pornography as a form of sex discrimination by allowing civil actions by victims who can prove harm.[5] The real threat to male dominance posed by this law propelled the liberals into the arms of the conservatives.[6] The right has always supported obscenity law; it embodies their concept of the pornography problem. The left has always criticized it as moralistic, anti-sex, homophobic, vague, overbroad, a "chilling" criminal sanction for expression of unpopular ideas, and a device for right-wing repression—indeed, as everything the same forces have said, falsely, of our proposed law. Once our proposal became a live possibility, this same obscenity law the liberals had long excoriated suddenly looked good. Now, anything that needed to be done about pornography could be done by obscenity law. Given a law that, unlike obscenity law, would actually be effective against the pornography industry, liberals faced the fact that U.S. obscenity law has done nothing against the industry and never will. Perhaps they noticed that the pornography industry, unstemmed by the prosecutorial efforts of three conservative administrations, has quadrupled in size since the U.S. Supreme Court announced its obscenity test in 1973.[7] Perhaps they noticed that obscenity doctrine is unworkable and unrealistic.[8] Perhaps they realized that no criminal law will ever be effective against a business that can be run from jail. The right likes how much obscenity law says, the left likes how little it does, so everyone is satisfied except those who want the pornographers, and the harm they do, stopped.

Another charge generated in the struggle over this proposed ordinance is that Andrea Dworkin and I are in bed with the right.[9] This fabrication, with the requisite sexual innuendo, emanated from liberals who defend pornography on the identical First Amendment ground conservatives do. Its sole function is to scare liberals off—which frankly does not take much. The right knows better than to embrace the sex equality the ordinance advances and they oppose. In fact, individual legislators on left and right have both supported and opposed the equality approach to pornography, but only one individual of the scores we have worked with closely identifies as conservative.[10] One person is not a wing or an organization. Frankly, this lie would be easier to survive if it were true. If civil rights laws against pornography had the right's resources, money, access, votes, and power behind them anywhere, they would have been in place for over a decade.

Together with politicians, journalists, and pornographers, judges left and right in the United States have also taken a single position on the sex discrimination law against pornography for the same reason: to make injury through pornography civilly actionable as sex discrimination violates the First Amendment.[11] This convergence is not publicly decried as an unholy alliance or an abandonment of marginalized and powerless groups by the left. It is hailed as an objective reading of the law. In other words, when people converge without regard to left and right to support this law, their convergence is stigmatized as "strange bedfellows,"[12] sinister and unprincipled, and attributed to the right. When forces align across left and right to oppose the measure, to silence violated women, and to bury recognition of their human rights, that is seen as a victory for the left, and moreover bipartisan, so it must be correct.

Only if one assumes that left and right relevantly diverge is it remarkable to find them together. The assumption that the political spectrum is defined by these polarities dates from the French Revolution.[13] The left/right distinction, even as it makes increasingly little sense of many political cleavages, is nonetheless taken as almost a natural fact, like North and South. Because left and right are widely considered polar political divisions, nice academic points are made by showing when extremes converge. But if left and right are not relevantly defined by distinction, their convergence makes no point.

Through the lens of a systemic analysis of sex inequality, left and right alignments in conventional politics share a deep, common, grounded bond, a common misogyny, a common sexualization of inequality that makes sexual abuse visible only as sex and invisible as abuse, inequality, or politics. This analysis exposes a new politics; recognizing these realities configures a new political geography.[14] Left and right become two moments, two strategies, in one system: male dominance. In this perspective, women as such do not inhabit the same political terrain men do. They live in a flatter world of male authority characterized by possession, exclusion, diminution, violation, marginalization, stigmatization, and foreclosure of opportunities on the basis of sex packaged in a variety of distracting political guises. Whatever difference left and right can and do make at times, neither the politics of left nor right addresses the deep structure of women's condition nor defines what must be done to change it.

This perspective illuminates the left-right convergence in two recent books on the subject of pornography: on the left, Edward de Grazia, *Girls Lean Back Everywhere: The Law of Obscenity and the Assault on Genius*,[15] and on the right, Judge Richard Posner, *Sex and Reason*.[16] Both treatments postdate the recent public exposure of pornography's concrete harms. Neither is part of the virtual academic cottage industry that has sprung up to exploit the attention to the topic created by this exposure, rushing to capitalize on the breaking of women's silence while doing everything volumes of words can do to re-impose it. Rather, these two books are products of two authentic lifetime commitments. De Grazia is a lawyer practicing at the line between pornography and art. Judge Posner is a theorist of the legal applications of means-ends rationality, centering on but not confined to economics. Both writers have a legal project as well as serious theoretical and political agendas that include pornography, but are not limited to it. De Grazia locates on the left, which shows how little class politics it takes to be there in the United States; Judge Posner locates on the right, in the forefront of libertarian conservatism. De Grazia is a modern liberal. Judge Posner correctly terms himself a classic liberal,[17] pursuing a diminished role for government and expansive liberties for those who can take them. That this characterization defines the right of the existing spectrum, yet also exactly describes the position of de Grazia and much of the left on the question of pornography, makes the point. On pornography, left and right are two cogs in a single machine, meshing to crush women.

Focusing on his treatment of pornography is fairer to de Grazia, whose whole book is about it, than to Judge Posner, who sets it within a sustained theory of sexuality, with one chapter on pornography and connections made throughout the text. The books are not comparable in other ways as well. De Grazia's book requires a lot of analysis to get at what he is saying; his position emerges more from his exercise of editorial prerogatives than from what he says in his own voice. Indeed, almost the entire book consists of selections from the work of others. Judge Posner, in contrast, says what he thinks; he even writes his own book. Posner's is more open to, and worthy of, theoretical engagement; de Grazia's is narrowly legal by comparison. but de Grazia's parade of actual historical materials, and the need to search out his argument like the murderer in a murder mystery, makes his book more difficult to analyze, if more fun.

De Grazia presents his argument substantially through exhibits, relying on choice and placement to convey his message. Much interpretation of what he is doing is required to get at what he is saying. He traces a history of censorship of erotic materials from engravings through printed books, to photographs, films, and videos, to the beginnings of computers, in a presentation that unfolds like a documentary film. It is made of bits and cuts, including interviews he did, other people's briefs, magazine articles, transcripts, parts of the materials at issue, and so on. And on. The author, as well as much about his sources, is largely concealed this way. The materials are placed in a uniform format beginning with the source's name. To find out when and where it was said, you have to dig around in the back.

The book is organized to showcase de Grazia's one smart moment: his defense of William Burrough's *Naked Lunch*[18] and Henry Miller's *Tropic of Cancer*.[19] The argument is: if material has value, it cannot be obscene. From this it follows that nothing can be done about it.[20] The reader can get bogged down in the parade of materials, fascinating in themselves, and think that de Grazia is not saying anything, but it is all strategized to convince the reader of this argument.

Although he never puts it this way, de Grazia clearly believes that censorship harms the censored. Authoritatively telling people that there are things they cannot say, or punishing them for saying them, destroys them. When the government restricts art and literature—genius for short—wives and publishers flee, reputations crash, health, friends, and houses vanish. Writers cannot write, contemplate suicide, commit suicide.[21] Censorship causes death. One person, after losing a Supreme Court case, "went into clothing."[22] Certainly the effects of silencing are real and serious, and the causal link between censoring art and harm to artists is real even if it is only proven through experience. If only de Grazia took the harms of pornography—

its silencing and other devastating consequences for women, which include murder—even a fraction as seriously, and viewed that causal connection half as sympa-
thetically.

Of the two authors, Judge Posner is the more self-conscious theorist. His views
on the larger issues of sexuality and politics underlie many common social attitudes,
laws, and policies. His book argues that the ends of sexuality are determined genetically through evolutionary biology,[23] and that these ends are pursued rationally to
maximize fitness through social organization and behavior, particularly economics.
He interprets regularities of women's sexual status and treatment as expressions of
such biological imperatives pursued economically.[24] His analysis of pornography is
situated within this larger theoretical edifice.

Sex and Reason is oddly reminiscent of Frederick Engels's combination of
largely unquestioned biologism with economic determinism,[25] leaving a similarly
unsatisfied sense that most of the important questions about women and men and
their society were resolved before the curtain went up. The natural base posited for
sexuality does most of the explanatory work. For Judge Posner, the biology comes
first, then the "theory of sexuality" proper. Biology is not theory to him; it is the
facts. But to locate sexuality in nature, and to see nature as fixed, is not prior to a theory of sexuality; it *is* a theory of sexuality. It takes the theoretical position that sexuality is fixed in nature. This should be justified as such, not bracketed at the outset.

Posner characterizes the opposing view as the social constructionist position of,
among others, radical feminists who are "strong believers in the plasticity of human
nature."[26] As someone who might be so described, I do not believe that human nature
is plastic but that, with regard to the inequality of women and men, there is no such
thing as human nature except socially speaking. It is not that human nature plays a
more or less determinative role, not that I would put different things in that box,
but rather that to posit a human nature and its contents is to both make and refer to
a social determination. Nature has no such box. Or, if anything is in it, it is not sex
inequality.

The point of human nature theories—Posner's is not the most rigid among them
but is also no exception—is to attribute a fixed bottom line, an unchangeability that
we must live within and keep in view, a baseline that no choice or policy can alter.
These theories set limits, telling us that "there have always been"[27] certain things, as
if no further explanation is needed, certainly not a social one; as if the fact that "there
have always been"[28] certain things necessarily points to biology. This assumption,
while not justified, does not in itself make such theories false, but the variability of
sexual facts across and within cultures and times, as well as the fact that the particular limits thus asserted reinscribe the unequal gendered social status quo, tends to undermine their claim to being prior to society. In other words, theories that attempt to
explain facts of women's inequality to men—say, rape or prostitution or sexual harassment or pornography—in terms of human nature are first and last theories of
what women must put up with. These theories cannot see the degree to which they
rationalize social inequality as natural because they think that they are scrutinizing
sex difference. They do not see that to do this, to assume socially situated gender behavior is natural, is to assume that gender *inequality* is natural. They cannot *prove* it
is natural, because it has never been found outside a social context. So they assume,

because it has seemingly never *not* existed, it must *be* natural. In other words, they *assume* that the socially *inferior* status of women is, at least in part, an expression of the biology of gender dimorphism. The assumption this entails that women are, at least in part, biologically inferior to men explains the insult of such theories to women's human status.[29]

Posner says we do not have to buy his biology to buy his economics.[30] Formally, this is true because the economics provides the means in a means-ends analysis. But without nature to set its particular ends, his theory would be radically incomplete.

As the empirical content of his construct of human nature, Judge Posner adopts many social beliefs about women and sexuality common on the right but also pervasive across political lines. One is that men have a stronger sex drive than women. That sex is a drive is assumed; that pleasure and reproduction drive men's drivenness is treated as a natural fact. Socially compulsive and compulsory masculinity is not considered as a competing explanation. Given no weight in this calculus, as is common for those who explain male sexual aggression with appeals to nature, is the clitoral orgasm, which, once it gets going, goes on for weeks, and no man can keep up with it, to no end of the frustration of some. (This underlies the often nasty edge to the query, "Did you come?", meaning, "Aren't you done yet? I am.") This does not figure in Judge Posner's relative sex drive calculations, although its existence is recognized widely, including in societies that aim to control and own women through clitoridectomy.

Posner believes that sexual preferences are largely genetically fixed.[31] He also uses terms like "highly sexed"[32] to describe individuals, as if he is observing a fact of an individual's genetic endowment, with no discussion of its potential social determinants, such as the relationship of childhood sexual abuse to promiscuity.[33] The judge concedes that what people experience as the erotic varies historically, across cultures, and sometimes even changes over the lifetime of an individual. He knows this is odd from a genetic point of view.[34] It is an embarrassment to a genetic theory of sexual scripts that, for example, the back of a woman's neck routinely produces erections in Japan and a flat nothing in the United States.[35] (Will racial theories of genetic sexual scripts try to solve this?)

The slighting of the social determinants of sexuality is most visible in his treatment of the determinants of homosexuality. In Judge Posner's view, social determinants create "occasional" or "opportunistic" homosexuals; biology creates the "real" ones.[36] Why homosexuality calls for explanation, while heterosexuality, with all its abuses, does not, is unexplored. The biological approach to the explanation of homosexuality minimizes the social facts of sexuality under conditions of gender inequality: women are abused, despised, objectified, and targeted sexually through presumptively exclusive sexual use by men, who are socially defined as sexual aggressors and actors, not to be acted-upon or aggressed-against, at least not as adults. Lesbianism can take a stand against this treatment and for women's equality, often intentionally and consciously, in a way an evolutionary explanation for sexual preference elides. Posner mentions this in passing,[37] as he does nearly every piece of evidence or argument against his positions, but here only to divide lesbians between real ones whose sexuality is biological and less real ones whose sexuality comes from their lives. This division subordinates women's experience to a social

Darwinism.[38] It is also circular: sexual preference can be argued to be biological because only what biology is said to produce counts as "real" sexual preference. As it
minimizes lesbianism as a choice for sexual equality, form of political resistance,
and affirmation of women, his approach also insures that no amount of evidence to
the contrary can falsify the hypothesis that sexual preference is biological. By denigrating as "not the real thing" a sexual behavior and identity that is often admittedly
socially and politically produced—how, again, does lesbianism protect the gene
pool?[39]—compelling evidence that sexual preference *itself* is social, not biological,
for everyone, can be dismissed.

Missing here, as well as elsewhere in Judge Posner's analysis, is the social fact
of male dominance—both as explanation and as something to be explained. Applied
to homosexuality among men, the biological analysis misses the possibility that
male homosexuality might be an instance of some men extending to sexuality the
higher social value placed on men in every other respect. Maybe some male homosexuality involves overconforming heterosexuality in the sense of affirming male
dominance, including over other men. At the same time, maybe some gay men want
more equality in sex and resist the fixed preferences and gender roles of heterosexuality and hate being made to be a man—meaning in part a sexual aggressor against
women—by social force.[40]

Most theorists of sexuality leave sexual abuse out of their theories. To his credit,
Judge Posner does not. This does not mean, however, that his sociobiological theory
explains it adequately. For example, the survival value of child sexual abuse is not
discussed.[41] Pursuing Judge Posner's sources does reveal a line of literature on how
girls feel about rape that suggests some of the hazards of the sociobiological approach. It seems that girls raped before puberty are not as traumatized by it as those
raped after, because the sacred gene pool is unsullied.[42] Feelings are biologically determined too. Are women most traumatized by rape midmonth, not too upset during
their periods? It is tempting to suggest that rape-murder of women after menopause
would be less traumatic because their contribution to the gene pool is over, but someone might test it.[43]

The same tradition has investigated visual cues to sexual arousal, thought to attract men more than women, studies to which Judge Posner refers repeatedly.[44] The
idea is that men are hard-wired to respond to pornography. It is hormonal, evolutionary by now. Although this work cannot measure any reality that is not also social, because there is no context outside male dominance in which this phenomenon has
been documented to occur, these studies give a patina of science and inevitability to
the same observations pornographers rely on and exploit to make bank deposits. As
Penthouse pornographer Bob Guccione puts what this science seeks to make into a
fact of nature: "Men traditionally are voyeurs. Women traditionally are exhibition-
ists."[45] Relax and enjoy this happy complementarity because there is nothing you
can do about it. Unconsidered is that men might be sexually conditioned to arousal
through visual possession and intrusion in sex-unequal societies in which pornography plays a powerful role—which then may even have hormonal or evolutionary
consequences. In this research, if something has physical effects, it has physical
causes. Similarly, it is not considered that the unupset raped little girls may be terror-

ized into silence, lacking in words, dissociated, split, or telling researchers what they can stand to tell them or think they want to hear.[46]

The same sociobiological researchers Judge Posner cites, in other studies he did not use, find that women differentially respond positively to visual cues for dominance, such as pictures of Lambourghinis and Brooks Brothers' suits.[47] What a surprise: visual subordination triggers men sexually, and visual cues to dominance (in which no one is actually dominated) attract women. This is equality? When men go about looking like Lambourghinis, women will doubtless find them irresistible. And when women go around raping either Lambourghinis or inhabitants of Brooks Brothers' suits, these researchers will have my undivided attention.

Studies suggesting that men rape because of their biology are not used to urge the decriminalization of rape, although that has arguably been largely accomplished anyway.[48] No one suggests that, since men are evolutionarily more aggressive, they are hard-wired to murder, and that laws against murder should therefore be eliminated. Nor do those who believe in biological theories, including Judge Posner, generally support biological intervention against these abuses. Exonerating abuse on biological grounds has been mostly confined to pornography.

Once the adaptational telos is established, Judge Posner's economic analysis kicks in. Rational man pursues choices for sex. As one reviewer of Posner's book put it: "It is not too far wrong to characterize the theory he offers as one of men's rational, if fervent, search for places to ejaculate."[49] Being a man in the sense of socially becoming a member of a dominant gender class is not among the ends that Posner's sexual man rationally seeks. In a reverse of de Beauvoir,[50] for Posner, one is born, one does not become, a man. What amounts to male power is always already there in the genetic endowment. His biology of sexuality—men acting, women acted upon; men raping, women getting raped; men buying and selling, women being bought and sold—is male dominance by another name. His fixed sexual preferences of men for women, of women for men, are compulsory heterosexuality by another name. His objectification of women through visual cues as the essence of heterosexual excitement is pornography by another name. Male dominance, in other words, is essential. Sex inequality in society is not what Judge Posner sets out to explain because, as a system of *social* force, he does not seem to know it is there. It is remarkable that one can still attribute what is, in fact, male dominance to the genes and be taken as making a serious contribution to policy and scholarship.[51]

Both Posner and de Grazia embody their main theses on pornography in the ways they write. Judge Posner's graceful writing style ranges flexibly from the familiar to the elevated but is profoundly non-sexually explicit. The closest to vernacular he comes is to say that a boy will sometimes "do okay"[52] in a sexual pinch for men who are otherwise heterosexual. He refers to sexual partners in sexual intercourse as "the penetrator" and "the penetrated," or to the penetrated as "the insertee."[53] In an obscenity case on which Judge Posner sat, his opinion for the panel observes that "the least unprintable of the descriptions reads as follows: 'Magazine entitled, Let's F . . .'"[54] Edward de Grazia, by contrast, includes in his book many materials that have been litigated for obscenity, which also seem selected for the purpose of clustering at the line between pornography and not.[55] Judge Posner is a reasonable sexual man. Edward de Grazia is as sexually explicit as mainstream publishing permits, attempting, by moving the reader sexually, to open the mainstream to more pornography.

As for women, Judge Posner discusses them but little. Edward de Grazia hides everything he can behind a woman, including his title and jacket cover. "Girls lean back everywhere . . . ," Jane Heap said in defense of *Ulysses*, meaning that women do everywhere what was challenged as obscene about the book.[56] The cover shows a woman with her hand slightly over her mouth, suggesting that censorship of pornography is about shutting women up (especially women with well-manicured nails). De Grazia may not know it, because awareness of sexual abuse seems not to enter his world, but this gesture is common among adult women who begin to speak about being sexually abused as children, particularly when their abuse included oral penetration. Fronting women like this is a favorite strategy of the left when defending pornography.[57]

Each author is gender-neutral in his way. Posner elides most social inequality behind biological determination or market forces. De Grazia makes women's place in a tradition of sex in literature seem equal, even egalitarian—obscuring entirely the role of sexual abuse in pornography, and of pornography in sexual abuse. Each makes it seem impossible that pornography is harmful to women in particular.

Judge Poster *is* persuaded that children are harmed by being sexually used to make child pornography.[58] That he had to carefully scrutinize research to reach this conclusion is a little chilling. Edward de Grazia openly wars against existing laws against child pornography in his footnotes, arguing essentially that it should be protected speech—or, at least, that high quality child pornography should be.[59] If Judge Posner's book is preoccupied with male homosexuality,[60] Edward de Grazia's shows a recurrent interest in sex between adults and children.[61]

Judge Posner interprets rape, intercourse, and masturbation as fungible in terms of the benefits men get from them.[62] Rape, he says, is "a substitute for consensual sex rather than an expression of hostility to women."[63] For this, he has probably never been called anti-male, or even anti-sex. This may be because he does not explore the possibility that misogyny is an aphrodisiac of male supremacy—that hostility to women may be common to some sex and rape. The observation that "most rapists want to have sex, not to make a statement about, or contribute to, the subordination of women,"[64] is seen to be enough to distinguish the sex from the subordination. But the experience of subordinating women may be much of what the rapist gets *sexually* out of rape. Wanting to have sex without being faced with a human being,[65] seeing women as sexual objects—which Posner says "in moments of sexual excitement even egaliatrian men" do—[66]is not seen as having anything to do with rape, as hostile, subordinating, or even dehumanizing.

In a parallel split, Posner argues that pornography is erotic not ideological, distinguishing between its "aphrodisiacal effect," meaning its sexual arousal value, and its "ideological effect," meaning its denigrating and rape-promoting potential.[67] As he puts this, "the audience for pornography is interested in sexual stimulation, not in sexual politics."[68] Again, what is sexually stimulating embodies or reveals no politics. Again, the possibility that the sexual politics of pornography, meaning its power disparities, may be precisely what is sexually stimulating about it, the possibility that the dehumanization of women makes pornography sexy (and helps create a sexuality of dehumanizing women), is not considered. He misses the feminist point: the politics of rape and pornography *are* their sexuality. Posner seems to be of the view that to be "morally indifferent" to sex,[69] and hence rational about its analysis, one must ignore its politics. A politics is not a morality. An analysis of power dynamics in power terms is no more morally based, and no less rationally descriptive of a rational system, than an analysis of market forces in market terms.

From their books, one gets the impression that Judge Posner has not seen much pornography and that Edward de Grazia bathes in it nightly. From such seemingly divergent experiential backgrounds, they converge on *ignorance of its contents* as the principled state of mind in which to consider what, if anything, should be done about it. The premium on ignorance—de Grazia's seems studied, Posner's actual—pervades their legal work on the subject as well as these two books. Judge Posner, for example, wrote a decision overturning an appeal of a conviction of *Hustler* for invading a woman's privacy—a woman whose situation might have led him to think more deeply about the women in the materials than he appears to have done in this book.[70] Robin Douglass won at trial her claim that *Hustler* had published nude pictures of her without her authorization. She lost on appeal not because the panel thought she had no privacy to lose—this was a miracle, as she had apparently consented to be in *Playboy*—but because the jury had been shown a "best of *Hustler*" selection. Judge Posner thought this may have inflamed them against the magazine. With pornography, reality produces bias, not realism. Only ignorance of it can produce the requisite rationality. At least Judge Posner recognized, for all the good it did Robin Douglass, that pornography does something—something that not even a properly instructed jury can be relied upon rationally to control.

When expedient, Edward de Grazia's legal work also places a premium on ignorance of pornography. He, too, tells us not to look when thinking about what to do—or, at least, sometimes. In *Mishkin v. New York*, which adjudicated whether sado-masochistic verbal and visual pornography written by formula with covers showing "scantily clad women being whipped, beaten, tortured, or abused,"[71] could be obscene, de Grazia represented an array of illustrious publishers in an amicus brief,[72] arguing that these materials must be protected as speech. None of the publishers had seen the materials, or so they said. Their argument was, what was in them did not matter; what mattered was that something of some value somewhere, from which these materials were indistinguishable, would be hurt someday if anything was done about the materials at issue. (Their side lost in this case.) The materials in *Mishkin* are unambiguously pornography, in contrast with most of de Grazia's book, which does not excerpt the *Mishkin* materials. Nor is his view that ignorance makes principle, so convenient when the materials show overt violence, inflexible. In his brief in *Oakes* a case on the boundaries of child pornography, de Grazia described the photos and specifically referred the Court to them as exhibits in the trial record.[73] It is an invitation to look. With photographs of the defendant's "partially nude and physically mature 14-year-old stepdaughter" wearing only bikini pants and a long red scarf[74] and prominently displaying her breasts[75]—photographs de Grazia calls "child nudes" and that the young woman had tried to destroy[76]—content suddenly matters. Violent sexual materials should be protected in spite of their content, but other sexual materials, including those of children, should be protected because of their content.

In their policy positions and ways of writing, then, Posner and de Grazia exemplify the two complementary strategies through which pornography historically has been protected. The conservative strategy is to cover it up. The liberal strategy is to parade it. Keeping it out of public view insures that those who want it can have it, unaccountable to anyone. But the more it is seen, the more it is normalized, the more women's status and treatment comes to correspond to it, the more its harm merges into the appearance of women's nature and becomes invisible, and the more consumers are hooked on it. If it is covered up, the harm will not be seen; if it is made public enough, the harm will not be seen either. Both strategies allow the harm to be done while protecting pornography from the perception that it harms anyone.

Centrally, both authors argue that pornography should be protected because it has value, or more precisely, when it has value.[77] But when, according to them, doesn't it? As a measure of value, Posner proposes that what is valuable is what an artist does.[78] Artists do art; that means, whatever they do cannot be pornography. (This would be news to artists like Anais Nin who made pornography on purpose, knowing exactly what they were doing—and, in her case, why they were doing it (money), how it differed from art ("no poetry"), "murdered" writers, and destroyed sex).[79] That work has artistic ambition is Posner's fallback position. He also allows value to be measured, in part, economically: what someone will pay for is valuable.[80] To de Grazia, too, pornography should be protected if it has value. What is valuable to him is what anyone sees value in. Anyone.[81] Entertainment is valuable. Sexual arousal confers value.

In the value argument, Judge Posner holds down the high end, the elite end, de Grazia the low end, the democratic end. In pornography, left and right come to this: male desire confers value, just the desires of different men. What men want is valuable, and what men value, they get. This, in essence, is their constitutional argument.

That materials are valuable because men value them is, actually, virtually axiomatic in the world of case law as well. The Seventh Circuit decision in *American Booksellers Ass'n v. Hudnut*,[82] written by Frank Easterbrook, another economic libertarian judge, illustrates. (Judge Posner did not sit on this case.) It held that Indianapolis' civil rights law against pornography violated the First Amendment. Merely quoting the query "If a woman is harmed, why should it matter that the work has other value?" was treated as enough to invalidate the civil rights approach.[83] The invisibility of the women harmed in and through pornography was so total, their insignificance so complete, their human status so nonexistent, that asking why the product of their abuse was more valuable than they were, was taken as a rhetorical question. The question has yet to be answered.

The *Hudnut* decision goes further: it takes harm to women as a measure of the power, hence value, of pornography as speech.[84] De Grazia would doubtless find this position congenial, although it turns existing First Amendment law on its head and goes far beyond anything suggested by Judge Posner. For instance, Judge Posner did not suggest that *Hustler*'s use of Robin Douglass was more valuable than her privacy was, or that the speech value of using women the way *Hustler* did was more important than the woman who was used without her permission.

Much of the left and right see pornography as what Judge Posner calls a "victimless crime,"[85] like witchcraft or heresy.[86] He is clear that in situations in which an "adult model is physically injured," suppression of materials made under these circumstances would be warranted.[87] De Grazia does not give even this ground. But it is unclear whether Judge Posner has considered the fact that physical injury to women can produce an artistic product. What if materials are harmful *and* aesthetic, the artistic snuff film with the wonderful camera angles, the visual stylization? Or, when a woman is forced to have sex for pornography by a gun at her head that is not fired?[88] If the resulting materials show no aggression, does this qualify as Posner's "physical injury"?

At this point, one wonders why coercion into pornography is not a good example of market failure. The victims bear the cost; the consumers get the benefits at an artificially low price; the producers reap inflated profits at the victims' expense. If coerced women were compensated for their injuries, if the real cost of production were paid, we would see if the pornography industry would survive. Judge Posner's failure to apply the kind of economic thinking he pioneered is puzzling.

But this is the author who writes that "[p]rostitution is itself a consensual activity."[89] If child abuse plus abductions and homelessness and poverty and forced drug addiction and physical assault and stigma and no police protection and being bought and sold and treated as a leper in society and being so vulnerable that anything anyone will pay to do to you can be done to you is consent, prostitution is consensual.[90] All of this and more are what it takes to get women into pornography. This kind of abuse supplies the missing link Judge Posner sought in one of his First Amendment decisions between "blood sport," which is illegal although expressive, and erotic dancing, which, according to him, is protected speech.[91] Pornography and prostitution, including erotic dancing, are blood sports of male supremacy. Edward de Grazia refers with a sneer to women who are violated through pornography as "victims,"[92] in quotes, then parades all the women he can find saying what a wonderful time they had. This is the pimp's line; it is good for business.

Given their lack of grasp of violence against women, it is not surprising that both men misstate the research on the harm of pornography, if not to the same degree. Social studies, laboratory data, and testimony from real perpetrators and real victims all support the conclusion that men's exposure to pornography makes women's lives more violent, dangerous, and unequal.[93] The connection varies in strength depending upon factors like the violence of the material, length of explore, and predisposing factors, but in a population of exposed normal men, it is never not there. And no population of real consumers is controlled as the experimental groups, by ethical fiat of the founders of the experiments, are controlled—by eliminating those who will most certainly act on the materials. Yet Posner repeatedly entertains, without embracing, the disproved catharsis hypothesis[94] and mistakenly writes as though the data on this question were in equipoise, or close.[95] This is noteworthy because Judge Posner seldom gets anything descriptively wrong.

De Grazia mouths the press lie that the Final Report of the Attorney General's Commission on Pornography,[96] which calmly reviewed the research to date and concluded that it substantiated these effects of exposure, is wild, exaggerated, and unsupported. In fact, it is cautious and measured. That Judge Posner even leans toward exonerating the harmful effects of pornography,[97] when the research he can usually read so well clearly establishes the opposite, testifies to the success of the public relations campaign to cast doubt on the existence of pornography's harms by distorting the research findings and discrediting the Commission.[98] Neither writer can grasp the concrete damage done to women through pornography, which has been documented in testimony and has even been conceded by the courts—including, prominently, the *Hudnut* court in a clear statement de Grazia edited out.[99]

It is with their evaluation of feminist work against pornography that any daylight between de Grazia and Posner disappears: they become one. Excerpted and affirmed, Posner becomes a part of de Grazia's book.[100] Now who is in bed with the right? Posner wrongly assumes that feminist work against pornography attacks the literary canon.[101] De Grazia wrongly assumes that it attacks all the works he has long defended. Common reflex is the ignorant assumption that a new civil rights definition of pornography[102] must pose the same problems as the old criminal definition of obscenity,[103] as if a test of material harm is the same as a test of moral content. Neither seems to have a grip *even on the words* of the new definition.[104] Neither intimates awareness of the common legal and social usage of the term "sexually explicit."[105] Neither grasps the fact that, under the civil rights ordinance, subordination must be proved as fact, not merely asserted as content.[106] Together or separately, these simple definitional requirements exclude virtually all the examples used to invalidate it. Put another way, civil rights work against pornography does not belong in de Grazia's history of the abuses of obscenity law at all, except as critique of that tradition.[107]

While both confuse the literary canon with the civil rights statutory definition, de Grazia makes a strategy of conflating literature attacked for obscenity with pornography, in order to protect both. It is, in fact, unclear whether there is some pornography he would restrict and only defends the kind of writing typically published by Grove Press, whom he has so often represented.[108] He does move from defending literature from false accusations of being pornography toward using literature as a means of defending pornography itself. In so doing, he moves from denying an unreal harm to denying a real one.

The two authors converge in complaining that the civil rights approach to pornography does not take the "value" of the materials into account, as obscenity law does. Because obscenity law criminalizes sexual materials defined as morally bad, it makes sense to allow their value—moral good—to outweigh it. The civil rights law, by contrast, defines pornography in terms of the sex discrimination—the real harm—it does. It makes pornography civilly actionable when coercion, force, assault, defamation, or trafficking in sex-based subordination can be proven.[109] To offset the value of the materials against their harms, as both writers urge, means concretely that when Linda "Lovelace" proves she was coerced into the film *Deep Throat*,[110] a court should weigh its literary worth against her injuries before granting relief, perhaps even before allowing her to go to trial. When a young girl is gang-raped by her brother and his friends, who hold up and read from pornography magazines and force her to imitate the poses exactly,[111] the value of those magazines, say in promoting anticlericalism, should be weighed against her assault. When a Native American woman is gang-raped by white men who repeatedly refer to the video game *Custer's Revenge*,[112] when a prostituted woman is raped by a man who insists she likes it because he saw it in a movie he mentions,[113] the value of the video game (an historical satire?) and the movie (a critique of fascism?) should be weighed against these women's rapes before anything can be done about the materials shown to cause them. When women prove that, due to pornography trafficked in their jurisdiction, they are harassed at work, battered in their homes, disrespected in school, and endangered on the street,[114] the literary, artistic, political or scientific value of the materials would have to be balanced against the women's equality they have been proven to destroy.

There is something monstrous in balancing "value" against *harm*, things against people, this on which left and right speak as one. It is not only balancing the value of human rights against the value of products that violate them. It is not only balancing rape, murder, sale, molestation, and use against pleasure and profits, or even aesthetics and politics. It is not only writing off the lives and dignity of human beings as if that were a respectable argument in a legal and academic debate. It is not even that this position that elevates the rights of pimps and predators over their victims and targets is part of current law. It is prior: when injury to women and children can be balanced against the "value" of pornography, women and children do not have human status—even though, pace de Grazia, women stand up everywhere.

Notes

1. The original attribution of this *statement* or view to me seems to be *Playboy's*. James R. Petersen, "Politically Correct Sex," *Playboy*, Oct. 1986, at 66, 67 ("the antiporn feminists have their own brand of mercurial language: Sex is Rape . . ."). Subsequent versions include Asa Baber, "A Significant Shift," *Playboy*, Apr. 1992, at 30 (claiming my *N.Y. Times* op-ed piece on rape implies that "all men are rapists"); James R. Petersen, "Mixed Company," *Playboy*, Feb. 1992, at 47, 137 ("The Catharine MacKinnons of the world view all sexuality as hostile."). It was subsequently published by Rush Limbaugh in its most pithy form. Rush Limbaugh, *The Way Things Ought To Be* 126 (1992) ("Ms. MacKinnon teaches, and I assume therefore believes, that all sex is rape, even the sex in marriage . . . You laugh or you disbelieve, but I assure you this is true. I don't make things up."). Limbaugh often stated words to this effect on his radio program. See also James R. Petersen, "Catharine MacKinnon: Again," *Playboy*, Aug. 1992, at 37, 38 (cutting and using quotations of my work out of context to attempt, among other things, to substantiate this lie). This false characterization has undoubtedly been given momentum, elevation, and credibility by repetition in legitimate venues, such as Wendy Kaminer, "Feminists Against the First Amendment," *Atlantic*, Nov. 1992, at 110, 114 (claiming that Andrea Dworkin and I suggest that, due to sex inequality, "there can be no consensual sex between men and women . . ."). For an attempt to raise *Playboy's* concept as articulated in Rush Limbaugh's precise words to the facticity of a legal citation, see Susan Estrich, "Teaching Rape Law," 102 *Yale Law Journal* 509, 512 n.10 (1992) ("For the position that all sex is rape, see, e.g., Catharine A. MacKinnon . . ."). This attribution was corrected by an errata sheet to indicate that this was the author's opinion. Id. at errata ("Replace with 'For an analysis that seems to me to imply that all sex is rape, see Catharine A. MacKinnon . . .'").

It is, of course, difficult to provide citations to pages on which something is not said. Discussions of sexuality in the context of an analysis of gender inequality can be found in Catharine A. MacKinnon, *Toward a Feminist Theory of the State* 126–54, 171–83 (1989).

2. Pornographers and the mainstream media have told the same lie far longer about

Andrea Dworkin, beginning in the late 1970s. Recent examples include Roundtable, "A New Sexual Ethics for Judaism?" *Tikkun*, Sept.–Oct. 1993, at 61, 62 (Kimmelman: "Andrea Dworkin suggested that all heterosexual intercourse is rape . . ."); John Casey, "The Case that Changes How We See Rape," *Evening Standard*, Oct. 20, 1993, at 9 ("The extreme radical wing of the feminist movement has long insisted that all men are rapists. One of its chief ideologues, Andrea Dworkin, argues in effect that all heterosexual intercourse is rape."); Richard Cohen, "The Wide Net of Sexual Harassment," *Washington Post*, June 15, 1993, at A21 ("In the lexicon of some radical feminists such as Andrea Dworkin, even willing sexual intercourse in marriage is a form of rape."); Richard Eder, "The Left and Right May Cheer Witty Debate of Culture," *L.A. Times*, Apr. 15, 1993, at E2 (book review) ("Andrea Dworkin's insistence on using rape for heterosexual intercourse in general . . ."); Suzanne Fields, "Tyson Jury Sends Strong Message," *Chicago Sun-Times*, Feb. 13, 1992, at 40 (editorial) ("Andrea Dworkin . . . stops just short of calling every episode of intercourse rape."); Wendy Kaminer, "Feminism's Identity Crisis," *Atlantic*, Oct. 1993, at 51, 67 ("Dworkin devoted an entire book to the contention that intercourse is essentially a euphemism for rape."); Charles Krauthammer, "Defining Deviancy Up: The New Assault on Bourgeois Life," *New Republic*, Nov. 22, 1993, at 20, 24 (including, in partial reference to Dworkin's work, "if there is no such as real consent, then the radical feminist ideal is realized: all intercourse is rape."); David Rubenstein, "Feminism That Degrades Women," *Chicago Tribune*, Jan. 31, 1992, at 15 (discussing Andrea Dworkin's views: "[i]f intercourse is virtual rape, women who seek it virtually seek to be raped."); David Sexton, "Focus the Sex War: It's So Bad Being a Man," *Sunday Telegraph Ltd.*, Nov. 7, 1993, at 21 ("In America, Andrea Dworkin proclaims that all sexual intercourse whatsoever is exploitation and violation and must stop if women are to become equal."). Stripping these false statements of their qualifiers, this campaign of defamation was then expanded by *Time* magazine: "Andrea Dworkin has simplified the discussion by asserting that every act of sex between a man and a woman, no matter what, is rape." Lance Morrow, "Men: Are They Really That Bad?," *Time*, Feb. 14, 1994, at 58. Challenged on the veracity of this statement, head of *Time*'s Research department Betty Satterwhite asserted the magazine's "confidence" in the statement and her assistant referred to Andrea Dworkin's *Intercourse* at pages 122, 126, and 133. When confronted with the fact that *Intercourse*, apart from being a work of literary criticism, is about intercourse, not "all sex," and that those pages did not support this statement in any case, Ms. Satterwhite stated that *Time*'s characterization was true of "her work as a whole." She remained, however, unable to point to a single example that substantiated it. Ms. Satterwhite also stated that *Time*'s "policy" gave them no obligation to demonstrate that what they published is true. Conversation with Betty Satterwhite, chief of *Time*'s research department (approx. Mar. 3, 1994). No further willingness to correct, or citation to supportive passages, was obtained from *Time*'s legal department.

3. A certain crescendo was reached in Camille Paglia, "The Return of Carry Nation," *Playboy*, Oct. 1992, at 36.

4. The Moral Majority has long supported obscenity law, See, e.g., *Public Hearings on Ordinances to Add Pornography as Discrimination Against Women, Minneapolis City Council, Gov't Operations Comm.* 34–35 (Dec. 12–13, 1983) [hereinafter "Hearings"] (statement of Eugene Conway, Morality in Media) (discussing obscenity law while saying he supports the ordinance, support he later withdrew in an unrecorded session, stating that obscenity law was enough).

5. See generally Andrea Dworkin and Catharine A. MacKinnon, *Pornography and Civil Rights: A New Day for Women's Equality* (1988) [hereinafter *New Day*].

6. At least, they warmed to obscenity law considerably. See, e.g., Appellee's Motion to Affirm or Dismiss at 16–17, Hudnut v. American Booksellers Ass'n, Inc., 475 U.S. 1132 (1986) (No. 85–1090). I have participated in scores of discussions in which liberals who criti-

cized the ordinance asserted that any real problem pornography poses is adequately addressed by obscenity law.

7. Miller v. California, 413 U.S. 15, 24–26 (1973).

8. See Catharine A. MacKinnon, "Not a Moral Issue," in *Feminism Unmodified* 146 (1987).

9. This charge began as a political critique by pornography's defenders, transmuted into an assertion of fact—the right opposes pornography, so whoever opposes pornography must be allied with the right. It was applied to the ordinance—"feminists allied with right-wing moralists"—in an article in *The Village Voice*. Lisa Duggan, Censorship in the Name of Feminism," *Village Voice*, Oct. 16, 1984, at 13 (purporting to report on the passage of the Indianapolis ordinance). This account, full of fabrications (from stating that Andrea Dworkin played no part in the ordinance work there to reporting that I wore "gold jewelry") and distortions, credited the passage of the Indianapolis ordinance to the "political activism" of Rev. Greg Dixon, a fundamentalist preacher. He had nothing to do with it. After the hearings on the law, at which Duggan admits that no right-wing support surfaced (isn't inventing dark conspiracies *based on* absence of evidence a right-wing methodology?), Duggan says its main sponsor called Dixon and "asked for his help" because the ordinance was "in trouble." Id. It seems that "during the final discussion before the vote many council members were equivocating." Id. Supporters of the bill were expressive during the debate, legislators "felt the pressure," and the measure passed. Id. This *post hoc ergo propter hoc* fantasy is based on ignorance of the legislative process both in general and in particular. Political scientist Donald Alexander Downs also crated this false account. Donald Alexander Downs, *The New Politics of Pornography* 124 (1986). Had either bothered to ask, they would have learned that enough votes for passage existed prior to the final vote. This right-feminist "alliance" did not exist, so pornography's defenders had to invent it. By force of endless repetition, it has become considered the *deus ex machina* of antipornography feminism. See, e.g., Pete Hamill, "Woman on the Verge of a Legal Breakdown," *Playboy*, Jan. 1993, at 138; Marcia Pally, "Misalliance Against Pornography," *Sacramento Bee*, Feb. 21, 1993, at F1; James R. Petersen, "Catharine MacKinnon: Again," *Playboy*, Aug. 1992, at 37. It is repeated by Judge Posner, in a passage excerpted by Edward de Grazia, in Edward de Grazia, *Girls Lean Back Everywhere: The Law of Obscenity and the Assault on Genius* 614 (1992). My favorite response to it is J. C. Smith's, who reportedly said, "if right-wing women would spend more time in bed with [Ann] Scales, MacKinnon, and Dworkin, and less time in bed with their right-wing husbands, the world would be a better place." Ann Scales, "Avoiding Constitutional Depression: Bad Attitudes and the Fate of Butler," *Canadian Journal Women and Law* (forthcoming 1995); see also Ann Scales, "Feminist Legal Method: Not So Scary," 2 *U.C.L.A. Women's Law Journal* 1, 5–10 (1992).

10. She is Beulah Coughenour, the Indianapolis legislator selected for her political skills, which were exceptional, by the moderate Republican (pro-affirmative action, pro-choice) Mayor William Hudnut, see William H. Hudnut III and Judy Keene, *Minister/Mayor* 146–47 (1987), to shepherd the ordinance through the City-County Council. Beulah Coughenour supported this human rights law out of an understanding that pornography harmed women and violated their equality. Even Downs learned this about her. See Downs, supra note 9, at 110–12. In Indianapolis the ordinance was modified significantly, most importantly by exempting from the trafficking provision materials that did not show what is considered violence, a feature we termed the *Playboy* exception. The fact that the Indianapolis ordinance covers *only materials that were made from, show, or are proven to cause violence*, Indianapolis and Marion County, Ind., Code ch. 16, § 16–3(g)(8) (1984) (defense from the trafficking provision for so-called nonviolent materials), has been routinely ignored in the press and case law, from *Hudnut* on, or misreported, even in scholarly literature. See, e.g., Deborah Rhode, *Justice and*

Gender 266–71 (1989). The definition of pornography is also routinely garbled and simply misquoted. See, e.g., Downs, supra note 8, at 114; Rhode, supra at 266. That a conservative legislator would preside over a compromise designed to save *Playboy*, certainly a left-right convergence, has produced no public comment whatsoever.

Using "conservative" as epithet, in effect requiring that only women who first present liberal credentials can work for women, shows no respect for the process of consciousness and organizing that has defined the women's movement, and no comprehension of the resulting politics of which the ordinance is a part. Downs is so dumbfounded at the "unusual alliance," Downs, supra note 8, at 109, of women uniting against their common oppression that he simply cannot see the organizing of women *as women* that facing sexual violence as sex inequality makes possible. But then, he also misses the sexual violence and the sex inequality.

Entirely obscured in the desperation to tar this civil rights initiative with a right-wing brush have been the progressive politics of its first defenders and longest and strongest supporters. Completely ignored are the African American liberal Democratic man who was one of the bill's first two sponsors in Minneapolis and the lesbians and gay men and African American women who have sponsored it, fought for it, and voted for it in legislative settings. Their invisibility in these accounts *is* politics as usual.

11. Compare, e.g., American Booksellers v. Hudnut, 598 F. Supp. 1316 (S.D. Ind. 1984) (Barker, J.) with American Booksellers v. Hudnut, 771 F.2d 323 (7th Cir. 1985) (Easterbrook, J.) (holding that Indianapolis antipornography statute defining pornography and prohibiting coercion, force, assault, and trafficking in pornography as sex discrimination is a violation of First Amendment right to free speech), *aff'd mem.*, 475 U.S. 1001 (1986) (6–3 summary affirmance).

12. See Jean B. Elshtain, "The New Porn Wars," *New Republic*, June 25, 1984, at 15; Hamill, supra note 9, at 138; Franklin E. Zimring, "Sex, Violence and the Law," *N. Y. Times*, Jan. 28, 1990, § 7 at 18 (reviewing Downs, supra note 9) (uncritically repeating "strange bedfellows" as fact); see also Downs, supra note 11, generally and at 97, 109 ("strange bedfellows"; "unusual alliance").

13. Thomas Carlyle, *The French Revolution: A History* 174 (1934). The *Oxford English Dictionary* defines "center" politically in these terms as well. *Oxford English Dictionary* 1036 (2d ed. 1989).

14. These politics are powerfully articulated in Andrea Dworkin, "Woman-Hating Right and Left, in *The Sexual Liberals and the Attack on Feminism* 28 (Dorchen Leidholdt and Janice G. Raymond, eds., 1990); see also Andrea Dworkin, *Pornography: Men Possessing Women* 98–99, 207–209 (1981) (articulating the left's attachment to pornography); Andrea Dworkin, "Why So-Called Radical Men Love and Need Pornography," in *Letters from a War Zone* 214 (1989).

15. De Grazia, supra note 9.

16. Richard A. Posner, *Sex and Reason* (1992).

17. Id. at 441.

18. See Attorney General v. A Book Named "Naked Lunch," 218 N.E.2d 571 (Mass. 1966) (Edward de Grazia for intervenor Grove Press, Inc.).

19. See Grove Press, Inc. v. Gerstein, 378 U.S. 577 (1964) (Edward de Grazia for Grove Press, Inc.); see also Jacobellis v. Ohio, 378 U.S. 184 (1964) (applying reasons given for reversal of judgment of obscenity conviction by several justices in companion case to *Grove Press v. Gerstein*).

20. See De Grazia, supra note 9, at 421–25.

21. See id. at 91, 109, 477.

22. Id. at 524.

23. "I see biology as explaining the drives and preferences that establish the perceived ben-

efits of different sexual practices to different people." Posner, supra note 18, at 7.

24. See, e.g., id, at 106–107.

25. Frederick Engels, *The Origin of the Family, Private Property and the State* (International Publishers Co. 1942) (1892).

26. Posner, supra note 7, at 438. Posner's theory of the relation between the biological and social in sex is well laid out on page 87. There, he opposes "a given" to "choice," as if biology is a given, a constraint, and society provides choices. Id. at 87. That society may be as, or even more, constraining than biology is not considered.

27. Id. at 29.

28. Id. at 7, 88.

29. Id. at 99 ("[T]he stronger male sex drive requires more spillways."); id. at 354–55.

30. Posner does notice some literature on the clitoral orgasm but says it does not support a stronger (never equal?) sex drive in women because "capacity for orgasms and desire for them are two different things." Id. at 92. How he knows women have *less desire* for orgasms is unspecified. He also notices separately the reality of clitoridectomy and its role in controlling women. Id at 214.

31. See id. at 100–102, 106, 295–98.

32. Id. at 125.

33. He does mention in passing that sexual abuse of children can produce promiscuity, id. at 396, but without connecting it to his discussion of individuals being "highly sexed" as a presumptively genetic trait.

34. Id. at 359.

35. For illustrative literature, see id. at 37 n.1, 359–60.

36. Id. at 179–80, 299–300.

37. Id. at 180, 299–300.

38. The common epithet that feminism is lesbianism in disguise contains an important truth. If a woman resists sexual subordination by men, her heterosexuality is often called into question. This is telling as to what heterosexuality is seen to be about, but it does not tell a biological story, unless (again) the subordination of women to men is supposed biological. It is a further problem for Posner's theory that the biological data on homosexuality he uses relies entirely on evidence collected on men.

39. Posner concedes that the genetic explanation for lesbianism is weak. Id at 102. He attributes much "opportunistic of male sexual companionship," Id. at 137, meaning the old canard that lesbians would not be lesbians if they could have a man, which serves to keep men central to women's sexual definition. He also notes the possible contribution of sexual abuse by men to women's choice to be sexual with women, but again sees this as producing "opportunistic" rather than "real" lesbians. Id at 299–300.

40. For a stunning example of this critique, see John Stoltenberg, *Refusing to be a Man* (1989).

41. Posner says it makes "biological sense," Posner, supra note 7, at 401, that stepfathers would be more likely to engage in incest than biological fathers, but he never addresses why an adult sexually abusing *any* child makes evolutionary sense.

42. Nancy W. Thornhill and Randy Thornhill, "An Evolutionary Analysis of Psychological Pain Following Human (Homo sapiens) Rape: IV, The Effect of the Nature of the Sexual Assault, 105 *Journal of Comparative Psychology* 243, 247, 251 (1991).

43. I thought I made this up until I read Nancy W. Thornhill and Randy Thornhill, "An Evolutionary Analysis of Psychological Pain Following Rape: I. The Effects of Victim's Age and Marital Status," 11 *Ethology and Sociobiology* 155 (1990) (asserting that reproductive-aged women are more severely traumatized by rape than older women or girls).

44. Posner, supra note 17, at 92 n.14, 94, 106, 123, 354.

45. De Grazia, supra note 9, at 577.

46. As it turns out, the child victims may not have told the researchers anything. Their care-takers may have "helped the child interpret the interview questions, or with very young vic-tims the caretaker gave the responses to questions based on the caretaker's perception of the effect of the assault on the child." Thornhill and Thornhill, supra note 43, at 245. The children were previously interviewed by social workers. The researchers themselves did not even at-tempt to interview the children, but "received the data in the form of computer printouts." Id. at 243, 245.

47. Douglas T. Kenrick et al., "Evolution and Social Cognition: Contrast Effects as a Func-tion of Sex, Dominance and Physical Attractiveness" 20 *Personality and Society Psychology Bulletin* 210 (1994).

48. No changes in the rape law, or anything else, has addressed the drastic disparity be-tween rape as a pervasive fact in women's lives and the legal system's inadequate response to it. See Catharine A. MacKinnon, "Reflections on Sex Equality Under Law," 100 *Yale Law Journal* 1281, 1298–1308 (1991). As to rape rates, Posner concludes that rape is decreasing based on one sample interview study that contradicts every other study on the subject, a study that has not been replicated. See Posner, supra note 18, at 33 n.39. Age cohorts studies and an-nual F.B.I. reports, supported by the experience of rape crisis centers, none of which Judge Posner mentions, document both that rape is far more prevalent than has been known and that numbers of rapes may be increasing. Diana E. H. Russell, *Sexual Exploitation: Rape, Child Sexual Abuse, and Workplace Harassment* 52–57 (1984); "Women and Violence: Hearing Before the Senate Comm. on the Judiciary on Legislation to Reduce the Growing Problem of Violent Crime Against Women," 101st Cong., 2d Sess. 27–46, 67–68 (1990) (testimony of Mary Koss). Posner's choice of study is particularly bizarre in light of the repeated cautions in the source he cites for it that its odd results are unreliable. See Tamar Lewin, "25% of Assaults Against Women are by the Men in their Lives," *N.Y. Times*, Jan. 17, 1991, at A12 (stating that Bureau of Justice Statistics sample study showing rape rate dropped from 1973 to 1987 "should not be considered conclusive" as against F.B.I. reports showing large annual increas-es, particularly as the sample population (64 rapes in 1987, 136 in 1974) was too small a num-ber from which to generalize).

49. Gillian K. Hadfield, "Flirting with Science: Richard Posner on the Bioeconomics of Sexual Man," 106 *Harvard Law Review* 479, 490 (1992) (book review).

50. See Simone de Beauvoir, *The Second Sex* (1961).

51. A sociobiology of race that offers genetic or evolutionary explanations for white su-premacy or racial inequality in society is generally criticized as science for bigots and raises tremendous controversy. It is not a recognized specialization in social science. No federal judge has yet written a book arguing for it.

52. Posner, supra note 17, at 114.

53. Id. at 43.

54. Sequoia Books, Inc. v. McDonald, 725 F.2d 1091, 1093 (7th Cir. 1983) (Posner, J.), *cert. denied*, 469 U.S. 817 (1984).

55. The definition of the word pornography used here and throughout is from the Model Antipornography Civil-Rights Ordinance:

  1. "Pornography" means the graphic sexually explicit subordination of women through pictures and/or words that also includes one or more of the following:
  a. women are presented dehumanized as sexual objects, things or commodities; or
  b. women are presented as sexual objects who enjoy humiliation or pain; or
  c. women are presented as sexual objects experiencing sexual pleasure in rape, incest, or other sexual assault; or

d. women are presented as sexual objects tied up or cut up or mutilated or bruised or physically hurt; or

e. women are presented in postures or positions of sexual submission, servility, or display; or

f. women's body parts—including but not limited to vaginas, breasts, or buttocks—are exhibited such that women are reduced to those parts; or

g. women are presented being penetrated by objects or animals; or

h. women are presented in scenarios of degradation, humiliation, injury, torture, shown as filthy or inferior, bleeding, bruised or hurt in a context that makes these conditions sexual.

2. The use of men, children, or transsexuals in the place of women in (1) of this definition is also pornography for the purposes of this law.

New Day, supra note 5, at 138–39.

56. De Grazia, supra note 9, frontispiece.

57. When women defend pornography, it seems as though pornography could not be hurting women. Fronting women thus has obvious strategic benefits for pornographers—and also makes women who are willing to perform this role comparatively valuable. The fact that some women are hurt less by pornography than others, and the fact that some women stand to gain by saying no women are, does not mean that many other women are not badly hurt by it—or, that all women, because they are women, are not limited and diminished by its existence in society.

58. Posner, supra note 17, at 395–98.

59. De Grazia, supra note 19, at 557, 582, 607, 609 (attacking laws against child pornography and defending sex photographs of children in artistic terms).

60. For a discussion of this aspect of Judge Posner's theory, see William N. Eskridge, Jr., "A Social Constructionist Critique of Posner's Sex and Reason: Steps Toward a Gaylegal Agenda," 102 *Yale Law Journal* 333 (1992) (book review); Pamela S. Karlan, "Richard Posner's Just-So Stories: The Phallacies of Sex and Reason," 1 *Virginia Journal of Social Policy and Law* 229, 243 (1993) (book review) (asserting that male homosexuality is a "central preoccupation" of *Sex and Reason*).

61. De Grazia, supra note 9, at 557, 582, 607, 609.

62. See Posner, supra note 19, at 366, 369, 373, 374, 384, 385 ("since rape is a form of intercourse . . ."). This is also the import of his view that men who cannot get women to have sex with them become rapists. Id. at 106, 107, 107 n.54, 368.

63. Id. at 366; see also id. at 370, 385.

64. Id. at 385.

65. Id. at 367.

66. Id. at 371.

67. Id. at 366, 367, 371.

68. Id. at 371.

69. Id. at 85.

70. Douglass v. *Hustler*, 769 F.2d 1128 (7th Cir. 1985), *cert. denied*, 475 U.S. 1094 (1986).

71. Mishkin v. New York, 383 U.S. 502, 505 (1966) (finding that instructions to the author included that he "deal very graphically with . . . the darkening of the flesh under flagellation . . ."). For the titles, see id. at 513–15.

72. Brief Amicus Curiae of Marshall Cohen et al. in support of Appellant, Mishkin v. New York, 383 U.S. 502 (1966) (No. 49) (representing Marshall Cohen, Jason Epstein (Random House), Paul Goodman, Warren Hinckle (Ramparts), Eric Larrabee, Walter Minton (G. P. Putnam's Sons), Norman Podhoretz (*Commentary*), Richard Poirier (*Partisan Review*), Barney

Rosset (Grove Press), Robert Silvers (*The New York Review of Books*), and William Styron).

73. Brief Amicus Curiae of the Law and Humanities Institute in Support of Respondent at 29, Massachusetts v. Oakes, 491 U.S. 576 (1989) (No. 87–1651).

74. Massachusetts v. Oakes, 491 U.S. 576, 580 (1989).

75. Commonwealth v. Oakes, 551 N.E.2d 910, 912 (Mass. 1990).

76. Id. at 912; John H. Kennedy, "High Court Set To Hear Mass. Child-Porn Appeal," *Boston Globe*, Jan. 16, 1989, Metro at 13.

77. Posner, supra note 17, at 381.

78. Id. at 378.

79. Anais Nin, *The Journals of Anais Nin (1939–1944)* 56–60, 66, 69–70, 72, 176–78 (1966). Posner notes that many legitimate artists have made pornography (Posner, supra note 17, at 360), but seems to be of the view, basic to obscenity law, that aesthetically superior materials cannot be pornography.

80. Posner, supra note 17, at 376.

81. De Grazia, supra note 9, at 441.

82. 771 F.2d 323 (7th Cir. 1985), *aff'd*, 475 U.S. 1001 (1986).

83. Id. at 325.

84. Id. at 329.

85. Posner, supra note 17, at 371. Posner makes a qualified exception for children. Id. at 395.

86. Id. at 381.

87. Id.

88. This happened to Linda "Lovelace," among others. See Linda Lovelace and Michael McGrady, *Ordeal* (1990).

89. Posner, supra note 17, at 380.

90. See generally Catharine A. MacKinnon, "Prostitution and Civil Rights," 1 *Michigan Journal of Gender and Law* 13 (1993).

91. Miller v. Civil City of South Bend, 904 F.2d 1081, 1100 (7th Cir. 1990) (Posner, J., concurring), *rev'd sub nom.* Barnes v. Glen Theatre, 501 U.S. 560 (1991).

92. De Grazia, supra note 9, at 584–85.

93. Hearings: See also Attorney General's Commission on Pornography, Final Report 31–46, 197–290 (1986) [hereinafter Final Report]; Pornography: Women Violence and Civil Liberties (Catherine Itzin, ed., 1993) [hereinafter Itzin]: Diana E. H. Russell, "Pornography and Rape: A Causal Model," 9 *Political Psychology* 41 (1988).

94. Posner, supra note 17, at 366 ("[B]y facilitating masturbation, pornography may actually reduce the demand for rape . . .").

95. Id. at 366, 368–71. Part of the problem here seems to be that, inexplicably, Judge Posner does not discuss the best search on pornography's harm, including that on the effects of nonviolent materials. See "Hearings," supra note 4; Final Report supra note 94; Itzin supra note 94.

96. Final Report, supra note 94.

97. Posner, supra note 17, at 370–71. He also discusses pornography as a "victimless crime," while apparently having considered the ordinance, which makes coercion, force, assault, and trafficking subordination civilly actionable. Id. at 371. Judge Posner, in a decision on nude dancing that pre-dated his book, noted of the ruling on the ordinance *Hadnut*, "[w]e held that the ordinance violated the First Amendment because it was an effort to control the way people think about women and sex." Miller v. Civil City Bend, 904 F.2d 1081, 1092 (7th Cir. 1990) (Posner, J., concurring), *rev'd sub nom.* Barnes v. Glen Theatre, 501 U.S. 560 (1991). *Hudnut* did so rule. However, coercion, force assault, and subordination are neither victimless nor thoughts.

98. This is discussed and documented in Itzin, supra note 94, at 11–12.

99. De Grazia, supra note 9, at 617. See American Booksellers Ass'n, Inc. v. Hudnut, 771 F.2d 323, 328–29 (7th Cir. 1985) ("[W]e accept the premises of this legislation. Depictions of subordination tend to perpetuate subordination. The subordination. The subordinate status of women in turn leads to affront and lower pay at work, insult and injury at home, battery and rape on the streets. In the language of the legislature, '[p]ornography is central in creating and maintaining sex as a basis of discrimination. Pornography is a systematic practice of exploitation and subordination based on sex which differentially harms women. The bigotry and contempt it produces, with the acts of aggression it fosters, harm women's opportunities for equality and rights [of all kinds].'"); see also Village Books et al. v. The City of Bellingham, No. C88–147OD, Memorandum and Order at 9 (D. Wash. Feb. 9, 1989) (in litigation on civil rights ordinance against pornography passed by referendum, ". . . it is undisputed that many social harms are caused by pornography."); Schiro v. Clark, 963 F.2d 962, 971–73 (7th Cir. 1992) ("This Court previously addressed the issue of pornography in [*Hudnut*]. There we accepted the premise of anti-pornography legislation that pornographic depictions of the subordination of women perpetuate the subordination of women and violence against women . . . The recognition in *Hudnut* that pornography leads to violence against women does not require Indiana to establish a defense of insanity by pornography."), *aff'd sub nom.* Schiro v. Farley, 114 S. Ct. 1341 (1994).

100. De Grazia, supra note 9, at 614–15 (quoting Richard A. Posner, *Law and Literature: A Misunderstood Relation* 334–35 (1988).

101. Id. at 615 (radical feminist movement against pornography a "danger to literary values").

102. See supra note 56.

103. Miller v. California, 413 U.S. 15, 24 (1973) (defining obscene works as those "which, taken as a whole, appeal to the prurient interest in sex, which portray sexual conduct in a patently offensive way, and which, taken as a whole, do not have serious literary, artistic, political, or scientific value").

104. E.g., Judge Posner, in the excerpt de Grazia uses, describes the project of "[a] group of radical feminists [that] invites us to consider the obscene less as a matter of excessive frankness in the portrayal of sex than as a point of view harmful to women . . ." Posner, supra note 103, at 334. Obscenity is already defined; the ordinance defines pornography. Obscenity is about a point of view; the ordinance makes *actual harm* civilly actionable. Judge Posner goes on to discuss the "sexually graphic," which is not statutory language. Id. at 335–36.

105. "Sexually explicit" is a term in common use, see, e.g., Posner, supra note 102, at 334, referring to an explicit presentation of sex. For example, in litigation by women whose photographs were used by *Penthouse* without their permission, *Penthouse* is referred to as "a sexually explicit men's magazine." Fudge v. Penthouse Int'l, 840 F.2d 1012, 1014 (1st Cir.), *cert. denied*, 448 U.S. 821 (1988). In litigation concerning prisoners' access to pornography, one court found that "sexually explicit publications" posed a danger to rehabilitation. Dawson v. Scurr, 986 F.2d 257, 262 (8th Cir.) (finding that the prison's rule provided "access to sexually explicit materials while advancing the legitimate penological interests in rehabilitation and security."), *cert. denied*, 114 S. Ct. 232 (1993); see also Carpenter v. South Dakota, 536 F.2d 759 (8th Cir. 1976), *cert. denied*, 431 U.S. 931 (1977). In a sexual harassment case, one court said, "Although Romero's actions were not sexually explicit, they were attempts to pressure and intimidate plaintiff into renewing their sexual relationship and thus his actions constitute conduct of a sexual nature." Fuller v. City of Oakland, No. C-89–0115, 1992 U.S. Dist. LEXIS 2546, at *31 (N.D. Cal. Feb. 10, 1992). Courts thus have no trouble distinguishing the sexually explicit from mere conduct of a sexual nature. Obscenity law similarly clearly distinguishes

"sexually explicit nudity" from mere nudity. See Erznoznik v. City of Jacksonville, 422 U.S. 205, 213 (1975).

Often, "sexually explicit" is deemed so clear that it is employed to define other unclear terms. See United States v. Western Electric, No. 82–0192, 1989 U.S. Dist. LEXIS 12513, at *1 (D.D.C. June 26, 1989) ("'[A]dult' audiotex programs [are] defined by Bell Atlantic as 'obscene, sexually explicit, lewd or indecent.'"); Young v. Abrams, 698 F.2d 131, 134 (2d Cir. 1983) ("Young defined X-rated films as those having 'more violence and more sexually explicit scenes than an R film [Restricted to adults] would have.'"); see also Heise v. Gates, 197 Cal. Rptr. 404, 407 (1984) (using "sexually explicit" to clarify "obscene" and "pornographic"). Rarely is the term defined itself, and then most often in laws criminalizing abuse of children. See 18 U.S.C. § 2256(2)(a)-(e) (1988) (sexually explicit conduct), *West Virginia Code* § 61–8C-1(c) (1994); or to limit access by children to sexual materials using adults, for example, *Georgia Code Annual* § 16–12–100(a)(4) (1994); *Michigan Comprehensive Laws* § 722.673, sec. 3(b) (1992); *Washington Review Code* § 9.68A.011(3) (1994).

The term is commonly used to describe that larger category of materials of which a smaller part may be obscene, in the same way that the Model Antipornography Civil-Rights Ordinance uses "sexually explicit" to describe a larger category of materials, of which a smaller part may be sex-discriminatory. For example, one court noted, "before a person may be found guilty of promoting obscenity, the materials he promotes must be more than sexually explicit, they must be obscene under the statutory definition." People v. P.J. Video, 68 N.Y.2d 296, 300 (Ct. App. 1986), *cert. denied*, 479 U.S. 1091 (1987). Courts often note that "sexually explicit as defined by the Supreme Court in *Renton* [is] expression that the Court held could be constitutionally regulated." MD II Entertainment, Inc. v. City of Dallas, No. 3–92–CV-1090-H, 1993 U.S. Dist. LEXIS 8487 at *27 (N.D. Tex. Apr. 15, 1993) (citing Renton v. Playtime Theatres, 475 U.S. 41, 49 (1986)). The term "sexually explicit" is merely used, not defined, in *Renton*, 475 U.S. at 49, by reference to the decision in *Young v. American Mini Theatres*, in which, also undefined, "sexually explicit" designated a category of materials presumably entitled to less First Amendment protection. 427 U.S. 50, 51 (1976).

106. The ordinance does not define pornography as graphic sexually explicit "depictions of" subordination, but as a practice of subordination. Women are often subordinated to make depictions of subordination, and as a result of the consumption of such depictions, but the subordination still must be proven to be *done*, not only shown. In addition, if materials criticize subordination, it will be difficult or impossible to prove that they subordinate.

107. Both also see us as obsessed with *Playboy*. See De Grazia, supra note 9, at 583; Posner, supra note 19, at 33, 365 n.33, 371–72. Discuss murder as the ultimate sex act in pornography, the sexualization of death and torture, the elements of objectification common to all pornography, and mention *Playboy* as part of it, and it will be said you are obsessed with *Playboy*. *Playboy* is such an icon, one of left and right's common nerves, that one need only touch it to be charged with obsession. For a discussion of "the *Playboy* standard," see Catharine A. MacKinnon, "More than Simply a Magazine: Playboy's Money," in *Feminism Unmodified* 134, 138 (1987). Both writers seem unable even to perceive that it is *the harm Playboy does* that is documented, analyzed, and made civilly actionable.

108. Grove Press, Inc. v. Maryland State Board of Censors, 401 U.S. 480 (1971); Grove Press, Inc. v. Maryland State Board of Censors, 397 U.S. 984 (1970); Grove Press, Inc. v. Brockett, 396 U.S. 882 (1969); Grove Press, Inc. v. Gerstein, 378 U.S. 577 (1964).

109. For texts of the ordinance with its causes of action, see *New Day*, supra note 5, at 99–142.

110. Lovelace and McGrady, supra note 89.

111. Press Conference Testimony at the Minnesota Press Club, Minneapolis, Minnesota,

July 5, 1984 ("I'm 15 and in the 9th grade. . . . Many of my friends and I have been attacked in and out of our homes with the use of pornography."). On questioning by the press, she described the events in the text.

112. *Hearings*, supra note 4, at 66–67 (testimony of Cu/s Lu/s).

113. Mimi H. Silbert and Ayala M. Pines, "Pornography and Sexual Abuse of Women" 10 *Sex Roles* 861, 865 (1984).

114. *Final Report*, supra note 94; "Hearings," supra note 4; see also "Massachusetts State Hearings on Bill H. 5194" Legislature's Joint Comm. on the Judiciary (Mar. 16, 1992).

7

The Visit and The Video: Publication and the Line Between Sex and Speech

David M. Estlund

INTRODUCTION

In the recent debates over the constitutional status of pornography, there has been a strand of argument to the effect that pornography is not covered by the First Amendment because it is relevantly like sexual activity itself, or alternatively, like vibrators or other sexual devices. As Fred Schauer puts the point, if a contact-free visit to a prostitute for sexual purposes (e.g., voyeuristic) is not covered by the First Amendment, then why think that a video with similar content and used for similar purposes is covered? This strategy would avoid the need to show that pornography is regulable on the traditional narrow grounds involving harm or obscenity. The argument contends that (at least hard-core) pornography is, in this sense, "not a free speech issue."[1]

I want to consider an interpretation of the First Amendment that would be able to meet Schauer's challenge, though it raises problems and questions of its own. One relevant difference between the voyeuristic visit and the video is that the video is published material. I want to consider what relevance this *has* under the First Amendment, as well as how much relevance it *should* have under a good constitution, and why. The basis for its actual relevance will be an interpretation of the press clause of the First Amendment. I will see how far it can be argued that the meaning of the press clause must be to protect publication in general—not just journalistic material, as the received meaning of "freedom of the press" would have it. The basis for thinking publication in general *ought* to be strongly protected in a good constitution will be located wherever the reader chooses to locate the rationale for a constitutional protection for speech. Arguments for freedom of speech tend to work equally well as arguments for a freedom of publication.

If the publication test is accepted as a sufficient condition for First Amendment coverage, then published material ought apparently to be protected as strongly as "speech," whether or not the published material can be found to count as speech. Published pornography, then, would indeed be a free-speech issue since it would be constitutionally protected as if it were speech. This would be the legal difference between the visit and the video. This way of distinguishing between them, however, is only valid if the publication test has acceptable implications elsewhere. This can only be tested by considering a reasonably precise account of what will count as published and what will not. Accordingly, I describe and evaluate a conception of publication for use in a strong constitutional protection such as the First Amendment, especially for its consequences in the area of sexual material.

One worry about a publication criterion is that it discriminates against material that is used only privately. By including published material, it may seem to exclude unpublished or unpublishable material. As I will argue in more detail later, the effects of the publication criterion are *entirely inclusive and not in any way exclusive.* It would not necessarily repeal, replace, or undercut any particular standing or proposed basis for inclusion. For example, certain kinds of material might receive other kinds of constitutional protection precisely in virtue of their private nature. Such a protection may be more, less, or equally as stringent as the protections of speech and press. No position on that matter is explored here.

It is sometimes easier to show that certain material is *covered* by the protections in the First Amendment to the Constitution than it is to show that is ultimately *protected* against censorship or other regulation. The importance of doing so is that if something is covered, then it may only be regulated or censored on relatively narrow grounds; that is what its being covered amounts to. As I shall use the term, material is protected under the First Amendment just in the case that (1) it is covered, *and* (2) in the circumstances where there are insufficient grounds of the narrower kind for regulation (and coverage alone has rendered any other grounds as without legal weight).

Even if published sexual materials are covered, countervailing considerations may cancel the protection. Unless some category of material is protected absolutely (and probably none is), a sufficient showing of sufficient harm, for example, will defeat the protection. I mean to leave open the question whether some whole category of published sexual material might have its protection canceled in this way. The claim is only that it ought to have a defeasible claim to protection, simply by virtue of being published, that is similar to whatever protection speech receives and for the same reasons. The account proposed here decides the question of coverage (versus protection) without any regard to the sexual nature of the material. It is highly neutral with regard to content or viewpoint in this respect.[2]

PORNOGRAPHY AS SEX ITSELF?

The law of pornography ought to come to terms with Frederick Schauer's argument that some pornography has no better First Amendment standing than prostitution. It is more like the exchange of a sexual favor for money, Schauer argues, than it is like speech or communication. Schauer's dichotomy of sex/communication is unfortunate since sex—even sex for money—falls easily within that capacious rubric. Schauer narrows his concept of communication, however, to material whose point is predominantly cognitive (another difficult term) or mental. Pornography is not a free-speech issue because it does not have a sufficiently mental point to count as the "speech" or communication" that the First Amendment addresses. I will argue that Schauer's mentality requirement is unacceptable since it would exclude much material that obviously is of a kind addressed by the First Amendment, such as horror films, slapstick comedy, tearjerkers, and much else. Sexual arousal is no less mental than fear, laughter, or tears, and they have involuntary physical correlates just as sexual arousal has.

His explanation of why some pornography ought not to be a First Amendment concern fails, but there is more to his argument than this. The strength of Schauer's idea lies in his attempt to push much pornography and some commercial sexual activity so close together as to defy any reasonable distinction in law. His best example is memorable: a man pays two females to perform sexually for him without touching him. The man is sexually aroused and perhaps satisfied by this encounter, and that is why he pays for it. They never touch each other, but the encounter is clearly a form of sexual activity. Furthermore, whether or not it counts as prostitution (as I shall call it), it is not the sort of activity whose regulation would usually be thought to raise any First Amendment questions. In any case, I will assume this for the sake of argument. The absence of interpersonal physical contact is no reason to exclude it from the category of sexual activity or to include it in the First Amendment category of speech. How, then, can the prostitutes' performance be reasonably distinguished from a videotape of the same performance, made and used for the same purposes?

When is this line crossed? Suppose there is just a glass barrier between the customer and the performer. Suppose there is an opaque wall, but a real-time, two-way video system. Suppose they are separated by miles, but retain the real-time video link.[3] Suppose the video link is not real-time, but a video recording played later. If the live encounter with the prostitutes is not speech for First Amendment purposes, how could the videotape be speech? One notable difference is that the videotape represents (in this case, depicts) something, and much material that is representational thereby counts as speech for First Amendment purposes. The live encounter with the prostitutes might also be representational, however. Prostitutes sometimes portray (represent) characters such as schoolgirls or harsh task masters, or simply feign pleasure to arouse their clients. In addition, "rubber goods" are usually representations of penises. Since we ought to grant that neither rubber goods nor prostitution is typically covered by the First Amendment, representation cannot be sufficient for coverage. Representation, then, does not mark a difference between what I shall refer to as The Visit and The Video. What relevant difference is there? Or is Schauer correct that, like prostitution, pornography is not even a free-speech issue?

I will first discuss Schauer's own analysis of the issue in more detail and criticize his exclusionary approach. Next, I will propose a conception of publication and consider its significance for the First Amendment generally. Third, the more specific case of sexually explicit activity and material will be considered, with special attention to the boundaries of the legal category of prostitution. The publication approach will be shown to have significant and useful implications in such difficult First Amendment areas as phone-porn and nude dancing, with a brief foray into "virtual reality" and cyberspace.

Schauer on Cognitivity and Communication

One natural reply to the attempts to separate pornography from unquestionably covered material on psychological grounds, is to dispute the psychology. This response has only limited value however. Even if a psychological dispute successfully pushed The Video back toward the vicinity of covered expression, it will tend to pull The Visit along in its train. Nevertheless, I consider the psychological question first, and then emphasize its limits against Schauer's ingenious dilemma.

Schauer's strategy is to defend an analysis of "communication," and then argue that "hard-core" pornography does not typically accord with it. It is instructive first to consider the development in his own view from a cognitivity requirement to a mentality requirement.

In an article on the subject, Schauer based his argument that hard-core pornography is not communicative on the claim that it is not "cognitive." He said the voyeuristic visit is "no more cognitive than any other experience with a prostitute," and that neither pornography nor the use of sexual "rubber products" "constitutes communication in the cognitive sense."[4] In a later book, he includes a nearly identical passage in which the phrase "no more cognitive" becomes "no more communicative," and instead of saying neither pornography nor the use of rubber products "constitutes communication in the cognitive sense," he later says, "neither involves communication in the way that language or pictures do."[5]

The change apparently reflects the recognition that much material that ought to be covered under the First Amendment's conception of speech has little or no cognitive content. Cognitive content, broadly conceived,[6] is that which falls within the province of the intellect[7] involves knowledge, belief, reasoning, inference, and interpretation. To limit the scope of the First Amendment to cognitive material so conceived would be vastly to narrow its protections as they currently stand. Much artistic material would apparently be excluded, including at least some dance, instrumental music, and abstract painting, sculpture, and film. Schauer never intended such a narrow category of protection.[8]

In the book, Schauer uses more inclusive terms by arguing only against material that has "neither propositional, emotive, nor artistic content."[9] This refinement allows him to retain the original strategy of disqualifying hard-core pornography by arguing that it involves predominantly a "physical rather than a mental experience.[10] Since it is predominantly physical, it is not significantly propositional[11] or emotive (and is not, in any case, artistic). Schauer's terminology (especially "cognitive," "intellectual") may seem to suggest a constitutional privileging of reason over the passion,[12] but this impression is at odds with his explicit inclusion of "the emotive" as "essentially an intellectual or mental process."[13] The privileged class includes emotive material and so does not privilege reason or the intellect. Rather, Schauer's root distinction is between the *physical* and the *mental*. "The emotive and the cognitive are distinguishable from the physical."[14]

Suppose we christen a third category of content, *visceral*,[15] to reflect Schauer's emphasis on material that produces primarily physical rather than emotional or intellectual effects. Whether or not sexual arousal is properly regarded as predominantly a physical rather than a mental effect, it does not seem relevantly different in this respect from laughter, crying, nausea, revulsion, shock, suspense, or fright. In all these cases, as with sexual arousal, there is an undeniable mental component to the experience, and the physical effects are largely involuntary. So Schauer's argument ought to apply to visceral material as a class and not just to sexually visceral material.

"The basis of the exclusion of hard-core pornography is not that it has a physical effect, but that it has nothing else" (182). Schauer does not mean to exclude all material that has some visceral content, even if it is sexual. It could be redeemed by having content of another kind, too— cognitive or emotive—or by having an independent claim to be artistic. Still, this qualified exclusion ought consistently to apply to the whole class of material that is predominantly visceral in content. Two difficulties are obvious: (1) Why discriminate against visceral material? and (2) Isn't much material that is predominantly visceral obviously and properly protected by the First Amendment?

Regarding the first difficulty, Schauer gives no explicit argument for excluding material with predominantly visceral content from First Amendment coverage. His indirect argument is that such an exclusion is the only way to explain our exclusion of prostitution or rubber goods from the scope of the First Amendment. That analogy will be criticized below. As for the second difficulty, underprotection, consider a range of material that is predominantly visceral in content and that is produced and used primarily for visceral purposes: tearjerkers, slapstick comedy, horror films, certain kinds of rock music ("thrash," "speed metal"). Material of these kinds, like explicitly sexual material, often has other aims and contents as well, but not always. Some material is aimed and used entirely to make people laugh. Stand-up comedy is often like this. An even better analogy would, like Schauer's paradigm case of hard-core pornography, take a nonverbal form. Consider silent cartoons, or other comic films with no (or inconsequential) dialogue. Or consider clowns at the circus. In consistency, Schauer ought to hold that none of these is speech for First Amendment purposes and may be banned or regulated without constitutional qualm.

It may well be objected that humor, or fright, or the other examples actually involve emotive content, thus falling within Schauer's scope of protection. The question then is why sexual arousal should not be regarded as an emotion. Its having physical aspects would not distinguish it from most other emotions. Indeed, this may be a more direct route to the weakness of Schauer's account. Once the scope of protected material is enlarged to include that which aims and is used to produce emotions, there is no longer any ground for excluding hard-core pornography, whose effect is primarily to produce the emotion of sexual arousal.

So the attempt to separate pornography from clearly covered material on psychological grounds apparently fails. Still, this point does not yet answer the difficult question of how it could be speech *while the hands-off encounter with the prostitute is not.* What is the constitutionally relevant difference between these that allows The Video to be protected but not The Visit to the prostitute?

I propose that the general ground for regarding pornography as covered is that it is (typically) published. It is an important fact about a prostitute's performances that they are not before a live audience. If they were, they ought to be regarded as covered by the First Amendment and, so, protected unless they met specified exceptions. Any representational aspect, then, drops out; coverage would still be triggered if the play-acting part of the performance were removed, leaving only an erotic dance or even merely an erotic show,[16] though still before a large audience. Such a show would differ from other clearly protected shows merely by having much sexual content. The suggestion here is that publication is sufficient for coverage under the First Amendment. Once it is covered, the state needs special and strong reasons to regulate it; it is presumed to be protected. In principle, the sexual content itself might be argued to provide special and strong reasons for regulation, or related reasons could be adduced, such as offensiveness, tendency to increase sexual discrimination, or abuse. However, in a clear sense, it will be much more difficult to justify regulating pornography if it is granted coverage under the First Amendment. It can no longer be excluded[17] in the way that playing tennis is.

PUBLICATION AND THE PRESS CLAUSE OF
THE FIRST AMENDMENT

I want to consider the basis for finding a broad freedom of publication in the First Amendment, via the press clause. First, I provide an interpretive argument about how to make sense of the existence of the press clause in addition to the speech clause. Second, I consider the historical arguments about the meaning of the press clause in the founding period. Third, I turn to the question of what rationale there is for a constitutional freedom of publication apart from historical and textual arguments. This can serve partly as an aid to constitutional interpretation, but also as a freestanding argument about what a constitution ought to be like.

Text

I take the main competitor to be the journalistic interpretation of the press clause. On this view, the freedom of the press is primarily a protection for published news and opinion. This interpretation faces a textual trilemma:

1. it regards the press clause as redundant after the speech clause, *or*
2. it says journalism wouldn't have been covered by the speech clause alone, *or*
3. it says the press clause adds stronger protection for journalism than for other speech.

The central problem with the journalistic interpretation is that journalism is already speech and so would have been clearly covered by the speech clause. Without some separate argument, the press clause should not be read as redundant unless absolutely necessary. The text clearly names two freedoms neither of which is to be abridged.

As for the view in (3) that the press clause adds additional protection for journalism, there is no textual support for this. The speech and press clauses are exactly parallel by all appearances.

If (1) and (3) are rejected, the only alternative for the journalistic interpretation is (2), the claim that journalism wouldn't have been protected by the speech clause alone. However, one would have to read the speech clause as extremely narrow to maintain (2). For example, one might say that the speech clause didn't clearly cover the printed word. This is not only an oddly narrow understanding of speech, but it would make a journalistic press clause very weak medicine. Nonjournalistic printed material, such as novels or textbooks, would still not be covered. Option (2), then, is also untenable, and the journalistic interpretation of the press clause is without textual support.

On a publication interpretation, the press clause is meant to protect published material of all kinds. This doesn't mean that there aren't exceptions allowed for strong reasons, but all published material would have a First Amendment claim against regulation.

There is a narrow and a broad publication interpretation, and I will be arguing for the broad. The *narrow publication reading* sees the press clause as protecting the publication only of speech. One could argue that this is not utterly redundant. A censor might limit a pamphleteer's circulation to some very small number on the ground that the small number is sufficient to allow her to say what she wishes. It might be seen as a separate issue whether one may publish what one says. However, this is something of a stretch. There isn't really a credible argument that a freedom to speak doesn't include a freedom to say the same thing to many people, or many times. The narrow publication reading still makes the press clause redundant.

The *broad publication reading* of the press clause sees it as protecting all publication (possibly subject to narrow exceptions), whether or not it might qualify as speech under the speech clause. This would relieve published materials of the need to show that they count as speech. Their protection would not depend on it.

Early History

In addition to these narrow textual arguments, the history of the speech and press clauses lends further support to a publication interpretation. The idea of freedom of press derives from the sixteenth- and seventeenth-century English system of licensed printing, the requirement that anything to be printed must first obtain the approval of Crown licensers.[18]

There are some distinctive features of material produced on a printing press: for one thing, the typography is usually standardized (unlike calligraphy); for another, it is easy to produce large editions of a single text. It is clear that the licensing system was motivated by the ease of producing large editions rather than by standardized typography or other distinctive features of printed material. Surely this was not the only manner of disseminating a message publicly: public posting of (handwritten or printed) bills, public speaking, and word of mouth, were among the other available means. But the printing press made it easier to reach a larger audience for most purposes. Whatever understanding of freedom of press the founders may have had, the very idea was owed to the rejection of licensed printing. It seems clear enough that the important thing about printing—from the standpoints both of those who would censor it and of those would resist censorship—was that it facilitated publication.

The intellectual background of the founders' ideas of free speech and press prominently featured the more general idea of free publication. John Milton, in his *Areopagitica—A Speech for the Liberty of Unlicensed Printing* (644), argued against the legal requirement of licensed printing and, in the process, defended the freedom to "write," "speak," and "publish," as well as "print." William Blackstone's influential *Commentaries on the Laws of England* (1769) argued that "the liberty of the press . . . consists in laying no previous restraints upon publications. . . . Every freeman has an undoubted right to lay what sentiments he pleases before the public: to forbid this is to destroy the freedom of the press." He argued that punishment after publication was no infringement of a person's free will, and, "[n]either is any restraint hereby laid upon freedom of thought or inquiry: liberty of private sentiment is still left; the disseminating, or making public, of bad sentiments, destructive of the ends of society, is the crime which society corrects."[19] Blackstone's argument supports the freedom to lay one's sentiments before the public. Whether or not Blackstone had the full scope of this idea in mind, it obviously goes beyond the freedom of printing, writing, or speaking. Since there are nonverbal printed ways, as well as nonprinted ways of laying one's sentiments before the public, the freedom Blackstone defends is a freedom of publication, even if the published material is neither spoken nor printed.

In 1720 John Trenchard and Thomas Gordon, in the open letters under the pseudonym, Cato, defended "freedom of speech" as "the great Bulwark of Liberty." They also argued "that freedom of the Press is one of the greatest bulwarks of liberty, and can never be restrained but by despotic governments."[20] Virginia's state constitution followed the language of Cato's *Letters*, but it didn't mention freedom of speech. It declared in 1776, that "the freedom of the press is one of the greatest bulwarks of liberty, and can never be restrained but by despotic Governments."[21]

We find similar language about publication in debates over whether to ratify the constitution, especially in proposals for a bill of rights:

> Resolved . . . that the people have a right to freedom of speech, of writing and publishing their sentiments, and therefore that the freedom of the press ought not to be restrained, and[22] the printing presses ought to be free to examine the proceedings of government, and the conduct of its officers.[23]

> Resolved . . . that the people have a right to freedom of speech, and of writing and publishing their sentiments; that the freedom of the press is one of the greatest bulwarks of liberty, and ought not to be violated.[24]

James Madison, in his first speech on the subject, combined the influential "bulwark' language of Cato's *Letters* with Blackstone's early emphasis on the freedom to publish one's "sentiments." Speaking on June 8, 1789, Madison proposed "The people shall not be deprived or abridged of their right to speak, write, or to publish their sentiments; and the freedom of the press, as one of the great bulwarks of liberty, shall be inviolable."[25] This was changed by the House committee to "The freedom of speech and of the press . . . shall not be infringed," and this was approved by the House and Senate on Sept. 25, 1789,[26] changing once more to become the First Amendment as ratified on December 15, 1791.[27]

Before the federal constitution was ratified, nine states put declarations of rights in their own state constitutions, and every one of these included freedom of the press. Only one of them, Pennsylvania, mentioned freedom of speech.[28] It is not as if the idea of a separate freedom of speech only occurred to the framers in these last few years since it had to be known to them through the letters of Cato, as we have seen. It does suggest, however, that the press clause had the wider and more solid following among lawmakers of the day.

This historical evidence suggests that, in the tradition leading up to the Bill of Rights, the primary interest to be protected by "freedom of the press" was an interest in *publishing* one's sentiments without government censorship. These texts also suggest that the freedom was to protect not just journalism but all printing, since it was all printing that had been subject to licensing. It may be that the main goal in protecting all printing from government censors was to allow commentary, criticism, and information about political affairs as a way to protect against bad government. This does not mean, nor is there any strong evidence, that the protection was meant to be limited to, or especially strong for material found to be of this political nature.[29]

For all this, however, there is no suggestion of a broad (all publication) rather than a narrow (only published speech) publication interpretation of the press clause. There's every indication that the protections were expected to apply to material that counted as speech apart from the fact of publication, though this may have included some nonverbal material such as editorial cartoons.[30] It is not entirely clear what protection, if any, was intended for published fiction, though the idea of laying one's sentiments before the public surely covers it.

There is a certain tension between the historical approach and the more text-based approach I applied earlier. The historical approach seems to suggest that the press clause was intended to protect published *speech*, despite the fact that after the speech clause such a narrow protection is pretty clearly redundant, as noted above.

There are, then, textual and historical resources to support interpreting the press clause as a broad protection for publication in general so that each citizen may "lay what sentiments he pleases before the public: to forbid this is to destroy the freedom of the press."

Rationale

Why should there be a constitutional rule against legal regulation of published material? Of course, we might well ask the same thing about constitutional protection for speech. However, if a constitutional protection for speech is defended in certain familiar ways, then the same case supports a constitutional protection for publication. This conditional argument leaves aside consideration of the merits of the familiar defenses of a protection for speech, and it also allows that the protection in question might admit of exceptions for special well-defined cases (such as "clear and present danger"). The kind of constitutional protection that speech should receive on the weight of these arguments should also be extended to publication.

Here is a familiar Justification for a constitutional rule against legally regulating speech. Call it, *the Collective-Power Rationale*:

> Speech is one of the most important ways that the power of government, or of the social orthodoxy generally, can be subjected to the reasoning of people across a wide social and economic spectrum. Where speech is used for this purpose, the collective power is likely to be exercised more wisely and fairly. Much of this kind of speech will be Mistaken, or uninformed, but the general run of opinion is bound to be better informed and more correct as a result of a freedom of speech, at least in the long run. Much speech will be used for other purposes and have no significant value in the guidance of collective power, but where this line should be drawn is among the fundamental questions that should be decided in public discussion, not prior to it.

This is just a sketch of a familiar line of argument, and its branches and siblings are abstracted out. It is merely stated here and not defended. The question is how this, or anything close to it, could be a good argument for a speech protection without also being a good argument for a publication protection. The argument is equally compelling if "publication," in the sense of "expressive material intentionally disseminated widely or in a public forum" is substituted for "speech." If the case for protecting speech admits narrow exceptions for cases of immediate danger or certain kinds of deception or whatever, then the conclusion about a protection for publication will be similarly qualified (and if it does not admit such exceptions, it will not be so qualified). The justification supports a protection for speech whether or not it is published and also supports a protection for publication whether or not it is speech.

A sharply different justification for constitutional protection of speech—one that places less emphasis on the imperatives of social deliberation—might be called, *the Self-Expression Rational*:

> Each individual has a deep interest in deliberately forming and acting on her own convictions, tastes, and tendencies. The ability to speak freely is necessary to the fulfillment of this interest. This is an interest whose exercise rarely harms anyone else directly. The danger produced by the freedom to speak is easily outweighed by the well-being the freedom promotes. Thus, society ought to be precluded from coercively restricting speech.[31]

Again, this is merely a sketch, and similar arguments can take different forms. Still, it is hard to see how anything similar could be a good argument for protecting speech without also being a good argument for protecting publication, whether or not it is speech. Whether the particular variant of this argument rests on the utility to the speaker, on the value for society of allowing such self-expression, or on rights of the speaker not to be interfered with, it seems certain to provide an equally good case for the freedom intentionally to disseminate expressive material widely or in a public forum, if, as in the case (arguably) of Thelonius Monk's music, the material is not speech.

These are only two examples, but it is hard to conceive of a plausible case for a free-speech principle that does not work as a case for a free-publication principle. This is no proof. What matters here is (1) whether there is a successful defense for a free-speech principle, and if so, (2) whether it is equally successful as a defense of a free-publication principle. Since the question whether a free-speech principle can itself be defended is beyond my scope here, the rationale for a free-publication principle is both conditional and inconclusive: if there is a defensible free-speech principle, then probably, for the same reasons, there is a defensible free-publication principle of similar scope and strength.

WHAT COUNTS AS PUBLISHED?

What counts as published? This question has two parts. What *kind* of material can count as published? And *how public* does it have to be? Surely not all material that is reproduced and distributed, such as pens and cars, can count as published. It might seem that only speech can count as published, but there is no difference between the narrow publication interpretation (which is redundant after the speech clause) and my broad publication interpretation unless there is a viable concept of publication that can include material regardless of whether it is speech. So there is this question of what kind of material is publishable as a conceptual matter.

A second part of the question attends to the issue of *how public* it has to be. That is, supposing some material that may or may not be speech is in the category of material that can count as published, it could only so count if it were made public, distributed, put on view, or some such thing. Presumably, exposing the material to one other person only would not usually be sufficient. What would? I begin with this question, then turn to the question of why pens are not publishable.

Dissemination

The paradigm case of publication is printed verbal material produced in a large edition and made widely available. I propose to sketch a theory of publication that can be applied to a wide variety of materials falling outside of the paradigm case. Clearly the idea of publication lying behind "freedom of speech or of the press" is not limited to printed material (consider broadcast journalism), to verbal material (consider editorial cartoons), or to material produced in large editions (consider public lectures).

The last component of the paradigm case, "made widely available," lies closer to the heart of the matter. Material that is made available only to one person is the clearest case of unpublished material. I shall assume that for some material that is made available to between one and fifty persons it will be difficult to say whether it should be regarded as published or not, but that above fifty it is clearly published. This number is chosen somewhat arbitrarily, and most of the account will be the same if the reader substitutes a preferred number to represent the smallest availability that is clearly sufficient to count as publication. The appropriate number may vary with different kinds of material as well, but I avoid these complications.

In some contexts, the number of people to whom some material is available does not seem the crucial issue in determining whether it is public or published. For example, in cases of very small availability but where the few are chosen randomly (or by first come, first served) from those who desire access to the material, some may

Figure 7.1. Produced Material

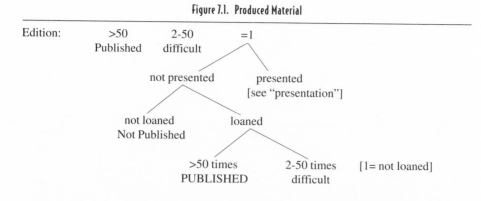

wish to regard the material as published. On the other hand, some may want to deny that material is published if its availability is limited to members of a private organization, even if that group is very large. I will try to avoid these questions by limiting my purview to material whose availability raises no questions about private membership or private circulation. I intend the account to apply primarily to material made available equally to whomever will pay for access to it (and I assume no exorbitant cost),[32] within the constraints of limited circulation or room capacity or life of the material.

So consider first material that is produced in editions, such as printed and recorded material. Call this *produced* material (Figure 7.1). Where the edition is larger than fifty, it is published, and where it is less that fifty, it is a more difficult case. In the case of an edition of one piece, it is not published unless it meets the criteria under loaned or presented materials as these are defined below.

An important subcategory here is material that is *loaned*, since this allows even an edition of one piece to be made widely available. Where the size of the edition multiplied by the number of people that can borrow each piece is greater than fifty, the material is published. Cases less than fifty are difficult, and where this number equals one, the material is not published.

Next consider material that is displayed or performed, such as dramatic theater, film, gallery art, live music, and so on. Call this *presented* material (Figure 7.2). Where the capacity per presentation multiplied by the number of presentations is greater than fifty the material is published. Where this number equals one, it is not published, and where it is between one and fifty, it is a difficult case.

There are special difficulties in the case of live presented materials. For material to count as having an audience greater than fifty, it must be the same material. Live performances, however, vary from one performance to the next, and so two performances to audiences of twenty-five may not really be two performances of the same material. This problem about repeated performances does not arise where the audience per performance is greater than fifty. I have stipulated that the cases between one and fifty will be put aside here as difficult. What, then, about the case of repeated live performances to an audience of one? The pertinent question on this analysis is whether the performance is too tailored to the audience to count as the same material each time. The answer will often be difficult, though not always, and varies from

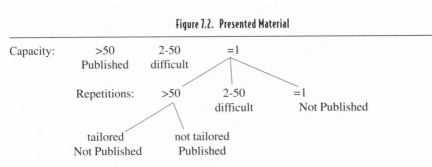

Figure 7.2. Presented Material

case to case. I will discuss this class of material in more detail in the context of specific kinds of sexual material. If it is tailored to audiences of one, then it is not published regardless of the number of performances.

In principle, tailoring can occur in performances to larger audiences, as when a
lounge singer joins a table of patrons midsong. I will assume that such tailored
episodes are outweighed by the fact of their presentation to a large audience. It may
as well be regarded as tailoring the performance to that particular audience rather
than as tailoring to any individual.

There are some cases of relatively narrow dissemination that should count as
published if they are made available in a public forum. For example, a person on a
street corner inviting passersby to browse through his portfolio of photographs is not
expressing himself less publicly just because no one chooses to look. On the other
hand, the idea of a public forum cannot be entirely separated from the question of the
size of the (at least potential) audience. A space (or channel, etc.) is presumptively
public only if there is a reasonable expectation that material posted there would be
available to some significant number of people. Thus, the man with his portfolio is
less likely to receive protection under a publication principle if he sets up in a dark
alley late at night. Dissemination in a public forum can, then, substitute for dissemination to a large number of people.[33]

Sexual material that fails the publication criterion because it is too tailored to a
single patron would become a publication if the same highly tailored performance
were simply also presented to a wide audience. In effect, prostitution counts as published expressive material if it is intentionally opened to public view. Then it would
be covered by the publication-based press clause, for example. Regulation of live sex
shows would raise serious questions of freedom of expression. The fact that the sex
involved is illegal under prostitution laws simply shows that prostitution laws may
be unconstitutionally overbroad in this way. On the other hand, the expressive interest might be legitimately limited in the case of public sex acts,[34] but I won't consider
the case for that view here.

Is a Pen a Publication?

One advantage of a publication criterion is that it gains coverage for art without the
need to argue that art is always speech. But this raises a challenge for the publication
criterion: many widely disseminated materials, such as pens and cars, are not ordi-

narily regarded as published, and it would be a liability for the publication criterion if it had to count them as covered under the First Amendment press clause. But if they are not counted as published, how is it that art counts as published without reverting to the fiction that all art is speech?

I take it for granted that not only verbal material counts as speech within any adequate construal of the speech clause. Instrumental music, visual arts, dance, pantomime, and so on, are often covered, and this is widely agreed. It is not so clear, however, that *all* instances of material in these media count as speech even under this broad legal understanding of that term. It is far from clear, for example, that Abstract Expressionist painting in America (the "New York School": Kline, Motherwell, DeKooning, Stella, etc.) was *saying* something. That is certainly possible, but not at all obvious, and possibly false. If we nevertheless assume that it has a claim to First Amendment protection, then on what grounds? To fit it under the speech clause, we must either expand the notion of free speech in an *ad hoc* way, or show that the material is speech in some real sense. Or, of course, we could let the protection be limited to material that could be shown to be speech and let the chips fall where they may. On this view, our best understanding of much art may or may not qualify it for First Amendment protection. Are we really as unsure about whether such art should be protected as we are about whether it must be understood as saying something?

The publication interpretation of the press clause promises an alternative. Let us assume that much music, visual art, and so on, is *not* speech in any defensible sense. This material is often obviously published, and this doesn't depend on a prior determination that it really is speech. But here's the problem: if art counts as published whether or not it counts as speech, why doesn't a mass-produced pen also count as published?

Is a pen a publication? This question is a challenge for the publication criterion. Pens and many other mass-produced objects are not ordinarily thought of as the kind of thing that admits of publication, but it is difficult to say why not. The strategy of limiting publications to expressive, communicative, cognitive, or some other such kind of material fails at both ends: at one end, there may be no such characterization that would cover everything that it should, especially the diverse forms of art, while excluding what it seeks to (e.g., The Visit); at the other end, it is hard to find such a characterization that does not cover too much, including pens and other mass-produced and creatively designed objects.

One approach to this problem would be to take a page from the book of the opponent. The argument that pornography fails to have cognitive, or artistic, or emotive content simply fails, as I argued earlier. Specifically, there is no more reason to deny that sexual arousal is an emotion than there is to deny that grief is. Now that pornography meets that criterion, perhaps the criterion can be used to exclude pens.

The danger is that this strategy makes the publication criterion otiose. If something has, for example, emotive content, shouldn't it be covered whether or not it is published? In reply, however, if The Video has the emotive content of sexual arousal, then so does The Visit. If we take for granted that The Visit is not covered under the First Amendment, then not all material with emotive content is covered.

Some such disjunctive criterion as "cognitive, emotive, or artistic" might serve as a necessary and sufficient condition for a kind of material's counting as publishable in principle. Let us use the term "expressive" to summarize them. Where many accounts go wrong, however, is in making expressiveness a sufficient condition for *coverage*. Those accounts cannot explain why The Visit is not covered but The Video is; the publication criterion can. Granted, almost anything, especially if it is intentionally made public, could be placed in the broad category of "expression." In the case of pens, however, the expressive component is usually very small, whereas it is the predominant characteristic of the prostitutes' performance. Material whose expressive component is too small should not be counted as publishable. That is, even wide and intentional dissemination of the material would not qualify as publication for the purposes of the press clause.

It is an implication of my view that the category "expression" should not be used to identify the material covered under the speech clause. Speech is covered whether or not it is published, and if all expression is "speech," then the press clause would never protect any material not already protected by the speech clause. (It would still, perhaps, protect the publication of such material, which is usually the issue anyway.) The main reason against counting all expression as speech for First Amendment purposes is that The Visit is undeniably expression. Of course, its protection could be canceled by an obscenity doctrine, but that analysis would yield no more protection for The Video than for The Visit. The publication approach exploits a relevant difference. Neither is speech, though both are expressive. Expression that is not speech is not covered under the speech clause, but is covered under the press clause if it is widely enough disseminated. Widely disseminated expressive material is publication whether or not it is speech and obtains protection on that basis.

Denying objects such as pens membership in the class of publishable materials when the expressive component is very small still leaves open the possibility that such material might be regulated for reasons that are impermissible on First Amendment grounds. Suppose the state sought to ban pens that didn't have a sufficiently "American" look, thereby suppressing pens popular with, say, certain ethnic or racial groups. We don't need to say pens are covered by the First Amendment in order to say that the state may not regulate the distribution of pens because of the state's disapproval of the pens' expressive content. Pens can be regulated much more freely than published material, but not on the basis of some real or imagined message that the state wishes to suppress.[35]

Material that is widely disseminated, then, does not count as published material unless it has a significant expressive component, whether cognitive, emotive, or artistic. This helps us to draw the lines where we (I?) would like them to be, but what justification is there for drawing the line between expressive and nonexpressive, publicly disseminated material? The guiding idea is the effort to grant coverage and so presumptive (but defeasible) protection to a class of materials that has a special likelihood of addressing matters of public concern. Material that has little if any expressive dimension can safely be placed outside of that category. The concept of publication I propose then is *expressive material that is intentionally publicly disseminated*. Such material, whether or not it counts as speech, qualifies for the same sort of protection as speech, but under the press clause of the First Amendment.

IMPLICATIONS FOR SEXUAL MATERIAL

There is no difficulty distinguishing between Schauer's example of a no-contact visit to a prostitute and a video containing similar activities that is made and used for similar purposes. The Visit is in the category of presented materials with an audience of one, which is unlikely to be repeated in an untailored form. Therefore, it is not published material. The Video is in the category of produced material and is probably produced in an edition larger than fifty, or if not, is made available by loaning or presenting to a total number of people greater than fifty. Hence, the Video is published material. The implication is that the Video is covered by the First Amendment and so may only be regulated or banned for the usual reasons constitutionally permitted as bases for regulation of speech, such as sufficient showing of harm or categorization as obscene. The prostitute's one-time private show gets no First Amendment protection unless it finds some other way into that amendment's concerns, such as by qualifying as political speech or nonobscene art. Neither seems likely.

No theory is well defended by its ability clearly to dispose of one case. It is helpful to consider a number of kinds of sexual material to test the implications of the above analysis. One natural area to consider concerns telephone pornography, ads for which are now familiar in magazines, weekly newspapers, and late-night television. The publication analysis implies that whether phone porn receives First Amendment coverage depends on whether the caller hears a recorded message (published), or a live interlocutor (tailored; not published). This may seem at first like an arbitrary distinction, but it is driven by the idea of publication. If that idea seems to cut too finely here, consider that this implication closely parallels the distinction between the in-person encounter with the prostitute and the video having similar content, aims, and uses. In both cases, the publication criterion gives some measure of protection to the published form and (barring other unusual protected features, such as political or artistic content) allows the state to treat the unpublished form as a case of sex for money. This analysis treats live phone pornography as more like prostitution than speech, but cautiously allows First Amendment coverage when it takes a published form, as in the case of a recorded message.

Consider the broad category of live sex shows. These range from nude dancing with artistic ambitions to straightforward sexual activity made available for viewing, and even touching.[36] The publication criterion boils the issue down to the size of the audience. The fare in a common strip joint is clearly published material. The more difficult cases concern live performances for an audience of one. If there is no pretense of *repeating* the show, then the material is clearly unpublished. Where there is some suggestion of a repeated show, there is good reason for a strong presumption that such performances are too tailored to the individual to count as successive performances of a single show. However, to be consistent, if there is good reason to regard the performances as just as undifferentiated and untailored as they would be if the audience were more than fifty per performance, this analysis must count the show as published. What is more likely is that such private shows are unabashedly tailored, and so should not be regarded as published.

Where a putative show for an audience of one involves physical contact between the audience member and the performer, the element of tailoring is too pronounced to allow that such an episode could be repeated with different single-member audiences in a way that should be counted as publication of a single show.

The publication criterion is well suited, I believe, to answer a difficult legal question: what is the difference, for First Amendment purposes, between a sex show and prostitution? As we have seen, the presence or absence of physical contact will not mark an appropriate line. The answer offered here is that sometimes there is no difference, but sometimes there is the fact of the publication of the sex show. Publication grounds at least minimal First Amendment protection.

Intentional Versus Unintentional Dissemination

I will only briefly note the need to limit the coverage of the press clause to only intentional as opposed to inadvertent dissemination of the material. The visit to the prostitute does not gain First Amendment coverage by being inadvertently broadcast over public airwaves (suppose a security camera that caught the action was accidentally patched into a public frequency, etc.). It doesn't matter whether we say that it only counts as published if the dissemination is intentional or that the intentionality requirement is additional to the publication criterion. The aim of the publication criterion is to mark off a range of material that might seek to address matters of public concern, on the model of political deliberation. The constitution's interest in this broad category is not that it is widely available, but that someone has intentionally *made* it so. Without that, there would be little reason to be especially sensitive to its possible bearing on public matters.

On Private Material

Consider a private letter, without political or artistic significance. On what basis can it claim First Amendment protection? The usual answer, I think, is that it is paradigmatically a case of speech. This answer is awkward in several respects. First, if it counts as speech under the First Amendment, then it is subject to the usual categories and exceptions. Speech is regulable if it is obscene, and the current standard of obscenity contains nothing that would prevent its being applied to private erotic letters. If the First Amendment is the whole basis of the protection of private letters, then they are apparently regulable when obscene. If that is the current state of the law about private letters, then my account is not much more repressive for its implication that private letters with no artistic or political significance receive no First Amendment protection. If the law protects private letters in some other way, such as a constitutional right to privacy, without use of the First Amendment, then this independent protection is in no way canceled by the publication criterion proposed here.[37]

I have said that an advantage of protecting publication as such is that art can receive much protection even without having to pretend that it is speech. What about *unpublished* art? There are two possibilities: either it would be protected by privacy, or protecting it would require resorting to treating it as speech after all. In the latter case, the publication criterion would have no special consequences for art.

Cybersex

Consider now several more difficult cases, in which new technology raises questions about the very idea of publication. First, consider the sort of noncommercial phone sex explored in the novel *Vox*.[38] Two people have a sexual tryst over the phone with neither receiving payment from the other. I will call this phone *sex* to distinguish it from phone *pornography*, which is characterized by a caller's paying for the provision of the live or recorded message. Phone sex is like privately made and kept videos or photographs, and ought to receive whatever protection it does in a similar way.

The case of phone pornography supplies an interesting intermediate case for the publication analysis. This account bases the distinction between recorded and live messages on the question of whether the message is tailored to the individual and so not truly published. Consider a message that is both recorded and tailored, on the model of phone messages commonly employed in other contexts. Upon calling a certain number, you hear the message, "Press 1 for a woman, or 2 for a man." After pressing one or the other, you hear, "Press 1 for heterosexual, or 2 for homosexual," and so on. Or suppose that at various stages in the recorded erotic message, the listener is asked to press a key to choose various "plot twists." The point is that the message could be highly tailored to the individual, with the degree of specificity limited only by the state of computer technology. It will soon be possible to produce computer-generated phone pornography that is nearly indistinguishable from a live conversation, just as home computers rapidly approach the ability to (apparently) converse naturally with their owners. This is an intrinsically difficult case for the publication analysis since it blurs the line between a single presented content and spontaneous live interaction.

Similar problems are generated by more sophisticated sexual uses of computer technology. There are already computer games that employ CD-ROM technology to create a highly interactive experience including high-quality photographic, audio, and video material. As this genre improves, it will become increasingly unlikely that any two users will pursue exactly the same "route" through the interactive options, and this might suggest to some that the experience is highly tailored and not published. On the other hand, if the question is not whether a single run of the software is published but whether the software itself is, then doubts are likely to recede. Such a program is as clearly published as any board game. Certainly, we should say the same thing about prerecorded phone pornography, however "interactive" it might be.

There are more exotic speculations about sexual uses of emerging "virtual reality" technology. Consider, for example, a full bodysuit in which the senses of touch, sight, and hearing are completely controlled by interactive computer software. Here, perhaps, is the limiting case, the final test for Schauer's attempt to assimilate pornography to sexual activity. If they can be separated here, they can be separated anywhere. Consider first a genuine sexual interaction in which one person requests a certain sexual favor of another and the latter obliges, for payment. Next consider one person in the virtual reality suit and another at the controls. The suited user verbally requests certain kinds of sexual "contact" and the person at the controls clicks the mouse to oblige, producing a tactile, audio, and visual environment for the suited user that approximates old-fashioned sexual interaction with a fantasy partner. This is highly tailored and not published (so long as the interaction is not opened to public view). Now remove the person at the controls and replace him or her with software that is exactly as obliging. Schauer bids us ask how this last scenario could enjoy any protection under freedom of expression that the first, nonvirtual interaction does not. The publication analysis asks whether the software program is intentionally disseminated widely or in a public forum and whether it has a sufficient expressive dimension. If so, it is a publication and should be covered under a constitutional protection. Since the protection for publication as such is principled and not designed just for this case and since this example is as difficult a version of Schauer's question as I can conceive, I believe the idea of freedom of publication provides an answer to Schauer's challenging suggestion that hard-core pornography is not even a free-speech issue.

Notice that, in this case, the publication analysis circumvents the mental/physical dichotomy on which many have rested arguments similar to Schauer's. In the virtual-reality example, the physical response is no more mentally mediated than it is in real sexual contact, and so that dichotomy provides no basis for treating the cases differently under the law. The closest the publication analysis comes to that distinction is in applying only to material that is expressive. Probably the virtual-reality program could be distinguished from a vibrator on those grounds, the former being publishable and the latter not, though I won't pursue the question further.

CONCLUSION

Let me summarize the publication interpretation of the press clause of the First Amendment as I have developed it. The publication interpretation of the press clause begins with a conception of expressive material that includes a broad range of contents, including cognitive, emotive, and visceral. Among other things it includes both The Visit and The Video with their predominantly sexual content. But, among other things, it excludes such things as mass-produced pens or cars. The second component of the publication interpretation is a criterion of how widely disseminated the material is. This criterion covers both produced material and presented material, and dissemination is allowed to take the form of editions, audiences, borrowers, downloads, and other forms. Material counts as published if it is both sufficiently expressive and sufficiently (intentionally) disseminated. Published material should be (and might be) covered by the press clause of the First Amendment and afforded the same kind of protection and exceptions as material that is covered only under the speech clause. Thus, when it is published, pornography would be better protected than prostitution (unpublished because not disseminated) or mass-produced sexual aids (unpublished because not sufficiently expressive). When it is not published, as in private letters or photographs, its degree of protection from legal regulation is unaffected by my analysis.

Notes

1. Schauer, *Free Speech: A Philosophical Inquiry* (Cambridge University Press, 1982), p. 184. Cass Sunstein follows Schauer in degrading the constitutional status of pornography on the basis of its lack of cognitive content ("Pornography and the First Amendment," *Duke Law Journal* 1986, no. 4 (1986: 606). However, Sunstein seems to grant that it is speech under the First Amendment, though "low-value" speech. Schauer's distinctive move is to argue that pornography may be regulated without scrutiny as to its "low value." Catharine MacKinnon gives a similar argument in *Only Words* (Harvard University Press, 1993), p. 184. She sees the viewer of pornographic pictures as in a sexual relationship with the models in those pictures. The women depicted really do the things that are documented in pictorial pornography. Men "experience this *being done* by watching it *being done*. What is real here is . . . that the materials . . . are part of a sex act" (p.17).

2. I take no stand on whether strong content neutrality is necessary in the final determination of *protection*.

3. We are not dealing in science fiction. The real-time remote video link exists right now via computer and modem. See information on the Internet: *World Wide Web*, "Virtual Dreams," [http://www.virtualdreams.com/].

4. "Speech and 'Speech'—Obscenity and 'Obscenity': An exercise in the Interpretation of Constitutional Language, "*Georgetown Law Journal* (1989): 923.

5. Schauer, *Free Speech* p. 182.

6. Cognitive content is sometimes defined as content that is either true or false. The criticism of Schauer is stronger if we allow him a somewhat broader use of the term.

7. See Schauer's unusually broad use of "intellect," which I avoid here, quoted in note 8.

8. "The emotive as well as the propositional or cognitive, is implicitly encompassed by the intellectual or communicative interpretation of the First Amendment" ("Speech and 'Speech,'" p. 923).

9. Schauer, *Free Speech*, p. 183.

10. Schauer, p. 923.

11. By "propositional," Schauer seems to mean what might be better called "cognitive." His is an imprecise use of the term since standard emotions are often propositional (even apart from whether they are cognitive). To fear that the sky will fall is to have a fear that has as its content the proposition, "the sky will fall." So propositional states are not properly contrasted with emotions. It is a separate question, and one much debated, whether cognition (belief, knowledge, reasoning) is properly contrasted with emotions, or whether instead many emotions are significantly cognitive. See, e.g., Phillippa Foot, "Moral Beliefs," in *Virtues and Vices and Other Essays in Moral Philosophy* (University of California Press, 1978), originally published in *Proceedings of the Aristotelian Society* 59 [1958–59]; Donald Davidson, "Hume's Cognitive Theory of Pride," in *Essays on Actions and Events* (Oxford University Press, 1980, originally published in *Journal of Philosophy* 73 [1976]; and Martha Nussbaum, *Upheavals of Thought: A Theory of the Emotions* (forthcoming Cambridge University Press).

12. Schauer cites Finnis's defense of the distinction between reason and passion (Finnis, "Reason and Passion: The Constitutional Dialectic of Free Speech and Obscenity," 116 *University of Pennsylvania Law Review* 222 [1967] as one that his distinction parallels "to some extent" (Schauer, "Speech and 'Speech,'" p. 923 n. 146).

13. "Speech and 'Speech,'" p. 924.

14. "Speech and 'Speech,'" p. 924. Schauer claims to find this basic distinction in the Court's own reasoning, though his citations provide no support. He offers only three terms from *Ginzberg v. U.S.* None of these, "erotically arousing," "titillation," or "sexual stimulation," is a clear appeal to the physical. The Court could easily have named physiological

effects such as erection, or at least used some such term as "physical," "bodily," or "biological" if that had been its point.

15. Sunstein uses this term in "Pornography."

16. Judge Richard Posner proposes protecting nude dancing on the basis of its being art and usually representational in some way. (See Miller v. City of South Bend, U.S. Court of Appeals, Nos. 88-3006 and 88-3244 (7th Cir. 1990); Posner's concurring opinion; and *Sex and Reason* [Harvard University Press, 1992], pp. 363–64.) On my account, this often strained finding is not necessary in order to trigger First Amendment coverage.

17. When tennis is played before a large audience, it raises interesting questions for my analysis. Certainly sporting events can be controlled and used for expressive and ideological purpose, but so, perhaps, could anything (at least if we include successful and unsuccessful attempts).

18. Blackstone gives a brief history of licensing laws, *Commentaries on the Laws of England*, Vol. IV, p. 152, n. *n* (any edition).

19. Blackstone, *Commentaries on the Laws of England*, Vol. IV, p. 152 (any edition).

20. Letter #15, Feb. 4, 1720, Cato's Letters, Vol. I (Russell & Russell, 1969), p. 100.

21. Anthony Lewis, *Make No Law* (Vintage Books, 1991), p. 51.

22. Note that this mention of the "proceedings of government" is added to the previous general protection of the press as a second conclusion from the "right to freedom of speech, of writing and publishing their sentiments."

23. Resolutions of Maryland, April 28, 1788, *The Debates on the Constitution*, Part Two (Library of America, 1993), p. 555.

24. Resolutions of Virginia, June 1788. See *Debates*, p. 561 Same words in Resolutions of North Carolina, Aug. 2, 1788, *Debates*, p. 568.

25. Lewis, *Make No Law* p. 50.

26. Lewis, p. 50.

27. Hamilton associates liberty of the press with "newspapers" in ed. 84, 1788. But what he says doesn't limit it to this.

28. Powe, *The Fourth Estate*, p. 26.

29. To say that a certain freedom is a "bulwark of liberty" is ambiguous. A bulwark is a first line of defense, but also a leading edge. The freedom may be useful in protecting other liberties, but to call one liberty a bulwark of liberty may just be to say that it is typically the first liberty to go.

30. See Lewis, *Make No Law*, p. 55, on a cartoon of Washington as an ass.

31. An example of this approach is, C. Edwin Baker, *Human Liberty and Freedom of Speech* (Oxford University Press, 1989).

32. For example, the lectures at the $100,000 Club (fund-raising banquet for George Bush) may not be properly regarded as published, even assuming anyone contributing $100,000 was eligible to attend.

33. Neither of these—wide audience or public forum—has any necessary connection to the material's having content that is of public concern. See Schauer, "'Private' Speech and the 'Private' Forum: *Givhan v. Western Line School District*," 217 *Supreme Court Review* 217 (1979), for this three-way distinction.

34. David Cole usefully calls attention to the fact that while publication of expressive material usually heightens the presumption of protection in existing First Amendment law, the opposite is usually the case with sexual materials. There, publication is precisely what is objected to. I share Cole's concern that this is an indefensible double standard. See "Playing By Pornography's Rules: The Regulation of Sexual Expression," 143, no. 1, *University of Pennsylvania Law Review* 111 (Nov. 1994).

35. Sunstein, *Democracy and the Problem of Free Speech* (Free Press, 1993), pp. 154–59,

for elaboration of the point in the text. Also see the Supreme Court case, R.A.V. v. City of St. Paul, 112 S. Ct. 2538 (1992), arguing that even less-protected categories of speech are protected from certain regulations based on government disapproval of a message.

36. For some accounts of what is or has been available in Times Square, see *Village Voice*, collected articles under the head: "Sleazy Does It: Savoring Times Square Before Disney Takes Over," July 18, 1995.

37. I would be troubled if there were no other basis of protection and would count that against the present view.

38. Nicholson Baker, *Vox: A Novel* (Random House, 1992).

Shaping and Sex:
Commentary on Parts I and II

David M. Estlund

The essential thing is to be what nature made us. A woman is always only too
much what men want her to be.

ROUSSEAU

Modern culture has been deeply impressed by the extent to which we ourselves are
the makers. Even Rousseau, who accepted the traditional view that nature provides
authoritative standards, knew that nature is not necessity. A constant question has
been what limits there are, if any, to what we can make. An intermittent question has
been, 'Who's this "we," paleface?[1] Just as Tonto may not share the Lone Ranger's
vulnerability to the attacking tribe, "we" are not all equally responsible for what our
culture has made. This challenge has been posed not only in the context of race, but
also of class, and increasingly, of gender and sexual preference. Even apart from
these questions, the practical question is, "What can be changed and what should
be?"

PART I: SHAPING SEX, PREFERENCE, AND FAMILY

The first part of this book concerns "shaping" or "construction" in the context of sex,
preference, and family. Many of the chapters in the book, including each of the essays in the first part, could as well have been placed in a different one of the four
parts. Their collection under the heading "Shaping" is intended to call attention to a
theme they have in common, encouraging the reader to isolate that theme for consideration and allowing the editors in their commentary to address that theme directly.

The essays by Moody-Adams, Nussbaum, and Okin share a concern with the
initial conception of the problems of sex, preference, and family. In some sense,
every chapter in the book is concerned with how we conceive these problems, but in

this part we call special attention not to the intellectual merits of alternative ways of conceiving things but also to what might be called the metaphysics of the conception of these issues and the political significance of those metaphysical questions. The following are at least partly metaphysical questions, as that branch of philosophical inquiry is usually understood:

> Is the very category "family" constituted partly by assumptions about the locus of certain social responsibilities, such as responsibility for the well-being of children? How could the family be responsible for the welfare of children when the state has such an overriding impact on what the family can do and be? (This is among the questions considered by Moody-Adams.)

> Are sexual desire and related emotions natural, precultural categories of human experience, or are they culturally produced and perhaps even susceptible to intentional change? (Nussbaum investigates this.)

> Is gender a natural division, or is it culturally produced and changeable? What sort of social world would be required for the eradication of gender? (Okin treats these questions.)

Moody-Adams

Michele Moody-Adams asks us to think of the prevailing concept of family (which she criticizes) as a moral concept, one that locates the final responsibility for the welfare of children in the head-of-household. If this is what a family *is* then that implies that the state, in the form of its collectively sovereign citizens, has at most a secondary responsibility for children's welfare. She argues that this is unfortunately close to the conception of the family in mainstream U.S. debates. If we treat this concept of family as "socially constructed," then we can choose to reconceive it. Thus we can directly face the question how much responsibility for children's well-being ought to be assumed publicly. A great deal, argues Moody-Adams.

Many will argue against Moody-Adams that if we emphasize public responsibility this will lead parents to neglect their responsibilities. As a result, the public will become overburdened with the care of other people's kids. The state will have neither the competence nor the political will nor, as a result, the financial resources to perform the task well. There are several difficulties with this objection.

First, even if publicly emphasizing the state's responsibility would have bad consequences, this would be no argument that it does not bear that responsibility. Still, of course, the state's *capacity* to care for children is certainly to the point. So, second, the charge that the state could not competently do it must be addressed. But that charge cannot be either defended or answered just as it stands. The evaluation must be case by case, policy by policy. There are many things the state can do to benefit children, some that it already does, and some that it could do but does not. Despite its rhetorical value, there is no simple answer to the question, Who is better at raising children, the state or the family?

Third, pessimistic predictions about the political will of the public to help children are both premature and partly beside the point. The public debate about what moral responsibility the public has is one of the major arenas in which the political will gets formed. It is a confused contribution to a will-forming political discussion to point out that there isn't the will for a proposed policy. The question under discussion is whether there should be, and many citizens will support it if they are solidly convinced that they morally should.

Fourth, the question of financial wherewithal is, in a wealthy society like ours, almost entirely determined by the question of political will. And political will is determined to an important extent by the merits of the moral case as the citizenry judges those merits. What are the merits of the assignment of great moral responsibility for child welfare to the public in its political role? Some might object that the state could not be finally responsible since, of course, the parents are. But the idea of "final responsibility" ought to be questioned. If the state has the ability to help children whose parents are negligent, who has final responsibility? Are the parents exonerated if the state is morally blamed for inaction? Obviously not. The negligent parent has no legitimate claim to public help in that case, but the child might have a claim to assistance against both the parent and the state.

Having said that, I want to turn to a context in which public negligence might actually exonerate otherwise blameworthy parents: abortion. Consider a public policy that denies a poor woman any additional welfare payment for the care of an additional child. Moody-Adams cites Mary Ann Glendon's question of "why pregnant women in the United States should be asked to make significant sacrifices (whether they abort or bear children), if absent fathers and the community as a whole are not asked to sacrifice too" (16).[2] This is posed as a question of fairness. How is it fair to ask just the mother to bear the burden of carrying the fetus to term when it would be possible to share this burden socially?

Of course, some burdens that could be publicly shared might not be the public's responsibility. The question is how this is determined. If I voluntarily venture into an unsafe neighborhood, the public accepts some responsibility for my safety. If a woman voluntarily engages in sexual intercourse, then, no matter how careful she is to avoid pregnancy, under the policy described above, the public refuses to accept any responsibility for her child's care. Can we tell just by looking that she is "finally" responsible for that child's welfare, but that I am not "finally" responsible for my own safety? The public has a great capacity to help in both cases. Its obligations cannot be read off some antecedently fixed obligations of the private citizens involved. Of course, this is not yet an argument that the public is responsible in either case.

Moody-Adams employs the language a of "social constructionism" in her title, and at some points in her argument (p. 6), arguing both to and from the claim that the family is partly socially constructed. She is not, however, directly addressing what *forms* the family might take (for that, see Eskridge and Minow, Part IV). Rather, her topic is the shape and place of the *concept* of family in the apparatus of moral responsibility for others. If this apparatus is itself socially constructed, as she also seems to believe, that language might suggest that there is no right or wrong way to do it. The thesis of social constructionism applied to normative concepts like responsibility in some ways recapitulates the older thesis of the "essential contestedness" of normative or political concepts, in which political discourse is no more than a power struggle. Moody-Adams plainly does not intend to subscribe to that form of social constructionism. Apparently, the value of that terminology for her purposes is its connotation that what is socially constructed can be socially reconstructed if we decide that it should be.

The idea of social constructionism arises in many essays in the book. Martha Nussbaum's essay employs the idea in a way that allows us to distinguish and critically consider several of its many different meanings.

Nussbaum

When it is claimed that something is socially constructed, there are a number of things that might be meant. The one thing that is almost never meant is the thing the words most naturally suggest, that some structure or entity (e.g., a barn) is created intentionally (e.g., raised) by some social group of people (e.g., friends and neighbors). In this sense of "socially constructed," here are some things that are certainly socially constructed: some barns, written legal codes, political parties, NATO, Woodstock, Earth Day, and this book. In that first sense, here are some things that are certainly not socially constructed: your sex, your sexual preference, your experience of sexual desire, your sexual organs. So when these are said to be socially constructed, something else must be intended.

Consider the meaning of a word, "leg." We might say that the meaning of the word "leg" is socially constructed when we reflect on the fact that the symbol or utterance has no meaning apart from the conventions of a linguistic community. Here "constructed" would mean something like "a product of human convention." The meaning of a word is not just constructed in this sense, but *socially* constructed, in that it is the product of the conventions of a particular social group.

"Social" may seem to be redundant since convention already either depends on or actually constitutes a form of sociality. But there is some value in emphasizing the social source of the construction, to distinguish the thesis of social construction from theses of construction that have nothing to do with convention. For example, even though truths of logic ("If all As are Bs and x is an A, then x is a B") or of mathematics ("The sum of even numbers is always an even number") are apparently not subject to human or social convention, it might be argued that they are facts about any possible faculty of reasoning or understanding and have no truth or existence independently of such faculties. Some philosophers hold this sort of view about especially math, logic, and morality. Kant held a version of this view about everything we could ever know or experience, and some philosophers follow him today. Nussbaum declares her sympathy for the views of one such philosopher, Hilary Putnam (p. 41, n.72). Never mind whether any of this is correct; it might be called a form of constructionism or constructivism. Still, this would not be (nor is it any support for) a thesis of *social* construction since society and sociality are entirely absent from the account.

The claim that something is socially constructed, then, might mean that it is the product of social convention. The meaning of the word "leg" is socially constructed in this sense, as is the meaning of every word. Legs, however, are clearly not socially constructed in either this sense or (usually) in the barn-raising sense of "socially constructed." Even if you think "leg" is a contingent, conventional, conceptual category, you should allow that iguanadons would have had legs whether or not any culture had ever devised that category. Later categorical schemes cannot affect what dinosaurs were like, and either they had legs or they did not. Their legs are not constructed even if the category "leg" is. If this argument works for dinosaur legs, it works for human legs.

It is jarring, then, to hear it even asked, as Martha Nussbaum does, whether the sexual organs are socially constructed. This jolt is really only different in degree from the rhetorical impact of her claim that human love, desire, and sexuality are socially constructed. A product of some social convention would not exist but for the existence of either that social convention or some certain alternative conventions. Sexual organs, legs, love, desire, and sexuality do not apparently depend on any particular social convention for their existence.

Even if their existence does not depend on social convention, however, perhaps their nature or constitution does. It seems very likely that sexual desire will be different in many ways—feel different, involve different associated beliefs and desires, lead to different behaviors, and so on—depending on the cultural significance of sex in the subject's society. But if that is the meaning of the claim that sexual desire or other emotions are socially constructed, or are "social and historical artifacts" (p. 45), then neither phrase can be used univocally to apply to both emotions and to sexual organs. There is no claim in Nussbaum's essay that the sexual organs are different in different cultural settings, though that is apparently her claim about emotions. Sexual organs and emotions alike are categorized and individuated differently in different cultures. Emotions, unlike body parts, are actually affected and changed by these cultural differences.

Recall that the meaning of the word "leg" is plainly a product of social convention. What about the proposition that legs are among the parts of a normal human body? Does the truth of this claim depend on social convention, or does it express a fact that is utterly independent of social convention? Let's start with what is certain: no social convention of language or meaning or categorization *changes the human body*, certainly not enough to determine the truth or falsity of the proposition that human bodies normally include legs. If there is social construction going on in the area of this proposition, it is not the construction of bodies but of something else.

Perhaps what is socially optional is not what the body will be like but whether to put into its own conceptual category the part of the body we think of as a leg. Perhaps categories, unlike the human body, are entirely up to us, to build and shape as we might (if not exactly as we will or wish). Legs are not socially constructed but perhaps the category "leg," much like the meaning of the word "leg," is socially constructed in the sense of being the product of social convention. The choice of categories is not just the same thing as the choice of meanings for words since two different societies could choose the same categories and give them entirely different names. But much as we can see how word meaning might be conventional, we can see how categorization might be.

However, the fact that categorization is something societies can do in different ways says nothing about whether all categories depend on social convention, with none being real or presocial. The former is obvious, the latter is deeply contested. There is no inconsistency in holding that, while societies can categorize as they might, some category schemes are objectively incorrect, others are objectively correct. Again, never mind for now whether this is true. The point is that it is not refuted by noting that different societies can categorize things in different ways. That would be possible even if there were objectively correct or incorrect categorical choices.

Realizing this, it looks as if Nussbaum's thesis that the emotions are socially constructed is apparently not as strong a claim as the language suggests. Here is a skeleton of the argument as I see it:

1. Different societies categorize and value things differently (leave aside whether objective correctness is possible).

2. Individuals apply, with only limited variation, the categories and values of their own cultural situation or nexus.

3. An individual's emotions are constituted by value judgments that are culturally learned.

4. Therefore, emotions will vary significantly across cultures, both varying within recognizably similar categories and falling into some different categories altogether.

5. Therefore, both the nature of some emotions (weaker conclusion) and the very existence of some emotions (stronger conclusion) are products of culture or social convention.

So how should we understand Nussbaum when she says, for example, that erotic love is socially constructed? She wants to draw the stronger conclusion, that "Plato and John Updike are not describing the same passion" (23). However, her argument requires that we identify erotic love in ancient Greece and erotic love in contemporary America, and then ask how different they might be. It is inconsistent to conclude that they are not both forms of the same emotion, erotic love. If they are both forms of the same passion, though different in important ways, the conclusion is the weaker one: erotic love does not owe its existence to culture or social convention; rather, the forms that erotic love can take are to a great extent culturally produced. This is probably correct, and her essay goes a long way toward establishing it. There is some question, though, whether it bears much relation to the thesis of social constructionism.[3] She writes, "What we have to get rid of here is the idea that there is some one *thing* beneath the surface that is simply being described in different language" (24). But this is ambiguous. First, there is the different language. Second, there are the cultural variations in the form erotic love takes. But, third, there is *the thing* that takes those different forms, what she calls "erotic love." If it is not erotic love in both cases, if it is so different in ancient Greece that we cannot accurately call it by any emotion name we have, then we have no argument that *erotic love* takes different forms, for we have not found erotic love in the ancient Greeks and probably cannot understand their sex lives at all.

At best, then, we should wink at the claim that the human body, or the sexual organs, are socially constructed, are social and historical artifacts. Either it is a vivid and dramatic characterization (which we could accept with a wink) of an important but moderate claim about cultural variation in conceptual frameworks, or it is a more problematic metaphysical claim that all reality is, in one way or another, made by mind. I believe Nussbaum's main conclusions in this essay depend only on the former, less radical view.

For Nussbaum, "the payoff of the position that emotions are not given in nature but are socially constructed is that emotions become a part of the domain of moral effort, so construed" (p. 25–26). It is important to distinguish two theses that are central to the idea of social constructionism. The first thesis is that whatever entity, category, or phenomenon that is said to be culturally constructed is *variant across cultures* and in that sense *not universal*. The second thesis, which is supposed to be supported by the first, is that the entity, category, or phenomenon is (comparatively) *subject to intentional change* and in that sense *not necessary*. The fact that something *is* universal in all known cultures past and present does not imply that it is *not* subject to intentional change. Cancer and sexism are (as far as I know) present in every known culture, even though it may well be possible to eradicate them in the future. The fact that something is *not* universal does not imply that it *is* more subject to intentional change. Tay-Sacks disease is especially prevalent in Jewish culture[4] and selfishness is more prevalent in some cultures than others, but neither of these facts strikes me as good evidence that either condition could be intentionally eradicated. Maybe either or both of them could be, but their cultural variability does not seem to offer any special reason to think so.

The question, then, is whether something's not being universal is *any reason at all* to think that it is more subject to intentional change than we should otherwise think it is. This depends on the entity, category, or phenomenon in question and on many other circumstances. Sometimes it is little or no reason (as in the cases of Tay-Sacks and selfishness), and sometimes it is some reason. Sometimes, for example, the cultural variability of a phenomenon may, in the circumstances, strongly suggest that it is not only culturally produced but *intentionally and optionally* culturally produced. Suppose we discover that something that happens to favor people who have greater influence over the content of the culture (say, men or capitalists or whites) turns out not to be present in cultures where the power structure is different. That kind of cultural variability is some reason, though far from conclusive reason, to suspect that the phenomenon is intentionally produced by the powerful in their own interests. Even this, the intentional and optional cultural production of something, does not generally imply that it can be intentionally changed. Some forces can, like toothpaste, be more easily released than recovered.

A similar point still applies to Nussbaum, who emphasizes the cognitivity of emotions as the root of their social construction. A cognitive or belief-like dimension of emotion is behind the cultural production of emotion on her view, and she takes it to support both alterability and cultural variability. But it does not support a claim of greater alterability. Beliefs are not obviously easier to change than other features of people. Which beliefs? Which other features? Does your depression become more tractable if we know that it depends on your mistaken belief that you are dying of cancer than it would be if it were produced by a dietary deficiency? I see no general reason to think so. Still, in some circumstances the intentional production of a phenomenon, especially where it seems to require constant intentional maintenance, can be good evidence that it could be intentionally changed. The possibility of change seems to be what is at stake in social constructionism. If so, the social constructionist project (if it has that much unity) may rest on a mistake. The claim that something is socially constructed is an effort to put a bridge between the claim that it varies across cultures and the claim that it can be intentionally changed. The bridge is the claim that it varies socially *because* it is intentionally constructed by culture or convention. This bridge does not quite span the distance since what is intentionally produced might be beyond intentional change. But more importantly, deciding to put so much effort into *this* bridge makes the vital mistake of conceding that if something is not intentionally produced, or even also not culturally variant, then it probably cannot be intentionally changed. In Nussbaum, the concession takes the form of holding that emotions are more changeable because they are culturally taught than they would be if they were produced entirely by nature. That should not be conceded. If the point is alterability, then social constructionism is a distraction. The important question is whether the male/female dichotomy, the homosexual/heterosexual dichotomy, sexual desire or its forms, and so on, can be changed through human effort to change them. If they can, this is of enormous importance since it gives birth to a new question for human societies: whether these things ought to be changed. Their being socially constructed or not is only a very uncertain guide to their susceptibility to change.

Okin

Susan Okin quite properly puts the emphasis on change. Without toiling over whether gender is socially constructed, or exactly what that would mean, she argues that gender can be done away with—and ought to be. Difference in biological sex ought to have "no more social relevance than one's eye color or the length of one's toes" (p. 44, and in her book, *Justice, Gender, and the Family*). In a gender-free society, "no assumptions would be made about 'male' and 'female' roles, and men and women would participate in more or less equal numbers in every sphere of life" (p. 45). This would extend to the structure of the family, where she advocates not only the absence of gender roles, but the absence of different parental or household roles even apart from gender. Thus, her main proposal in this essay is to look to homosexual couples as a model for the household and family of the gender-free society. One does not need to find any fault in the role-free distributions of labor and responsibility that may be more common in homosexual households in order to wonder why this ought to be held out by Okin as an ideal toward which we ought to try to move our whole society. Similarly, while there is nothing wrong with an approximately equal distribution of males and female across the many "spheres of life" outside the family, we might ask why this is an ideal toward which we should move.

The easiest part to agree with is that there should be no strong social pressures, "expectations," or "assumptions" (2) on women or men to adopt certain social or family roles simply because of their biological sex. Okin's goal is more than this, namely, that the sexes should be about equally represented in every sphere of social life. Which of these should we count as an absence of "gender roles?" I believe there are just two different proposals here: call the first the absence of normative gender roles, or the absence of gender *rules*; call the second the absence of *de-facto* or descriptive gender roles, or the absence of gender *patterns*. Okin advocates both absences, which means that she advocates the absence of gender patterns even if these are not produced by social pressures, assumptions, or expectations based on sex. It is easy to understand why she disapproves of gender rules, but it is less clear what is wrong with gender patterns that are not produced by gender rules.

It is possible that if there were no gender rules then this would eradicate gender patterns. Okin, however, does not mean just this. She values the absence of patterns separately, in addition to the absence of rules. This is clear from her very ideal of a gender-free society. If a person's sex is to be utterly without social relevance, then there could not be any significant correlation between sex and social role. If, for example, teachers, pediatricians, and social workers tended to be predominantly women even after sex-based social pressures were removed, then we could not expect our conceptions of femaleness to be entirely unaffected by this fact. Elsewhere Okin argues (following Amy Gutmann) that "sex should be regarded as a relevant qualification in the hiring of both teachers and administrators until these proportions have become much more equal."[5]

This may be the reason Okin values the absence of gender patterns even if they were not caused by gender rules. She may believe that patterns produce rules. If women freely choose to settle into certain role patterns, then over time there will come to be expectations and even pressures on future women to adopt those same patterns. After all, there is always social pressure not to be different. There is also a powerful tendency to follow role models one identifies with. We might hope that women would not feel different for choosing a role that is uncommon for women, so long as it is not uncommon for people. And we could hope that women would not have any special affinity for female role models. That is, we could *hope* that gender was socially insignificant in these ways. But if there are distinctive patterns in the way genders occupy social roles, even if these are, at first, freely chosen, gender may become far from socially insignificant. Women may well come to identify themselves *as* women again, with all the social expectations and assumptions this would entail.

If that is the problem with gender patterns, then the root value is women's freedom to choose their social roles; this would be lost over time as patterns produced rules. The problem is how to let women choose as they will, but also to make sure that they do not choose any gender-specific patterns. Maybe women's free role choices (those in the absence of gender rules, social antipattern efforts, or prejudice) would produce no differential gender patterns; that would be perfect. Is this something Okin is prepared to predict, and with what evidence? How can we know in advance that equal opportunity for members of gender (or racial) groups will produce anything near equal representation of those groups in every social role? If this is not a prediction but a prescription, then we ought to keep close track of the individual freedom that might have to be traded off for this group-based criterion of equality.

The choice between diminished occupational freedom and oppressive gender rules may be one we have to face, or it may not. It is important to consider first what could be done to allow free choice and the gender patterns this may produce without permitting the development of strong sex-based pressures toward certain social roles.

Under what circumstances can differential role patterns exist for certain groups without producing strong social norms that tend to reproduce those patterns? Consider the category of gay men in America. It is widely said that gay men are disproportionately represented in certain professions; they make up a larger fraction of those professions than their fraction of the general population (or, in male-dominated professions, greater than their fraction of the general male population). Many professions in the arts are apparently disproportionately gay in that sense.[6] No doubt this produces a certain cultural association between the ideas of male homosexuality and the social role of artist, thus shaping the very idea of male homosexuality in our culture to some extent. However this pattern came about, whether it depended on different patterns of discrimination across different professions or not, it is not clear to me that these patterns have created additional repressive assumptions and expectation pressuring gay men to choose professions in the arts. Certainly a pattern like this leads to stereotyping, but that is not the same thing as social pressure to conform to the stereotype. The stereotype might yet reproduce the pattern even without creating pressure to conform if people's simple expectations make it emotionally more difficult for a gay man to be very unlike the stereotypical gay man. Ignoring the other sources of discrimination against gays, has the stereotype of arty gay men significantly obstructed their entry into non-arts careers?

I do not have good evidence about which of these social pressures this professional pattern has produced or whether they are very strong and repressive. There is an important point either way. If those pressures do not exist or are not very repressive, then we might ask whether gender patterns could also exist without excessive role-restricting pressures. On the other hand, if the pressures on gay men that are caused by these professional patterns are fairly strong, we need to appreciate the dilemma this produces. It may be that those undesirable social pressures could only be avoided if, somehow, gay men were dislodged from this professional pattern. But how should this be done? And is this really preferable to the original situation? It would certainly be preferable if we could know that the pattern were largely the product of stereotyping and other undue social pressures, but that is far from clear. Since the pattern might be one that would survive in conditions of relatively free occupational choice, is it clear that we should strive for a society in which this pattern is destroyed, in which members of groups defined by sexual preference are approximately equally represented in all social roles?

Reflection on this example about gay men should increase our willingness to consider the possibility that women (and, of course, men) might freely choose occupations and roles in a pattern that involves gender-based differences. I believe that there can be no good reason to deny that this would happen (or to assert it) from a situation in which choices are far from free. And once we acknowledge that it might happen, Okin's goal of a gender-free society, with equal gender representation across all social roles, looks like a mixed blessing at best.

If we turn to the structure of a gender-free family, the same problem appears. Unless we have good reason to deny that women would freely[7] choose roles at home in a gender-patterned way, then the social goal of no gender patterns in the family threatens its own form of oppression: intentional social stigmatization of individuals who adopt gender-typical roles, designed to discourage that choice. There is a certain amount of this already, even though it coexists with an opposing stigmatization of deviance from traditional gender roles. It is impossible to say which of these is stronger.

One last question about Okin's ideal of the gender-free family concerns her ideas about just distribution of labor in the home. One can distinguish several different possible positions on adult roles in the family:

1. Avoid forced or pressured roles of any kind;

2. Avoid unfair distributions of domestic labor;

3. Avoid genders in their traditional roles;

4. Avoid the traditional roles, regardless of which genders occupy them.

(1) and (2) are pretty uncontroversial. Okin advocates (3) and (4) as well. She believes that traditional gender roles are both pressured and unfair—so the uncontroversial (1) would imply (3); and (2), also uncontroversial, would imply both (3) and (4). It is not clear, however, whether traditional roles are to be avoided just because they tend to be unfair and pressured. We can try to imagine the closest possible thing to those traditional roles without the pressure or the unfairness. Here is a try: one role involves primary responsibility for the care of the children and the general management of the household. The other role involves primary income-producing responsibilities, where these are met by work outside the home. To avoid unfairness, suppose that, apart from work time outside the home, the second partner does about as much domestic work as the first partner does during the time spent at home (not overall). Also, assume some version of shared legal rights to wealth and assets, including cases of death and divorce. However, to keep it traditional, suppose that the income-producing partner's work at home is mostly of a traditionally male kind: building, repair, car work, yard work, and so on. Adjust the arrangement further if necessary to make it both fair and recognizably traditional. Each role has great advantages and great disadvantages for its inhabitant. But fairness does not require an arrangement that is as good for each person *in every respect*. It is sufficient (though probably not even necessary) for fairness that the arrangement be freely chosen and approximately equally advantageous for each person overall.

Uncontroversial positions (1) and (2) are no longer any support for avoiding the roles this thought experiment produces, (I will call them "free, fair, traditional roles") so long as there is also no gender-based social pressure on either partner to choose one rather than the other. This is already true for gay and lesbian led families. Okin celebrates the lower incidence of the traditional (she calls them "gendered") roles in homosexual households, despite the obvious absence of gender-based social pressure that would taint those roles. Perhaps she is assuming that those roles must be unfair (and if so, it would not matter which gender occupied which role in a heterosexual partnership). But as the above thought experiment suggests, this is either a failure of imagination or only a criticism of a narrow range of possibilities within a traditional division of domestic labor: the ones that would be unfair even if freely chosen. That would not be a general critique of the traditional gender roles more broadly conceived, just a critique of unfairness itself in that subset of cases where it is present.

If straight partners could arrange free, fair, traditional roles, one might still worry about whether a pattern of this kind would, over time, produce expectations incompatible with genuine freedom. If so, we're back to the dilemma discussed above. Here as there, and for the same reasons, this may not count decisively against a traditional pattern of domestic roles. In the case of gay and lesbian partners, the acceptance of traditional roles could not possibly produce gender-based role patterns and, so, could not produce gender-based conservative pressures. It is hard to see, then, why free, fair, traditional roles for homosexual partners should be avoided at all.

Okin's main point is not to praise gay couples for avoiding traditional roles, but rather to argue that, insofar as they happen to avoid those roles, they are worthy models for heterosexual families: "The reason gay and lesbian families may be, at least in one important respect, a model to be followed, is that they are *far* less likely than heterosexual families to practice anything resembling a gendered division of labor" (54–55). Does this mean that a "gendered" or traditional arrangement could never be free and fair? I have explained why I doubt that. A slightly different reason Okin gives several times is that traditional gender roles provide "far from the best kind of environment in which children can learn . . . to develop the sense justices" (55). But that obviously depends on whether traditional gender roles are always unjust. If they can be free and fair, then they can be a fine model for children.

PART II: SEX

Sex is a perennial social problem. Sexual desires may be greatly shaped by social conventions and circumstances, but that does not mean that they readily conform to any intentionally imposed social standards. Although success has been mixed, prostitution, homosexuality, adultery, promiscuity, premarital sex, pornography, and masturbation have been relatively resistant to social efforts to eradicate them. Are there good reasons for socially encouraging some forms of sexual activity and expression, and discouraging others? Are the reasons ever sufficient to justify putting these standards into law?

Part II groups together several essays that bear on legal regulation of sexual activity. Rosenblum and Macedo discuss how the problem of regulating continuing sexual relationships looks from liberal, democratic, and communitarian points of view. Rosenblum uses the case of polygamy to test theories that promote congruence between sexual relationships and political forms. Macedo presses liberalism toward its limits, advocating the use of state prestige and power to encourage valuable forms of sexual life, concentrating on the homosexual case. MacKinnon and Estlund each discuss the constitutional legal issue of how or whether to regulate certain kinds of sexually explicit expressive materials. MacKinnon discusses books by Richard Posner and Edward DeGrazia, arguing that the similarities between the left and right are more telling than their differences when it comes to their complicity with pornography's subordination of women. Estlund argues that the idea of publication allows us to see why there should be more constitutional difficulty about regulating a sexually explicit video than there is about regulating a voyeuristic visit to a prostitute.

Rosenblum

Feminist writers have long argued that traditional gender roles within the family are unjust, but that does not always get them in the door politically. Liberal political theory has a strong tendency to protect the internal affairs of families from state interference much as other nonpublic associations are relatively free to arrange their own collective rules and activities. Not everything that takes place in a family home is a family matter, of course. Parents are legally required to see that their children get a state-approved education. Drug use, violence, criminal conspiracy, and many other possible family activities are nevertheless treated as public business. Why aren't all the economic, authority, and work arrangements between the adult partners also public business? It is difficult to think of a justification for excluding these that also justifies making the *sexual* arrangement a matter of public concern, which is how it is treated in much of the United States today in certain respects—anal and oral sex,[8] polygamy, and other things are prohibited by law even when they are consensual. If those things are not too private for the law to regulate, then why think the state should take no position on whether traditional gender roles in the family are permitted by justice?

One way to press the charge of internal family injustice across the liberal threshold of family privacy is to show that what is going on in there matters for the well-being of the political community as a whole. If some family form were sufficiently popular and destabilizing of social or legal order, or destructive of social justice in the larger community, then even many liberal theorists would think the state is permitted to intervene in certain ways. Rosenblum wonders just where the threshold is.

She considers the case of polygamy. Few Americans object to its legal proscription, yet it is difficult to see how such intolerance can be justified in a liberal framework. In Mormon communities, polygamous marriage was severely patriarchal, but that may be avoidable in other contexts. Rosenblum studies the history of U.S. courts confronting Mormon polygamy and other unorthodox marital arrangements preferred by insular and voluntary communities On one hand, there is a deep liberal reticence about reaching a legal hand into family or marital choices, except to prevent direct harm to individuals. On the other hand, what goes on there may be of the first importance for politics if it influences the capacities and aspects of character that a successful political order requires. Thus, the state's legitimate interest in a certain measure of congruence between private and public forms of life is sometimes offered as a reason for interference in family and sexual relations. To the liberal privacy approach Rosenblum opposes the "democratic sex" approach, which finds citizen building to favor public intervention in those relations. She uses the tension she finds between liberal family privacy and democratic sex to raise important questions about contemporary feminist (as in Okin) and communitarian appeals to the value of congruence between the moral order within the home and that of the larger political community. Is the democratic sex (or congruence) approach a recipe for shoring up faltering private moral foundations of democratic citizenship, or is it a pretext for inserting some people's preferred ideals of family life through an ill-guarded crack in the liberal political door? Rosenblum does not offer an answer, but raises the question in a compelling form.

How could it be a legitimate reason for state action that certain arrangements of the family are corrosive of the moral fabric of our citizenry? The congruence theorists may answer that it is not just any part of the moral fabric that is threatened, but certain key threads of citizen character that make a just, liberal democracy possible. This can easily look like a truck-sized loophole in contemporary liberalism. It would allow moralism to reach into any area of life so long as it is based on the understanding that a certain kind of (private) life or activity will tend to produce worse (or better) citizens (by publicly acceptable standards of a good citizen). The clause requiring "publicly acceptable standard of a good citizen" would at least be an advantage over more unbridled attempts to put moralism in statesman's clothing. Still, I cannot help wondering if the face-to-face community of the missionary position has salutary effects on citizen empathy, and whether there might be some ingenious way to discourage other sexual positions through public policy. The argument from character is not easily contained.

That sobering question cannot refute the congruence theorists by itself, of course. What if certain forms of relatively private life *do* produce citizens without the kind of character a just, liberal democracy requires. Is a citizen who notices this morally bound by liberal principles to stand back? That would be one committed liberal. Most contemporary liberal philosophers would doubt that such a commitment could be required by any adequate theory of the justification of political authority. In the dominant contractualist strand of theory, for example, liberal limits on state power are secondary to the overriding interest every citizen has in maintaining an effective order of political authority. If liberal limits undermine the state's ability to stave off chaos, then the limits cannot be justified to individuals interested in some measure of security and cooperation. Liberals will either deny that a given device of state intrusion is required to maintain political order or, failing that, become a little less liberal. The latter would not be an abandonment of principle in favor of pragmatism or any such thing. Principle itself requires the modern liberal to prefer viable government to individual privacy if they conflict. (Which do you prefer?)

So the question whether certain forms of family life can undermine the political order is not a question that even most liberals can place outside of legitimate political concern, despite its menacing sound to liberal ears. Nevertheless, many inquiries into whether certain family forms produce better citizens than other forms may be inappropriate as reasons for state action. If the very viability of a stable political order is not at stake, then a liberal will balance the prospect of producing better citizens against the threat to an individual's scope to make many important decisions about the form of her life and family herself, without the pressure of coercively backed, majority-supported inducements to become more what the state would like her to be. (Of course, it is hard to say exactly where this balance lies.) Even if there is no necessary conflict between being an ideal citizen and having profound control over the shape of one's life, there is a conflict between having that sort of control and being shaped, by state devices, into an ideal citizen.

Unless limitless improvement of citizens, as citizens, is required to avoid the collapse of political life altogether (and this is a serious question), then a liberal political philosophy will be led, on principle, to prefer something like privacy to most opportunities for making better citizens. Congruence between sexual and family arrangements on the one hand, and the imperatives of politics on the other, is not ordinarily a liberally permissible reason for state action. There is much in private life that is within the grasp of legitimate legal power, however, including physical and psychological protection of certain kinds and enforcement of civil and human rights. These public prerogatives do not leave such things as family forms and marital arrangement untouched, though much scope for choice remains.

Macedo

Stephen Macedo argues that even a robust political liberalism permits the use of law to encourage "the valuable forms of sexuality." The valuable form he concentrates on is marriage. Paying special attention to the case of gay couples, Macedo wonders whether liberalism so prevents us from being judgmental that we cannot even use public power "gently and unobtrusively" (97) to encourage monogamous homosexual marriage. His arguments, however, are meant to extend to encouraging marriage more generally. He argues that evaluative judgments are unavoidable and appropriate. Moreover, he argues that these evaluative judgments may legitimately be put into law.

The question is not whether gay marriage should be legally allowed. Macedo assumes, and I agree, that of course it should. Nor, I think, is the central question in his essay whether some kinds of sexuality are more valuable than others. Assume that some are. We can leave aside the question whether there are reasons other than their value that might justify legal measures designed to encourage or discourage certain forms of sexuality (e.g., economic considerations, population needs, civil rights enforcement, crime reduction). The question is just whether the following is a legitimate reason for encouraging one form of sexuality (such as monogamous marriage) through the law: it is a more valuable form of sexuality.

A legal measure might either legally require the preferred form, or prohibit it, or provide moderate incentives to adopt it. Macedo is not defending legal requirements or prohibitions here, only other incentives provided by law, and he plainly thinks this makes all the difference in a liberal framework. Liberals have traditionally argued especially against the legitimacy of legally prohibiting behavior that harms no one else. Such arguments do not yet show anything wrong with more indirect legal measures to influence such behavior. Consider, for example, tax breaks for married individuals. They do not legally proscribe the harmless personal choice of staying single. Perhaps, then, no liberal should object to these measures, whatever the reason behind them.

Notice, however, that a tax break is just a tax differential. You pay more if you are not married than if you are married, other things equal. And you are legally required to pay under threat of jail and/or legally imposed fines. The state requires that you either get married, or be legally forced to pay higher taxes than married people. If you are unmarried, you might well ask what justifies the use of coercive state power to require you to pay more than your married neighbor. Could this tax differential be justified by the superiority of married life?

Perhaps Macedo has in mind legal measures to provide incentives in a manner even more "gently and unobtrusively" than through tax incentives. Consider a public education campaign with the slogan, "Get married; it's good for you." I turn to the role of this kind of value judgment in law shortly, but first let us look for the coercion this still involves. On one hand, no one is legally coerced to get married by this campaign. On the other hand, every tax payer is legally required to pay her share of the cost of this campaign, even someone who does not believe marriage would be good for her, given her circumstances and options. What is the point of this campaign? Surely, a slogan or a ten-second ad will not convince anyone that marriage is good for them. The point of such a campaign would be publicly to express the government's official desire for more people to marry, and to stimulate and endorse more effective persuasive activity by citizens (e.g., your mother, your neighbors, the Republican party) who already believe this. Even without deciding whether or not such a campaign could be justified, there are at least two things about it that call for liberal scrutiny. First, the taxation to support this family values campaign is coercive, as is all taxation. Second, the social pressure that is the goal of such a campaign is mobilized against those who make the harmless personal choice to stay single. I repeat that neither of these is meant to show that the campaign could not be justified, nor have I said that it could.

Consider now the reason for the legal measures encouraging marriage: that married life is more valuable than unmarried life. This might mean marriage is valuable for the married person, or it might mean marriage is valuable for the larger community, or it might mean some more objective kind of value, or some combination. Macedo's "argument for marriage claims that more stable commitments promote public as well as private welfare" (94). If the value claim is about what is good for the person, then it is unclear why one citizen (or many) should be able to impose this) judgment on another (unless there is some pressing public impact at stake). The point is not whether someone would have to be unreasonable to reject, say, a scientific finding that marriage improves life expectancy. The point is rather that, unless life expectancy is at the center of some urgent problem that fundamentally threatens the political order, it should be up to the individual, in light of whatever advice or evidence she chooses to credit, whether to choose (as she might conceive it) a longer expected life with less flexibility and independence, or a shorter expected life of a more independent kind. To say it should be up to her is not to say that there is no correct or incorrect choice in the circumstances. It is rather a point about the proper and improper uses of our political power over other people. It is hard to see how I could have the authority to employ coercive public power I share equally with others, to legally institute the views of some of us about what is good for the others. If we put the problem this way, it is no answer for Macedo to point out that the coercion employed does not actually coerce anyone to get married.

If the claim about the value of married life is about what is good *for the polity* in someone's living a certain way, then as I said above (in discussing Rosenblum), we must trade this value for the polity against the loss of individual scope in which to shape and live one's own life in accordance with one's own reasonable convictions. The result of this balancing act is that just any claim that some way of living, such as marriage, would make people better for the community is not a liberally permissible reason for legal measures to encourage it. Such considerations are put out of bounds by the interest people have in retaining that scope for their own and others' free conscientious choices, so long as their having this scope is compatible with a stable and mutually beneficial political order. Where that very order is in question, the liberally protected space finds its boundary.

Macedo's work, here and elsewhere, shows a deeper appreciation of the arguments for contemporary liberalism than do most communitarian critics. And there is much to learn by asking, with Macedo (as I understand him), how much communitarian thought could be accommodated without leaving the liberal paradigm. And it does not matter at all whether he should be counted as a liberal or as a communitarian, or as both at once. What should be understood, though, is that, for better or worse, Macedo's view is really not very liberal as these things go. In his other writings, Macedo associates himself with the "political liberalism" of John Rawls, who insists that, at least in the most important matters, only considerations that are acceptable to all reasonable and conscientious citizens count as reasons for coercive state action. Here, however, Macedo's reasons for state action are simply the value of the form of life the action would encourage, just the sort of reasoning political liberalism seems to repudiate. Perhaps Macedo subscribes to political liberalism only insofar as it would block partisan reasons for *legally requiring* marriage, for example. However, he gives no reason for blocking such reasons only there, while endorsing their use to support indirect legal (but still coercive) measures to institute controversial value judgments through, say, tax incentives.

Perhaps Macedo believes that political liberalism should only constrain the reasons we can use in the limited range of questions that Rawls himself concentrates on: what Rawls calls constitutional essentials and matters of basic justice. Rawls neither endorses nor (more importantly) argues for such a limitation. Even if political liberalism's strictures applied only in that limited way, however, it would still need to be shown that the matter at hand—legal encouragement of marriage solely on the ground that it is a more valuable way of life—is neither a threat to constitutional essentials (such as freedom of thought or association) or to basic justice.

Perhaps Macedo believes that the conceptions of meaning and value that he would use in legal efforts to make people better could not be rejected by any reasonable citizen. Formally, that is the political liberal's trademark, though substantively, one is less liberal in this framework as one counts fewer possible positions reasonable. (I do not suggest the absurd idea that the most adequate view is the most liberal one.) Of course, it may be that liberalism is indefensible just where it departs from Macedo. However, there is no new argument in Macedo against the more neutral, more liberal, liberalism I have sketched, and which he apparently rejects.

MacKinnon

Left-leaning critics of Catharine MacKinnon's efforts to establish legal mechanisms for regulating pornography often try to discredit her by showing that her efforts are supported by many on the right. But if MacKinnon's guilt is established by this kind of association, then these critics can themselves be assumed to be in bed with the many right-wing critics of MacKinnon's work. If she is "in bed"[9] with the right, and her left-wing critics are also in bed with the right, it follows that they are in bed with MacKinnon, something that will certainly be denied on all sides. In this critique of Posner and De Grazia, MacKinnon turns the bedfellows argument against her critics and modifies it, arguing that her leftist and rightist critics are not even relevantly different from each other.

If there is a question for those on the left about the political valence of MacKinnon's writings and legal work, it should be whether her work tends to promote the very aims of conservatives that are leftists' *reasons* for opposing conservatives. Even this is a bit silly since what really matters is how good the reasons are, not whether they count as leftist or rightist. However, it is sometimes a clue to the flaws in a position to see that it is characteristic of a larger point of view that one has reasons for opposing. So what is supposed to be conservative about MacKinnon's antipornography project?

Some seem to think that her project is conservative by virtue of its willingness to regulate speech through law. One answer to this[10] is that almost any remotely sensible person, including leftists, would advocate regulating lots of speech (even in viewpoint-discriminatory ways): consider perjury, criminal conspiracy, defamation, false advertising. This is correct as far as it goes, but it does not settle the issue. In American history, at least, there is a decent case for seeing the proregulation forces as largely conservative, the two major battlefields being sexually explicit material and radical political dissent. In both cases, it has been mainly the defenders of orthodoxy and status quo who have sought to ban and punish speech. If so, this does not prove that contemporary proregulation efforts are conservative, but it raises a legitimate question. For several reasons, the answer to that legitimate question, however, is that MacKinnon's work is not conservative.

Pornography is argued by some to have important value as social and political dissent.[11] If it does, that is certainly a strong reason against regulating it, though it would not be conclusive if pornography nevertheless harms women in a sufficiently direct way. Is there an antidissent dimension to the motives of the antipornography movement today? Here is where we must know our left from our right. Many religiously motivated conservative opponents of pornography plainly fear the challenge that much of pornography represents to the orthodox and highly gender-regimented conception of marriage and family. Virtually all pornography implies a value for sexual activity outside of long-term emotional commitments and apart from procreation. Insofar as this challenges traditional ideas of marriage, it challenges one of the strongholds of gender hierarchy in the society at large. The right certainly opposes pornography partly for this reason. MacKinnon clearly does not oppose pornography for this reason; no one is a more energetic opponent of the existing power relations between the genders. She would, however, deny that pornography has much power as dissent: it might not celebrate exactly what the right wants as compared with the left, but it celebrates precisely what men want, she argues, whatever the consequences might be for women, and that is entirely orthodox. Whoever is correct about the dissident power of pornography, feminist critics of pornography are seeking neither to protect the status quo nor to return to some previous and preferable arrangement between the sexes. They are not conservative or reactionary in the way that opponents of social and political dissent have often been.

The second way in which regulation of speech (beyond the patently necessary regulations) has usually been conservative is in efforts to constrain the forms of sexual life, activity, and expression that are socially accepted. Existing obscenity law is a testament to the political power of this socially conservative point of view. There is often a connection between the antidissent and the anti-sexual freedom sentiments, but they are also separable in principle. Feminist opponents of pornography are not antidissent, but are they, in a word, antisex?

MacKinnon addresses this charge here, though in a puzzling and ineffective way. She considers the charge, which can be found coming from both the left and the right, that she has argued that all sex is rape. If that were true, then, since she deplores rape she would plainly be antisex. While it might not be clear from her piece in this volume, the charges by *Playboy* magazine, Rush Limbaugh, and others that MacKinnon thinks all sex is rape are not made from whole cloth. Since many readers are likely to think *Playboy* and Limbaugh are pretty handy with whole cloth—a likelihood not lost on MacKinnon when she concentrates on those two sources—it is worth looking more closely at the basis for the charge. MacKinnon calls it a "libel" (103) and a "lie, rather than a mistake, on the assumption that they have both read my work, which may be giving them too much" (102). She suggests that it is a part of "an escalating litany of increasingly defamatory names" (102), and another case of someone being "slandered" for simply asking "whether sex equality has been achieved" (102).

The question whether the accusers might actually believe their charge (in which case it would not be a lie), and if so, on what basis, is made more interesting by MacKinnon's second footnote. In addition to *Playboy* and Limbaugh, the charge that MacKinnon thinks all sex is rape has also come from Wendy Kaminer and Susan Estrich, legal scholars widely regarded as feminists.[12] Of course, the charge may still be false, but for the moment, what about MacKinnon's charge that it must be a lie in the mouth of anyone who has read her works? Even after noting that the same charge has come from feminists Kaminer and Estrich, MacKinnon writes, "The line between those who wield this libel and those against whom it is wielded cuts across left and right. It divides those who want to maintain and advance under male supremacy from those who want to end it. It draws a line of sexual politics" (103). If *Playboy* and Limbaugh could not really believe the charge if they had read her work, then surely Kaminer and Estrich could not believe it. If you start with the premise that *Playboy* and Limbaugh are lying, then you are led to the conclusion (and MacKinnon apparently embraces it) that these noted feminists are lying, too. On the other hand, if Kaminer and Estrich could really think that MacKinnon argues that all sex is rape (and it seems clear to me that they could), then surely *Playboy* and Limbaugh could also think so. Then there would be no reason to suppose any of them were lying.

Rather than trying, on the basis of her own text, to explain how someone might have come to this interpretation and explaining how the interpretation does not hold up, MacKinnon writes: "It is, of course difficult to provide citations to pages on which something is not said (145, n. 2)"[13] While "[women] *do* say [that] sexuality occurs in a context of gender inequality" (102), how could that possibly be mistaken for the view that all sex is rape? It is easy, as I hope to show, to find parts of MacKinnon's work that many honest readers believe amount to the argument that all sex is rape. If so, this disposes of MacKinnon's charge that those critics are lying. It still leaves the question whether their interpretation is correct.

MacKinnon, like many other feminists, will sensibly allow a distinction between rape and what is legally regarded as rape (since the law might get it wrong). How does MacKinnon understand the category of rape outside of its fallible legal definition? "Politically," she writes in *Feminism Unmodified*, "I call it rape whenever a woman has sex and feels violated."[14] Now consider this political conception of rape along with MacKinnon's view: "What is understood as violation, conventionally penetration and intercourse, defines the paradigmatic sexual encounter."[15] And, "the degradation and violation and domination of women . . . defines the social meaning of female sexuality in societies of sex inequality."[16]

One can plausibly infer from these views that ordinary sex is, and is understood as, violation. When women experience sex as violating, that is rape (though not legally); therefore, ordinary sex is rape. There are at least two ways in which "all sex is rape," understood in one natural way, is too simple an interpretation. First, her critique of the "paradigmatic sexual encounter" may be limited to heterosexual intercourse and perhaps not to every case of that, even in an unequal society. Where she extends the critique to female sexuality as a whole under gender inequality, it is apparently a consequence of intercourse's being paradigmatic of that sexuality. Second, her view is explicitly about sex in conditions of sex inequality, and so not, in a stronger sense, about *all* sex.

Of course, the critics who accuse her of arguing that all sex is rape may well understand all this. First, "sex" is often used to refer to intercourse, and it is usually understood to mean intercourse unless specifically qualified (because, as MacKinnon emphasizes, intercourse is paradigmatic sex in present conditions). There is usually no ambiguity when it is said simply that two people had sex. Furthermore, it is absolutely clear that none of the critics in question were suggesting that MacKinnon believes that even nonintercourse sex acts are rape. No one would understand the proposition that all sex is rape, by itself, in that way. Second, since "all sex" does not unambiguously mean sex under all possible social conditions, when she is charged with holding that all sex (intercourse) is rape, she has not necessarily been charged with holding that intercourse would be rape even under different social conditions. "All sex," if limited to intercourse, is literally unclear as between all sex in present conditions, all sex past and present; all actual sex past, present, and future; and all possible sex. It is certainly possible that the view attributed to MacKinnon under the phrase "all sex is rape" is the view that all intercourse under present conditions is rape. And that is pretty close to her view. (It is somewhat unclear in her work whether homosexual intercourse is exempted from this critique.)

While the resulting view does not include all sex, in its strongest possible sense, as rape, the view is radical enough to suggest an explanation for her otherwise odd refusal in this essay to try to clear up just what she does think. After persuasively arguing that the all-sex-is-rape view is pinned to her because it would so effectively discredit her views, it would hardly save her reputation to point out that her actual view is only that in our society ordinary heterosexual intercourse is rape.[17] It is surprising (and fortunate) that her actual views have not made her more of an intellectual outcast than they have. And it is no wonder that sometimes, as in this piece, she soft-pedals those views. It is serious soft-pedaling to suggest that there is no more truth to the all-sex-is-rape attribution than this:

> For allegedly *saying* this, or what is said to amount to this, women are vilified, shunned, unemployed, unpublished, scorned, trivialized, stigmatized, marginalized, threatened, ignored, personally hated by people we have never met, and unread. All this for what we *do* say: sexuality occurs in a context of gender inequality, a fact no hate propagandist has yet tried to rebut. (102)

Is MacKinnon's critique of ordinary heterosexual intercourse under gender inequality antisex? It is not antisex any more than a Marxist critique of labor as it exists under capitalism is antilabor.[18] It is not just another in a long line of efforts to suppress sexuality through censorship. It is not antidissent, it is not antisex, it seeks neither to preserve the status quo nor to return to a better time. I conclude that there is nothing conservative (in the present sense) about MacKinnon's critique of existing sexual relations nor in her motive, which is based on that critique, for legally regulating pornography. The critique of existing sexual relations is certainly discomfiting. Even if it is accurate, however, there is good reason for wondering whether regulation of pornography is an effective means of reform and whether it is likely, in its effects, to be liberating for women or not.

Estlund

Catharine MacKinnon is one of several writers who argue that pornography is sex. She writes, "Pornography is masturbation material. It is used as sex. It therefore is sex."[19] Sex itself is not generally protected by the First Amendment, so why should pornography be? MacKinnon asks us to see the viewer of pornographic pictures as in a sexual relationship with the models in those pictures. The women depicted really do the things that are documented in pictorial pornography. Men "experience this *being done* by watching it *being done*. What is real here is . . . that the materials . . . are a part of a sex act."[20]

This raises a good question: why should it make a legal difference whether the model and the man are in the same room with nothing but space between them, in different rooms separated by a glass partition,[21] far away with a real-time video connection,[22] for with the time-shifted video connection of a videotape? If a visit to a prostitute for voyeuristic sexual purposes is not (or should not be) protected speech, why should we think a videotape of the same performance, and used for the same purposes, is (or should be) protected? Frederick Schauer posed precisely this question in 1979,[23] and its power has been neglected by critics. David Estlund[24] explains the importance of this argument and the inadequacy of certain answers to it. He also proposes a constitutional argument that would support a difference in law between the voyeuristic visit, on the one hand, and the pornographic video, on the other. (As the author of the article, I shall limit myself to brief introductory comments here.)

The proposal for distinguishing the visit from the video involves interpreting the freedom of the press in the First Amendment as extending coverage to all published material regardless of whether it is speech. The video is typically published, and the visit is typically not. Material is published if it is (1) publishable in principle, which requires that it be expressive material, and (2) widely enough disseminated. Material that is covered may not all be protected since there may be narrow grounds for regulation of even covered material. But apart from those narrow exceptions, if any, published material ought to be protected as if it were speech, whether it is or not. There are historical and textual arguments for this reading of the press clause, as well as another rationale for such a protection: if one of the main reasons speech is protected is that there is a significant amount of speech that bears on matters of public or political concern, then that is exactly as good a reason for equally protecting the class of material that is intentionally published whether or not it is speech.

An interesting dichotomy between material that is tailored to the individual viewer and material that is repeated or disseminated in such a way that it is not tailored is also a source of difficulty for this analysis. Sexual uses of electronic technologies, for example, provide a number of borderline cases. Consider, for example, the service available on the Internet in which a paying customer at his computer directs a video camera at a remote location to "capture" desired images of a nude model in real time.[25] Estlund's analysis can treat a given episode as too tailored to count as a publication. But suppose the pictures that result from this process are available not just to the person directing the camera but also to anyone who chooses to link into this service at that time. Any distinction in law must face borderline cases, but sometimes they are so numerous and so central to the aims of the theory that the theory cannot survive them. These particular examples will be problems for lots of theories, of course, since they are bound not to fit neatly into our existing categories of commercial and private sexual activity and expression. Sexual use of computer technology is just one way in which our very concept of sexuality is changing, and law and legal theory are struggling to keep up.[26]

Notes

1. I take this second question from the title of a paper given by Naomi Scheman at University of Wisconsin, Philosophy Department Colloquium, circa 1985. She takes it from a story in which Tonto queries the Lone Ranger's suggestion, at the sight of some charging Native Americans, that "we're in trouble."

2. Mary Ann Glendon, *Abortion and Divorce in Western Law: American Failures, European Challenges* (Harvard University Press, 1987), p. 53.

3. Nussbaum never shows sympathy for the kind of social constructionism associated with Michel Foucault, in which interpersonal power is the central cause. On Nussbaum's view of the social construction of emotions, the central point is the cognitive dimension of emotions, which allows them to be culturally produced through teaching and learning.

4. Culture is relevant because insular marriage and reproductive practices are part of the cause.

5. *Justice, Gender, and the Family*, p. 177.

6. Posner discusses the evidence on this question, and cites some literature, in *Sex and Reason* (Harvard University Press, 1992), pp. 303–305.

7. By "freely" here I mean if there were both no effective social effort to produce a certain distribution and no employment discrimination based on prejudice against women.

8. Five states criminalize only same-sex sodomy, while an additional eighteen criminalize it for all.

9. MacKinnon engages with the "bed" analogy in several places, especially her n. 10 and accompanying text.

10. See, e.g., Cass Sunstein, "Porn on the Fourth of July," *New Republic*, Jan. 9, 16, 1995, p. 43, and Mari Matsuda, "Public Response to racist Speech: Considering the Victim's Story," in *Words That Wound*, ed. Mari Matsuda (Westview Press, 1993), pp. 35–35.

11. See Lynn Hunt, ed., *The Invention of Pornography: Obscenity and the Origins of Pornography: 1500–1800* (Zone Books, 1993).

12. It has also been made by many other feminists. See Carlin Meyer, "Sex, Sin, and Women's Liberation," *Texas Law Review*, 72 no.5 (April 1994), and Strossen *Defending Pornography* (Scribners, 1995), and references therein.

13. MacKinnon does undermine this rhetoric by referring the reader in the next sentence to pages 126–54 and 171–83 of *Toward a Feminist Theory of the State* (Harvard University Press, 1989).

14. *Feminism Unmodified* (Harvard University Press, 1987), p. 82. She continues, suggesting that this is neither the actual nor even the best *legal* way to define rape, however: "I'm not talking about sending all of you men to jail for that."

15. *Feminist Theory of the State*, p. 137.

16. 100 *Yale Law Journal* 1302–1303 (1991).

17. Or, if even my interpretation seems strained to you, substitute only "for women it is difficult to distinguish the two under conditions of male dominance" (*Feminist Theory of the State*, p. 174).

18. I leave aside here whether the views of *some* of its proponents might be fairly characterized as antisex. For that argument, see Myer, "Sex, Sin, and Liberation," and Strossen, *Defending Pornography*, and references therein.

19. *Only Words* (Harvard University Press, 1993), p. 17.

20. *Only Words*, p. 17.

21. Melanie Bush, *Village Voice*, "Workers' (Show) World," July 18, 1995, p. 15.

22. *World Wide Web*, "Virtual Dreams," http://www.virtualdreams.com/. Pornography-related sites on the Internet disappear regularly, sometimes from censorship, usually from unmanageable demand. This site was offering its software and service for a fee at the above Web address as of September 17, 1996.

23. Schauer, "Speech and 'Speech'—Obscenity and 'Obscenity': An Exercise in the Interpretation of Constitutional Language," 67 *Georgetown Law Review* 899 (1979).

24. Estlund is also the author of these comments.

25. *Web*, "Virtual Connections."

26. See issue of *Yale Law Journal* (May 1995) devoted to emerging technologies and the First Amendment.

Part III

PREFERENCE

8

The Economic Approach
to Homosexuality

Richard A. Posner

I want to summarize, and at the same time refine and extend, the economic analysis of homosexuality presented in my book *Sex and Reason*,[1] and relate analysis to the debate between essentialist and social-constructionist theories of homosexuality. I do not suggest that economics has the last word to say on homosexuality as a social phenomenon, but I do think that it can contribute to our understanding of the phenomenon and of proposals for reforming laws and social practices affecting it.

THE APPROACH DESCRIBED AND APPLIED
Homosexual Preference and Behavior

The basic assumption of economics, or at least of the brand of economics that I peddle, is instrumental rationality: the individual chooses the means that are most suitable, as a matter of both costs and benefits, to his ends, the latter usually being assumed to be given to him rather than freely chosen by him.[2] The choice of means need not be and often is not conscious, so there is no paradox in referring to rational choice by animals. And since as Martha Nussbaum and others have emphasized recently, emotion and reason are not necessarily antagonistic, there is also no paradox in supposing that sexual behavior, despite the intense emotions that precede and accompany it, may be rational.

The first step toward an economic theory of homosexuality is to distinguish between sexual desire, comprehending both appetite and preference, on the one hand, and sexual behavior, on the other hand. The first half of this opposition, which consists of both drive (sexual desire in the "push" sense) and attraction (sexual desire in the "pull" sense), determines ends; the second is a menu of means. The more intense a person's sexual appetite is, the more he will value sexual activity over other activities, while the structure of his sexual preferences will affect the value he attaches to different forms and objects of sexual activity and also to a variety of (in the sense of number—not of large differences among) sexual partners. Appetite or drive thus primarily affects substitutability between sexual and nonsexual activities, while preference primarily affects substitutability among different sexual activities. I believe that in general though of course not in every case, men have a greater interest in sex than women, a greater desire for frequent sex than women, and a greater taste for variety of sexual partners, by which I mean not a taste for bisexuality (though that may be true also) but a taste for multiple partners of the preferred sex. The empirical support for these assumptions, controversial though they are in feminist circles, is considerable, and there is a respectable although not conclusive biological theory that explains the empirical data.[3]

The difference between sexual desire and sexual behavior is not only important to economic analysis but also helpful in exposing an ambiguity in the concept of homosexuality. The concept could refer to a preference (strong or weak) for same-sex relations, or alternatively to the fact of engaging in same-sex relations (whether often or seldom), or even to some combination of preference and behavior—maybe the only "real" homosexual is one who both prefers same-sex relations and acts on his preference. I do not think it is fruitful or even possible to decide which meaning of homosexuality is best; indeed, the meaning of the word is highly mutable—for reasons that I believe are essentially economic. More on that later. For now, just so that the reader will understand what I am talking about, it is enough to note that in ordinary American English a "homosexual" is anyone who, other things being equal, prefers someone of the same sex as a sexual partner to someone of the opposite sex. In the language of economics, this "preference homosexual," as I will call him (or her), will buy more same-sex than other-sex relations if the full price (comprehending nonpecuniary as well as pecuniary factors) is the same. The perfect bisexual would then be one who will buy the same amount of each type of sex if the full price is the same. When I use the term "homosexual" I shall mean a preference homosexual unless I indicate otherwise.

The emphasis that I am placing on the distinction between homosexual *preference*[4] and homosexual *behavior* may seem misplaced in an economic analysis. Economists are known for their distrust of people's declared motives and their consequent insistence on inferring preferences from behavior ("revealed preference," or putting one's money where one's mouth is). But my approach is consistent with the revealed-preference tradition.[5] Homosexual preference in my analysis is inferred not from what a person says about his sexual preferences but from the behavioral choices that he makes *when confronting an equal price for heterosexual and homosexual relations.* The empirical measurement of homosexual preference so defined is obviously very difficult, but the conceptual focus on preference-revealing behavior is clear.

Homosexual preference as I am defining it is not uniform. Some people have a strong aversion to engaging in homosexual behavior; in my terms, they will avoid it even if it is much cheaper than heterosexual behavior. Other people have a strong aversion to engaging in heterosexual behavior. Kinsey devised a scale of zero to 6 to represent the range of homosexual preferences. A zero has only heterosexual preference, a 6 only homosexual preference. A 3 is a perfect bisexual, indifferent to the sex of his partner.

The preference spectrum probably is bimodal, in much the same way that "handedness" is bimodal. The vast majority of people are right-handed, a small minority are left-handed, and a tiny minority are ambidextrous, yet some right-handed people can write with their left hand without too much difficulty while some left-handed people can write with their right hand without much difficulty. If there is strong social pressure to write with the right hand, most left-handed people can learn to do so, but they will never be comfortable doing so. Similarly, the vast majority of people appear to have a strong heterosexual preference, although some of them regard a homosexual relationship as somewhat substitutable for a heterosexual one. A small minority, no greater than 3 to 4 percent of males and 1 to 2 percent of females,[6] have a strong homosexual preference but again some of these consider a heterosexual relationship substitutable although inferior. The number of people who are bisexual in the sense of regarding male and female sexual partners as being of essentially the same desirability, or even closely substitutable, is very small.

In an economic analysis, the values, shaped in part by location on the Kinsey scale, that people place on the various ends of sex, such as pleasure, cementing a relationship, disguising one's sexual preference, establishing, expressing, or reinforcing dominance, and producing children, determine, along with the different costs of the different kinds of sexual behavior, the amount and kinds of that behavior that people engage in. Obviously a man who has a strong homosexual preference will set a high value on homosexual relations. But if threat of punishment, religious scruples, fear of disease or of social ostracism, or desire for children cause the expected cost of such relations to exceed the expected benefit, he may, despite his preference, substitute heterosexual for homosexual relations. Or he may decide to forgo all sexual relations.

I can make the analysis a little more concrete by supposing a society which is intolerant of homosexuals and in which AIDS is rampant. (Some might think this an accurate description of our society.) A man who had a strong homosexual desire might nonetheless engage in a certain amount of heterosexual intercourse because he wanted children, because he wanted to pose as a heterosexual in order to avoid the social stigma and occupational and other economic discrimination that might be visited on a known homosexual, because AIDS made his preferred form of homosexual intercourse (for example, anal intercourse without condoms) too costly, or because repression made it costly for him to find other homosexuals with whom to have a relationship. Yet even in such a society a person of strong *heterosexual* preference might sometimes engage in *homosexual* behavior if he had a strong sex drive (implying a preference for another sexual activity, rather than a nonsexual activity, as a substitute for a most-preferred sexual activity that is unavailable) and the cost of heterosexual intercourse was very high, as it might be if he were confined to a sexually segregated institution such as a naval ship or a prison.

I hope I have indicated the basic character of the economic analysis. Even without the formalization dear to the modern economist, the analysis yields interesting, testable, and to some extent supported hypotheses about homosexual behavior. The most dramatic is the well-substantiated substitution of safe sex for unsafe sex by male homosexuals in the wake of the AIDS epidemic.[7] The cost of unsafe sex having risen, there was substitution toward safe sex. This involved a greater use of condoms in anal intercourse, a reduction in the average number of sexual partners per male homosexual, and a tendency to substitute relatively safe activities such as oral intercourse and mutual masturbation for anal intercourse, which (if unshielded) is much more likely to transmit the AIDS virus. Safe sex is not a perfect substitute for unsafe sex even when it is perfectly safe. If it were, we would expect not only complete rather than partial substitution of safe for unsafe sex, but also that the substitution would have occurred *before* the AIDS epidemic, since other sexually transmitted diseases were rampant among homosexuals before AIDS came on the scene. Since safe sex must therefore be perceived by homosexuals as costly, we should expect that AIDS has caused not only some substitution toward safe sex but also some reduction in the amount of homosexual sex, though not as great a reduction as would occur if safe sex were not an option. One alternative to sex is abstinence, so the more costly sex is, the more abstinence we should expect.

Many examples of rational homosexual behavior can be organized around the concept of sexual search cost, defined here as the cost incurred in matching up with a suitable sexual partner. It is not just an information cost. If it were, it would be zero rather than, in my formulation, infinite if a person were confined in a place where he knew there were no potential sexual partners for him.

The concept of sexual search cost is helpful in explaining why homosexuals are concentrated in cities, and not all cities but usually just one or several per country, depending on the size.[8] If homosexuals were distributed proportionately equally rather than concentrated in a small number of locales, the cost of search would be very high because the fraction of the total population that is homosexual is so small. To take an extreme example, a man might be the only homosexual in his village, so that to find a sexual partner of his preferred type he would have to incur substantial time and travel costs. These costs are greatly reduced if homosexuals cluster in a few places where, because of their concentration, there is a large homosexual population to search over.

This analysis is incomplete in two respects. First, the example of the village that contains a single homosexual, while useful for exposition, rather loads the dice. Suppose the village has two homosexuals. Then it can be argued that each is at least as well off as he would be in a city that had a large population of homosexuals. Although he would have many more potential sexual partners to choose among in the city, he would face much greater competition there for the sexual partner of his choice. This assumes, however, what is always perilous in dealing with male sexuality, indifference to variety in sexual partners. (And we should therefore expect less geographical concentration of lesbians than of gay men, since women, including lesbians, have on average less taste for variety of sexual partners.[9]) Experience with the dating, cohabiting, and marriage markets suggests, moreover, that satisfactory matching of sexual partners requires search across a large sample of possible partners because of the highly idiosyncratic character of persons when viewed as candidates for an intimate relationship. If satisfactory homosexual sorting requires a large sample to search over, the effect of a concentrated population of homosexuals in reducing search costs is likely to dominate the costs of increased competition. Of course much homosexual (also heterosexual) sex is of the "spot market" kind—the anonymous encounter in the restroom, or with a prostitute—and here the relational aspect is minimized. But anonymous sex implies a large number of potential sexual partners, for which a large concentration of the relevant population is necessary.

Second, we must consider the phenomenon of pairing off. Suppose that precisely as a consequence of low search costs in cities in which homosexuals are concentrated, the homosexuals in those cities pair off in couples, leaving few unattached homosexuals for newcomers to date. Then the opportunities for the newcomers might not be much better than in the small towns from which they had come. But because men have, as I believe and have been emphasizing, a greater desire for variety of sexual partners than women do, male homosexual couples tend to be less stable than heterosexual (or lesbian) couples are.[10] This may be changing as a result of AIDS, which has raised the cost, especially to (male) homosexuals, of having multiple sexual partners. We might therefore expect that large cities would be losing some of their attractiveness to homosexuals. Another benefit of city life for homosexuals is that it is easier to escape detection in a big city. So we can expect that tolerant societies have less geographical imbalance in their homosexual population than intolerant ones do, since the benefits of concealing homosexual preference are smaller in tolerant societies.

The concept of sexual search costs may help explain why many though of course not all homosexuals have an "effeminate" manner, in the sense of gait, posture, speech, mannerisms, or style of dressing recognizably distinct from the corresponding ensemble for the "straight" man. Women are easily distinguishable from men even in casual encounters because of gross physical differences especially of shape and voice. But homosexuals are not easy to distinguish from their heterosexual counterparts, so the adoption of a distinctive manner[11] enables sexual preference to be signaled (as in a memorable passage in Proust, describing the first meeting between Charlus and Jupien), thus reducing the costs of homosexual search. The signal is not entirely clear, because some heterosexual men are effeminate.[12] But the unclarity may actually be valuable to homosexuals in a repressive society, because then "straights" cannot be certain that an effeminate man is a homosexual. This point suggests the possibility that there might be less, rather than (as one might expect) more, effeminacy in a tolerant society than in an intolerant one. This is an example of a point to which I shall return, that economics supports, though only in part, the social constructionists' view of homosexuality.

The substitutability of sexual practices is often ignored in discussions of public policy, for example, policy toward AIDS. Conservatives, observing that homosexuals and bisexuals are a major source for transmission of the disease, suppose that measures to repress homosexuality would reduce the spread of the disease. This is not clear. One effect of repression is to increase the benefits of (heterosexual) marriage to persons of homosexual preference, since such marriage both facilitates the concealment of homosexual preference and provides an alternative sexual outlet that is more desirable the more costly the preferred alternative of homosexual relations is made. Consistent with this hypothesis, it appears that homosexuals are in fact more likely to marry in repressive than in tolerant societies.[13] A married homosexual may engage in homosexual relations on the side, contract AIDS, and transmit it to his wife—especially since his proposing that they have safe sex could be a tip-off to his double life. From the standpoint of controlling AIDS, therefore, it might make sense to legalize homosexual marriage, which by lowering the cost of durable homosexual pairing off would reduce homosexual promiscuity, a factor in the rapid spread of AIDS in the homosexual community. A further point is that a reduction in the social stigma of homosexuality would reduce the incentive of homosexuals to cluster in cities, where they can form their own insulated communities. This is potentially important from the standpoint of public health because the concentration of a potentially infective population, unless the concentration results from or has the effect of quarantining that population, can accelerate the spread of a disease by increasing the number of persons exposed to it. Concentrating the homosexual population reduces the search cost of homosexuals who desire sex with multiple sex partners, a recognized risk factor for AIDS; encouraging that population to disperse (encouragement that homosexual marriage might provide) would therefore reduce homosexual promiscuity and with it the spread of the epidemic.

Some conservatives who are concerned about the AIDS epidemic support the laws, found in about half the states of the United States, criminalizing sodomy. They believe that the effect of those laws is to induce abstinence from homosexual acts or at least to reduce the number of such acts. But simple economics can help us to see that a more realistic goal of policy would be to forbid only those homosexual acts that are likely to transmit AIDS. Although historically "sodomy" meant anal intercourse, most American sodomy statutes explicitly forbid oral as well as anal intercourse and impose the same penalty on both practices. (Hardwick of *Bowers v. Hardwick* fame had been caught engaging in oral, not anal, intercourse and charged with sodomy.) This is a mistake. Homosexuals should be encouraged to substitute oral for anal intercourse, because it is very difficult to transmit the AIDS virus by oral sex. For the same reason they should be encouraged to substitute anal intercourse with condoms for anal intercourse without—yet both are punishable with equal severity under the existing sodomy laws.

Although if sodomy laws are to be retained they should be confined to unshielded anal intercourse, in order, as I have said, to channel homosexual behavior into safer forms, the economic case for their retention is very weak. As with other consensual crimes, the costs of enforcement are very high—so high that the sodomy laws are virtually unenforced. And cost is not the only factor; public support for criminalizing voluntary sexual relations between adults, even when the relations are homosexual, is weak. The benefits of an unenforced law are low, and here probably negative; the sodomy laws contribute to an atmosphere of hostility toward homosexuals that undermines efforts to contain the AIDS epidemic, for the reasons noted above.

Were sodomy laws enforced, they would impose heavy costs on homosexuals, much as forbidding vaginal intercourse would with respect to heterosexuals. Because of AIDS and other serious sexually transmitted diseases, characteristic homosexual practices such as unshielded anal intercourse impose external costs, by increasing the risk of disease to future sexual partners (and to *their* future sexual partners) of a person who might become infected through such practices. Hence an act of homosexual intercourse, even when between fully competent and consenting adults, cannot be considered Pareto superior to the no-intercourse case because it does not make at least one person in the world better off and no one worse off. But since sexually transmitted diseases are preventable at moderate cost by safe sex, it is unlikely that a policy of banning homosexual intercourse, even if such a policy were enforceable at reasonable cost, would increase social welfare in the economic sense, which emphasizes the satisfaction of preferences. A more direct way of dealing with the externality problem, and a method now employed by a number of states, is to criminalize the knowing exposure of one's sexual partners to the AIDS virus.

Opportunistic Homosexual

Thus far I have been discussing the behavior of persons of predominantly homosexual preference. The other half of the picture is composed of persons of predominantly heterosexual preference who nevertheless engage in homosexual behavior when the cost of heterosexual behavior is prohibitive. We should not be surprised that heterosexuals in prisons, navies and merchant marines, monasteries, boarding schools, and other sexually segregated institutions frequently resort to homosexual acts because their heterosexual opportunities are highly limited or even nonexistent. Preferring as they do heterosexual to homosexual sex, these "opportunistic" homosexuals like to play the insertive role in oral and anal intercourse because that is closer to the male role in heterosexual sex, and they prefer teenage boys to grown men because the former are physically more like women, being, typically, smaller and more delicate than grown men and having less body hair, softer skin, and higher-pitched voices. In other words these men seek, in good economizing fashion, the closest possible substitute that they can find for their preferred, but prohibitively costly, sexual activity.

The character of opportunistic male homosexuality—also the concept of sexual substitutability and the relation of drive to object—is nicely captured in this passage about Brendan Behan, the Irish poet and playwright, by his biographer:

> Where matters of sex were concerned, he was attracted to his own as well as to the opposite sex. It was more an excess of appetite than a particular preference for one sex or the other. He was, in fact, sexually attracted to women more than men. But long periods of his life had been spent in Borstal or in prison, and in the confinement of such male enclaves he had experimented in order to assuage an unusually active sexual drive . . . Brendan, contrary to having any regret about his wide range of sexual indulgence, would assert that it was a necessary activity in prison or after "forty days at sea": "Listen, Ben, for Jasus' sake, do you see that young soldier over there, you'd take him before you'd take Eleanor Roosevelt."[14]

We should distinguish among sexually segregated institutions along the dimension of voluntariness. Imprisonment is (at least if one ignores the decision to become a criminal) involuntary. Becoming a priest is voluntary. (Service on naval ships is sometimes involuntary, more often voluntary.) We should therefore expect a higher fraction of priests than of prisoners to be persons of predominantly homosexual preference. The cost of being denied heterosexual opportunities is lower for such persons than it is for persons of predominantly heterosexual preference, so the former are

more likely to self-select into a career in which heterosexual opportunities are reduced. It is true that in medieval Europe, boys were frequently steered into the priesthood, and girls into nunneries, by their parents, rather than choosing freely. Yet the
selection bias described above might still operate. Suppose, as was common among
medieval families from which priests and nuns were recruited, that dowries were demanded in marriage. Then fathers of teenage girls would tend to steer the less marriageable girls into nunneries, because such girls would require larger dowries; and
among these less marriageable girls lesbians would probably be overrepresented,
since some lesbians have a "masculinate" manner that is unattractive to men.
Likewise, fathers of boys would tend to steer their less marriageable sons into the
priesthood, because these boys, among whom homosexuals would tend to be overrepresented, would not do well in competition for brides having large dowries.

  Since, however, homosexual acts are more disapproved within the clerical community than within the prison subculture, the frequency of homosexual acts may be
greater in prisons than among priests at the same time that the fraction of persons with
a predominantly homosexual preference is larger among the latter. This point illustrates the difference between homosexual preference and homosexual behavioral—
indeed, in this particular example the two phenomena are correlated negatively.

  Signaling is a pertinent consideration when we consider homosexuality in the
American Catholic priesthood today. Because priests are not permitted to marry, the
priesthood is a good place for a homosexual to "hide"; his status as a bachelor is less
likely to be taken as evidence of homosexuality than if he were permitted to marry.
Many bachelors, of course, are heterosexual. But because the fraction of bachelors
that is homosexual is undoubtedly much higher than the fraction of married men that
is homosexual, bachelorhood is often considered evidence of possible homosexuality. (Notice that as the marriage rate declines in a society, this signal becomes weaker.) As a society becomes more tolerant of homosexuality, so that the benefit of the
closet declines, the percentage of homosexual priests will decline; likewise, of
course, if the priesthood were opened to married men, as Andrew Greeley and other
prominent American Catholics advocate.

  The sexually segregated institution is only the most dramatic illustration of the
general proposition that the prevalence of homosexual behavior is an inverse function of the sexual availability of women to men. The less available that women are to
men for sexual activity, the higher the price (not necessarily or even primarily pecuniary) of heterosexual sex and hence the greater should be the substitution toward
homosexual sex. There is more competition for women in a polygamous society[15]
than there is in a monogamous one. In a polygamous society, men are not limited to a
single wife. The result is a scarcity of women, particularly for younger men, who on
average have fewer resources with which to obtain a wife. We should therefore expect opportunistic homosexuality to be greater, other things being equal, in a polygamous than in a monogamous society and to take the form primarily of pederasty, that
is, a sexual relationship between a man and a boy. That is the form of homosexual
behavior preferred by persons of predominantly heterosexual preference because, as
I said, boys are more like women than grown men are. Moreover, we expect the ped-
erasts in the polygamous society to be found primarily among young rather than
older men, because it is the former who cannot afford wives.

Female prostitution, it is true, would be an alternative to pederasty as a way of meeting the sexual demands of bachelors. But in a polygamous society women are costly because of their scarcity relative to the demand, so prostitution is likely to be expensive. In an economic sense, the cost of prostitution includes the opportunity that the woman gives up by being a prostitute. The more she is in demand as a wife, the more she gives up, hence the higher the compensation that she will demand for working as a prostitute. Of course if there is slavery the price of prostitutes may plummet.

Even a monogamous society may have an imbalance in favor of women that, by driving up the price of heterosexual (including marital) sex, increases the demand for what I am calling opportunistic homosexuality. In ancient Athens the widespread practice of female infanticide and the sequestration of nubile girls in order to satisfy the demand for virgin brides limited the access of young bachelors of the citizen class to sexual partners of the same class but opposite sex. One is therefore not surprised that pederasty (as celebrated for example in Plato's dialogues on love) appears to have been common in the citizen class.[16] But perhaps one *should* be surprised, because prostitution was also common, making the situation unlike that of a polygamous society, a prison, a naval vessel, and other familiar sites of opportunistic homosexuality, where access to women is prohibitively costly. It is true that the prostitutes of Athens were foreign or lower-class women and so could not fully satisfy the romantic longings of the young men of the citizen class, and that, consistent with this point, Platonic and other ancient Greek pederastic literature emphasizes the mental and spiritual aspect of the pederastic relationships rather than the physical, though this emphasis may contain a large measure of rationalization. It is also true that while many men today, and doubtless in ancient Athens as well, would not consider any sort of boy a substitute for any sort of woman, we have no reason to suppose that pederasty was universal among the citizen class in Athens or even that it was a dominant social practice—only that it was more common, hence more likely to be socially approved or at least tolerated, than it is in a society such as ours in which girls are not killed at birth or sequestered until marriage. And it is true, finally, that in the citizen class of ancient Athens marriage was characteristically a relationship between radically unequal persons—an older man, educated, active in the world, and a young woman (often a teenage girl), uneducated and home-bound—and that this inequality, exemplified by the fact that Athenian husbands and wives were not expected to take any of their meals together and that child tending was considered a task for male slaves rather than for the child's mother, must have reduced the affective value of marriage and may thereby have shifted the focus of romantic theorizing to socially more equal relationships. One of these was the relationship between a young bachelor and his *gymnasium* boy lover.

Yet with all these points granted, the puzzle of widespread pederasty in a society in which prostitutes were plentiful and cheap persists. If a compassionate relation sealed by sex was sought, why did the young bachelors not pair up with each other, rather than chase boys?[17] One can easily imagine opportunistic homosexuality between men of the same age and status emerging in a society, such as that of ancient Athens, in which men were considered superior to women. From such a premise it would be natural to infer that relationships among men are superior to relationships between men and women (and *a fortiori* women and women—the Greeks thought lesbianism unnatural) and that the relationship could be completed, sealed, perfected by physical intimacy, like the exchange of blood in a "blood brotherhood." There is a demand for compassionate relationships; and sex, as I argue in *Sex and Reason,* can cement such a relationship. If companionship with women is infeasible, men will substitute companionship with men and may cement it with sex. Endowed as they are with a superfluity of procreative capacity, many men are sufficiently sexually indiscriminate to incur little cost from the eroticization of the male bond. On this interpretation, the very absence of compassionate marriage, and other forms of compassionate relationships with women, increases male bonding, and male bonding is incipiently or potentially homoerotic because of the function of sex in sealing relationships.

The analysis is incomplete, however, because it points to homosexual relations between men of the same age, not to pederasty, which appears to have been the dominant form of opportunistic homosexuality in the ancient Greek world. But if same-sex relations are more pleasurable for a heterosexual man when the sexual object is boyish and therefore more like a woman, he will trade off this benefit of pederasty against the companionate benefit of a more equal relation and may therefore choose the former, although Plato's *Symposium* suggests that for some men in ancient Greece the compassionate benefit of equal-age same-sex relationships exceeded the sexual cost.[18]

Another element in Greek pederasty may have been the rivalrous.[19] Men compete for women, both to spread their seed and to establish a hierarchy of male power. Competitive masculinity is a dimension of sexuality different from companionship but also missing from relations with prostitutes. Greek-style pederasty provided an outlet for this aspect of male sexual desire. Something like this also figures in homosexual activity in prisons. It is distinct from the domination-subordination theme that I discuss at the end of this chapter because my interest here is not in the relative position of man (over) and boy (beloved)—the *erastes* and the *eromenos*—but in the relative position of the competing men. However, like my previous point this one does depend in part on the boys' resembling women, because the competition is a substitute for a heterosexual competition.

Given the salience of pederasty in Athenian culture, or at least in elite circles of that culture, it may seem curious that the ancient Greeks lacked a distinct idea of homosexuality in the modern American sense, that is, as a strong preference for same-sex over opposite-sex relations. (Similarly, men in macho societies will frequently deny that there are any homosexuals in their society.) There are, I conjecture, two reasons for the difference, both of which are congruent with and indeed support the economic approach. First, the more common that opportunistic homosexuality is, the less likely are people to be aware of the existence of homosexual preference. Opportunistic homosexuals, remember, are persons of heterosexual rather than homosexual preference. Since preference homosexuals appear to be a small minority in all societies, homosexual behavior in a society in which opportunistic homosexuality is common will tend to be dominated by persons of heterosexual rather than of homosexual preference, making the latter inconspicuous. Second, the emotional distance in the average Athenian marriage would have reduced the cost to preference homosexuals of marrying, since they could fulfill their (meager) marital duties at low cost to themselves.[20] With homosexuals able to fit smoothly into the basic institution of the society, their homosexual preference lacked social significance—was unremarkable and therefore unremarked, much like left-handedness today.

With the rise of compassionate marriage, conceived of as marriage between at least approximate equals, homosexuals found it more costly to marry; marriage now involved a degree of intimacy difficult to achieve without a bond of mutual sexual desire. Companionate marriage tends to extrude what I am calling preference homosexuals from a basic social institution, namely marriage, making them more conspicuous and thus for the first time riveting public attention on the existence of a class of persons whose sexual preferences differ from those of the majority. A further point is that adultery is a more serious offense in a regime of compassionate marriage, and homosexual activity by a married man is a form of adultery.

It may seem odd that until almost the end of the Victorian era, men whom we today would call homosexuals tended to be thought of as normal men of vicious, unbridled appetite. But in a society that placed a high premium on virginity and hence tended to the sequestration and sexual anesthetization of marriageable (and married) women, many men of strong sexual appetite would lack adequate heterosexual outlets and some of them would turn to homosexual sex (others of course to female prostitutes). These men would differ from ordinary heterosexuals only in tending to have more intense sexual appetites and—a closely related point, especially in an economic analysis—to lack "self-control" (because the stronger an impulse is, the more difficult, or in other words costlier, it is to repress it). Because Victorian like ancient Athenian marriages were often deficient in intimacy, men of homosexual preference like Oscar Wilde could have successful or at least unremarkable marriages. So again awareness that there was a class of men of distinctly homosexual preference was muted. The salient category was sodomites, not homosexuals.

I have been considering the demand of the opportunistic homosexual for a woman substitute but one must also consider the demand of the preference homosexual for male sex partners whether or not themselves preference homosexuals. I conjecture that a handsome heterosexual man will have, on average, more homosexual experience (opportunistic on his side) than a heterosexual man who is not handsome. Men, whether heterosexual or homosexual, attach more value to good looks in a sexual partner than women do. So a handsome man will have more of a competitive advantage over homely men in the homosexual than in the heterosexual sex market.

Lesbianism

I have thus far focused almost entirely on *male* homosexuals. I shall not apologize for failing to give equal time to both sexes. Male homosexual activity and preference as well appear to be far more common than female homosexual activity and preference, and have far more often been the subject of government regulation; England for example had no laws against lesbian sex at a time when homosexual sodomy was a capital offense. Moreover, male homosexuality has been made socially problematic by the AIDS epidemic in a way that lesbianism has not—lesbian relations do not transmit the AIDS virus. But economics does have something to say about lesbianism. As

with male homosexuality, we should expect the relative costs of heterosexual and homosexual behavior to affect the relative prevalence of these behaviors among women
of homosexual preference. Since prostitutes have difficulty forming durable, emotionally adequate relationships with men, it is no surprise that lesbianism is common
among prostitutes.[21] Whether, overall, opportunistic homosexuality is more common
among women than among men is difficult to say. On the one hand, since the demand
for sex appears to be on average weaker among women than among men, women are
less likely to encounter the problem of unavailability of preferred sexual outlets and
therefore are less likely to substitute a less preferred outlet. On the other hand, precisely because the demand for sex is on average weaker among women than among
men, we can expect women to be more likely to substitute toward same-sex relations
if there are nonsexual reasons to do so. Together these two points suggest the following pair of testable hypotheses: the "sexual revolution" of the 1960s and 1970s, by expanding the heterosexual opportunities of women (in part by reducing the cost of sex
to women—the contraceptive pill being the key factor in this cost reduction), reduced
the amount of opportunistic lesbianism; the feminist movement of the 1970s and
1980s (and continuing into the 1990s), by promoting hostility toward men by some
women, has increased the amount of opportunistic lesbianism.

Normative Analysis

Although I have now broadened my canvass to take in lesbianism, the focus has remained on positive rather than normative economic analysis—on explaining phenomena rather than on changing public policy, though I veered into the latter subject
when I was discussing AIDS-actuated public policies toward male homosexuality.
Economics has value in the normative as well as the positive domain of sexual analysis. Although I have already discussed homosexual marriage, I want to add that an
economic analyst, at least one of free-market bent, is unlikely to place much emphasis on expanding so heavily regulated an institution as marriage. It is true that modern marriage is a matter of free choice and is dissoluble almost as easily as a contract
of partnership. But the contracting parties' freedom is constrained because the married couple is not permitted to make a legally enforceable agreement on all the terms,
including duration and the consequences of dissolution, of their "contract." There is
an economic argument for deregulating marriage, thereby transforming it in the direction of cohabitation contracts, where the parties choose their own terms. Then the
strong statement of commitment implicit in a decision to marry under the present
legal regime for marriage would give way to an equally strong, if not indeed
stronger, commitment implicit in a decision to marry, or (if one wants to reserve the
term "marriage" for the familiar, regulated institution) cohabit, by a contract ter-
minable only by death, serious wrongdoing, or other dramatic change of circumstance. There should have to be protective provisions for children in any potentially
procreative union. But with that important proviso (of limited but, because of the
possibility of adoption and of artificial insemination, not negligible applicability to
homosexual unions as well as heterosexual ones), I do not believe that there is a persuasive economic basis for resisting an evolution from status to contract, resulting in
an essentially uniform treatment for homosexuals and heterosexuals.

Other important issues in public policy toward homosexuality include job discrimination, with specific reference to the exclusion of homosexuals from the military; child custody; and age of consent (in this country invariably higher for homosexual than for heterosexual relations, in those states that do not forbid homosexual intercourse). Here again I think the economic perspective is helpful, but, even more clearly than before, not decisive. I have already discussed, in reference to AIDS, the issue of retaining the sodomy laws. I shall further illustrate normative economic analysis of homosexuality with the ban on homosexuals in the armed forces,[22] leaving the other topics to the discussion in *Sex and Reason*.[23] Apart from symbolic issues and (what is closely related) the implications for the self-esteem and social acceptance of homosexuals generally, there are two obvious costs of the ban. First, to the extent enforced it reduces the field of selection, thus forcing the government to pay higher wages or other compensation to military personnel because there is less competition for positions; in other words, the ban reduces the supply of applicants for military jobs, although, in part because it was porous even before the recent modifications,[24] probably not by much. More important are the costs of enforcing the ban; they are not trivial. There is, however, a potentially offsetting benefit: to the extent that heterosexuals do not want to serve beside homosexuals, the removal of the ban would increase military personnel costs; the government would have to pay higher wages to hire and retain heterosexual personnel. This effect, which need not be completely offset by the greater supply of potential recruits from the homosexual population, implies that even if the leadership of the Department of Defense had no hostile feelings toward homosexuals, and indeed believed (on good evidence) that they make just as good soldiers as heterosexuals do, it might maintain the ban on homosexuals in order to minimize overall personnel costs, in just the same way that, were it not for the laws forbidding racial discrimination in employment, a nonbigoted employer might refuse to hire blacks because his white workers would demand a wage premium for incurring the perceived disutility of working in proximity to blacks. The very symmetry between these hypothetical arguments for racial discrimination and for discrimination against homosexuals will for many people condemn the latter form of discrimination without regard to economic considerations. But I wish to abstract from other considerations.[25]

Which means that I also want to abstract from the question whether the relaxation of the ban against homosexuals in the military would reduce operational effectiveness by impairing the morale of heterosexuals. That is an issue, in the first instance at least, of military science or art, rather than of economics, and I will not try to address it here. I have merely pointed out that even if the issue were ignored, there might be an economic argument for retaining the ban. Other arguments might outweigh it; it is enough for my purposes here to point out that economic analysis does not tell us whether, on balance, the ban on homosexuals in the military should be retained or abolished.

This is a general point about the economic analysis of sexual practices. Suppose it is the case—it is the case in this country today—that there is a large reservoir of apparently unreasoning fear of and hostility toward homosexuals, so that many people would derive utility from measures to repress homosexual activity. Should that utility be weighed equally with the utility that homosexuals derive from homosexual activity, in deciding whether repressive measures are efficient? The answer to that question is "no" for those who, like John Stuart Mill or Ronald Dworkin, reject, as illegitimate sources of public policy, what Mill called preferences with regard to the "self-regarding" conduct of other people and Dworkin calls "external preferences." But to defend this position (as I tried to do in *Sex and Reason*) would carry me outside the boundaries of economics as they are generally understood today and therefore outside the scope of this paper.

ECONOMICS AND THE SOCIAL CONSTRUCTION
OF SEXUALITY

I promised to relate the economic analysis of homosexuality to the debate between essentialists and social constructionists over the nature of homosexuality. There are two related but distinct axes of debate. The first and less important is over whether homosexual preference is more or less fixed or innate, on the one hand, or a matter of choice on the other. There is increasing evidence that the strong homosexual preference that marks a person in our society as "a homosexual" (or a lesbian) is probably genetic, if not genetic, congenital; if neither, then the product of physical or psychological factors impinging on persons in their infancy.[26] It is of no importance to my economic analysis which it is. The analysis would be affected if homosexual preference, like homosexual behavior, were chosen. But that seems extraordinarily unlikely.

Although many homosexual-rights advocates resist, primarily it seems on political grounds,[27] genetic and other biological theories of homosexuality, none of those advocates as far as I know claims or believes that homosexual preference is something one adopts or cultivates, as one might cultivate a taste for classical music or fine wines. If they thought this they would be playing into the hands of the religious right, which believes that homosexuality can be prevented if potential homosexuals are prevented from engaging in homosexual behavior, which might give them a taste for it—and can even be "cured" by society's somehow inducing homosexuals to confine themselves to heterosexual behavior until they develop a taste for it. This idea of preference following behavior is reminiscent of the argument that Hamlet makes to his mother—that if she refrains from sexual relations with her husband one night it will strengthen her will to refrain the next, and the next, and eventually every night.

The center ring in the debate over social construction is a debate not over the mutability of individual sexual preference,[28] or even over the relative importance of nature and culture in shaping not only human behavior; certainly the economist readily acknowledges the significance of social forces in affecting costs and benefits. The testing case is the mutability of human nature at the deep level that includes sexual preference. A representative social-constructionist thesis, in which the influence of Foucault is palpable, is that homosexuality was invented little more than a century ago by European psychiatrists, so that when we speak of the "homosexuality" of the ancient Athenians we are necessarily speaking of a different phenomenon from twentieth-century American homosexuality—further evidence being that the effeminacy that some believe to be a "natural" characteristic of homosexuality was not a feature of Greek homosexuality.[29]

As should be plain from my earlier discussion of types of homosexuality, I believe that economics provides qualified support for the social constructionists' analysis of homosexuality. If by "homosexuality" we mean not a particular class of preferences or a particular class of acts but a concept or definition prevailing in a particular society at a particular time, ancient Greek homosexuality is indeed a different phenomenon from modern American homosexuality. I have argued that the Greek concept probably was dominated by the practice of pederasty by opportunistic homosexuals (that is, heterosexuals by preference), while the American concept is dominated by the practices of "real" homosexuals in the sense of persons who have a strong homosexual preference. And not only is effeminacy a characteristic associated with "preference homosexuals" (or with the male partners of opportunistic homosexuals) rather than with opportunistic homosexuals. I have pointed out that it is likely to be adopted consciously as a signaling strategy by preference homosexuals who, especially in a society intolerant of homosexuality, may have difficulty identifying each other and may use the ambiguous signal of effeminacy to reduce sexual search costs without completely giving themselves away to the "straights."

If any social constructionists believe that no men or women had strong preferences for same-sex over different-sex relations until the word "homosexuality" was coined in the second half of the nineteenth century,[30] I think they simply are wrong. A person can have a feeling without being able to name it—infants have feelings before they can speak, and animals have feelings; the second example is particularly important, given the insistent parallels between human and animal sexuality—given that we *are* animals. You can't have a desire for a pizza before the pizza is invented, but you could be hungry before then;[31] I think sexual orientation is more like hunger than it is like desire for an invented product like a pizza. If all—and it is not a little—that social-constructionism is taken to entail is that the expression (or concealment) of homosexual preference in particular sexual practices and mannerisms, the geographical dispersion or concentration of homosexuals, the amount of homosexual behavior, and the culturally dominant concept of homosexuality are different across societies and epochs and that many societies lack a distinct concept of homosexual preference (for which the word "homosexuality" was coined) because the practice of homosexuality in those societies is dominated by heterosexuals,[32] I agree against anyone who suggests that Plato and Freud were talking about the same thing when they discussed the sexual desire of males for males. In between these positions is Martha Nussbaum's suggestion that the social conditions in ancient Athens increased not only the demand for pederasty, but also the desire for it.[33] In my analysis, sexual preference is a constant, and changes in social conditions alter behavior merely by changing the costs and benefits associated with different forms of sexual behavior. So scarcity of women might induce pederasty, or savage punishments for sodomy induce homosexuals to marry, without any effect on preference (disposition, inclination). This is the point where, in my analysis, social construction runs out.

I similarly do not believe, as might a more convinced social constructionist, that the preference of Athenian bachelors for boys over each other reflected an inability, in a society in which heterosexual relations were virtually by definition relations between unequals (a dominant male and a subordinate female), to visualize sexual relations between equals, such as two adult males of the citizen class. If that were true, we would expect opportunistic male homosexuality to be less pederastic the more sexually egalitarian the society was. I do not believe that this pattern holds. But here is an excellent example of a case in which economic analysis and radical constructionism generate incompatible—and testable—hypotheses.

William Eskridge, in a learned and fascinating review of *Sex and Reason*, invokes Foucault to support a less radical version of the social construction of human sexuality than I have been considering so far, yet a version that Eskridge considers antithetical to pragmatism and that he offers in criticism of the pragmatic character of the reforms in the legal treatment of homosexuals proposed in my book.[34] I suggested that the ban on homosexuals in the military be relaxed rather than eliminated altogether, and while I urged that homosexuals be permitted to form domestic partnerships I fell short of advocating that homosexual marriage be authorized. My position strikes Eskridge as pragmatic in taking existing attitudes and institutions for granted as a baseline from which to make strictly incremental changes. A social constructionist perspective, he believes, would demonstrate the mutability of the baseline—that there is nothing natural about hostility to homosexuals or about heterosexual marriage, that these are social constructs which will change as fast as society changes. The suggestion that pragmatism and social constructionism are opposed is at first glance puzzling. For is it not the pragmatic project "to refloat the world, to make it less stationary and more transitional, to make descriptions of it correspondingly looser, less technical, more uncertain"?[35] What better description of the social-constructionist project could be imagined?

The difference is this. Social constructionists, when they turn normative, tend to be Utopian. Sensing the fluidity of all social arrangements, they believe that a slight nudge might bring about a social revolution. Pragmatism does not entail incrementalism or venerate the status quo, but neither does it teach that the rejection of foundationalism entails a denial of the stubbornness of attitudes or the inertia of institutions. A pragmatic reformer is concerned with what works and therefore cannot ignore public opinion or political realities merely by noting that the things he wants to change are not rooted in nature but instead are "mere" social constructs. I agree that hostility to homosexuals and limits on who may marry are social constructs, that they do not have the weight of nature or the moral law behind them. Hostility to homosexuals is not a feature of all human societies and therefore is unlikely to have a biological basis; and while heterosexual marriage is closely connected to human biology, the recognition of marriage between homosexuals would not violate any biological imperative. What the authors of the Bible thought about homosexuality is not likely to move the pragmatist, who sees nothing in principle to prevent a sudden overthrow of established attitudes and institutions and knows plenty of cases in which fears of the consequences of radical changes—such changes as allowing religious or political freedom or dismantling the laws segregating the races or admitting women into the legal profession—proved to be unfounded. But hostility to homosexuals in American society today is no less a brute fact for not having a credible biological or supernatural basis, and it is a fact that any responsible policy maker must take into account in considering proposals for reform. It is not the case that attitudes that do not have a biological basis are always easy to change. We must not ride Blake and Emerson and Nietzsche to the conclusion that every feature of the social landscape is no stronger than the facades of a Potemkin village, no more stable than the turn of a kaleidoscope. Ethnic and religious hatred are examples of tenacious though irrational beliefs that the serious political reformer must treat as hard social facts though not accept as permanent realities; and they happen to be examples that hatred of homosexuals resembles. The immediate establishment by legal fiat of complete equality between homosexuals and heterosexuals may be as unrealistic in the contemporary American setting as complete racial and sexual equality would have been in 1850. Social constructionism has not abolished reality, pragmatically defined as the domain of the—temporarily—impossible.

Notes

This paper appears in somewhat different form as chapter 26 of my book *Overcoming Law* (1985) and was revised in November 1994. I thank Janet Halley, Lawrence Lessig, and Martha Nussbaum for many helpful comments on a previous draft.

1. Richard A. Posner, *Sex and Reason* (1992) (hereinafter cited by title only); see index references to "Homosexuality" and "Homosexuals." (In the book, as in this paper, I use the term "homosexual" as a noun without pejorative intent, though I realize that most male homosexuals prefer to be called "gays." When I use the term "homosexual" it will usually refer to a male rather than to a female, for reasons I shall explain.) The central economic chapter in *Sex and Reason* is chapter 5. With only a few exceptions the works cited in this paper were published after *Sex and Reason*.

2. I do not suggest that instrumental rationality is the only tenable conception of rationality. See Robert Nozick, *The Nature of Rationality*, ch. 5 (1993).

3. For the empirical support, see Edward O. Laumann et al., *The Social Organization of Sexuality: Sexual Practices in the United States*, chs. 3, 5 (1994); *Sex and Reason*, ch. 2; for the theory, see id. ch. 2; Richard Green, *Sexual Science and the Law* (1992); Simon LeVay, *The Sexual Brain* (1993); David M. Buss and David P. Schmitt, "Sexual Strategies Theory: An Evolutionary Perspective on Human Mating," 100 *Psychological Review* 204 (1993), esp. 210–12.

4. Advocates of homosexual rights prefer the term "orientation," because they think "preference" connotes choice or mutability, and though many of them are made anxious by biological theories of homosexuality they deny that one chooses to be homosexual as one might choose to be a lawyer or a Methodist. I agree that homosexuality is not chosen, but as economists tend to take preferences as given rather than chosen (and to focus on choices given preferences), "preference" and "orientation" have similar connotations in an economic analysis of homosexuality.

5. Some economists believe that revealed-preference theory enables economics to dispense with the concepts of utility and utility maximizing. I do not think so, for reasons powerfully marshaled in Amartya Sen, "Internal Consistency of Choice," 61 *Econometrica* 495 (1993), but the issue is not important to my analysis of homosexuality.

6. *Sex and Reason* 294–95. Even lower estimates are suggested by recent large-scale sex surveys in England and France, summarized in ACSF Investigators, "AIDS and Sexual Behaviour in France," 360 *Nature* 407 (1992); and Anne M. Johnson et al., "Sexual Lifestyles and HIV Risk," 360 *Nature* 410 (1992); by a substantial new survey of American men, John O. G. Billy et al., "The Sexual Behavior of Men in the United States," 25 *Family Planning Perspectives* 52, 59–60 (1993); and by Laumann et al., note 3 above, at 293 (2.4 percent male, 1.4 percent female). A comprehensive review of the data from sex surveys concludes that "only about 2–3% of sexually active men and 1–2% of sexually active women are currently homosexual." Tom W. Smith, "American Sexual Behavior: Trends, Socio-Demographic Differences, and

Risk Behavior," p. 6 (National Opinion Research Center, University of Chicago, GSS Topical Rep. 25, version 1.2, Oct. 18, 1993); see also id. at 33 (tab. 8). The usual objection to inferring the percentage of homosexuals from surveys is that "closeted" homosexuals will conceal their sexual preference from however skilled an interviewer. If so, this would imply that the more tolerant the society, the larger the percentage of homosexuals that would be revealed by surveys. There is no such relation. Surveys of sexual practices in the Scandinavian countries, which are more tolerant of homosexuality than the United States is, reveal a lesser frequency of homosexual behavior than the U.S. survey data do. The Scandinavian data are summarized in Mads Melbye and Robert J. Biggar, "Interactions between Persons at Risk for AIDS and the General Population in Denmark," 135 *American Journal of Epidemiology* 593, 600 (1992).

7. For discussion and references, see Tomas J. Philipson and Richard A. Posner, *Private Choices and Public Health: The AIDS Epidemic in an Economic Perspective*, ch. 2 (1993). For more recent evidence, see Laumann et al., note 3 above, at 435 (tab. 11.29B).

8. For empirical evidence, see ACSF Investigators, note 6 above, at 408; Johnson et al., note 6 above, at 411; Laumann et al., note 3 above, at 306–308.

9. *Sex and Reason* 91–92; cf. Lillian Federman, *Odd Girls and Twilight Lovers: A History of Lesbian Life in Twentieth-Century America* 246–48, 254 (1991); Marilyn Frye, "Lesbian 'Sex,'" in *Lesbian Philosophies and Cultures* 305, 313 (Jeffner Allen, ed., 1990).

10. *Sex and Reason* 305–307; Laumann et al., note 3 above, at 316.

11. Not necessarily an effeminate one. Other methods of signaling homosexual preference have become as or more common in contemporary American society. See, e.g., "Clothing," 1 *Encyclopedia of Homosexuality* 246 (Wayne R. Dynes, 1990).

12. Which suggests, by the way, that having an effeminate manner is not entirely voluntary.

13. Michael W. Ross, *The Married Homosexual Man: A Psychological Study* 110–111 and tab.11.1 (1983).

14. Ulick O'Connor, *Biographers and the Art of Biography* 77 (1991).

15. Technically, in a polygynous society, that is, one in which men are permitted to have more than one wife but women are not permitted to have more than one husband. The vast majority of polygamous societies are polygynous.

16. *Sex and Reason* 38–45, and references cited there—especially K. J. Dover, *Greek Homosexuality* (2d ed., 1989).

17. I consider and reject a possible noneconomic answer to that question at the end of this paper.

18. Achilles and Patroclus, in the *Iliad*, may illustrate this kind of homoerotic relationship. Eva Cantarella, *Bisexuality in the Ancient World* 10–11 (1992).

19. The competitive aspect of the Greek sexuality is emphasized in John J. Winkler, *The Constraints of Desire: The Anthropology of Sex and Gender in Ancient Greece*, chs. 2–3 (1990).

20. See, for example, Cantarella, note 18 above, at 90. Most homosexual men are capable of having full intercourse with women (that is, are capable of penetration and ejaculation), even if they don't enjoy it.

21. *Sex and Reason*, 179.

22. The ban has been modified by the Clinton Administration, but the extent to which the modification signifies a real change in military policy toward homosexuals and lesbians is as yet unclear.

23. Except to note that lowering the age of consent to sexual intercourse might facilitate the spread of AIDS to teenagers.

24. See 22 above.

25. I take a broader view of the issue in *Sex and Reason* 314–23. Here I confine myself to economic analysis except for a glance at social constructionism at the end of the paper. For

background to the debate over homosexuals in the armed services, see Jeffrey S. Davis, "Military Policy Toward Homosexuals: Scientific, Historical, and Legal Perspectives," 131 *Military Law Review* 55 (1991).

26. Besides evidence cited in *Sex and Reason*, see Green, note 3 above, at 63–84; LeVay, note 3 above; J. Michael Bailey et al., "Heritable Factors Influence Sexual Orientation in Women," 50 *Archives of General Psychiatry* 217 (1993) (and studies cited there); Dean H. Hamer et al., "A Linkage Between DNA Markers on the X Chromosome and Male Sexual Orientation," 261 *Science* 321 (1993). For a good popular summary of the evidence, see Chandler Burr, "Homosexuality and Biology," *Atlantic Monthly,* March 1993, p. 47, and for a skeptical view of it, William Byrne and Bruce Parsons, "Human Sexual Orientation: The Biologic Theories Reappraised," 50 *Archives of General Psychiatry* 228 (1993). The evidence consists of studies of identical twins, comparisons of the brains of homosexual and heterosexual men who died from AIDS, the lack of any authenticated "cures" for homosexual preference, the fact that homosexual preference appears to be found in all human societies despite enormous differences in sexual mores and methods of child rearing, the existence of homosexuality in many animal species, the self-reported experience of homosexuals of having been aware of their sexual preference from the earliest period of their sexual awareness, and, most recently, indirect but powerful evidence that there is a gene predisposing to male homosexuality, transmitted through the maternal line. See Hamer et al., above. I find particularly telling the evidence that identical twins have a much greater concordance of homosexuality than fraternal twins. See *Twins and Homosexuality: A Casebook* (Geoff Puterbaugh, ed., 1990). Since fraternal twins, like identical twins, are ordinarily raised in the identical familial and social environment, any differences in their sexual orientation are likely to be due to genetic factors.

27. The political economy of the homosexual-rights movement raises fascinating issues, which I shall not discuss here. See Philipson and Posner, note 7 above, ch. 8, for some conjectures based on the economic theory of interest groups.

28. Although Janet E. Halley, "The Politics of the Closet: Towards Equal Protection for Gay, Lesbian, and Bisexual Identity," 36 *UCLA Law Review* 915, 934–46 (1989), argues for that mutuability, as do also a number of moral conservatives. See, e.g., Dennis Prager, "Homosexuality, the Bible, and Us," *Public Interest* 60, 73–75 (Summer 1993). Prager fails to distinguish between opportunistic and preference homosexuality, and argues most unperceptively that the fact that many homosexuals have dated or even had intercourse with women shows that homosexual preference is not biologically determined. He refers to none of the biological evidence.

29. David M. Halperin, "One Hundred Years of Homosexuality," in Halperin, *One Hundred Years of Homosexuality and Other Essays on Greek Love* 15 (1990).

30. Cf. id. at 30. For powerful criticism of the radical constructionist view of homosexuality, see Richard D. Mohr, *Gay Ideas: Outing and Other Controversies*, ch. 7 (1992). Although I have used the term "radical constructionist" and would describe myself as a "moderate constructionist," it is common to equate social constructionism with radical constructionism, just as it is common to equate feminism with radical feminism.

31. Cf. Hilary Putnam, *Renewing Philosophy* 111–14 (1992), pointing out that it is one thing to say that we made the Big Dipper, and quite another to say that we made the stars.

32. What I have been calling "opportunistic homosexuals."

33. Martha C. Nussbaum, "Constructing Love, Desire, and Care," in [this volume], ch. 20.

34. William N. Eskridge, Jr., "A Social Constructionist Critique of Posner's *Sex and Reason:* Steps Toward a Gaylegal Agenda," 102 *Yale Law Journal* 303 (1990).

35. Richard Poirier, *Poetry and Pragmatism* 40 (1992).

9

The Sexual Economist and Legal Regulation of the Sexual Orientations

Janet E. Halley

Judge Richard A. Posner offers a two-part argument in his contribution to this volume, "The Economic Approach to Homosexuality." First, he argues that economic analysis of human sexuality supports a claim that heterosexual preference is an essential, transhistorical feature of most human beings while homosexual preference is a similarly fixed characteristic of very few human beings.[1] Human sexuality is "constructed" in the limited sense that different cultural settings induce individuals with intrinsic preferences for same or cross-sex contacts to seek sexual outlet in behavioral repertoires that, though they are transhistorically homosexual or heterosexual, manifest striking plasticity from culture to culture. Second, he argues that, given this moderated social-constructivist view of human sexual variation, a sexual economist can predict the aggregate social response to various sexual incentives and deterrents and thus draw up socially optimal regulations. The precise form of social constructivism he adopts is doubly necessary to make his economic analysis of homosexuality work: positing intrinsic, transhistorical, "real" preference heterosexuals and "real" preference homosexuals enables him to make predictions about how individuals will respond to changes in sexuality regulation; positing plasticity in the meaning and availability of sexual behaviors gives regulation something to do.

The sweep of Judge Posner's argument derives in large part, then, from a controversial premise about the kind of thing that human sexual orientation is. This essay critiques that premise, in three parts: first, it indicates how Judge Posner's model of human sexual orientations enables him to offer a simple economic analysis of sexuality regulation; second, it paces through Judge Posner's revealed-preference analysis to show how it forces the conclusion that homosexual and heterosexual preferences are human givens; and third, it critiques his assessment of the social costs and benefits of sexuality regulation as incomplete because it does not take into account the legal and economic production of sexual agents.

THE RELATIONSHIP BETWEEN ECONOMIC ANALYSIS OF
SEXUALITY AND SOCIAL CONSTRUCTIVISM

Judge Posner proposes that regulation of sexuality should be maintained or adopted only if it is efficient, or rational in an economic sense. To be rational, sexual policy must be based on an assessment of whether a specified sexual behavior is valuable as a general matter or not. An economic assessment of the costs and utilities of various sexual activities as a general matter necessarily includes but cannot be limited to the costs borne and utilities enjoyed by sexual actors. (For instance, the social value of unsafe sex *given HIV* includes the pleasure both parties enjoy in the primary contact, discounted by the risk that they will transmit the virus to either partner *and* the risk of transmitting the virus to the partners' partners *and* the risk of transmitting the virus to the partners' partners' partners and so on. If a behavior is valuable as a general matter, the question for policy is whether and how to create incentives likely to guide self-interested sexual actors to engage in it. If it is harmful as a general matter, the question is whether and how to deter the behavior. If regulation can promote valuable or deter costly behavior, it is rational, and Judge Posner is prepared to recommend it as a legal reform.

An economic analysis of sexuality thus depends at every stage on some assessment of what sexual actors are like. In order to give due weight to the utilities enjoyed by sexual actors, the sexual economist needs to know how people value their sexual activities. And in order to calibrate incentives and deterrents, the sexual economist needs a predictive apparatus that will foretell how self-interested sexual actors would calculate their costs and utilities under "what if" schemes of sexuality regulation. The conceptual virtue of internal consistency would also encourage the sexual economist to invoke the same model of sexual actors at both steps.

An economic analysis of sexual regulation thus needs a fairly thick set of assumptions about what human beings are like as *assessors of sexual value before* they begin to cope with the particular sexual regulations that they do (or, in the policy shop, can be imagined to) face, and a fairly thin set of assumptions about what human beings are like as *erotic actors*. It requires the former to be stable and the latter to be plastic. A fairly mild form of sexuality constructivism corresponds best with these requirements.

As Carole S. Vance points out, sexuality constructivists "differ in their willingness to imagine *what* was constructed."[2] She proposes a spectrum of sexuality constructivisms differentiated by the degree to which they disturb the assumption that everything about sexuality is natural:

> At minimum, all social construction approaches [to sexuality] adopt the view that physically identical sexual acts may have varying social significance and subjective meaning depending on how they are defined and understood in different cultures and historical periods . . .
>
> A further step in social construction theory posits that even the direction of sexual desire itself, for example, object choice or hetero/homosexuality, is not intrinsic or inherent in the individual but is constructed. Not all constructionists take this step; for some, the direction of desire and erotic interest are fixed, although the be-

havioral *form* this interest takes will be constructed by prevailing cultural frames, as will the subjective experience of the individual and the social significance attached to it by others.

The most radical form of constructionist theory is willing to entertain the idea that there is no essential, undifferentiated sexual impulse, 'sex drive' or 'lust,' which resides in the body due to physiological functioning and sensation . . . This position, of course, contrasts sharply with more middle-ground constructionist theory which implicitly accepts an inherent sexual impulse which is then constructed in terms of acts, identity, community, and object choice.[3]

Vance astutely describes the following scale of constructivist operations, each of which etches deeper into any assumption that sexuality as we know it is natural:

1. Culture creates the meaning of sexual acts;

2. Culture creates the repertoire of acts and identities that belong to homosexual and heterosexual orientations;

3. Culture creates homosexual and heterosexual orientations themselves;

4. Culture creates sexuality more generally; or

5. Culture creates sex itself.

Measured on this scale, Judge Posner's constructivism is the quite modest position (2): culture (and thus law) can shape the meaning of sexual acts and the repertoire of acts and identities that belong to homosexual and heterosexual orientations, but sex, sexuality, and homosexual and heterosexual orientations are ineradicable elements of the human condition.[4]

What if one tried to do an economic analysis of sexual regulation using a stronger form of constructivism—for example, position (3), which proposes that culture and not nature supplies homosexual preference and heterosexual preference? Such an analysis would have to take into account a feedback loop that Judge Posner is able to close: if culture shapes not merely the deeds but the desires of sexual actors, not merely the modes of satisfying homosexual and heterosexual desire but the status of having homosexual and heterosexual orientation, then law can, too; and if law shapes not only people's sexual behavior but also their sexual preferences, the assumption upon which Judge Posner's economic justification of sexual regulation rests—that he can predict the assessments of sexual value that individuals bring to the sexual marketplace—evaporates. Regulation (particularly if it increased or decreased the amount of homosexual or heterosexual preference people entertained) would need to be included as a variable in the calculation of its own social utility. Economic analysis would still be conceivable, but it would have to assess complex, perhaps even chaotic, dynamics quite different from the neat linear patterns described by Judge Posner. It would be far less determinate, and far less likely to invalidate or authorize particular regulations of sexuality. And it would have to address a question Judge Posner is able to avoid: what is the value, to individuals and to the collectivity, not only of various sexual acts but of the human categories homosexual and heterosexual (and of the idea that they are natural)?

INFERRING THE REAL PREFERENCE HOMOSEXUAL

Judge Posner uses economic analysis to derive his empirical claim that, though sexual orientation and behavior are subject to cultural shaping in a sexual market, basic human homosexual and heterosexual preference is not. Here, as in the policy assessment that arises from this empirical claim, the distinctively economic cast of the argument derives from his assumption that sexual actors are economically rational: they will take advantage of sexual opportunities only when the perceived advantages exceed the perceived costs. Social and legal policy can modify individuals' assessments of the utilities and costs of heterosexual and homosexual object choices. For instance, proheterosexual social policy can convince more people of the utilities of cross-sex genital contacts to orgasm and can thereby induce more people to engage in them, while antihomosexual social policy can make same-sex contacts to orgasm more costly and can convince more people to avoid them. Social and legal policy is capable of rearranging people's behavior, but on Judge Posner's model of sexuality constructivism, it cannot alter the underlying distribution of intrinsic homosexual and heterosexual preference. Those preferences are exogenous to the sexuality marketplace.

If the sexual economist reads back from behavior, through the costs and benefits imposed by the social world in which it occurs, he can (sometimes, not always) reveal intrinsic, preference for same- or cross-sex contact. In order to draw such inferences, Judge Posner makes a number of assumptions about what sexual preferences are like and how sexual actors seek to satisfy them. Human sexuality is composed of unconscious desire and conscious desire, assisted in an unspecified way by fantasy but *satisfied* by means of *behavior*. Of all possible behavioral options, the bull's eye is genital contact to orgasm—everything else is a substitute.[5] Moreover, Judge Posner assumes that unconscious and conscious desire in human beings can have the characteristic of being sex-preferential—of being focused on the same sex as the person harboring them or on a different sex. If a person's desires are preferentially homosexual, he or she will anticipate and experience more satisfaction in homosexual genital contacts to orgasm than would a person whose desires are preferentially heterosexual, and vice versa.

In estimating the utility of available sexual opportunities, an individual who prefers same-sex contacts (supposing such a preference to exist) would place a higher value on those promising genital contact to orgasm with a person of the same sex than on those promising genital contact to orgasm with a person of a different (in common parlance, "the opposite") sex. The converse would be true for an individual whose sexual desires are heterosexual (again, supposing such a preference to exist). But in deciding whether to exploit any given sexual opportunity, the actor will take into account other, secondary utilities—low search costs, procreation, social approval, legal privileges, and so on—and will discount all the relevant utilities by the relevant costs—high search costs, procreation, social ostracism, legal sanctions and obstacles, and so on.

Given all these assumptions, Judge Posner seeks "testable hypotheses" that isolate individuals' intrinsic preference structures. In an imagined world in which society and law provided people with equally costly sources of sexual satisfaction in

intercourse with persons of the same sex and with persons of a different sex, homosexual preference would be manifested whenever a person consistently preferred the
former. If such an interpretive opportunity were ever to offer itself, Judge Posner
would label such persons "preference homosexuals." Others who, when faced with
the same options, consistently preferred heterosexual contacts, would reveal themselves to be "Preference heterosexuals."

That entirely hypothetical exercise to one side, Judge Posner looks for real-
world "revealed preference" tests. Actual episodes and patterns of human behavior,
examined as rational choices among options bearing different costs and benefits,
permit the identification of *some individuals* as *real* preference homosexuals; other
individuals as *real* preference heterosexuals; and others as *real* preference bisexuals.
Real preference homosexuals can be identified, for instance, when social discrimination against homosexuals makes acts of intercourse with persons of the same sex
more costly than heterosexual contacts. Under those (depressingly familiar) circumstances, the people who nevertheless engage in same-sex erotic contacts indicate that
they maintain a stronger interior preference for them than people also faced with
those costs, who instead avoid homosexual acts. Homosexual behavior against a
backdrop of discrimination reveals *real* preference homosexuality.

An interesting consequence of antihomosexual discrimination in this scheme of
inference is that it blocks a symmetrical inference from heterosexual behavior: such
behavior, since it is less costly under a regime of antigay discrimination, creates
equally valid inferences that the person engaging in it is a real preference heterosexual or a real preference *homosexual* who is acting opportunistically, substituting heterosexual sex for his or her preferred object choice in order to avoid social sanctions.
Even married men with children may not be real preference heterosexuals: they may
instead be merely *opportunistic* heterosexuals whose behavior masks their real preference homosexuality. Conversely, in single-sex institutions such as jails where the
cost of heterosexual genital contact may be extremely high, real preference heterosexuals may seek to satisfy their sexual desires in homosexual contacts: unable to
satisfy their real preferences, they accept a substitute in homosexual contacts and
should be deemed merely opportunistic homosexuals.

It is important to see how this analysis makes homosexual and heterosexual preference intrinsic to persons and exogenous to the sexual marketplace and its volatili-
ties. Unconscious desire and conscious desire are intrinsic preference elements,
existing prior to behavior. They are focused in some distinctive way on sex-of-object
choice. Homosexual and heterosexual behavior, then, represents a selection from a
menu of options for satisfying already existing and invariant unconscious and conscious desire. Everything on that menu of options is external to, and merely indicative
of, the sexual preference personality it reveals.

It is important to note, however, that the sexual economist has *assumed* that real
preference homosexuality and real preference heterosexuality not only exist but ex-
haustively represent the preferences that choices of sexual object reveal. If those assumptions are suspended, reading back from behavior to real preference homosexuality and heterosexuality becomes impossible or misleading: actual choices may
reveal something else that is not represented in the assumptions—what Amartya Sen
calls an "unconnected preference."[6] Take for example Judge Posner's description of

a "Kinsey 3"—someone rated on the Kinsey scale as having equally strong patterns of homosexual and heterosexual fantasy and behavior, a "perfect bisexual." To fit such individuals into a conceptual scheme in which intrinsic sexual preference is marked by sex-of-object choice, Judge Posner determines that such a "perfect bisexual" is "*indifferent* to the sex of his partner." But this is a point at which the assumption that sexual preference is exogenously homosexual or heterosexual operates to obscure the possibility that *having* a sex-of-object choice, and the personality structure that accompanies it, may themselves be what sexual actors "really prefer." Someone who tests out as a Kinsey 3 may, for instance, have heard of the character "the bisexuals" and aspire to maintain that character. Such a person's behavior will reveal not an intrinsic preference but a *project*. Moreover, unlike Judge Posner's real preference bisexual, who approaches each sexual contact as if she were afflicted with lust for the first time, a more autobiographically astute bisexual calls on the resources of memory, self-reflexivity, and performativity and weaves a narrative of her sexual encounters that makes the sex of one partner important *inasmuch as* it is not like the sex of another partner. In that sense, the self-narrating bisexual is *more* interested in the sex of his or her sexual companions than people who show up at the extreme ends of Kinsey's sexual-orientation scale.

This alternate view of what a bisexual is doing dislodges more than Judge Posner's assumption that she is indifferent to the sex of her erotic partners. More fundamentally, it breaks the chain of inference from behavior to preference—or at least creates ambiguity about what inferences behavior will sustain; and more fundamentally still, it calls into question the assumption that homosexual and heterosexual preferences are intrinsic personality features bearing an exogenous relationship to behavior. Judge Posner supposes that *having* preference bisexuality is independent of, temporally proceeds, and determines the economics of behavioral choices. But for my hypothetical bisexual—and a lot of professed bisexuals these days describe themselves in terms consistent with my hypothesi[7]—sex-of-object choice intervenes complexly in the composition of the sexual personality that the person "has." Indeed, to the extent their bisexuality is not an internal given preference but a project, it is doubtful we should continue to reify it as *a* personality.

To recapitulate: Judge Posner wants us to read back from the behavioral patterns of "perfect bisexuals," discounted for the costs of search and so on, to an *a priori*, intrinsic sexual preference personality constituted as indifference to sex-of-object choice. But we can't make that inference because sex-of-object choice may itself be intrinsic to a bisexual's sexual preference personality. Indeed, bisexuality may involve shifting self-conceptions and much self-conscious behavioral tacking over time that call into question whether there *is* a sexual preference personality *there* to reveal.

I want to make a similar assertion about reading back from or to real preference homosexuality or heterosexuality. There, of course, what Judge Posner takes to define an *a priori*, intrinsic sexual preference personality is not indifference to sex-of-object choice, but strong preference of one sex over the other. But what if behavior emerges not from homosexual or heterosexual preference but from an unconnected preference, a preference for something not represented in the homo/hetero dichotomy?

In the picaresque of sexual preference examined in Judge Posner's essay, the effeminate gay man and the mannish lesbian cut important figures in part because they suggest desires, other than intrinsic homo/heterosexual preference, that people's sexual choices might reveal. Though in his book *Sex and Reason*, Judge Posner argued that effeminacy in gay men is biologically committed, he now views it primarily as a signaling device instrumentally adopted to cope with searching for sexual outlets under discriminations.[8] That is, men wishing to indicate that they want same-sex erotic contacts mimic women because other men who want same-sex erotic contacts understand what that signal means. A trace of the biological argument remains, however, when Judge Posner speculates that medieval fathers of mannish daughters might have despaired of obtaining appropriate matches for them, dispatched them to nunneries instead, and *thereby* concentrated the population of (real preference) lesbians in convents.[9] At any event, in Judge Posner's inferential scheme male effeminacy and female mannishness are physical manifestations of homosexuality imposed by nature or adopted by art. Any stray effeminacy that remains among real preference male heterosexuals is greatly to be lamented, as it makes its bearers into targets for opportunistic homosexuals—that is, real preference heterosexuals substituting a male anus for the preferred female vagina but holding out for some peripheral resemblances to the preferred object.

These formulations seem to me to draw on an impoverished notion of the relationship between sex and gender. Judge Posner assumes as a norm perfect transparency from gender to sex: male bodies are normatively masculine unless they are *eff*eminate; female bodies are normatively feminine unless they are mann*ish*. The resulting analysis provides two clues that something is amiss. First, the assumption of sex/gender transparency precludes any acknowledgement of mannish men or effeminate women, who disappear into the norm. Second, sex/gender opacity—male effeminacy, female mannishness—stands out as a deviation that requires explanation and that remains inexplicable until Judge Posner refers to heterosexual relatedness as the paradigm of erotic interaction. Male bodies fuck feminine genders, and masculine genders do whatever-it-is-that-lesbians-do to female bodies: homosexual eroticism is subtly recuperated to the paradigm of heterosexual interaction.

The mechanism of this recuperation is an assumption that the fucker has as his or her object sex, for which gender, when discordant, is a mere substitute. The error here resembles Judge Posner's exclusion of the possibility that bisexuality indicates not *indifference* to but a *project with respect to* sex-Of-Object-Choice. Here he excludes *priori* and as a matter of assumption the possibility that people engage in projects of maintaining some relationship between the sex they belong to because of the shape of their genitals and the gender they occupy because of certain aspects of their demeanor, dress, and so on. He thus excludes the possibility that, in different individuals, the sex/gender relationship may be transparent or opaque, stable or shifting. If aligning sex and gender is a project, slippages can occur or be induced. Sometimes those slippages will be perceived as failures—a macho football player is startled and his voice becomes soprano; other times slippages will ironize the very project of having a gender—my favorite example, of course, is me, serving as best man at my brother's wedding wearing a tux.[10]

And just as bisexuals can be imagined to have incorporated sex-of-object-choice into the very heart of their preference structure, as an object of preference in itself (notwithstanding Judge Posner's claim that their behavioral choices reflect a preference personality indifferent to sex-of-object-choice), so Judge Posner's real preference homosexuals and heterosexuals can be imagined to have incorporated *gender*-of-object-choice into their preference structure (notwithstanding Judge Posner's claim that their behavior univocally manifests a strong preference for *sex*-of-object-choice to the exclusion of other preferences). Why assume that it is the *sex* of one's object choice that forms the object of erotic attention, and not his or her *gender* or, indeed, the *particular relationship he or she maintains between his or her sex and his or her gender?* We know that the male sex partners of preoperative male-to-female transsexuals often deny that they are having homosexual sex: the conscious (at least) object of their erotic attention is not the sex but the gender of their lovers.[11] We know from recent work on the history of butch/femme relations among lesbians in the United States, that conscious desire often attaches not to the sex or gender of the loved one, but to her *gender liminality*.[12] Though Judge Posner reads bisexuals as free of sexual preference, they can just as readily be read to be saturated with it. Though he reads real preference homosexuals as chiefly motivated by a desire for same-sex erotic contacts to orgasm and as instrumental users of gender discordances, it is just as plausible that, in any given case, their real preference is for gender discordance itself.

But what about Judge Posner's strongest case, the persistence of homosexual conduct even in social and legal worlds that make such conduct extremely costly? Don't the individuals who brave acute antigay discrimination in order to have same-sex genital contacts to orgasm thereby indicate that they value those contacts more highly than others do? Sure, but nothing compels Judge Posner's claim that that valuation univocally maps onto their *intrinsic* preferences. Something else may provide the intrinsic structure of their desire. Eve Kosofsky Sedgwick provides a helpful reminder of the vast array of sexual Preferences that may underlay behavior but are ignored by the homo/hetero dichotomy:

> Even identical genital acts mean very different things to different people.
>
> To some people, the 'nimbus of "the sexual" seems scarcely to extend beyond the boundaries of discrete genital acts; to others, it enfolds them loosely or floats virtually free of them . . .
>
> Some people like to have a lot of sex, others little or none.
>
> Many people have their richest mental/emotional involvement with sexual acts that they don't do, or even don't *want* to do.
>
> For some people, it is important that sex be embedded in contexts resonant with meaning, narrative, and connectedness with other aspects of their life; for other people, it is important that they not be; to, others it doesn't occur that they might be . . .
>
> Some people like spontaneous sexual scenes, others like highly scripted ones, others like spontaneous-sounding ones that are nonetheless totally predictable.

> Some people's sexual orientation is intensely marked by autoerotic pleasures and histo-
> ries—sometimes more so than by any aspect of alloerotic object choice. For others the
> autoerotic possibility seems secondary or fragile, if it exists at all.[13]

Nothing precludes the operation of unconnected preferences along any of these
axes—for lots of sex, or little, or none; for fantasy without action or for action without fantasy; for homey sex or sex at arms' length; for scripted sex or improvisational
sex; for autoerotic or alloerotic sex—as the intrinsic *a priori* preference that undergirds a secondary, culturally saturated election of homosexual or heterosexual action. Indeed, the "something else" that underlies the behavior noticed by the sexual
economist may not even belong to the domain of "the sexual": persistent election of
same-sex erotic objects notwithstanding heavy socially imposed costs may satisfy a
preference for the perpetuation or interruption of childhood cathexes on a gendered
parent, for independence or separation, for community or loyalty, for rebellion, dignity, adventure. Elements that Judge Posner assigns to the presiding center of sexual
personality—the desire for genital contact to organs and the inflection of that desire
by homosexual or heterosexual object choice—may be secondary, facilitative, mere
utilities to which different individuals and different cultures assign different values;
the core *differand*, if it exists at all, may be buried somewhere else, perhaps even in
the welter of costs and utilities he deems merely secondary.[14] Though these possibilities may seem bizarre and unfamiliar, they really represent nothing more than what
philosopher Edward Stein aptly designates "sophisticated essentialism," that is,
essentialism about differences in human sexuality that does not assume that "our
commonsense categories of sexuality [will] get used in an advanced theory of sexual
orientation."[15]

REASSESSING THE SOCIAL COSTS OF REAL
SEXUAL PREFERENCE CATEGORIES

As Judge Posner indicates, any supposition that sexual orientations are socially
constructed has its costs, particularly that of possibly conceding the feasibility of a
project cherished by today's religious right: devising antigay policies that will prevent the "conversion" or "recruitment" of people who would otherwise be heterosexuals to homosexuality.[16] But of course the antihomosexual impulse of the religious
right does not depend on the model of sexual orientation it adopts: if laboratory researchers were ever to verify the empirical truth of real preference homosexuality by
finding *the* gene that unilaterally causes *it*, the religious right will be just as happy to
pursue its antihomosexual agenda through genetic fingerprinting, gene therapy, and
perhaps even selective abortion, sterilization, and other startling measures.[17]

Moreover, unless and until someone manages to show rather than merely assume that homosexuality and heterosexuality in humans arises from real, intrinsic,
presocial structures of the body or the personality, such an assumption has its own
costs. These costs appear primarily in the social understanding not of homosexuality
but of heterosexuality, and in the social and legal treatment not of homosexuals but
of heterosexuals.

According to Judge Posner's sexual economics, antigay discrimination in a society whose men and women are just about equally available as sexual partners has an asymmetrical effect on the certainty with which real preference homosexuality and real preference heterosexuality can be assigned: the people readily identified as homosexuals are probably real preference homosexuals, but people readily identified as heterosexuals are more illegible. They could be real preference heterosexuals doing what comes naturally, or they could be mere opportunistic heterosexuals—that is, real preference *homo*sexuals who have found that their preferred sexual contacts are too expensive and have decided to settle for substitutes.

This source of uncertainty appears to leave undisturbed Judge Posner's sexuality macroeconomics in that his policy analysis *assumes* real preference homosexuality and real preference heterosexuality in order to predict how *entire populations* will respond to the various costs and benefits associated with sexual behavior by society and law. Moreover, real preference sexual personality has a handy way of stripping any ambiguous erotic content from sexual "substitutions" by guaranteeing that objects accepted as "substitutes" are not actually "desired." Thus if male real preference heterosexuals are suddenly subjected to scarcity of women, by being thrown in jail for example, Judge Posner insists that they will become opportunistic *and not real* homosexuals in that they will hold out for the "insertor" role with effeminate partners in order to secure the closest possible substitute for what they really prefer, vaginal intercourse.[18] Male real preference heterosexuals living in a culture that makes sex with women accessible but emotionally chilly and that makes sex with men accessible and emotionally rewarding—ancient Greece, for example will have sex with men not because it pleases them erotically but because they are thereby able to satisfy a basic human need for companionship.[19] Judge Posner approximates the outermost limit of this line of thinking when he concludes that male real preference homosexuals are physically capable of vaginal intercourse with women "even if they don't enjoy it."[20]

These formulations drive a conceptual wedge between sexual desire and the rational selection between substitute means for satisfying it: though the former is truly sexual, the latter is not. The distinction is analytically reassuring, as it makes the machine of economic analysis run smoothly. It might even be personally reassuring, inasmuch as it suggests that anyone interested in knowing whether he or she is a real or merely an opportunistic heterosexual or homosexual needs only to strip away the detritus of coolly rational strategizing in order to lay bare the simple structure of his or her sexual desire. But it is incoherent: the sexual actor who accepts a substitute must nevertheless desire it. And the resulting incoherence is not merely conceptual: a social system that seeks to frustrate the direct satisfaction of some desires by driving them into masked satisfactions must be in some ways inescapably unstable.

No one supposes that people with small incomes who therefore live in mobile homes actually prefer mobile homes to more permanent architectural forms. In the housing market, mobile homes are clearly substitutes for other kinds of housing, and this is true even though those who find that mobile homes are all they can afford may actually desire them. But in a sexual economy regulated by legitimate antigay discrimination and analyzed by a conceptual system that makes rigid distinctions between heterosexual and homosexual personality and between exogenous desire and endogenous substitution, every individual person who acts like a real preference heterosexual is suspect. Such a sexual economy has no vocabulary to describe the quality of desire that attaches to a sexual substitute except that of appearance: representation, imitation, semblance, counterfeit, duplicity, appropriation, emulation, mirroring, simulation, fakery, forgery, imposture, impersonation, mimesis, parody, pastiche, sham, feigning, pretense, bluff, speciousness, dissembling, masquerade.

Reified models of sexual orientation like that offered by Judge Posner have the effect of setting the stage for crisis on the confusing middle ground occupied jointly by real preference heterosexuality and its opportunistic doppelganger. In the soporific lulls between crises of real-preference identification, moreover, the reification of sexual personalities works to obscure the ways in which sexual personality involves the interpretation of its representations. Reading one's own sexuality and that of others, and mutually acknowledging and obscuring representations of sexual selfhood, are themselves sexual practices tightly woven into the fabric of sexuality. A sexual economics aiming to understand how sexual actors value sexual opportunities would need to take under consideration not only the value people assign to different kinds of genital contact, to access to procreation, and so on, but also the benefits they derive from, and costs they associate with, different kinds of sexual knowledge and ignorance. Not only that: it would need to recognize that, whenever law regulates sexual behavior, it may be tampering with the values associated with sexual knowledge and sexual ignorance. An assumption that sexual preference exists as a given, exogenous personality type frames the analysis to exclude these issues and, thus, delivers an anorexic economic analysis of sexuality.

Take, for example, the economic analysis of sodomy laws, which Judge Posner offers as an exemplar of what economic thinking can do to increase the social benefits of sexuality regulation.[21] He identifies the huge social cost of HIV transmission as a proper focus of the sexual economist and takes the sodomy statutes as the most promising place to undertake legal reform. Throughout his analysis, he assumes that the sexual transmission of HIV is virtually entirely a gay male phenomenon—but of course it isn't: a growing proportion of new HIV infections in the United States occur in heterosexual vaginal and anal contacts, and those contacts appear to be the primary means of HIV transmission abroad.[22] And Judge Posner assumes that sodomy statutes target only homosexual contacts—but of course they don't: eighteen states criminalize fellatio, cunnilingus, and anal intercourse without regard to the sex of the participants, while only four maintain sodomy statutes that prohibit same-sex conduct alone.[23] What makes the sexual transmission of HIV a problem only of *gay men* is a practice of selective notice; and what makes the sodomy laws regulations of *homosexual* conduct is selective enforcement. Though Judge Posner concludes that statutes criminalizing the knowing transmission of HIV should replace sodomy laws, his proposal is subject to the same practices of selective noticing and selective enforcement that structure his analysis.

Sodomy law and Judge Posner's proposed substitute for it produce not only the salience of homosexuality but also the invisibility of heterosexuality. Heterosexuality drops from sight, and as it does so, becomes immune from regulation. Depending on what else you want out of a regulatory system, this feature of the social group populated by real preference and opportunistic heterosexuals is either a good thing (because it keeps the vice squad busy over there and not over here) or a bad thing (because it enables people to participate in the creation of social norms on an implicit guarantee that they will never themselves have to adhere to those norms or suffer the stigma of being designated a normative outlaw and because it thus allows important collective decisions to be made on the basis of unexpressed promises). Invisibility and immunity can produce a kind of blissed-out ignorance, the social attitude enjoyed by the James Moseley when he took the stand to admit performing cunnilingus with his wife at her request; after he was convicted of felonious consensual sodomy on the basis of that testimony, he ruefully reflected, "I had no idea I was incriminating myself."[24] Right.

What might it mean to inhabit a systematically unexamined social class populated by real and fake members and bestowing immunity from legal harms on all of them? An alarming example is available in the military's new policy on sexual orientation. This policy is directly based on the assumption that, while most servicemembers are real preference heterosexuals, a small minority of recruits are real preference homosexuals willing to live as opportunistic heterosexuals at least in the sense that they will pass for heterosexual. It declares that real preference homosexuality (described as a "propensity to commit homosexual acts") is inconsistent with military service purports to permit individuals with such a preference nevertheless serve in the military as long as they do not manifest their preference in behavior and establishes a procedure for determining when servicemembers' behavior can be considered to manifest real preference homosexuality.[25] This legitimation of an unstable social group confounding real preference heterosexuals with opportunistic heterosexuals whose real preference is homosexual, *combined with* severe sanctions for any behavior deemed to manifest real preference homosexuality, combined with the epistemic instability of real preference heterosexuality produces an extremely volatile social situation in the barracks. It suggests to a very energetic cohort of young men who have already demonstrated a willingness to defer to authority (1) that each of them has a real preference sexuality, most likely homosexual or heterosexual; and (2) that legal mechanisms of noticeable crudity can, and if set in motion, will reveal what that real preference sexuality is. Young men living under such regulations are less likely to scrutinize the uneven and unstable composition of the group to which they like to think they belong than to focus on the more cathartic and epistemically satisfying project of periodically imposing exile on others.

This likelihood was confirmed indirectly by the public debates leading up to adoption of the new military policy, when prime-time television allowed us to observe many of these young men as they expatiated on the value to them of maintaining the ban on gays in the military. Their worries were quite strikingly focused less on the cot than on the shower; less on actual unwanted contact than on the rebarbative qualities of *being seen*. They conceded that real preference homosexuals would serve side by side with them no matter what legal apparatus governed their relations; their goal, overall, seemed to be to forget that distasteful circumstance. They wanted policy to take account of the fact that they place a high value on *not knowing* that a *known* homosexual *knows* them.[26] Given the fact that they had to have real preference homosexuals in the shower with them, they wanted these parvenues to appear in the guise of opportunistic heterosexuals. They wanted precisely the companionship that would raise the most acute doubts about their own real preferences.

What are the economic justifications for paying attention to young men of such sublime incoherence? As Judge Posner indicates with some distaste, our problem is that they can make us pay for their unhappiness. He points ruefully to the law and economics axiom that antidiscrimination law drives up the cost of doing business by making majority workers less happy and thus more expensive. For an example he looks to laws dismantling Jim Crow in the workplace, which saddled employers with a white workforce that "demand[ed] a wage premium for incurring the perceived disutility of working in proximity to blacks."[27]

The economic cost of antidiscrimination may have an important role in deciding how much fairness we want, but it is important to get the calculus of the cost right, and the narrow social-constructivist view Posner takes of sexual orientation, and of race, risks getting the cost wrong. Think of Dilcey with Melanie's baby at her breast. Whites saw no disutility in quite intimate workplace proximity with blacks and, in fact, they actually preferred it as long as those who were known to be black were maintained in a materially subordinate position by the tasks they did, the wages they drew (if any), and the opportunities they could look forward to. Workplace segregation was never a goal of Jim Crow laws, which aimed instead to preserve workplace *hierarchy* by race. When the racial division of labor came under legal attack, whites demanded increased compensation not for putting up with increased proximity to blacks but for giving up a favorable wage spread. They demanded a premium in exchange for a premium.

If that is true, the race economist would want to ascertain the social costs not only of whites' wage premium under antidiscrimination but also of their wage premium under Jim Crow. And the inquiry would not be limited to whether antidiscrimination actually increased the cost of compensating whites, but would also seek to understand how whites entered into the antidiscrimination marketplace with a premium in the first place. In the latter inquiry, it could not be long before the race economist encountered the fact that race groups did not preexist law as primordially distinct labor pools; they were *produced as such* by quite noticeable legal and social mechanisms, including miscegenation statutes, race-identification law, and a rich array of associated cultural practices.[28] The costs and benefits of maintaining that production through wage differences are surely part of the whole picture.

Judge Posner's analogy is conceptually daunting because the military policy on sexuality sets up not only a "sexuality division of labor" (and thus does what Jim Crow workplace rules and later antidiscrimination law did for race) but also a system for generating the social groups whose labor exacts different prices (and thus functions like antimiscegenation law, race-identification law, and related cultural practices). Achieving an economic analysis of a cultural system with so many moving parts would doubtless be difficult. But if a regulatory system produces the very desires, interests, and identities that economic analysis describes as "bargaining positions" and that cultural criticism designates "subject positions," the relationship between economics and constructivism is much richer than Judge Posner is willing to concede.

Notes

1. A terminological note. Revealed *preference* analysis when applied to sexuality seeks to disclose what common language describes as sexual *orientation* (a deeply embedded erotic disposition) as opposed to sexual *preference* (a more adventitious or trivial selection from a menu of sexual options). My use of the terms "real preference homosexuals," "real preference heterosexuals," and so on, cooperates with the lexicon of economic analysis here—I hope without creating any implication that I suppose sexual orientations to be matters of "mere" preference.

2. Carole S. Vance, "Social Construction Theory: Problems in the History of Sexuality," in Dennis Altman, Carole Vance, Martha Vicinus, Jeffrey Weeks et al., eds., *Homosexuality, Which Homosexuality?* 13, 21 (London: GMP Publishers, 1989).

3. Id. at 18–19 (emphasis in original).

4. Though Vance and most participants in essentialist/constructivist debates assume that the premier source of any essential human characteristics is nature, it is helpful to distinguish, as Posner does, causation from kind. Posner, "The Economic Approach to Homosexuality," this volume, p. 186. It doesn't matter for his economic analysis whether the personality type at issue is given by nature or social forces, as long as sexual preference is established logically and temporally prior to the exertions of personality in behavior.

5. Indeed, the implicit paradigm throughout is the orgasm a man experiences when he inserts his penis somewhere. For a feminist analysis of this assumption in Posner's book *Sex and Reason*, see Gillian K. Hadfield, "Flirting with Science: Richard Posner on the Bioeconomics of Sexual Man," 106 *Harvard Law Review* 479 (1992).

Judge Posner's assumption that sexual desire is uniform and is distinct from its appearance in heterosexual and homosexual forms is repeated by this volume's table of contents, which proposes to examine the problems involved in "Shaping" "Sex" *before*, and *without reference to*, those involved in "Shaping" "Preference." This ordering stipulates that preference merely inflects sex. As Judge Posner's use of this ordering suggests, it poses a risk that heterosexual norms will be installed, without examination, in the battery of analytic assumptions about sex.

6. Amartya Sen demonstrates that, when revealed preference analysis posits a binary choice, it cannot construe the action of subjects who have actually entertained "unconnected preferences." Sen, "Behavior and the Concept of Preference," 40 *Economics* 241, 247–49 (1973).

7. For an astute assessment of bisexual identity, see Naomi Mezey, "Dismantling the Wall: Bisexuality and the Possibilities of Sexual Identity Classification Based on Acts," 10 *Berkeley Woman's Law Journal* 98 (1995).

8. Richard A. Posner, *Sex and Reason* 301 (Cambridge, Mass.: Harvard University Press, 1992); Posner, "Economic Approach," p. 177, 187.

9. Posner, "Economic Approach," p. 180.

10. An episode all the more cherished because it never occurred. The classic consideration of gender performativity is Judith Butler, *Gender Trouble: Feminism and the Subversion of Identity* (New York: Routledge, 1990).

11. See Suzanne J. Kessler and Wendy McKenna, *Gender: An Ethnomethodological Approach* 17 (Chicago: University of Chicago Press, 1978). For similar denials involving not transsexualism but mere gender passing, see Donna Minkowitz's gripping analysis of the amours of Brandon Teena, "Love Hurts," *Village Voice*, Apr. 19, 1994, at 24, 27.

12. See Sue-Ellen Case, "Towards a Butch-Femme Aesthetic," in *The Lesbian and Gay Studies Reader*, ed. Henry Abelove, Michele Aina Barale, and David M. Halperin, at 249 (New York: Routledge, 1993).

13. Eve Kosofsky Sedgwick, *Epistemology of the Closet* 25–26 (Berkeley: University of California Press, 1990).

14. As another means of testing the depth to which sexuality is socially constructed, Judge Posner proposes cross-cultural analysis, but the queries he proposes are too narrowly constrained to answer his question. For instance, he regards as unfriendly a relatively deep social-constructivist hypothesis (position [4] in my redaction of Vance's description of sexual constructivisms) that opportunistic homosexuality in ancient Greece took the form of pederasty because of cultural constraints requiring that the erotic lay in, and articulated, unequal social relationships. To the extent that such an account explains not only the categories homosexual and heterosexual but more fundamentally the category of *the erotic* as historically contingent, it is indeed inconsistent with Posner's assumption that genital contact to orgasm is the paradigm object of human erotic attention everywhere. But it is quite indecisive for the truth-value of either hypothesis that other cultures might present male pederasty in a direct rather than an inverse relationship with sexual egalitarianism. Posner, "Economic Approach," pp. 187–88. To insist on the probative value of such comparisons is to miss the slippage between causation and correlation. Particularly in the cross-cultural study of sexuality, equibus need not be paribus.

15. Edward Stein, "Conclusion: The Essentials of Constructionism and the Construction of Essentialism," in Stein, ed., *Forms of Desire: Sexual Orientation and the Social Constructionist Controversy* 325, 330 n. 10, 336 (New York: Routledge, 1992).

16. Posner, "Economic Approach," p. 186. Not all social-constructivist models of sexual orientation concede this much individual malleability, however.

17. I discuss this and related problems in "Sexual Orientation and the Politics of Biology: A Critique of the Argument from Immutability," 36 *Stanford Law Review* 503 (1994).

18. Posner, "Economic Approach," p. 179.

19. Posner, "Economic Approach," pp. 181–82.

20. Posner, "Economic Approach," p. 190 n. 20.

21. See Posner, "Economic Approach," p. 178.

22. The Journal of the American Medical Association (JAMA) reported in 1994 that heterosexual transmission of HIV generated the "largest proportionate increase in reported AIDS cases in the United States" from 1991 to 1992, increasing 130 percent while "all other exposure categories combined increased 109 percent" during that period ("Heterosexually Acquired AIDS," 271 *JAMA* 975, 975 [1994]. "Heterosexual transmission . . . accounts for greater than 75 percent of the cumulative number of HIV infections in adults worldwide" (David B. A. Clemetson et al., "Detection of HIV DNA in Cervical and Vaginal Secretions: Prevalence and Correlates Among Women in Nairobi, Kenya," 269 *JAMA* 2860 [1993].

23. My tally is based on Evan Wolfson, "When the Police Are in Our Bedrooms, Shouldn't the Court Go in After Them?: An Update on the Fight Against 'Sodomy' Laws," 21 *Fordham Law Journal* 997, 997–1011 (1994); Halley, "Reasoning About Sodomy: Act and Identity In and After *Bowers v. Hardwick*," 79 *Virginia Law Review* 1721 (1993), App. B; and a review in March 1996 of *Lesbian and Gay Law Notes*, an exhaustive monthly report of legal developments touching on sexual orientation, sexuality, and AIDS. It appears that the only major repeal since 1993 is an injunction recently issued to block enforcement of the Tennessee same-sex sodomy statute, *Campbell v. Sundquist*, No. 01A01-9507-CV-00321, 1006 WL 29326 (Tenn. Ct. App. Jan. 26, 1996). The *Campbell* decision may be reversed on appeal, and in any event, it leaves the Tennessee statute still technically "on the books," but for now I am counting Tennessee as a repeal state.

24. Joyce Murdoch, "Laws Against Sodomy Survive in 24 States," *Washington Post*, Apr. 11, 1993, at A20. Moseley's conviction was later reversed. *Moseley v. Esposito*, No. 89-6897-1 (Ga. Sup. Ct. Sept. 6, 1989).

25. 10 U.S.C. § 654 (1993).

26. See Kendall Thomas, "Shower/Closet," 20 *Assemblage* 80 (1993).

27. Posner, "Economic Approach," p. 185.

28. On the involvement of law in the generation of race as a social category and in the management of race distinctions, see e.g., F. James Davis, *Who is Black?: One Nation's Definition* 31–50 (University Park: Pennsylvania State University Press, 1991); Leon Higginbotham, Jr., and Barbara K. Kopytoff, "Racial Purity and Interracial Sex in the Law of Colonial and Antebellum Virginia," 77 *Georgia Law Journal* 1967, 1989–2020 (1989); Edmund S. Morgan, *American Slavery, American Freedom: The Ordeal of Colonial Virginia* 308–37 (New York: W. W. Norton, 1975); Winthrop D. Jordan, *White over Black: American Attitudes Toward the Negro, 1550–1812* 855–98 (Chapel Hill: University of North Carolina Press, 1968). Miscegenation laws were declared unconstitutional under the California constitution in 1948, *Perez v. Sharp*, 198 P.2d 17 (1948), and under the federal constitution only in 1967; *Loving v. Virginia*, 388 U.S. 1 (1967).

10

Homosexuality and the Constitution

Cass R. Sunstein

> Decisions of individuals relating to homosexual conduct have been subject to state intervention throughout the history of Western Civilization. Condemnation of those practices is firmly rooted in Judeo-Christian moral and ethical standards. . . . Blackstone described "the infamous crime against nature" as an offense of "deeper malignity than rape."
>
> Chief Justice WARREN BURGER, concurring
> in *Bowers v. Hardwick*, 478 U.S. 186 (1986)

> I'm going to make you my girlfriend.
>
> Heavyweight champion MIKE TYSON,
> to his challenger Razor Ruddock

I. INTRODUCTION

A True Story

In 1958, Richard Loving, a white man, and Mildred Jeter, a black woman, were married in the District of Columbia.[1] Soon thereafter they returned to their home in Virginia. They were promptly indicted. Their crime was to have married in violation of Virginia's prohibition on interracial marriage. They pleaded guilty to the charge and were sentenced to a year in jail. The trial judge suspended the sentence on condition that the Lovings leave Virginia and not return for twenty-five years. The judge said: "Almighty God creates the races white, black, yellow, malay and red, and he placed them on separate continents. And but for the interference with his arrangement there would be no cause for such marriages. The fact that he separated the races shows that he did not intend for the races to mix."

The Lovings challenged the miscegenation law on constitutional grounds. They claimed that the law deprived them of the "equal protection of the laws." Thus was born the most aptly titled case in the entire history of American law, *Loving v. Virginia*.[2]

In the United States Supreme Court, the legal issues were relatively straightforward. In 1954, the Court had decided *Brown v. Board of Education*.[3] There the Court had made clear that racial discrimination is constitutionally unacceptable and that "separate but equal" is not equal. The Brown Court held that under the Constitution, the government could not discriminate against blacks. This was the issue in *Loving*: Was the ban on racial intermarriage a form of discrimination in the relevant sense?

On this question, there was sharp dispute. Virginia thought that the answer was, "Clearly not." Virginia's lawyers argued that miscegenation laws punished whites and blacks equally. They claimed that there was no discrimination against blacks. The only relevant discrimination was against people who sought to participate in mixed marriages, and such people were racially diverse, including members of all races. Unlike in *Brown*, where racial separation marked racial inequality, here separation was truly equal. Discrimination against people who seek to participate in mixed marriages is not "racial discrimination" at all. It does not draw a line between blacks and whites. It is a form of discrimination, to be sure—but not at all of the form that justifies special judicial skepticism under the Constitution. Because blacks and whites were treated exactly alike, that kind of skepticism was unwarranted.

From the standpoint of the 1990s, the argument may seem odd, even otherworldly. But if we linger over it, we will see that its logic is straightforward and even plausible. How did the Supreme Court respond? The key sentence in *Loving v. Virginia* says that "the racial classifications [at issue] must stand on their own justification, as measures designed to maintain White Supremacy." This striking reference to White Supremacy—by a unanimous Court, capitalizing both words and speaking in these terms for the only time in the nation's history was designed to get at the core of Virginia's argument that discrimination on the basis of participation in mixed marriages was not discrimination on the basis of race.

The Court appeared to be making the following argument. Even though the ban on racial marriage treats blacks and whites alike—even though there is formal equality—the ban is transparently an effort to keep the races separate and, by so doing, to maintain the form and the conception of racial difference that are indispensable to white supremacy. Viewed in its context—in light of its actual motivations and its actual effects—the ban was thus part of a system of racial caste. Virginia really objected to racial intermixing because it would confound racial boundaries, thus defeating what the district judge saw as "natural" differences produced by God's plan.

In a world with miscegenation, natural differences between blacks and whites would become unintelligible; the very word "miscegenation" would lose its meaning. Indeed, in a world with racial mixing, it would be unclear who was really black and who was really white. The categories themselves would be unsettled—revealed to be a matter of convention rather than nature. In such a world, white supremacy could not maintain itself. And because this was the assumption behind Virginia's law, the law stood revealed as an unacceptable violation of the equal protection principle.

A Hypothetical Story

Now let us imagine a hypothetical case. Two women seek to marry. They are prevented from doing so by a law forbidding same-sex marriage. They argue first that the relevant law violates the right to be free from sex discrimination. This seems to be a good strategic choice on their part. It is of course well-established that laws discriminating on the basis of sex will be subject to careful judicial scrutiny, and will generally be invalidated. By contrast, it also seems clear that laws discriminating on the basis of sexual orientation will be subject to deferential judicial scrutiny, and will generally be validated.[4] Our hypothetical couple would therefore do very well to argue that they are subject to discrimination on the basis of sex, not sexual orientation. They might try to establish this argument by saying what seems clearly true, that if one of them were a man, there would be no barrier to the marriage. The law therefore seems to contain explicit discrimination on the basis of sex. It treats one person differently from another simply because of gender. It is therefore a form of sex discrimination.

This argument appear straightforward; but under current constitutional law, the argument gets nowhere. The prohibition on same-sex marriage, it is said, discriminates on the basis of sexual orientation rather than on the basis of sex. There is no sex discrimination, because women and men are treated exactly the same. If a man wants to marry a man, he is barred; a woman seeking to marry a woman is barred in precisely the same way. For this reason, women and men are not treated differently. From this we see that the complaint in our hypothetical case is "really" about discrimination on the basis of sexual orientation, not at all about discrimination on the basis of sex. Since discrimination on the basis of sexual orientation is subject to highly deferential "rational basis" review, under which almost all statutes are upheld, the barrier to same-sex marriages and relations is constitutionally acceptable.

This is indeed the answer offered by current constitutional law. Thus concluded the Supreme Court of Missouri, as against an argument of this kind. According to the Court:

> The State concedes that the statute prohibits men from doing what women may do, namely, engage in sexual activity with men. However, the State argues that it likewise prohibits women from doing something which men can do: engage in sexual activity with women. We believe it applies equally to men and women because it prohibits both classes from engaging in sexual activity with members of their own sex. Thus, there is no denial of equal protection on that basis.[5]

It will readily appear that this is the same answer offered by the state of Virginia in the *Loving* case.[6] To the extent that *Loving v. Virginia* is now believed inapposite, it is for the following reason. We can now see that a law forbidding racial intermarriage is an effort to promote white supremacy. The separation of the races, especially in matters of sexuality and marriage, was part and parcel of the subordination of blacks to whites. That separation was part of the creation of a fixed category of racial differences. No one really denies this. It seems clear that if racial mixing were common, no one would know who is black and white, indeed the categories would lose much of their meaning. (It even seems reasonably clear that issues of sex discrimination are at work in this context, since the availability of black women to white men was common, and since the miscegenation laws seem especially inspired by the effort to prevent black men from having relations with white women.) The effort to promote "white purity" was conspicuously intended to prevent the various results that would come about from racial mixing. The Supreme Court's reference to "White Supremacy" was thus both necessary and sufficient to defeat Virginia's argument. It was readily shown that the miscegenation laws were connected to that constitutionally unacceptable social institution.

At least for participants in the current legal system, it is much harder to say this for same-sex relations. Exactly how is the prohibition on same-sex marriage an effort to promote male supremacy? How can the one have anything to do with the other? We can see that racial intermarriage was objectionable because of its effects on the racial difference, deemed natural and desirable, but thought (by the 1960s) to have social consequences only because of social institutions productive of something like a caste system based on race. Surely, it might be suggested, the question of same-sex relations raises no analogous issues.

I believe that it is puzzlement about such matters that accounts for the failure to see that *Loving v. Virginia* is a relevant or even decisive precedent for the view that the prohibition on same-sex relations is impermissible sex discrimination. In the end, however, I think that *Loving v. Virginia* is in fact a decisive precedent. Very briefly: A ban on racial intermarriage is part of an effort to insist that with respect to gender there are just "two kinds." The separation of humanity into two rigidly defined kinds, white and black, is part of what white supremacy means. Even though some people have darker skin color than others, and even though genes do diverge, this separation is in important respects a social artifact.

To say that there are just "two kinds" of people, black and white, is hardly a simple report on the facts; the division of the world into two kinds is emphatically social. Whatever we may be say about genes and colors, that particular division is the construction of a distinctive social state of affairs. It is tempting to think that the same cannot be said for the separation of humanity into two kinds, women and men. Perhaps that separation is genuinely ordained by nature; perhaps it is not a social artifact at all, or at least not at all in the same way. Who would deny that the distinction between men and women is fundamental in this sense?

But perhaps this argument goes by too quickly. It is indeed true that some people are black and others are white; this is no less true, or less "factual," than the division of humanity into men and women. The question is what society does with these facts. I believe that the prohibition on same-sex marriages, as part of the social and legal insistence on "two kinds," is as deeply connected with male supremacy as the prohibition on racial intermarriage is connected with white supremacy. Same-sex marriages are banned because of what they do to—because of how they unsettle—gender categories.

This is not merely a philosophical or sociological observation; it is highly relevant to the legal argument. It suggests that, like the ban on racial intermarriage, the ban on same-sex marriages is doomed by a constitutionally illegitimate purpose. The ban has everything to do with constitutionally unacceptable stereotypes about the appropriate role of men and women.

Moreover, the ban has constitutionally unacceptable effects. It is part of a system of sex-role stereotyping that is damaging for men and women, heterosexual and homosexual alike, though in quite different ways. Indeed, one of the most interesting issues has to do with the distinctive ways in which the ban differentially harms heterosexual men, gay men, heterosexual women, and lesbians. I will offer a few very brief speculations on this point below.

The rest of this essay comes in three parts. Part II discusses the constitutional background and sets out an anticaste principle, designed to help explain why and when sex discrimination is constitutionally illegitimate. I spend a fair amount of space on the appropriate conception of sex discrimination. This subject is both of considerable interest in its own right and of great importance to an understanding of the issue of sexual orientation. What I say in Part II also bears on the appropriate conception of equality in the theory of democratic politics. Part III connects the legal attack on gender caste with the issue of same-sex relations. Here I argue that bans on same-sex relations are a form of sex discrimination and therefore constitutionally unacceptable. Part IV discusses the properly limited role of courts in the Constitution, and indicates how judicial limitations might bear on enforcement of the anticaste principle. It also suggests that these limitations apply to the President and all others charged with constitutional interpretation (though to a lesser degree). These points bear on some issues in democratic theory as well.

II. THE CONSTITUTION AND DEMOCRATIC THEORY: BRIEF NOTES

In applying the Constitution to issues involving homosexuality, we have a range of options. I discuss them briefly here.

Privacy

It is perhaps most tempting to apply the right of privacy—a form of "substantive due process"—to sexual autonomy in homosexual relations. As a practical matter, this route has been foreclosed by the Georgia sodomy case, *Bowers v. Hardwick*,[7] in which the Supreme Court held that the right to privacy does not extend to same-sex sodomy. *Bowers* is of course much-maligned. But the case has at least a degree of plausibility in light of the controversial foundations of (a) any form of substantive due process, as a matter of constitutional interpretation and (b) the ordinary roots of any constitutional "privacy" rights in Anglo-American traditions, which often have refused to recognize the legitimacy of homosexuality.

Both of these are largely legal difficulties. But there are philosophical problems as well. The fundamental problem for homosexuals is not well-described as a simple absence of "privacy"; the closet can furnish a degree of privacy, but it is hardly a full solution to current problems. The closet is made necessary by the presence of discrimination in both public and private spheres. For this reason the emphasis on privacy rights misconceives the basic issue. The lack of privacy against public and private intrusion is one problem, to be sure; but it is a problem mostly because of deeper problems of inequality. A resort to rights of privacy is therefore a misleading foundation for constitutional law or philosophical thinking in this area.

Equality and Irrationality

Equality Vs. Due Process. The equal protection clause, designed as an attack on traditions, is a far more promising source of new constitutional doctrine. Most generally, the due process clause is associated with the protection of traditionally respected rights from novel or short-term change. It has a large Burkean feature. It is backward-looking. By contrast, the equal protection clause is self-consciously directed against traditional practices. It was designed to counteract practices that were time-honored and expected to endure, in at least muted forms. It is based on a norm of equality that operates as a critique of past practices.[8]

Irrationality. Under the equal protection clause, the Supreme Court has invalidated certain forms of discrimination on the ground that they are irrational—unconnected with any legitimate public purpose. This idea is connected with an interesting conception of democracy: the distribution of benefits or the impositions of burdens must reflect a conception of the public good. The Court has also disqualified certain conceptions has reflecting "prejudice" or "hostility." When legislation is founded merely on prejudice, it cannot qualify as rational.

We should think of the category of "prejudice" as a placeholder for a complex moral argument; the term is usually a conclusion masquerading as an analytic device. But in some important cases, lower federal courts have said that discrimination on the basis of sexual orientation can indeed be irrational, because it is a simple product of prejudice or irrational fear. Thus, for example, some courts have said that the exclusion from the military of people with homosexual "orientation"—unaccompanied by homosexual acts—is irrational and therefore unconstitutional under the equal protection clause. This is an unusual step in the law, since the legislature is usually given the benefit of every doubt against claims of irrationality (for democratic reasons), and since there are widespread moral convictions here and at least debated empirical issues.

The claim of "irrationality" is intriguing, and if endorsed by the Supreme Court, that would represent an important step in this area. For present purposes I offer two notes. First, the Court has been highly reluctant to invalidate laws on grounds of irrationality, identifying that notion with a kind of legislative absurdity, which the Court is understandably reluctant to attribute to the United States Congress. Second, the idea of "irrationality" really depends on a judgment that the grounds lying behind legislation are invidious. It is not simple to explain why the judgments that underlie discrimination on the basis of sexual orientation are invidious; to make that claim, one has to make a moral argument, one that opposes other moral arguments. The claim of "irrationality" disguises the necessary moral argument. While the claim of "irrationality" seems modest, it depends at bottom on relatively adventurous claims.

Equality and Suspect Classes

Perhaps it should be argued that discrimination on the basis of sexual orientation is analogous to discrimination on the basis of race, and therefore to be invalidated except in the rarest of circumstances. This is a highly plausible argument, though a great deal would have to be said in order to make it fully.

We can start by observing that the Supreme Court has granted "heightened scrutiny" to laws that discriminate against certain identifiable groups. When the Court grants heightened scrutiny, it is most skeptical of legislation, and the burden of every doubt operates on behalf of groups challenging the relevant laws. In deciding whether to grant heightened scrutiny, the Court has not been altogether clear about its underlying rationale. The Court appears to have looked, above all, at the likelihood that the group in question will be subject to prejudice, the existence of past and present discrimination, and the group's lack of political power. In this way, it has moved well beyond the defining case of discrimination against blacks to include discrimination against women, illegitimates, and sometimes aliens. The Court has not decided how discrimination against homosexuals should be treated. Let me offer a brief overview of the traditional factors and of how they might apply here.

It seems clear that discrimination on the basis of sexual orientation is especially likely to reflect prejudice (subject to the qualification above, noting that prejudice is a complex category, a placeholder for a moral argument). When government disadvantages homosexuals, it seems plausible to think that it will often do so because of an unreasoned or visceral belief in their sickness or inferiority, or because of sheer ignorance of relevant facts. In this way, discrimination on the basis of sexual orientation seems closely akin to discrimination on the basis of race and sex. In all of these settings, prejudice—understood as stereotypical thinking based on factual falsehoods and often rooted in simple hostility—is likely to account for discrimination.

It seems clear too that homosexuals have been and continue to be subject to public and private discrimination. For most of American history, disclosure of a homosexual orientation was grounds for systemic social harms. Even today, homosexuals must often keep their orientation secret in order to be free from discrimination or even violence. In many sectors of the economy, homosexuals cannot easily obtain jobs if their sexual orientation is disclosed.

Attention to the history and operation of the Constitution suggests that homosexuals may well be politically powerless in the constitutionally relevant sense. Often they have difficulty in making alliances with other groups by virtue of the existence of widespread prejudice and hostility against them. Precisely because they are often anonymous (that is, unknown to be homosexual) and diffuse (that is, not tightly organized), they face large barriers to exerting adequate political influence. The *diffusion* and *anonymity* of homosexuals can serve as a major obstacle to political influence. For this reason, it is probably not decisive that homosexuality—unlike race and gender—can be concealed; the ability to conceal can actually make things worse from the standpoint of exercising political power. This problem, severe in itself, is heightened by the fact that people who challenge discrimination on the basis of sexual orientation are often "accused" of being homosexual themselves, with possible harmful consequences for reputation in general. The existence of widespread hostility directed against homosexuals can thus make it difficult for homosexuals and heterosexuals alike to speak out against this form of discrimination.

One problem with the issue of "political powerlessness" is that relevant judgments depend on some controversial and usually unarticulated claims about how much political power is appropriate for the group in question, and about the legitimacy of usual bases for legislative judgments on matters affecting the group. It might be thought that homosexuals have a good deal of political power, for they can influence elections, even elections of the President. But the same is true of blacks and women, and the potentially large electoral influence of both groups does not exclude them from the category of groups entitled to particular protection against discrimination. The reason is that the prejudice in the constitutionally relevant sense is likely to operate in the political process. The conclusion is that the category of political powerlessness looks like an inquiry into political science; but it really depends on some normative judgments about the legitimacy of the usual grounds for government action.

The Supreme Court has sometimes said that it disfavors discrimination based on "immutable" characteristics; but this is a confusing claim. In fact the emphasis on immutability has obscured analysis. In the historical debate over race discrimination, the key point was that blacks were made second-class citizens (see below), not that race is immutable. Homosexuality may or may not be immutable in the relevant sense; but even if it is not, mutability is not decisive. For one thing, immutable characteristics are not an illegitimate basis for adverse governmental action. Blind people can be told not to drive. Even if there were a biological predisposition toward certain criminal behavior, we could surely punish that behavior, so as to deter and stigmatize it; a biological predisposition is thus not a basis for immunity from the criminal law if the underlying conduct can legitimately be punished.

So too it should not matter, for equal protection purposes, if skin color and gender could be changed through new technology. Discrimination on the basis of race would not become acceptable if scientists developed of a serum through which blacks could become white. In addition, some physical conditions, like blindness, are immutable, but not for that reason an illegitimate basis for state action. Immutability is neither a necessary nor a sufficient basis for treatment as a "suspect class." The real question is whether legislation disadvantaging the relevant group is peculiarly likely to rest on illegitimate grounds; heightened scrutiny is a way of testing whether it does. I do not think that on this count, discrimination against homosexuals is less troublesome than discrimination against blacks and women. But here too any judgments turn on complex moral arguments.

Despite its plausibility, the argument that homosexuals are entitled to special protection from discrimination is unlikely to be accepted by the Court that decided *Bowers v. Hardwick*, and in any case perhaps we can build even more narrowly and precisely on existing law.

Equality, Sex Discrimination, and Homosexuality

To approach this possibility, consider Chief Justice Burger's striking concurrence in the *Bowers* case. There the Chief Justice offered an approving reference to Blackstone's suggestion that sodomy is "an offense of 'deeper malignity than rape,' a heinous act, 'the very mention of which is a disgrace to human nature,' and 'a crime not fit to be named.'" It might be worthwhile to linger for a moment over the suggestion that consensual sexual relations among men are of "deeper malignity than rape."

Under what premises could this possibly be so? Why did both Blackstone and the Chief Justice think it worthwhile to compare the two crimes, and to assert the comparatively greater malignity of consensual sodomy? I think that the answer closely links the problem of discrimination on the basis of sex with that of discrimination on the basis of sexual orientation; that rape has often seemed far less violative than sodomy of human nature, and that this says a good deal about the character of sex discrimination and sex differences; and that the Chief Justice's comment inadvertently helps explain why *Loving v. Virginia* is so precise a precedent for the subject under discussion. But to say this is to get a bit ahead of the story. Let me turn more generally, then, to the equality principle of the Fourteenth Amendment.

III. THE ANTICASTE PRINCIPLE

In General

At the origin, the central target of the Fourteenth Amendment was not irrational distinctions on the basis of race, but the system of racial caste. For those who ratified the post-Civil War amendments, the problem was that the law had contributed to a system of caste based on race, thought to be a morally irrelevant characteristic. Those who framed and ratified those amendments were aware that the system of racial hierarchy had often been attributed to nature. Thus in the aftermath of the American Civil War, it was expressly urged, "God himself has set His seal of distinctive difference between the two races, and no human legislation can overrule the Divine decree."[9] In the same period, antidiscrimination law was thus challenged squarely on the ground that it put the two races in "*unnatural* relation to each other."[10] The post-Civil War amendments were based on a wholesale rejection of the supposed naturalness of racial hierarchy. The hierarchy was thought to be a function not of natural difference but of law, most notably the law of slavery and the various measures that grew up in the aftermath of abolition. The animating purpose of the Civil War amendments was an attack on racial caste.

We might similarly understand the problem of sex discrimination as amounting to the creation of a system of caste, based on gender and often operating through law. That system, like the racial caste system and others as well, is often attributed to "nature" and "natural differences." Consider here Mill's remarks: "But was there any domination which did not appear natural to those who possessed it? . . . So true is it that unnatural generally means only uncustomary, and that everything which is usual appears natural. The subjection of women to men being a universal custom, any departure from it quite naturally appears unnatural."[11] A principal feature of the caste system based on gender consists of law and social practices that translate women's sexual and reproductive capacities into a source of second-class citizenship. Those capacities are often made, again by law and social practices, into objects for the use and control of others.

In these circumstances, I suggest that building on the racial analogue, the appropriate equality principle in the area of sex equality is an opposition to caste. The legal objection should be understood as an effort to eliminate, in places large and small, the caste system rooted in gender. A law is therefore objectionable on grounds of sex equality if it contributes to a caste system in this way. The controlling principle, to be vindicated through law, is not that women must be treated "the same" as men, but that women must not be second-class citizens. As discussed below, the difference between the two points is critical.

The concept of caste is by no means self-defining. I will have to offer a brief and inadequate account here, one that is designed to provide a preface to the discussion of discrimination on the basis of sexual orientation.[12] Of course I do not suggest that the caste-like features of all societies containing sex inequality are the same. Certainly the American system of sex discrimination is far less oppressive than most systems of racial and gender caste. But I do claim that the caste-like features are what justify social and legal concern.

The motivating idea behind an anticaste principle, broadly speaking Rawlsian in character, is that without very good reasons, social and legal structures ought not to turn differences that are irrelevant from the moral point of view into social disadvantages. They certainly should not be permitted to do so if the disadvantage is systemic. A difference is morally irrelevant if it has no relationship to individual entitlement or desert. Race and sex are certainly a morally irrelevant characteristic in this sense. A systemic disadvantage is one that operates along standard and predictable lines in multiple important spheres of life, and that applies in realms that relate to basic participation as a citizen in a democracy. These realms include education, health care, freedom from private and public violence, wealth, political representation, and political influence. The anticaste principle means that with respect to basic human capabilities and functionings, one group ought not to be systematically below another.

A particular concern is that self-respect and its social bases ought not to be distributed along the lines of race and gender. An important aspect of a system of caste is that social practices produce a range of obstacles to the development of self-respect, largely because of the presence of the morally irrelevant characteristic that gives rise to caste status.

In the area of sex discrimination, the problem is precisely this sort of systemic disadvantage. A social or biological difference has the effect of systematically subordinating the relevant group—not because of "nature," but because of social and legal practices. Prominent among these practices is social and legal control of women's sexual and reproductive capacities. The resulting inequality occurs in multiple spheres and along multiple indices of social welfare: poverty, education, health, political power, employment, susceptibility to violence and crime, and so forth. That is the caste system to which the legal system should be attempting to respond.

Are Women Different? Does It Matter If They Are?

We are now in a position to make some general observations about the important and vexing matter of sex "differences"; these will bear directly on the issues raised by homosexuality. It is often said that women and men are different and that the differences help both to explain and to justify existing social and legal inequality. It is often claimed, for example, that women are different from men and that different treatment in law is therefore perfectly appropriate. Indeed in many legal systems, including that in America, the basic social and legal question is: Are women different from men? If not, have they been treated similarly?[13]

However widespread, this approach will not do. The question for decision is not whether there is a difference—often there certainly is—but whether the legal and social treatment of that difference can be adequately justified. Differences need not imply inequality, and only some differences have that implication. When differences do have that implication, it is a result of legal and social practices, not the result of differences alone. Since they are legal and social, these practices might be altered even if the differences remain. In any case inequality is not justified by the brute fact of difference.

An analogy may be helpful here. The problems faced by handicapped people are not a function of handicap "alone" (an almost impenetrable idea—what would current handicaps even mean in an entirely different world?), but instead of the interaction between physical and mental capacities on the one hand and a set of human obstacles made by and for the able-bodied on the other. It is those obstacles, rather than the capacities taken as brute facts, that create a large part of what it means, socially speaking, to be handicapped. "Nature" is quite irrelevant. It would be implausible, for example, to defend the construction of a building with stairs, and without means of access for those on wheelchairs, on the ground that those who need wheelchairs are "different." The question is whether it is acceptable, or just, to construct a building that excludes people who need an unusual means of entry. That question may not be a simple one, but it cannot be answered simply by pointing to a difference. The same is true for sex.

We can go further. Differences between men and women—especially those involving sexuality and reproduction—are often said to explain sex inequality, indeed to be the origin of inequality. But it might be better to think that at least some such differences are an outcome of inequality, or its product. Certainly some of the relevant "real differences" between men and women exist only because of sex inequality. Differences in physical strength, for example, undoubtedly have a good deal to do with differences in expectations, nutrition, and training. These differences cannot solely be attributed to women's sexual and reproductive capacities. Indeed, the degree of difference between men and women is notoriously variable across time and space. The variations are sufficient to show that what we attribute to nature is often a social product.

Even differences in desires, preferences, aspirations, and values are in significant part a function of society and even law—in particular of what society and law do with sexuality and reproduction. Preferences are often adaptive to the status quo, and a status quo containing caste like features based on sex will predictably affect the preferences of men and women in different ways. It will lead to distinctive processes of preference formation, inclining men and women in different direction in both the public and private spheres. The point suggests that it is wrong to base sex discrimination policy only on what women currently "want." Existing preferences will be partly an artifact of a discriminatory status quo.

I cannot adequately discuss this complex subject here. I suggest only that many of the sex differences that are said to justify inequality— physical, psychological, and more—are really a product of inequality. This is of course an empirical claim. In light of our current knowledge, we cannot say precisely how much of sex difference is artifactual in this sense. But we know enough to suggest that nature is not responsible for anything like all of what we see.

We can go even further. It is possible that some or even many of the differences between men and women, even if not themselves a social product, are noticed, or have anything like their current social meaning, only because of inequality. It is at least possible that the differences between men and women have such foundational status only because of the ways in which inequality and social practice make gender crucial. I do not claim that women are "the same" as men, or that law should try to make them "the same." I claim only that some gender differences are noticed and have consequences in significant part because of sexual inequality.

Some people go so far as to argue that there is nothing in the simple biological facts to establish that there are just two sexes.[14] On this view, the brute biology of the matter could mean that there is one sex, or three, or five, or ten. As counterintuitive and even bizarre as this may seem, I think that it is right. The fact that men and women really are different—and this is indeed a fact—does not mean that the division of human beings into two and only two categories is compelled by biology. That division is social and sometimes legal. I will return to this issue below. Whether or not this last point seems at all plausible, I hope that I have said enough to suggest the enormous difficulties in the effort to approach the law of sex equality through the lens of "differences." It is especially odd to attribute all or most social and legal practices involving gender to "nature." And if constitutional law is to do something about sex inequality, it should look to the matter of caste rather than the matter of difference.

On Sex Difference and Sexual Orientation

Now let us examine the relationship between sex discrimination and discrimination on the basis of sexual orientation. As I have noted, the ban on same-sex marriages is not now thought to raise a problem of sex inequality under the American Constitution. But might the legal ban (and the social taboo) not be a product of a desire to maintain a system of gender hierarchy, a system that same-sex marriages tend to undermine by complicating traditional and still-influential ideas about "natural difference" between men and women? Here is my thesis: In terms of their purposes and effects, bans on same-sex marriage have very much the same connection to gender caste as bans on racial intermarriage have to racial caste. I am speaking here of the real-world motivations for these bans, and I am assuming, as does current law, that impermissible motivations are fatal to legislation. The claim from neutrality is implausible in this context for exactly the same reason that it was implausible in *Loving*. To say this is not to say that the ban on same-sex marriages is necessarily unacceptable in all theoretically possible worlds. In our world, the ban is like a literacy test motivated by a discriminatory purpose, or a veterans' preference law designed to exclude women from employment.

In this space, I will not be able fully to defend this thesis, on which much work remains to be done. Certainly the thesis is not belied by the fact that some "macho" cultures do not stigmatize male homosexuality as much as (say) the United States.

Even in such cultures, a sharp distinction is drawn between passivity and activity in sexual relations, and cultural understandings of passive and active operate in highly gendered terms. Thus the passive role is both stigmatized and identified with femininity, whereas the active role is socially respectable and identified with masculinity. In such cultures, sex-role distinctions have somewhat different manifestations, but sex discrimination is fully operative in thinking both about men and women and about sexuality.

My claim about the reasons behind the ban on same-sex marriages is in part an empirical one; and it has suggestive empirical support in psychological studies. For example, one social psychologist, capturing much of the general view, finds that "a major determinant of negative attitudes toward homosexuality is the need to keep males masculine and females feminine, that is, to avoid sex-role confusion . . . .[15] The evidence taken as a whole suggests that the prohibition on homosexual relations is best seen as an effort to insist on and to rigidify "natural difference," in part by crisply separating gender roles.[16] This occurs largely by ensuring that there are firm and clear lines, defined in terms of gender, about sexual (and social) activity as opposed to sexual (and social) receptivity or passivity.

Thus it is that the definition of men as essentially active, in social and sexual arenas, and of women as essentially passive in both places, helps undergird the caste system based on sex. It simultaneously helps account for the prohibition of same-sex relations. The social opprobrium directed against homosexuals is an outgrowth of the ways in which, for heterosexuals, the existence of homosexuality draws into question familiar ideas about the sex difference.

There appear to be important distinctions here between the reasons that underlie the stigmatization or prohibition on male homosexual relations on the one hand and those that account for bans on female homosexual relations on the other. The evidence suggests that the social stigmatization of male homosexuality comes in large part from the perceived unnaturalness of male passivity in sex. It is this feature of male homosexuality that accounts for the social opprobrium directed against it. Thus it is well-established that the male heterosexual opposition to male homosexuality stems largely from the desire to stigmatize male sexual passivity (especially male receptivity in anal intercourse). We might speculate that subjection to sexual aggression of this kind is especially troublesome because, socially speaking, it turns men into women, and in this way complicates ordinary views about the sex difference. Thus it is a familiar part of violent male encounters that the victim will be feminized, as in the boxer Mike Tyson's remark to a challenger, "I'm going to make you my girlfriend." I suggest that far from being an oddity, this comment says something deeply revealing about the relationship between same-sex relations and the system of caste based on gender. The comment is tightly connected with Chief Justice Burger's approval of Blackstone's statement about the greater malignity of sodomy than rape.

The ban on lesbian relations stems from quite different concerns. Part of the purpose of such bans is to ensure that women are sexually available to men; the institution of lesbianism has been problematic (or invisible) largely for this reason. Another part of the concern stems from the fact that lesbianism also complicates gender difference by creating a sexually active role for women, one that also undermines existing conceptions of natural difference. It is for this reason familiar to see that socially active women—women prominently in politics or public life—are often stigmatized as a lesbian. Indeed, a charge of lesbianism is a standard delegitimating device operating against women who have assumed stereotypically male social roles. There is thus a close connection between the caste system based on gender and the prohibition on lesbianism.

I claim that considerations of this sort help to maintain the legal and social taboo on homosexuality, in a way that might well be damaging to both men and women, and to both heterosexual and homosexual alike, though of course in very different ways and to quite different degrees. The distinction between the rigid categories "male" and "female," with the accompanying social and sexual traits "active" and "passive," has especially conspicuous harmful effects for gay men and lesbians. But for all of us, the categories and the traits are much too crude to account for social and sexual life when both of these are going well. For heterosexual women as well, the distinction can be highly damaging, because it is rigidly confining and untrue to the complexity of their experience, even when their sexual attraction is directed to men. The damage is closely connected to the caste-like features of the current system of gender relations. For heterosexual men, very much the same is true, since a degree of passivity in society and in sexual relations is both an inevitable and a desirable part of life, and since it is such an unnecessary burden to be embarrassed by or ashamed of this.

Speculative and brisk as they are, these various points suggest that the division of gender into "two kinds" may be as artificial and unfortunate for gender as it is for race. There are men and women, to be sure. But the division of humanity into only "two kinds," with accompanying features, is far too rough a basis for understanding the diversity of human character, in both the private and the public spheres. The insistence on two kinds in turn undergirds the system of caste based on gender; it is also part and parcel of practices of discrimination against same-sex relations. For this reason, the prohibition on such relations is a form of discrimination on the basis of sex, just as the prohibition on miscegenation was a form of discrimination on the basis of race. Both prohibitions are invalid under the equal protection clause.

PRUDENCE AND CONSTITUTIONALISM: THE EXAMPLE OF ABRAHAM LINCOLN

Abraham Lincoln always insisted that slavery was wrong.[17] On the basic principle, Lincoln allowed no compromises. No justification was available for chattel slavery. But on the question of means, Lincoln was quite equivocal—flexible, strategic, open to compromise, aware of doubt. The fact that slavery was wrong did not mean that it had to be eliminated immediately, or that blacks and whites had to be placed immediately on a plane of equality. On Lincoln's view, the feeling of "the great mass of white people" would not permit this result. "Whether this feeling accords with justice and sound argument, is not the sole question, if indeed, it is any part of it. A universal feeling, whether well or ill-founded, can not be safely disregarded."[18] What is most striking about this claim is the view that the inconsistency of a "feeling" with justice or sound argument may be irrelevant to the question of what to do at any particular point in time.

On Lincoln's view, efforts to create immediate social change in this especially sensitive area could have unintended consequences or backfire, even if those efforts were founded on entirely sound principle. It was necessary first to educate people about the reasons for the change. Passions had to be cooled. Important interests had to be accommodated or persuaded to come on board. Issues of timing were crucial. Critics had to be heard and respected. For Lincoln, rigidity about the principle would always be combined with caution about introducing the means by which the just outcome would be brought about. For this reason it is a mistake to see Lincoln's caution with respect to abolition as indicating uncertainty about the underlying principle. But it is equally mistaken to think that Lincoln's certainty about the principle entailed immediate implementation of racial equality.

The point is highly relevant to constitutional law, especially in the area of social reform. As it operates in the courts, constitutional law is a peculiar mixture of substantive theory and institutional constraint. The best substantive thinking might call, for example, for a constitutional right to welfare, or for a vigorous and immediately vindicated anticaste principle. But because of institutional constraints, courts might be reluctant to vindicate that right or to enforce that principle. Constitutional rights might therefore be systematically under-enforced by the judiciary, and for good institutional reasons. To reach this conclusion in any particular area, we would of course have to spell out the substantive principle and the institutional constraints in some detail. But often there is plausibly a difference between the real extension of a constitutional principle and the judicial enforcement of that principle. There might therefore be some space, or gap, between what courts are (properly) willing to require and what the Constitution is (properly) interpreted to mean.

In the area of welfare rights, the point seems readily visible. Let us suppose that the Constitution should be interpreted to create such rights, on the theory that the equal protection of the laws so requires. Judicial enforcement of welfare rights might call for a difficult managerial role. Courts would have to oversee complex institutions in order to ensure vindication of the relevant rights. Because of the distinctive nature of the welfare problem, creation of the subsistence rights might have harmful adverse effects on other programs with a plausible claim to the public fisc. To say the least, courts are not in a good position to see those adverse effects. The managerial role is thus one for which they are ill-suited. The point applies in many areas of social reform in which courts are asked to act.

In the area of sex discrimination, such managerial issues are not always present. Suppose, for example, that the ban on same-sex marriage is challenged on equal protection grounds; here ongoing judicial supervision of complex institutions is not really at issue. But there is nonetheless reason for caution on the part of the courts. An immediate judicial vindication of the principle could well jeopardize important interests. It could galvanize opposition. It could weaken the antidiscrimination movement itself. It could provoke more hostility and even violence against gays and lesbians. It could jeopardize the authority of the judiciary. It therefore seems plausible to suggest that at a minimum, courts should generally use their discretion over their docket in order to limit the timing of relevant intrusions into the political process. It also seems plausible to suggest that courts should be reluctant to vindicate even good principles when the vindication would compromise other interests, at least if those interests include, ultimately, the principles themselves.

Consider, for example, the issue of abortion. Suppose we think that restrictions on abortion violate the right of privacy, or (in an argument more congenial to that offered here) that such restrictions deny women the right to equal protection of the laws. Is it therefore clear that *Roe v. Wade* was rightly decided? Surely not. A precipitous vindication of the relevant principle might well be a mistake. Indeed, it is for this reason—not because of any supposed abuse of interpretive authority—that *Roe* may have been wrong when initially decided. It seems at least reasonable to think that the *Roe* decision prematurely committed the nation to a principle toward which it was in any case steadily moving, and that the premature judicial decision had a range of harmful consequences. These included the creation of the Moral Majority, the death of the Equal Rights Amendment, the galvanizing of general opposition to the women's movement, the identification of that movement with the single issue of abortion, the dampening of desirable political activity by women, and the general transformation of the political landscape in a way deeply damaging to women's interest.[19] Ideas of these sort suggest that even if discrimination on the basis of sexual orientation is often a violation of the equal protection clause, courts should be cautious and selective in vindicating that principle.

In the area of homosexuality, we might make some distinctions. The argument I have offered here—for the proposition that same-sex relations and even marriages may not be banned—is quite adventurous. If the Supreme Court of the United States accepted the argument in 1994, or even 1995, we might expect a constitutional crisis, a weakening of the legitimacy of the Court, an intensifying of homophobia, a constitutional amendment overturning the Court's decision, and much more. Any Court should hesitate in the face of such prospects. It would be far better for the Court to start cautiously and to proceed incrementally.

The Court might, for example, conclude that the equal protection clause forbids state constitutional amendments that forbid ordinary democratic processes to outlaw discrimination on the basis of sexual orientation. The Court might say that such amendments, of the sort that has been enacted (and invalidated judicially) in Colorado, do not merely discriminate on the basis of sexual orientation, but also disfavor a defined group in the political process, in a way that involves issues of political equality. A judicial ruling of this kind would be quite narrow. Or the Court might say—as some lower courts have done—that government cannot rationally discriminate against people of homosexual orientation, without showing that those people have engaged in acts that harm any legitimate government interest. Despite its problems, "rationality" review might well be the best route here. Narrow rulings of this sort would allow room for public discussion and debate, before obtaining a centralized national ruling that preempts ordinary political process.

We can go further. Constitutional law is not only for the courts; it is for all public officials. The original understanding was that deliberation about the Constitution's meaning would be part of the function of the President and legislators as well. The post-Warren Court identification of the Constitution with the decisions of the

Supreme Court has badly disserved the traditional American commitment to deliberative democracy. In that system, all officials—not only the judges—have a duty of fidelity to the founding document. And in that system, we should expect that elected officials will have a degree of interpretive independence from the judiciar. We should even expect that they will sometimes fill the institutional gap created by the courts' lack of factfinding ability and policymaking competence. For this reason, they may conclude that practices are unconstitutional even if the Court would uphold them, or that practices are valid even if the Court would invalidate them. Lincoln is an important example here as well. Often he invoked constitutional principles to challenge chattel slavery, even though the Supreme Court had rejected that reading of the Constitution in the *Dred Scott* case.

Whatever the Supreme Court may say or do, it is therefore crucial for elected officials, most importantly the President, to insist that discrimination on the basis of sexual orientation is incompatible with constitutional ideals. The President has far broader room to reach such conclusions than does the Court. But a President determined to end such discrimination would not do well if he insisted on immediate vindication of the principle. Instead he should be pragmatic and strategic. Following Lincoln's example, he should insist, in all contexts, that this form of discrimination is wrong, and wrong because it violates the most basic ideals of the American Constitution. Indeed, it is both right and good for him to show the connection between discrimination on the basis of sexual orientation and other forms of discrimination, most notably discrimination on the basis of sex.

In implementing the relevant principles, however, there is room for caution and care. Like the Court, the President can be selective about putting relevant issues on the agenda. He can use especially egregious cases—involving, for example, discharge of qualified soldiers from the military, or discrimination against people with AIDS—to give weight to the principle in contexts in which it seems most acceptable. He can start slowly and with the easiest areas. One of his major goals should be educative.

A relatively radical attack on the prohibition on same-sex marriages might come many years down the road, when the basic principle has been vindicated in many other and less controversial contexts. In this way, the attack on discrimination against homosexuals might well become an important part of the attack on the caste system based on gender. But even if the principle is held firmly in view, and even if it is seen as part of constitutional mandates, its vindication in American law and life need not be immediate—largely because an immediate insistence on principle would compromise so many other social goals, including those that underlie the principle itself.

CONCLUSION

In almost all countries, including the United States, there is a system with caste-like features based on gender. This is the target of the equal protection clause, rightly understood. If we shift our attention from the unhelpful and misleading question of difference to the relevant question of caste, we will see a tight connection between discrimination on the basis of sexual orientation and discrimination on the basis of sex.

In the long run, I believe, the ban on same-sex relations will be seen as having the same relationship to male supremacy as did the ban on mixed marriages have to white supremacy. *Loving v. Virginia* is therefore a key case for those seeking to use the Constitution to counteract both sex discrimination and discrimination on the basis of sexual orientation.

This does not mean that current courts should require states to allow same-sex marriages. Under contemporary conditions, a judicial holding of this sort would probably be a large mistake, even though the basic principle is sound. Elected officials, including the President, have somewhat more flexibility. As part of their constitutional duty, elected officials and citizens themselves should clearly state the basic governing principle, which is that discrimination on the basis of sexual orientation is morally and legally unacceptable. But in producing social reform in this area, public officials should be selective, strategic, and occasionally cautious. This course may well disappoint people who are firmly committed to the basic principle and who conflate caution with ambivalence. The conflation is unnecessary and misleading. If we are to dismantle the system of caste based on gender—a system that goes so deep into both law and life—we should sometimes be cautious about implementation even as we stand firm on principle.

Notes

1. The idea that there is an analogy between the *Loving* case and cases involving the ban on sex-sex relations has been well-discussed elsewhere. Versions of the argument are made in Andrew Koppelman, "The Miscegenation Analogy," 98 *Yale Law Journal* 145 (1988); Sylvia Law, "Homosexuality and the Legal Meaning of Gender," 1988 *Wisconsin Law Review* 187. I am much indebted to these treatments here, especially to Koppelman's ingenious essay.

2. 388 U.S. 12 (1967).

3. 347 U.S. 483 (1954).

4. The Court has not yet resolved this issue, however. Lower courts generally, though not unanimously, apply "rational basis" review of laws discriminating on the basis of sexual orientation.

5. State v. Walsh, 713 S.W. ed. 508, 510 (Mo. 1986).

6. See Kippelman, supra note 1, to whom I am indebted here.

7. 478 U.S. 186 (1986).

8. The general point is defended in Cass R. Sunstein, "Sexual Orientation and the Constitution: A Note on the Relationship Between Due Process and Equal Protection," 55 *University of Chicago Law Review* 1161 (1988).

9. U.S. Congress 1873–74, 22.

10. Id. at 983 (emphasis in original).

11. Mill, *The Subjection of Women*, reprinted in J. S. Mill, *On Liberty and Other Essays* (J. Gray, ed., 1991).

Compare this description of attitudes in prerevolutionary America: "So distinctive and so separated was the aristocracy from ordinary folk that many still thought the two groups represented two orders of being . . . Ordinary people were thought to be different physically, and because of varying diets and living conditions, no doubt in many cases they were different. People often assumed that a handsome child, though apparently a commoner, had to be some gentleman's bastard offspring." Gordon Wood, *The Radicalism of the American Revolution* 27 (1991).

12. There is more detail in C. Sunstein, *The Partial Constitution* (1993).

13. On how these questions are at work in American law, see C. MacKinnon, *Feminism Unmodified* (1987); C. MacKinnon, *Toward A Feminist Theory of the State* (1989).

14. See Thomas Laqueur, *Making Sex* (1992).

15. See MacDonald and Games, "Some Characteristics of Those Who Hold Positive and Negative Attitudes Toward Homosexuals," 1 *Journal of Homosexuality* 9, 19 (1974), cited in Koppelman, supra note #1, at 159 n. 86. See also Whitley, "The Relationship of Sex-Role Orientation to Heterosexuals' Attitudes Toward Homosexuals," 17 *Sex Roles* 103 (1987).

16. Id.; see also Koppelman, supra note 1.

17. I draw in this section on the discussion in Alexander Bickel, *The Least Dangerous Branch* (1965). Koppelman, supra note 1, also discusses the issue of prudence, but reaches a different conclusion.

18. *Collected Works of Abraham Lincoln*, 256 (Roy Basler, ed., 1953).

19. Some of these claims are made in Gerald Rosenberg, *The Hollow Hope* (1992).

11

Natural Law, Morality, and Sexual Complementarity

Paul J. Weithman

Natural law theorists have characteristically shared two commitments. They have insisted that the truths of normative ethics are in some way based on ends that are both natural for human beings to pursue and naturally good for them to attain. They have also insisted that the laws which govern human communities must in some way be based on those ethical truths. As with any family of ethical theories, theorists in this family have elaborated their shared commitments in interestingly different ways. The resulting natural law theories differ in their accounts of how ethical truths are grasped, how justification of these truths depends on knowledge of natural teleology, and how civil laws should encourage people to live in accord with them.

The most recent revival of natural law has come at the hands of John Finnis and Germain Grisez.[1] Finnis and Grisez draw on traditional natural law theory. They are, however, no exception to the generalization that the philosophically interesting differences among natural law theorists lie in their diverse elaborations of shared commitments. Finnis and Grisez offer accounts of moral epistemology, of moral obligation, and of the moral responsibilities of political communities that are decidedly nontraditional. Despite their theoretical differences with other natural law thinkers, Finnis and Grisez are decidedly traditional in the norms of sexual and reproductive ethics they defend. Thus both are opposed to contraception, to voluntary sterilization, to abortion, and to homosexual activity.

Finnis has recently argued, in a paper called "Law, Morality, and 'Sexual Orientation,'"[2] That all homosexual activity is wrong, that the attempt to share love through homosexual activity is the pursuit of an illusion and that political communities may legitimately discourage homosexual activity through a wide variety of legislative restrictions. The arguments Finnis offers for these claims draw both on claims that have long been relied on in the natural law tradition and on elements that are distinctive to Finnis's own natural law theory. In this essay, I provide a rigorous formulation of Finnis's arguments, showing the presuppositions on which they rely. I criticize both Finnis's attack on the licitness of homosexual activity and his defense of legislative restrictions on it. I argue that Finnis fails to show homosexual activity wrong, and he fails to show that political communities have a compelling interest in denying legal recognition to committed, lifelong, and exclusive homosexual relationships.

I

Finnis's argument against the licitness of homosexual activity is found in a long paragraph in the middle of his essay. Because I want to examine it carefully, the argument is worth quoting in full:

> The union of the reproductive organs of husband and wife really unites them biologically (and their biological reality is part of, not merely an instrument of, their *personal* reality); reproduction is one function and so, in respect of that function, the spouses are indeed one reality, and their sexual union therefore can *actualize* and allow them to *experience* their *real common good—their marriage* with the two goods, parenthood and friendship, which (leaving aside the order of grace) are the parts of its wholeness as an intelligible common good even if, independently of what the spouses will, their capacity for biological parenthood will not be fulfilled by that act of genital union. But the common good of friends who are not and cannot be married (for example, man and man, man and boy, woman and woman) has nothing to do with their having children by each other, and their reproductive organs cannot make them a biological (and therefore personal) unit. So their sexual acts together cannot do what they may hope and imagine. Because the activation of one or even each of their reproductive organs cannot be an actualizing and experiencing of the *marital* good—as marital intercourse (intercourse between spouses in a marital way) can, even between spouses who *happen* to be sterile—it can do no more than provide each partner with an individual gratification. For want of a *common good* that could be actualized and experienced *by and in this bodily union*, that conduct involves the partners in treating their bodies as instruments to be used in the service of their consciously experiencing selves; their choice to engage in such conduct thus disintegrates each of them precisely as acting persons. (1066–67, emphasis original)

On first reading, Finnis's argument is difficult to understand for several reasons. The argument is, as he himself acknowledges, presented elliptically and a number of its crucial premises are suppressed. Some of the concepts Finnis employs, most notably that of a "biological unit," seem unusual if not bizarre. The paragraph seems to juxtapose two arguments. The first half of the passage is an argument for the weak claim "their sexual union therefore *can* actualize and allow them to experience their real common good" (emphasis shifted), a conclusion that Finnis tries to prove but on which he does not subsequently rely. In the second half of the passage, the order of the sentences obscures the order of the argument, for the sentence that begins with the phrase "because the activation" seems to support rather than follow from the sentence that precedes it. The juxtaposition of the last two sentences is perplexing. Finnis moves from the claim that homosexual unions cannot realize "the marital good" to the claim that they cannot realize *any* common good without intervening argument.

Throughout the passage, Finnis conveys the impression of engagement in a multifront war. The claim that "the common good of two friends who are not and cannot be married . . . has nothing to do with their having children by each other" seems at first blush an *obiter dictum* directed at Stephen Macedo (1066, n. 46) since the second conjunct and not this claim seems to do the sentence's argumentative work. Other of Finnis's claims are directed against those who deny that parenthood is part of the "intrinsic fulfillment" (1065) of marriage, still others against those who think him unable to account for the licitness of a sterile couple's sexual activity. Finnis's parenthetical claim that human "biological units" are also "personal" is a preemptive strike against those who would accuse him of a crudely physicalist account of human sexuality. There is nothing inherently wrong with simultaneously doing battle on a number of fronts. The strategy does, however, pose problems for those war correspondents and analysts whose job it is to discern the main lines of attack.

Despite these initial difficulties of interpretation, Finnis's argument against the licitness of homosexual activity is philosophically interesting, both in its own right and as an instance of natural law argumentation. While I believe that his argument fails to establish its conclusion, it is important to grasp the argument's interest and sophistication to see what parts of it bear the burden of proof. My primary task in the next section will be to reconstruct the argument, trying to bring its presuppositions and most interesting features to light.

Fulfilling this task entails ascribing to Finnis concepts he himself does not employ and claims he does not explicitly endorse; my task in this section is to elaborate these. In particular, my interpretation requires imputing to Finnis an idea that he does not explicitly discuss but that I believe is central to his argument: the idea of a *complementary union*. To grasp this idea, note the commonplace that human beings unite in performing activities of various kinds. They unite, for example, to engage in scientific and dramatic pursuits, in worship and in games, in work, in play, in conversation, in order to listen to a speaker or to enjoy entertainment. Let us say that groups united in activity are complementary unions if and only if (i) performance of the activity in question engages the diverse attributes and capacities of the participants, or requires their accumulated efforts, and (ii) the end of the activity could not be realized unless it were pursued in ways that draw on or accumulate the diverse capacities and attributes of more than one participant.

Quite clearly the question of whether some union is complementary is independent of questions about how it is governed. Some complementary unions may be cooperative activities in which all participants are aware of and do or could approve the terms of cooperation; others may be activities coordinated by a leader who decides on the rules of the activity and the division of rewards without attending to actual or hypothetical consent. What is essential to a complementary union is that those united *complete* or *complement* one another in their collective activity by bringing to the activity what some other participants lack. Orchestras performing symphonic concerts and athletic teams playing games are paradigms of complementary unions, for in each case, play draws on the diverse attributes of the performers and the end of these activities could not be attained without such diversity. The unions of those attending worship or listening to a lecture are less obviously complementary. Yet when members share their ideas, impressions, and feelings in subsequent conversation, when they draw mutual support from taking part in collective prayer or when they learn from one another in a question period, the requisite diversity of capacities is engaged and the activity is one requiring diversity.

I believe Finnis thinks of complementary unions as having two important logical features.

First, since the fact that some group is a complementary union entails that it is capable of collective activity in pursuit of some end, it can be considered an agent, an entity (in this case, a corporate entity) capable of performing action. The fact that a group is a complementary union therefore entails, Finnis thinks, that it is in respect of that activity a "unit" or "one reality." It entails, Finnis thinks, that that group is "really united" with respect to the activity in virtue of which it is a complementary union.[3]

Second, a group is capable of realizing a common good, Finnis thinks, only if that group is a complementary union. To see why he might think this, note that common goods are not simply goods enjoyed or experienced by all members of a group. They are also goods realized in the group's collective activity, and they provide the point or the explanation of that group's engagement in the activity in question. If such a good could be realized in the solitary activity of the members, then the availability of this good through group activity would not explain why members were engaged in the activity together. So if they are to provide the rationale of a group's collective activity, common goods must be goods that individual group members cannot realize in their solitary activities. If common goods cannot be realized in solitary activity, it must be because they can be realized only in pursuits that draw on a diversity of capacities and attributes or on the cumulative efforts of a number of persons. Therefore, if some common good is the end or point of an activity, then it is such that it can be realized only if pursued in ways that draw on a diversity of capacities and attributes or that accumulate the efforts of a number of persons. Moreover, if that common good is, in fact, realized by a group, then the group's activity must be of that kind. So if a common good is realized by a group, that group must be a complementary union.

Let us exploit the notion of a complementary union to define what we might call a *sexually complementary union*. A union is sexually complementary if and only if (i) performance of the sexual activity in question engages the diverse sexual attributes and capacities of two adult partners, and (ii) the end of the activity could not be realized unless it were pursued in ways that draw on the diverse sexual capacities and attributes of two adult partners. Finnis would, I believe, endorse what we might call *the sexual complementarity condition*. This is condition on the realization of common goods by sexual unions, where two people are in sexual union just in case they are engaged in activity that essentially involves sexual contact—what Finnis calls the "activation" of the sexual organs of at least one of them. According to the sexual complementarity condition, two adults are capable of realizing a common good by and in a sexual union only if the union is sexually complementary.

What might this condition have to recommend it? Suppose two adults realize a common good through a sexual union. If that common good is the point of or the rationale for the partners' collective activity, then it must be a good that cannot be realized in solitary activity. Therefore, that good can be only be realized through collective activity that *ex hypothesi* entails sexual contact. If this is so, then it must be that it cannot be realized except through activity drawing on the diverse sexual capacities and attributes of the partners. And since the group in question achieves the good in sexual union, it must be engaged in such activity. The supposition that two adults realize a common good through their sexual activity therefore entails (i) and (ii). Hence, the union of the two is sexually complementary.

II

With the sexual complementarity condition in hand, it is possible to sketch the outlines of Finnis's treatment of homosexual activity.

If the sexual union of two people is to "actualize and allow them to experience their common good," then their union must satisfy the sexual complementarity condition. Finnis thinks that husband and wife in voluntary and uncontracepted sexual union satisfy this condition because of the natural complementarity between men and women. Each, he would say, can complement or complete the other by supplying what the other lacks to engage in the activity of procreation. Because they constitute a complementary unit capable of procreation, spouses become "one reality," a single "biological unit." Their "natural complementarity" is sexual, so the sexual union of husband and wife satisfies the sexual complementarity condition. It *can* allow them to realize their common good, a good that Finnis would say, includes not just procreation but also parenthood and friendship. Moreover, Finnis would argue this natural complementarity and consequent unity can be experienced even by sterile couples. They can enter into a complementary union and become "one reality" even if procreation is impossible.

With homosexual couples, Finnis would argue, things are different. He would claim that there is no sexual complementarity between man and man or woman and woman: their *sexual union* is not itself an instance of one partner supplying what the other lacks so that they can together achieve some end that neither could attain singly. The sexual union of a homosexual couple therefore, Finnis would say, fails the sexual complementarity condition; hence, there is no common good that can be realized through their sexual union. Therefore, Finnis says, homosexual activity can provide the partners only with individual sexual gratification. It is because individual gratification is a good each of the partners could realize through solitary activity that Finnis says "homosexual acts have a special similarity to solitary masturbation" (1062-63). It is because Finnis thinks partners in homosexual acts can realize only individual gratification that he thinks partners in such acts inevitably use their own and one anothers' bodies as instruments or means to gratification. And it is because he thinks there is no common good available through homosexual union that Finnis thinks homosexual couples who believe they realize one are in the grip of an illusion.

This rough interpretation captures the main lines of Finnis's reasoning. To see that it does so and to facilitate assessment, let me provide a more rigorous formulation of the argument. This formulation accommodates his text by including claims that he makes in the order he makes them.[4]

Suppose that Finnis thinks

(1) If the members of a group are united and act in the way members of their kind naturally unite and act to perform some function, then they are a complementary union.

From (1) and the properties of a complementary union, it follows that

(2) Groups constitute one reality of the sort that has a given function if they are united and act in ways groups naturally unite and act to perform that function.

Finnis explicitly says that

(3) "Reproduction is one function."

And it seems quite plausible that

(4) The voluntary and uncontracepted union of the reproductive organs of a husband and wife in certain intentional states[5] is the way husband and wife naturally unite and act to perform the function of human reproduction.

From (2), (3), and (4) it follows that

(5) A husband and wife in the requisite intentional states whose reproductive organs are voluntarily and uncontraceptively united are one reality of the sort that has the function of human reproduction: "in respect of that function, the spouses are indeed one real it."

Perhaps Finnis also thinks that

(6) Whatever is one reality with a biological function is one biological reality with that function.

and that

(7) Two things are united in one biological reality when and only when they are really united biologically, when and only when the union makes of them a "biological unit."

Then it follows from (5), (6), and (7) that

(8) "[t]he [voluntary and uncontracepted] union of the reproductive organs of husband and wife really unite them biologically": it makes of them a biological unit of the sort that has the function of human reproduction.

I believe Finnis would argue that

(9) Parenthood fulfills the function of human reproduction if and only if accompanied by friendship.

Perhaps he also would say of sentient or conscious units that

(10) The fulfillment of a function can be actualized and experienced by units of the sort that has function when they act in the way such units naturally act to perform that function.

From (4), (9), and (10) it follows that

(11) Parenthood and friendship can be actualized and experienced by units of the sort that has the function of human reproduction when their reproductive organs are voluntarily and uncontraceptively united and when the constituents of the unit are in the requisite intentional states.

From (5), (8), and (11), it follows that

(12) Spouses' "sexual union therefore can *actualize* and allow them to *experience*" parenthood and friendship.

Finnis characterizes marriage as

(13) "the real giving to each other of two people in biological, affective, and volitional union in mutual commitment which is both open-ended and exclusive" (1067).

Perhaps he thinks that

(14) Two people really give to each other in biological union only if they are "really unite[d] biologically" by their sexual union.

and that

(15) Two people are "really unite(d] biologically" by their sexual union only if their sexual union is a sexually complementary union.

From (15) and the properties of complementary unions, it follows that

(16) Two people are "really united biologically" by their sexual union only if their union makes of them "one reality."

Since husband and wife are sexually complementary, that "one reality" is a unit of the sort that has the function of human reproduction. So from (13), (14), (15), and (16), it follows that

(17) Being married entails that a husband and wife constitute by their sexual union a unit of the sort that has the function of human reproduction.

Suppose that Finnis thinks, as seems plausible,

(18) If being married entails that a husband and wife are continuously or episodically a unit of some sort, then the good of marriage includes the good of units of that sort.

and

(19) The good of a unit includes whatever fulfills the function of units of its sort.

Then from (17), (18), and (19) it follows that

(20) So the good of marriage includes the goods of parenthood and friendship.

And from (12) and (20), Finnis's first conclusion follows:

(21) "The sexual union [of husband and wife] therefore can *actualize* and allow them to *experience* their *real common good—their marriage* with the two goods, parenthood and friendship, which . . . are the parts of its wholeness as an intelligible common good."

What of the argument against homosexual conduct? As I mentioned at the outset, Finnis argues against the licitness of all orgasmic homosexual activity. He argues *a fortiori* against the licitness of such activity in a range of very difficult cases for his position: cases in which those engaging in such conduct do so in the context of a loving relationship. In the most difficult of these cases, partners may love one another so that they want their sexual union to achieve the intimacy of marriage. So

(22) Suppose that two people of the same sex intend, hope, or believe their sexual union to achieve a "real giving to each other . . . in biological, affective, and volitional union."

From (14) and (22), it follows that

(23) They intend, hope, or believe themselves to be "really unite[d] biologically" by their sexual union.

From (15) and (23), it follows that

(24) "Their sexual act can [ ] do what they . . . or imagine" only if their sexual union is a sexually complementary union.

But Finnis would assert that

(25) Two people of the same sex cannot be sexually complementary.

So

(26) The sexual union of two people of the same sex is not a sexually complementary union.

From (24) and (26), it follows that

(27) "Their sexual acts together cannot do what they may hope and imagine."

Moreover, from (26), it follows that a homosexual union fails the sexual complementarity condition. So

(28) Two people of the same sex cannot realize a common good by and in their sexual union.

But if there is no *common* good that can be realized through an activity, then any goods realized must be individual goods or gratifications. So, from (28), Finnis thinks it follows that

(29) The sexual union of two people of the same sex "can do no more than provide individual gratification."

If the end of a sexual union of two people is individual gratification, Finnis would argue, then it must be that partners in that union treat their own and/or their partners' bodies as means to their own and/or their partners' gratification. So if (28) and (29) are true, then

(30) "For want of a *common good* that could be actualized and experienced *by and in this bodily union*, that conduct involves the partners in treating their bodies as instruments to be used in the service of their consciously experiencing selves[.]"

What argument does Finnis offer that this is morally bad? He says that "the attempt to express affection by orgasmic non-marital sex" is pursuit of "an illusion" (1065) or a "fantasy' (1067). These remarks raise the possibility that Finnis thinks sexual activity in committed homosexual relationships is morally *tragic*. Partners in such a relationship, I have supposed, devote energy and attention to nurturing a relationship they take to be like heterosexual marriage. But because that relationship cannot be "what they may hope and imagine" (1066), Finnis might think, the partners' lives are as objectively tragic as the life of someone who forsakes all else to write a "great American novel" that is in fact of no literary merit. He might also think the partners' devotion of energy and resources to their relationship is irresponsible if the energy and resources could have been devoted to pursuit of a nonillusory end.

While Finnis may think that there are dimensions of tragedy and irresponsibility to some homosexual relationships, the real point of his argument lies elsewhere. Crudely put, I believe he might argue that human beings are essentially embodied and human agency is essentially the agency of embodied persons. Acting as if the body is an instrument for the production of pleasure implies an alienation of one's agency from one's body. The integrity or wholeness of human beings as agents is therefore compromised if they treat their bodies as "instruments to be used in the service of their consciously experiencing selves." So, from (30), Finnis thinks it follows that

(31) Two peoples' "choice to engage in [homosexual] conduct thus disintegrates each of them precisely as acting persons."

Since Finnis would maintain that it is morally bad to choose in ways that "disintegrate" oneself and/or another "precisely as acting persons," then he would conclude that the choice to engage in homosexual activity is morally bad.[6]

III

The sexual complementarity condition and the ideas of complementary and sexually complementary unions make it possible to reconstruct Finnis's argument in a fairly rigorous form. The argument thus reconstructed fits the language of his text and the order in which he makes his points. There is, therefore, some justification for supposing that, in its essentials, it is the argument he had in mind. In the next section, I will raise some objections to the argument; before doing that, I want to note three points about it.

First, note the features of Finnis's argument that make it appropriate to describe it as a natural law argument. As I remarked at the outset, natural law theories typically have at their core claims about natural teleology and their normative commitments typically depend on claims about the ethical value realized by the fulfillment of natural functions or the performance of characteristic activities. Finnis's argument as I have presented it appeals to just such claims. Premise (2) asserts that agents (in this case, groups) fall into kinds in virtue of their being united and acting in a way that is natural to members of that kind. Defense of (9) would appeal to two different sets of natural human characteristics. Defense of the claim that friendship partially fulfills the function of reproduction would, I believe, appeal to the claims that human beings have a natural capacity and need for relationships in which they are uniquely loved, and that that capacity is naturally engaged and the need naturally felt in acts of intense physical intimacy. Defense of the claim that parenthood, rather than simply procreation, fulfills the function of reproduction would appeal to the claim that those in such relationships find authentic satisfaction in jointly giving themselves to others. The argument also depends crucially on (19), the claim that units or agents realize their goods by the perfected or fulfilled exercise of their natural functions. Finally, the notion of sexual complementarity and the sexual complementarity condition fit with Finnis's view that the reproductive organs of women and men are naturally suited to the joint performance of the natural function of reproduction.

The second point to note about the argument concerns Finnis's description of a copulating couple as a "biological unit" of the sort that has the function of reproduction. This ascription of the function of reproduction to units comprised of husband and wife signals an advance within the recent history of the natural law tradition. Natural law thinkers earlier in this century often relied on the "perverted faculty argument" to demonstrate the moral illicitness of various sexual practices, prominently including contraception. According to that argument, procreation is the natural function of semen,[7] of the human genitalia, or more generally of the "reproductive faculty." The wrongness of contraception was then said to be located in the misuse of the faculty or organs so that they were kept from fulfilling their natural function.[8]

The perverted faculty argument is notoriously subject to difficulty. One of these difficulties concerns the general moral principle on which the argument seems to depend, a principle forbidding interference with the reproductive organs' performance of their natural function. This principle, in any form strong enough to support the desired conclusion, seems vulnerable to obvious counterexamples. Natural law theorists do not object to the removal of a diseased uterus and ovaries, for example, even though such surgery impedes the functioning of a woman's reproductive organs by removing them. Moreover, the principle seems suspiciously *ad hoc*. Its defenders are faced with the task of drawing a principled distinction between the reproductive organs, whose frustration the principle forbids, and other organs whose operation it is permissible to impede.

A more fundamental difficulty with the perverted faculty argument is that it seems to be motivated by a crudely physicalist understanding of sexual morality. One of the functions of moral principles is to single out certain states of affairs as morally relevant, or as morally decisive. Thus utilitarian principles single out as morally relevant facts about the happiness of sentient creatures; the textbook example of a deontological principle singles out as morally decisive the fact that some agent has made a promise. A moral principle strong enough to underwrite the perverted faculty argument against contraception must single out as morally decisive the fact that the reproductive organs have been frustrated in the performance of their natural functions. But it is hard to see, without a great deal more philosophical argument than proponents of the perverted faculty argument have provided, why facts about the natural functions of the reproductive organs are even morally *relevant*, let alone morally *decisive*. To suppose they are morally decisive is to suppose that there can be cases in which the intentions of agents are irrelevant to the moral worth of an act. It is to repose the moral worth of those acts in their physical properties.

Finnis's description of a sexually joined couple as a unit is part and parcel of his attempt to find an alternative to the perverted faculty argument that avoids these difficulties. The moral weight in his arguments is home not by natural functions, which it is illicit to frustrate, but by the goods realized when agents act on their choice to pursue or eschew what he calls "basic goods." As we have seen, Finnis argues that when a husband and wife engage in voluntary and uncontracepted sex, they realize the common good of their relationship. Whether or not Finnis's arguments against homosexuality, contraception, and abortion are sound, the moral principle on which they rely—enjoining respect for "basic goods"—is far more plausible than the principle on which the perverted faculty argument relies. A principle that implies the moral relevance of acting against some good is far more plausible than one that implies the moral decisiveness of frustrating natural function.[9]

The description of a couple as a "biological unit" is a natural concomitant of this shift of moral weight from functions to goods. The goods on which Finnis focuses in sexual ethics are goods realized, not by the sexual organs or faculties, but jointly by a sexually united couple. He therefore thinks that the agent engaging in the activity or function which brings about that good is the copulating couple considered as a single unit. His description of a copulating couple as a "biological unit" and his ascription of reproduction to that unit are therefore of a piece with his attempt to avoid difficulties that beset earlier arguments.

The third point concerns Finnis's inference of (31) from (30) and his argument that it is morally wrong to choose in ways that "dis-integrate" the self. The natural law theory of Finnis and Grisez is innovative in its treatment of moral worth and obligation, their treatment of these matters has drawn critical fire from other natural law thinkers.[10] It might therefore be thought that it is at this point that Finnis's argument against homosexuality is most vulnerable. But regardless of how exactly he defends the move from (30) to (31), I am inclined to agree that there is something both alienating and morally bad about treating one's body as nothing more than an instrument for producing one's own or another's pleasure. Therefore, I am inclined to agree that if the inferences leading Finnis to (30) are correct, the impermissability of homosexual activity follows, even if it does not follow in exactly the way that Finnis and Grisez suggest. Where Finnis is wrong, I shall argue, is in supposing that those earlier inferences are sound. It follows that if the most original elements of his natural law theory leave his argument against homosexual activity open to attack, they do so in a very different way than his critics might think. The problem is not with his claim that acts having certain features are morally wrong. It is that his account of moral wrongness forces him to argue that homosexual acts have features that in fact they lack and lack features that in fact they have.

IV

Those who criticize natural law treatments of homosexual activity are often tempted by what we might call the "sterility objection." According to this objection, any principle strong enough to imply the illicitness of homosexual sex can be exploited to show that that of sterile heterosexual couples is illicit as well. Since natural law theorists are typically committed to the licitness of the latter and the imperinissability of the former, it is alleged that natural law arguments against homosexual activity fail. But if the notion of sexual complementarity is assumed cogent and if Finnis is granted (25), then he has the resources to respond to this objection. This suggests that any force the sterility objection has against Finnis's argument depends on the force of objections to (25) and to the notion of sexual complementarity. I therefore want to pursue this objections and leave sterility aside.

Consider (25), the claim that two people of the same sex are not sexually complementary. Perhaps Finnis takes this claim as obvious. After all, he might ask, what could it mean to say that two people are of the same sex except to say that they are sexually identical? And if they are sexually identical, then they do not have the diverse sexual capacities and attributes and hence are not sexually complementary.

No doubt there is a sense of 'identical' in which two people are sexually identical if they are of the same sex. It is not clear, however, why (25) follows from the fact two people are sexually identical in this sense; seems to require that two people of the same sex not have *any* diverse sexual capacities and attributes. This claim would follow if it were the case that the only sexual capacities and attributes persons have, or the only ones relevant to their sexual complementarity, were the capacities and attributes necessary for performing the function of reproduction. But why suppose that?

Finnis does not, to my knowledge, provide a general theory of functions. It is therefore hard to know how functions differ from other activities. It is therefore hard to know why sexual identity, diversity, and complementarity must be defined with reference to any sexual *function* at all, rather than with reference to sexual activity. Even if it is granted that these notions must be defined with reference to a function, it is hard to see why that function must be reproduction.

The following argument for this claim might initially seem attractive. Suppose that if F is the function of unit U, then U realizes its good in the activity of fulfilling function F. So, if F is the function of a sexual union, then the common good of the sexual union is realized in the activity of fulfilling F. By the sexual complementarity condition, if F is the function of a sexual union, then a union engaged in the activity of fulfilling F is a sexually complementary union. This might suggest that sexually complementary unions must be defined by appeal to the functions, fulfillment of which actualizes the common good of sexual unions. If it were assumed that reproduction is the function of every sexual union and the only function in which the common good of sexual unions can be realized, then perhaps the notion of sexual complementarity would have to be defined with reference to the function of reproduction. The problem with this argument, however, is that it begs the question. What is at issue is whether nonreproductive sexual unions, including homosexual unions, are unions in which common goods can be actualized.

For purposes of argument, let us grant Finnis what assumptions he needs about identity, diversity, and complementarity for (25) to be obviously true. But then the sexual complementarity *condition* is far from obvious. Recall that the sexual complementarity condition is a condition on the possibility of realizing common goods "by and in" sexual unions. According to the condition, common goods can be realized by and in a sexual union only if the union is sexually complementary. Then the sexual complementarity condition entails that two people can realize a common good by and in their sexual union only if by their union each supplies what the other lacks so that they become a unit of the sort that has the function of reproduction. It entails that two people can realize a common good by and in their sexual union only if one is biologically male and the other biologically female. Is the sexual complementarity condition true when so understood?

It seems possible that two men or two women in an exclusive relationship could realize the goods of that relationship by and in the giving and receiving of sexual pleasure. Sexual activity might be occasions for partners to know one another with great emotional intimacy by showing their feelings to one another, by developing their feelings with one another, and by sharing their vulnerabilities. Moreover, it seems possible that one of the ways partners express the special and exclusive character of their relationship is through their sexual activity, since by sharing sexual activities, they share with one another what *ex hythothesi* they share with no one else. It therefore seems possible that the common good of an exclusive and emotionally satisfying relationship be fostered by and in a sexual union between two men or two women. If this is possible, then there is a common good that can be realized by and in sexual unions between two males and two females, at least on one plausible interpretation of "by and in."

Granting Finnis the assumptions he needs about sexual complementarity and identity if (25) is to be obvious therefore makes the sexual complementarity condition unacceptably strong. The condition could, of course, be construed more weakly so that the "diverse sexual attributes and capacities" to which it refers are not limited to reproductive attributes and capacities. It might also refer to diverse sexual needs and desires, and capacities for giving and receiving love in sexual activity. The condition could thereby be weakened so that a sexual union of two men or two women could satisfy it. This would require an interpretation of 'sexually complementary' according to which the question of whether two people are sexually identical in the relevant sense can*not* be settled by determining whether both are male or both female, that is, an interpretation according to which (25) is false. Finnis's argument depends on both (25) and the sexual complementarity condition. The problem is that interpreting (25) so that it is, as Finnis seems to think, obviously true requires interpreting the sexual complementarity conditions so that it is false. Interpreting the latter so that it is true requires interpreting the former so that it is false.

Note, moreover, that Finnis's argument for (21) depends crucially on his characterization of marriage as "real giving to each other" and on his use of sexual complementarity to elucidate what he means by "real." According to (15), two people really give themselves to each other in a biological union only if their union is sexually complementary. From this it follows that they really give themselves only if, by their sexual union, they become "one reality" (16). From (16) and the sexual complementarity of husband and wife, it is alleged to follow that that one reality has the function of reproduction (17). Claim (13), elucidated by appeal to the notion of sexual complementarity, therefore leads Finnis to very strong conclusions about the nature of marriage.[11] The move to (17) depends on the strong reading of "sexual complementarity," according to which two people are sexually complementary only if they are of different sexes. If, as I have suggested, this reading of sexual complementarity is too strong, then (17) and Finnis's strong conclusions about the nature of "real giving," fail to follow.

Finally, (29) says that homosexual unions "*can do no more* than provide each person with individual gratification" (emphasis added). This is a claim that Finnis thinks he needs if he is to defend (31), the claim that two peoples' choice to engage in homosexual activity "dis-integrates them precisely as acting persons." The argument for (29) also depends on (25) and the sexual complementarity condition. If, as I have argued, these cannot both be true, then it seems Finnis lacks an argument for (29) and hence for (31).

Finnis is clearly committed to (29), but need he be? Does he really need (29) to defend (31)? Perhaps he could rely on the following argument:

(29')   The common good of partners in committed, lifelong, and exclusive homosexual relationships can be actualized and experienced without orgasmic sexual activity.

(29")   Therefore, the common good of partners in committed, lifelong and exclusive homosexual relationships does not depend, either logically or causally, on what good is realized through the partners' orgasmic sexual activity.

(29''')   Therefore what good is realized in orgasmic sexual activity is not part of the "intrinsic fulfillment" (1065) of committed, lifelong, and exclusive homosexual relationships.

(29'''') Therefore orgasmic sexual activity is chosen as a means to the common good of partners in committed, lifelong and exclusive homosexual relationships.

(30')   Therefore two peoples' choice to engage in homosexual activity entails a choice to "treat their bodies as instruments to be used in the service of their consciously experiencing selves[.]"

Perhaps Finnis would think that the same considerations that allow him to move from (30) to (31) would allow him to move from (30') to (31). This argument might therefore seem to support Finnis's conclusion without the difficulties that I believe his own argument encounters.

The inferences from (29''') to (29'''') and from (29'''') to (30') turn on the notion of a means. This notion needs to be explained before the inferences can be assessed. Rather than pursue this issue, however, I want to turn briefly to the real problem with the argument, which lies in (29'). Finnis might defend (29') by claiming that partners in a homosexual relationship can realize the common good of their relationship by and in conversation, loving care for one another, committed and exclusive companionship, and the paternal kisses and touches of which Finnis thinks Plato would have approved (1061). Orgasmic sexual activity, he might maintain, is unnecessary. But is this correct?

If two people are sexually complementary, then they bring different sexual capacities and needs to their sexual union. It certainly seems possible that the sexual union of two people who are sexually complementary could allow the partners to realize a good that they cannot realize in conversation, kissing and hugging, or in any other way but sexual union. Finnis seems to believe that two people are sexually complementary if and only if they complement or complete one another with respect to the function of procreation. I suggested above that this interpretation of sexual complementarity is too strong and that two men or two women can be sexually complementary. It therefore seems possible that some elements of the common good of a relationship between two men or two women could be realized only in orgasmic activity between them. Since (29') excludes this possibility, (29') is false. The argument for (30') is no stronger than the argument for (30).

V

In addition to arguing that homosexual activity is immoral, Finnis argues that political communities have a "compelling interest in denying that homosexual conduct— a 'gay lifestyle'—is a valid, humanly acceptable choice and form of life, and in doing whatever it *properly* can . . . to discourage such conduct" (1070, emphasis original). He therefore thinks communities may enact legal restrictions on "the advertising and marketing of homosexual services, the maintenance of places of resort for homosexual activity, or the promotion of homosexualist "lifestyles" via education and public media of communication, or to recognize homosexual "marriages" or permit the adoption of children by homosexually active people, and so forth" (1076).

Finnis's argument for these claims turns on the function he assigns political communities in moral education. The role of political communities in moral formation is, he insists, solely subsidiary. Its task is to facilitate other communities' performance of their educative functions and to provide a "social environment conducive to virtue" (1073). The subsidiary functions of the political community determine what interests it properly has and which of those interests are compelling. As Finnis recognizes, political communities can perform their function without discouraging every act, or every sort of act, that is immoral. This implies as Finnis also recognizes that political communities have no compelling interest in criminalizing or discouraging immoral acts as such.[12] In this, Finnis thinks, he departs significantly from Aristotle and perhaps Aquinas (1073 ff.).

Since Finnis thinks both that the political community has the function of facilitating the educative work of other communities and that the political community suffers harm if the work of these communities is impeded, he thinks that political communities do have a compelling interest in discouraging conduct that threatens that work or the institutions which properly do it. In particular, Finnis argues, political communities have a compelling interest in discouraging behavior the toleration of which would threaten the integrity or stability of families. It is in virtue of this interest in protecting the family that he thinks political communities have a compelling interest in discouraging homosexual conduct and in denying that it is a "valid, humanly acceptable choice an form of life."

How does Finnis think the toleration of homosexual conduct threatens families? He says:

> All who accept that homosexual acts can be a humanly appropriate use of sexual capacities must, if consistent, regard sexual capacities, organs and acts as instruments for gratifying the individual "selves" who have them. Such an acceptance is commonly (and in my opinion rightly) judged to be an active threat to the stability of existing and future marriages; it makes nonsense, for example, of the view that adultery is *per se* (and not merely because it may involve deception), and in an important way, inconsistent with conjugal love. (1070)

Consider the case of homosexual marriage. Finnis seems to think that if a political community recognized homosexual marriage, the community would thereby give public assent to the proposition that

(32) Homosexual acts can be a humanly appropriate use of sexual capacities.

Public acceptance of this proposition threatens "the stability of existing and future marriages" Finnis thinks, because (32) implies that

(33) Sexual capacities, organs, and acts are instruments for gratifying the individual "selves" who have them.

Therefore, Finnis concludes, any political community that publicly accepts the former "must, if consistent" publicly accept the latter.

One minor difficulty with Finnis's argument is that (33) is a very strong claim, one that does not follow from (32) and is far stronger than he needs for his purposes. Given the possibility of sexual acts in which one partner lovingly and selflessly gives pleasure to the other, what more plausibly follows from (32) is the claim that

(33') Sexual capacities, organs, and acts are instruments for gratifying one or the other of the partners in a sexual union.[13]

Earlier, when arguing against (29'), 1 argued that homosexual acts can be humanly appropriate because in performing them partners realize a common good they can realize in no other way. These acts are therefore not instruments or means for gratifying one or the other sexual partner. Therefore another difficulty with Finnis's argument is that (33') does not follow from (32) either. A political community could recognize homosexual marriage, thereby accept (32) and simultaneously deny (33'). Instead of (33'), that community could publicly affirm—through clearly articulated educational policy, for example—the proposition that sexual acts are acts wherein adult couples in committed, lifelong, and exclusive relationships can actualize and experience their common good.

Suppose for the sake of argument, however, that my previous criticisms of Finnis are wrong, that (33') or (33) does follow from (32) and that any political community publicly affirming the former must publicly affirm the latter. Suppose further, for the sake of argument, that political communities do have a compelling interest in the stability of heterosexual marriages of some form.[14] Does it follow that existing political communities like the United States or any one of the states have a compelling interest in denying legal recognition to committed, lifelong, and exclusive homosexual relationships?

To defend an affirmative answer, Finnis would have to defend a number of causal claims. He would have to defend the claim that a political community's public affirmation of (33) or (33') would result in a significant number of citizens' accepting (33) or (33'). He would have to defend the claim that their acceptance of (33) or (33') is causally connected to at least some of the marital instability that he thinks political communities have a compelling interest in preventing. And he would have to defend the claim that those who accept (33) or (33') do so or are likely to do so *because of their society's legal recognition of homosexual marriage*. These claims would be extremely difficult to sustain, and not simply because of the difficulties that ordinarily attend causal claims in the social sciences.

To see the difficulty, suppose that the United States granted homosexual marriage legal recognition, thereby publicly endorsing (32). Suppose further that some years after legal recognition was extended, social scientists put forward widespread acceptance of (33) and/or (33') as an explanation for American sexual behavior and patterns of divorce. Would it follow that the acceptance of (33) and/or (33') resulted from the legal recognition of homosexual marriages?

Obviously anyone answering in the affirmative would have to rule out the possibility that (33) and/or (33') were widely accepted even before homosexual marriages were legally recognized. While I cannot prove it, I suspect that a significant number of Americans, at least a significant number of younger Americans, already accept (33), (33'), and/or some relevantly similar proposition. Indeed, it seems at least as likely that homosexual marriages will be legally recognized and (32) publicly affirmed *because a significant number of people antecedently accept (33) or (33')* as that a significant number of people will come to accept (33) or (33') as a result of the legal recognition of homosexual marriages.

Consider, moreover, the conditions under which social scientists might put forward widespread acceptance of (33) or (33') as an explanation of the widespread marital instability that Finnis thinks the political community has an interest in preventing. Perhaps a significant number of those who divorce or who report that their marriages are not what they had hoped cite disappointment in their sexual lives, the loss of romance, or the end of infatuation as reasons for their dissatisfaction. Is widespread acceptance of (33) or (33') an important cause of this phenomenon?

I would conjecture that one of the most important causes of such sexual dissatisfaction and disappointment is the prevalence of fantasies about sexual satisfaction and illusions about what (or who) constitutes an appropriate focus of sexual attraction. It may be that the belief set of anyone who accepts these fantasies implies a proposition like (33) or (33'). Social scientists may therefore find it useful to postulate widespread acceptance of one or both of those propositions. If I am correct, however, this is a greatly abbreviated explanation. Sexual dissatisfaction within marriage, if it exists, is really rooted in the prevalence of sexual illusions that the dissatisfied pursue and the sexual fantasies they are trying to fulfill. If this is true, then widespread acceptance of (32) is responsible for the acceptance of (33) or (33') only if it is responsible, in whole or in part, for the prevalence of sexual fantasies among the married. This is *prima facie* implausible since the vast majority of the married, it is reasonable to suppose, are heterosexual. It seems highly unlikely that fantasies that are supposed for the sake of argument to induce marital dissatisfaction are in fact caused by the beliefs married, heterosexual persons hold about the licitness of homosexual activity.

There is also another and far more plausible explanation of the prevalence of such fantasies, if prevalent they are. Popular culture encourages sexual fantasy and illusion by its portrayal of heterosexual satisfaction, by its presentation of some objects of desire as appropriate, and in particular by its gross commodification of women. Given the power of the media by which it is propagated, popular culture seems a far more likely culprit for the prevalence of these fantasies than what attitudes people would come to hold about homosexuality as a result of the recognition of same-sex marriages.

Finnis's argument that political communities have a compelling interest in discouraging homosexual activity by denying recognition to homosexual relationships depends on the claim that such recognition fosters attitudes threatening to marriage. The grounds Finnis provides for that claim, however, fail to establish it. Finnis's argument also depends on the claim that political communities have a compelling interest in preventing activity the toleration of which fosters attitudes that threaten marriage. I have suggested that popular culture fosters such attitudes by promulgating heterosexual fantasies and, in particular, by commodifying women. If this conjecture is correct, then Finnis would seem to be committed to the view that political communities have a compelling interest in discouraging citizens' consumption of popular culture.

VI

This has been a paper of limited aspirations. I believe that (32) is true and that (30), (30'), and (31) are false, yet I have neither defended the first nor attacked the latter three. I think (33) and (33') false, but I have serious reservations about employing public power to bring about agreement among adult fellow citizens. My reservations are rooted in the belief that securing agreement would require severe restrictions on the continual creation and spread of popular culture and in the belief that the liberal conception of political legitimacy is fundamentally correct.[15] I have not, however, defended these beliefs. I have fewer reservations than some other liberals about the public's use of its educational power to persuade children and adolescents of the falsity of (33) and (33'), yet I have not discussed the philosophy of education. Instead, I have contented myself with arguing that Finnis has not adequately defended his claims. There are, I believe, two important lessons to be drawn for the sexual ethics of natural law theory from even this modest conclusion.

The problem with Finnis's argument against the licitness of homosexual activity, I have suggested, does not lie in what is most original in his natural law theory. It lies instead in his claim that two people of the same sex are not sexually complementary and so cannot realize a common good in their union. These claims are, I believe, the staples of natural law arguments against homosexual activity. If they cannot be sustained, then natural law thinkers committed to the wrongness of homosexual activity will have to find some other line of reasoning to support their position. Those who think that that position can be supported only by a strong reading of sexual complementarity must concede that prohibitions on homosexual activity are indefensible by natural law arguments.

Finnis also argues that political communities have a compelling interest in discouraging homosexual activity and may therefore deny recognition to homosexual marriages. As we saw, he departs from earlier natural law thinkers by asserting that political communities have no compelling interest in discouraging immoral acts as such. Rather, their interest in discouraging homosexual activity is founded, Finnis thinks, on the subsidiary role political communities play in sustaining a public moral environment supportive of the family. Thus Finnis's argument requires that there be causal connections between, for example, the recognition of homosexual marriage and the prevalence of attitudes that destabilize families. I have argued that these causal connections do not obtain and that his argument for a compelling interest in the discouragement of homosexual activity fails. The problem with his second argument, in contrast to the first, *is* therefore connected with innovative elements in his theory. This suggests that natural law thinkers who want to argue for a compelling public interest in discouraging homosexual activity must rely on traditional defenses. They must maintain that political communities have a compelling interest in discouraging immoral acts as such and they must maintain that all homosexual activity is immoral. One of the many problems they will face in doing so is that traditional arguments for the latter claim are unsuccessful.

Notes

1. Beginning three decades ago with the publication of Grisez's seminal article, "The First Principle of Practical Reason," *Natural Law Forum* 10 (1965): 168–96; see also John Finnis, *Natural Law and Natural Right* (Oxford University Press, 1980).

2. John Finnis, "Law, Morality, and 'Sexual Orientation'" *Notre Dame Law Review* 69 (1994): 1049–76; page references to this article will subsequently appear parenthetically.

3. Here I believe Finnis shares a thought with Hobbes. Hobbes wrote, "A multitude of men, are made One Person when they are by one man, or one Person, Represented; so that it be done with the consent of every one of that Multitude in particular. For it is the Unity of the Representer, not the Unity of the Represented, that maketh the Person One. And it is the Representer that beareth the Person, and but one Person: And Unity, cannot otherwise be understood in Multitude." *Leviathan* Book I, ch. XVI. The thought that Hobbes and Finnis share is that "a multitude of men, are made One Person" or one unit if that "multitude" is capable of acting as one. Finnis and Hobbes differ, of course, on the necessary conditions for this occurring.

4. The first half of this reconstruction closely follows the more elaborate reconstruction of the first half of Finnis's argument that I present in the appendix to my "A Propos of Professor Perry: A Plea for Philosophy in Sexual Ethics," *Notre Dame Journal of Law, Ethics and Public Policy* (1995): 75–92. I am grateful to the editors of the journal for their kind permission to reuse certain ideas, sentences, and turns of phrase from that article.

5. Exactly what these intentional states are would be very difficult to specify, and Finnis himself does not allude to them. I have imputed this qualification to him assuming that there are some states he would exclude as part of permissible sexual union, even if they do not com-

promise its voluntariness. One might be the state induced by moderate chemical intoxication; another, perhaps, is the state of objectifying one's spouse. Still another, I believe, is the state of regarding sexual union as a means to some independently specificable end like pleasure or the production of children. Still others include the intentional states of those who deliberately contracept, those who engage in sexual activity hoping, believing, or intending that their partner is employing contraception and those who have undergone elective sterilization.

6. The arguments for (31) and for the wrongness of the choice to engage in homosexual activity are difficult to state precisely. At page 1067, note 47, Finnis says that the whole argument can be found at Germain Grisez, *The Way of the Lord Jesus*, vol. II (Franciscan Press, 1993), pp. 634–39, 648–54, 662–64. The arguments to which Finnis refers draw, in turn, on the elements of Grisez's very complicated moral theory, which are laid out in the previous volume of that work. See, for example, Germain Grisez, *The Way of the Lord Jesus*, vol. I (Franciscan Press, 1986), pp. 214–15, for a moral principle presupposed by the arguments of volume II that Finnis cites; I am grateful to Germain Grisez for this reference.

7. See John Noonan, *Contraception* (Harvard University Press, 1986), p. 366.

8. See, e.g., *The Ecclesiastical Review* 79 (1928): 527–33; also John C. Ford, S. I., and Gerald Kelly, S. I., *Contemporary Moral Theology II: Marriage Questions* (Newman, 1963), p. 319, quoted critically at Richard McCormick, S. I., *The Critical Calling* (Georgetown University Press, 1989), p. 276.

9. The moral principle on which the perverted faculty argument depends implies that we can infer an act is wrong from the fact that it frustrates certain natural functions. Since Finnis thinks that it a mistake to infer an 'ought' (or an 'ought not') from an 'is,' he accuses proponents of the perverted faculty argument of a fallacy (cf. 1068–69). My treatment of the perverted faculty argument, by contrast, does not depend on Finnis's claim that it is *always* a mistake to infer moral from factual claims. It depends on the much weaker claim that facts about the frustration of the natural faculties are not morally decisive in the way that the perverted faculty argument requires.

10. See, e.g., Jean Porter, "Basic Goods and the Human Good in Recent Catholic Moral Theology," *Thomist* 57 (1993): 27–49.

11. Indeed, Finnis says that civil laws manifest "a failure of understanding" if they omit contraception from a list of conditions that prevent the consummation of marriage; see p. 1068, n.50.

12. Thus he acknowledges, for example, that political communities can perform their functions without passing laws against "secret and truly consensual adult [homosexual] acts"— acts that Finnis considers immoral. He therefore says that criminalizing such behavior falls outside the scope of what he deems "proper discouragement" of homosexual activity (1076).

13. I imputed the weaker claim to Finnis above when I reconstructed his argument for (30).

14. I include the "of some form" qualifier merely to avoid debate about the acceptability of traditional divisions of labor within marriage and of the unequal opportunities partners have traditionally had legally to exit marriage. Clearly these matters are not germane to the point at issue. While I agree with Finnis that political communities have some interest in the stability of heterosexual marriages of some form, it may be that we disagree on the strength of interest. We almost certainly differ on what interest this entails since I do not think the interest in marital stability is grounded on political communities have an interest in maintaining environments conducive to the virtues Finnis has in mind. Unfortunately, I cannot pursue this matter here.

15. For a clear statement of this conception, see Jeremy Waldron, "Theoretical Foundations of Liberalism," in his *Liberal Rights* (Cambridge University Press, 1993), pp. 35–62.

Part IV

FAMILY

12

All in the Family and In All Families: Membership, Loving, and Owing

Martha Minow

I: ALL IN THE FAMILY—WHO IS THE FAMILY?

Introduction

The first part of my title, "All in the Family," refers to the television show by that name because it captures the theme I would like to sound here. Otherwise known as the Archie Bunker show, the central character exhibited gross racial, ethnic, and sexual prejudices—and yet the show itself celebrated the capacity of human beings to grow and change within families. What interests me here in particular is the shift in the constellation of people treated as family over the years the show was on the air. Initially, Archie and his wife Edith shared their home with their daughter and her husband—not quite a nuclear family, but a rather traditional extended family. Over time, however, Archie meets Edith's lesbian cousin. He also learns to deal with divorce. Ultimately, Edith dies, Archie's daughter separates from her husband and they both move away, and Archie becomes the custodian of a niece who is half-Jewish. All inside this "family," then, the variety of shifting relationships mirrored the variety of potential family memberships in the larger society. Once a show exhibiting the prejudices of a white ethnic patriarch toward his diverse society, "All in the Family," over time, brought that diversity inside the family itself.

Both the growing diversity in groups across this nation who claim to be families and diversity within the families themselves carry consequences for the three basic issues in family law: (1) who is in "the family," (2) what benefits accompany family membership, and (3) what obligations accompany family roles. It may once have seemed that these questions had obvious and uncontroverted answers. It may once have seemed that "family" referred to a natural or obvious social entity created by the biological ties of parent and child and the divine or contractual ties of marriage.

I am skeptical of all stories of a past golden or untroubled age, however, and I do mean to dispute any claim that "family" as defined by law is natural or obvious. Certainly it is a legal rule, not a natural fact, that creates the presumption that a child born to a woman who is married is the child of the woman's husband. Rules about marriage eligibility and practices have also undergone sufficient historical changes to reveal the political, religious, and social choices embedded in that institution.

Scholars have also shredded the myth of the homogenous family with historical and sociological studies revealing enormous variance in the structures and functions of families. Finally, and perhaps most telling, the myth of the homogenous family portrayed in television sitcoms has been challenged on television itself—consider not only "All in the Family," but also "My Two Dads," "The Brady Bunch," and "Kate and Allie," not to mention an oldie but goody, "My Mother the Car."

Today there can be no doubt that the variety of social practices poses new and pressing questions for legal definitions of family, family benefits, and family obligations. No neutral answers, tethered to "nature" or consensus, are available. Instead, the legal rules inevitably register choices, and the immediate task is to articulate and debate the considerations that should influence those choices.

In this essay, I will sketch those considerations while documenting the challenge to conventional understandings posed by the current diversity of groupings that are candidates for family status. Locating the ambivalence over pluralism within American history and constitutional traditions would help; so would clarifying the preconditions for tolerance. In this spirit, I will first address what considerations should guide legal definitions of families and distributions of benefits based on family status. Then I will reconsider this discussion while examining legal obligations based on family status.

Nothing Natural About It: Legal Regulation and Family Diversity

The most basic evidence that regulation of families reflects cultural choices is the constant theme in American culture that "the family" is in crisis—and hence, someone should do something about it. Newspapers over the past few years abound with stories about dramatic shifts in American families. Historians tell us that Americans have worried about the family for over three hundred years; the Puritans began it all by "decrying the increasing fragility of marriage, the growing selfishness and irresponsibility of parents and the increasing rebelliousness of children."[1] Wary that I may be seen as just another decrier in this tradition of bemoaning the family in crisis, I suggest two specifically recent patterns of change. The first is increased gap between legal or conventional definitions of family membership and actual lived practices—diversity of groups that seem themselves as families. The second is an apparent rise in the numbers of families composed internally by people with contrasting religious, ethnic, or racial identities—diversity within families. While the first raises directly questions for legal rules about who is "family" and what benefits should attach family membership, the diversity within families exposes further complications. Each development, in turn, exposes the unavoidable choices for contemporary family law.

Diversity of Families

More than a year ago [1991], a *New York Times* headline announced, "Only One U.S. Family in Four is 'Traditional'" compared with 40 percent in 1970.[2] The term "traditional" here referred to a married man and woman living with their children. If the children are *their own*—not stepchildren under eighteen—the percentage is even smaller; only 8 to 10 percent of all households are families of this sort, with a wife who does not work outside the home.[3]

Lawful family membership traditionally depended upon marriage, birth of a child to its biological parents, or adoption. Yet today, different groupings of people are increasingly claiming legal family status. The Massachusetts highest court accepted the claim by an unmarried woman to unemployment benefits offered to the legal spouse of someone who had to move for employment purposes; the woman claimed that her cohabitation of thirteen years should entitle her to those benefits.[4] A few years ago, New York accorded to the gay lover of a man who had died the legal protection against eviction from a rent-controlled apartment that the law grants to spouses of deceased leaseholders.[5] Thus, the question I pose is which kinds of groups should be defined legally as families, and what benefits should accrue because of this family status?

No responsible discussion of these questions can begin without first acknowledging how they implicate social and political choices about distributing privileges. No factual answer can resolve those choices, nor is it possible for the government to be neutral in the face of an array of social relationships. As long as the terms "family," "parent," and "spouse," carry legal significance, they depart from their social meanings and even from the meanings people intend when they apply these terms to themselves.

For example, the legal rules defining "family" for immigration purposes notably chafe people's actual practices of family life—no doubt reflecting a public policy to restrict immigration rather than a conscientious effort to define "family." The Immigration Reform and Control Act of 1986 affords amnesty to undocumented individuals who meet its requirements—but many of these people have spouses or children who do not.[6] The eligible individuals must choose whether to stay in this country without their relatives or to leave the country, and the ineligible individuals must choose whether to remain illegally.

In addition, the Immigration and Naturalization Service (INS) treats as a "family unit" for its general practices only those immediate family members who regularly reside in the same household.[7] As law professor Carol Sanger notes,

> The INS definition of family unity fails to acknowledge that for a variety of reasons many children in this country live with nonparental relatives outside the family home . . . [A]ssume a 14-year-old boy, excludable because he assisted another alien in entering the country illegally, lives with his uncle. The boy will not be considered a member of his father's family group because the boy is functionally part of another family. If, however, the uncle is also applying for legalization and seeks a waiver on behalf of his nephew, the application cannot be granted in the name of family unity because the nephew is not a member of the uncle's biological family.[8]

This kind of scenario is especially likely among families of immigrants who migrate in waves, often with male relatives arriving first and sending later for other immediate family members. Moreover, many immigrants share households and treat as family members nieces or nephews, grandparents, or cousins, which the INS will not include under its definition of family unit.

Extended families face special burdens from other governmental programs as well. Eligibility rules for food stamps and other government poverty programs often pose choices between living with family members or living apart from them. The United States Supreme Court has found no defect in regulations that deny separate household eligibility for food stamps to parents who live not only with their own children but also with their siblings, even though unrelated families that share living space may be eligible.[9] The irony here is that the government's policy works against the goal of encouraging relatives to turn to relatives when they face difficult economic times. To counter this, New York began an experiment recognizing kinship ties by supporting foster care with relatives, but faced a crisis when the numbers of participating families seemed too many and too expensive to include. Yet attentiveness to cultural variety especially calls for recognizing relationships between grandparents and grandchildren or other extended family ties.

Another major discontinuity between law and social practice arises for gay and lesbian people. Some would say that this is fine, that the law should not recognize relationships that are immoral, unnatural, or (in a somewhat circular argument) illegal. Rendering gay and lesbian relationships illegal is, of course, a social and political choice, and it is one currently under challenge around the country and, indeed, around the world.

For gay and lesbian activists, it is a form of illegitimate discrimination to deny lawful marriage for gay and lesbian couples, to deny adoption and foster care to gay and lesbian individuals, and to disadvantage homosexual parents in contests over custody of their biological children. They advocate that it should be unlawful for employers, insurance companies, and other entities to ignore these family roles or punish gay and lesbian people because of them—as a state attorney general did recently in withdrawing a job offer to a woman because she had undergone a religious marriage ceremony with another woman.

These calls for legal recognition and protection are increasingly successful. As small sign of the times, or should I say, the stars, the *Star Tribune* in Minneapolis recently started publishing announcements of gay or lesbian "domestic partnerships" on what had previously been its wedding and announcement page.

Many people, however, still believe that gays and lesbians should be excluded from the privileges of family membership. It will not do, however, to support this view with reference to nature, convention, or even religion. many religions are themselves struggling with these questions; some are performing marriages for gays and lesbians, some are ordaining gay and lesbian clergy. Disagreements over these issues are intense and volatile; they involve the central issues of politics—who's in or out, and who gets what. Finding sufficiently shared assumptions with which to resolve these disagreements is itself a challenge, and in our society, that challenge will inevitably turn to the legal system—since it is all that we have in common.

It is important to recognize that the resolutions of those conflicts will, in turn, affect cohabiting heterosexuals and potentially other groups as well. For example, claims by lesbian partners of women with children to a kind of equitable parenthood *or in loco parentis* right based on performing the functions of a parent could, if recognized, produce legal protection for other informal but functional family relationships—such as those between aunts who care for children and boyfriends and the children of their girlfriends. New rules in these contexts will also reflect the eroding significance of biology to lawful family membership in light of new reproductive technologies. For if a woman who contributes no genetic material to the fertilized egg she carries to term can become the lawful mother, why cannot her cohabiting female lover also become a lawful parent for that child?

New reproductive technologies, gay and lesbian couples, immigrants, applicants for food stamps—these may each sound marginal to family law and to legal definitions of family. But if you continue to think that the core legal definitions of family are still safe and uncontested, think again. Consider single parent households—whether never married or divorced, and stepfamilies—or the term I prefer, blended families. By 1989, nearly 25 percent of all children in this country lived in single parent families, and over half of all African-American children lived with one parent.[10] As a result of the combined rates of divorce, separation, and births to unmarried people, more than half of all white children and three-quarters of all black children born in the 1970s and 1980s are expected to live for some portion of their childhoods with only their mothers.[11] The number of children living with unmarried parents doubled between 1980 and 1985.[12] The sheer decline in the use of the term "illegitimate child" indicates a change, as bearing and keeping children become more socially acceptable for unmarried people—whether moviestars or not. Our rates of single-parent—and divorce—households remain the highest in the world.

Furthermore, numerous families are now created through remarriage, typically following divorce. Reflecting the increase, the Census Bureau counted stepfamily households for the first time in 1990. One observer predicts that half of all young people will live in blended families by the year 2000, given current rates of divorce and remarriage.[13]

For single parent households, blended families, adoptive families, gay and lesbian families, and extended families, social practices often do not match legal definitions of family or law enforcement of family roles. The rules may say that children of unmarried fathers are eligible for child support from their fathers but not for public benefits they would receive if their fathers had married their mothers.[14] Unmarried fathers may be counted as members of the family for some legal purposes even if there is no cohabitation, or not counted even if there is. Divorced fathers remain fathers, but it is unclear in some legal circumstances when they remain members of "the family." States also lack clarity about the legal and financial obligations, if any, of a stepparent: if that person has not adopted the child, should the law give no recognition of their relationship if, for example, the stepfather obtains a divorce and then wishes to visit his ex-wife's child?

While it is socially recognized that the blended family composed of a mother and her children, a father and his children from another marriage, and the former spouses or lovers of each adult may act as one "family"—perhaps an extended family—when, if ever, should the law recognize such practices? Should the law enforce duties for stepparents, for example? In her vivid study of two such groupings in Silicon Valley, California, anthropologist Judith Stacey called them "Brave New Families," and found people turning to one another as if they were extended families despite divorces and subsequent remarriages.[15]

While some people continue to turn to one another despite divorce and remarriage, others wish to excise their former relatives after a divorce. As one teenage character reports in a recent short story, "Trouble is all those divorces really mess up the photograph albums . . . Mom butchered ours. There's only about two pictures left of Dad in all twelve albums."[16] Should private efforts at emotional excision produce comparable legal results, or should the law assure that Dad stays, in some way, part of the family?

Related questions surround changes in adoption of children. Shifting from an era of sealed documents—part of the myth that no adoption had happened—some adoptive parents now meet the birth mothers, and some experiment with "open adoption" in which an adopted child maintains ties with both the biological and adoptive parents. If these groups of people function as a kind of extended family, should the legal definition of who is a parent be modified? Or should law preserve the notion of exclusive parenthood and terminate all legal ties with the biological parent after adoption?

My own intuition favors expansive definitions. I am not alone. The American Home Economics Association defines a family unit as "two or more persons who share resources, share responsibility for decisions, share values and goals, and have a commitment to one another over time . . . regardless of blood, legal ties, adoption, or marriage."[17]

Yet these definitions do not match most current legal rules defining family, marriage, or parenthood. Should the rules change to reflect these views or instead continue to discipline or constrain them? Should shifting legal and informal practices defining family membership also alter the benefits and obligations attached to family roles? I hope I have demonstrated that the answers to these questions are not obvious or answerable by reference to nature or convention. But before I defend an expansive, or tolerant, view, we need to consider the additional complication of diversity *within* families.

Diversity Within Families

One function of families in this society is to nurture cultural diversity; in private homes and communities, families engage in varied religious, ethnic, and lifestyle practices that reflect and in turn support the national commitment to liberty. Respecting the autonomy of each family in many ways ensures the continuation of social diversity as parents raise their children according to their own values and traditions. We could enforce this diversity, but we do not: our legal system does not pursue the route taken by several other multicultural societies which assign each person a "personal law," or the specific legal rules accompanying his or her religious tradition, such as Hindu, Moslem, Jewish, or Christian.

Perhaps we do not have such rules because we believe, in a certain sense, that every family is characterized by diversity. If the birth of a child is the triggering act in the creation of a family, surely this involves the diversity of generations. Any two people who come together in marriage join two distinct family cultures, embedded ways of squeezing the toothpaste, expressing disagreements, and relating to others. The Sunday after my sister married her husband—with whom she had lived for the prior six years—she rolled out of bed and asked when he was going to the delicatessen to get the cold-cuts. He looked at her with confusion, asked why he should go, she burst into tears, and two hours later realized that as a child, growing up, my Dad would go out every Sunday to the delicatessen and pick up cold-cuts. My sister also realized that she does not even like cold cuts, but she found she had brought to her new family—the one created by her marriage—a set of expectations about which she had not even been conscious and which certainly surprised her husband.

But specific forms of diversity within families in this country reflect the transcendence of higher barriers and more profound separatisms than those that distinguish delicatessen-going families from others. The history of racial segregation in families is a striking example. The legacy of slavery and racism included legal rules against interracial marriage and restrictions against interracial adoption. The 1967 Supreme Court decision in *Loving v. Virginia* rejected state efforts forbidding interracial marriage.[18] It was a landmark case for racial justice as well as for the constitutional status of family law.

Interracial adoption, long unheard of, became an experiment in the 1960s and remains a subject of controversy. My colleague Elizabeth Bartholet argues that opposition to it reflects a segregative spirit that should have no place in American law and too often consigns nonwhite children to foster care or institutions rather than assuring them parents of their own race.[19] In a refreshingly courageous judgment, the Supreme Court in 1984 rejected a divorced white father's challenge to a white mother's custody of their child solely on the grounds that the mother was cohabiting with (and later married) an African-American man.[20] The Court reasoned that "[t]he effects of racial prejudice, however real, cannot justify a racial classification removing an infant child from the custody of its natural mother found to be an appropriate person to have such custody."[21] Thus, at least in theory,[22] the legal system is not supposed to bow to prejudices against racial diversity within families.

Similar but less high profile patterns have emerged with religious diversity *within* families. The longstanding practice of religious matching by adoption agencies—through which a child born to parents of a particular religion would be matched with adoptive parents of the same religion—is much in decline, and legally unacceptable if it produces unequal treatment and delays in the adoption process. And while religious institutions and clergy may decline to approve or perform interreligious marriages, secular marriages remain available for unions of men and women from different religions. If, however, those couples have children and then divorce, special problems may arise over the children's religious upbringing and practices. Consider three examples:

A mother seeks and obtains a restraining order prohibiting her ex-husband, a Mormon, from engaging their children in any religious activity, discussion, or attendance during visitation. The appellate court lifts the restraining order "due to the absence of evidence of harm to the children and our resulting belief that the order represents an unwarranted intrusion into family privacy."[23]

A mother seeks a restraint against the father from causing or allowing their children to violate the Jewish Sabbath and dietary laws during their visits with him. The court denies it on the grounds that such an order would violate the father's constitutional right to freely exercise his own religion.[24]

A mother obtains physical custody of a child but the father obtains "spiritual custody," meaning he is entrusted with inculcating a religious tradition no longer observed by the custodial parent.[25]

I will examine the rationales in these cases in some detail because they illuminate how diversity *within* families can pose challenges to the very definition of family and to the privileges or benefits accompanying family membership. They also show the complications that come with a tolerance for interreligious families.

In a post-divorce situation with parents of different religions, what should the law treat as the family unit—that is who is in the "family"—for purposes of protecting family privacy or balancing interests within the family? What privileges of parenthood should be preserved in this circumstance? In addressing this question, can the state maintain neutrality toward religion and toward two parents while also protecting children?

In the first case, the custodial mother left the Mormon church when she separated from her husband, and she sought then to restrict the husbands ability to require the children to engage in Mormon religious activities. The court treated the question as concerning the risk of harm to the children; the court rejected testimony by an expert that conflicting views would be harmful to the children because the expert had not examined the particular children involved.

The court treated religion as a matter of ultimately individual choice. Parental prerogatives remain unconstrained by the governmental obligation to guard children from harm in the absence of evidence of physical or emotional problems to the children arising from exposure to two religions. Perhaps most striking is the court's decision to define "the family" to include both divorced spouses and their children in one unit. The court endorses the "salutary judicial disinclination to interfere with family privacy without the evidentiary establishment of compelling need."[26]

Who is in the family entitled to such privacy? Note that the ex-husband is included in this protected sphere: "The rationale that supports judicial respect for family privacy does not lose its force upon the dissolution of marriage where, as here, a family relationship—even a disharmonious one—continues between the former spouses in connection with the rearing of their minor children."[27]

The dissenting judge in this case, however, painted a contrasting picture. This judge brought out unrebutted evidence at trial that the mother developed the belief that the father was sexually molesting their daughter: "She appealed to her bishop for help and was rebuffed, being told that the issue was not a 'moral' one. The crisis in confidence experienced by the mother led to a dissolution from husband and a break with the Mormon Church."[28] The mother joined a different church, and perceived that the children experienced confusion in reconciling the beliefs of the two parents, compounded, in her view, by the husband's presentation of Mormon materials during his visits with the children. The dissenting judge viewed the reasons for the mother's separation from both husband and church as relevant to the assessment of the children's best interests; that judge also urged a reading of the court's duty to guard children from harm as including future, not only past harm. This dissenting view exposes the trouble with the majority's definition of the divorced couple and their children as one family unit entitled to family privacy and raises a sharp question about the court's justification for seeking a neutral stance with regard to the conflict presented in the case.

In the second case, a mother sought to restrain her husband from causing the children to violate Jewish traditions, including dietary laws, during his visits with the children. Here the court reasoned that it "must neither violate the mother's or the children's constitutional right to religious freedom *nor permit the imposition upon the father of the mother's religion which imposition would violate the father's consti- tutional right of freedom of religion.*"[29] The court reasoned that the mother could not use the court to impose her religious practices on her ex-husband, even though she has the right to select the religious upbringing of the child. In essence preserving the father's privilege to influence the children's religious upbringing, the court stated that it intended to promote a strong relationship with the noncustodial parent, while also remaining impartial toward religion.

The court acknowledged the risk of harm to the children from confrontation with conflicting values, but nonetheless concluded that society is pluralistic and that each individual must balance the conflict between conflicting commitments to the state and to one's own ethnic or religious heritage. Here, the court made much of the choices already made by the mother—not only had she divorced and remarried, she herself had also converted from Christianity to Judaism. The court reasoned that she created a "personal pluralism" with "voluntarily obtained dichotomies"—and thus the children would share that pluralism.

In this light, the court treated as self-interest—beyond parental privilege—the mother's effort to shield the children from alien influences or temptation to depart from their religious practices. The court also suggested that the father try to be sensi- tive to their views "so as not to have them see him as a contradiction in their lives." But the court would not grant to the custodial parent a power to be used to exclude the father's contrasting religious views and practices as a factor in the children's lives. The court thus curbed the mother's privileges in deference to the father's and expressed confidence that the children would be able to choose their religious prac- tices in light of their mother's guidance when, later, they gained independent reason.

In the third case, the noncustodial parent has spiritual custody of the child, thus exercising the prerogative to determine the child's religious upbringing. This case marks an exception to a usual practice of according to the custodial parent the right to determine the child's religious upbringing and training. Yet even if the custodial parent is granted that right, the courts must struggle with the competing claims of a noncustodial parent to religious freedom and to a right to expose the child to his reli- gious practice.

As these three cases indicate, diversity within families complicates analysis of who is within the family, and what benefits accompany family membership. Parental prerogatives, such as guiding a child's religious upbringing, become complicated when the parents themselves disagree. The secular state, committed to neutrality about religion, then faces a special problem. How can it avoid imposing any particular religious—view that is, how can it remain neutral—while still performing its function of protecting children? The usual judicial answer, demonstrated by these cases, is to turn to the language of children's interests and harms, to consider the testimony of psychologists, and to count on a notion of individual choice for parents and for children as they grow into people capable of mature independent reason.

Yet, this usual judicial answer actually demonstrates the impossibility of neutrality in these cases, for the emphasis on individual choice of religion neglects the possibility that the sheer fact of being posed with a choice about religious identity alters the child's relationship to religion. Some religions do not treat religious identity as a choice but instead an inheritance. Others treat choice itself as a threat to the religion's integrity. Even the child who reaffirms the religion of his custodial parent in the face of exposure to his noncustodial parent's religion has a different relationship to religion than one who had no such sustained exposure. The difficulty is not just the legal system's, but the children's, and the parents'. This impossibility of judicial neutrality toward religion in these cases mirrors the impossibility of avoiding choice in the legal definitions of "family" and articulations of benefits of family membership.

We face choices about who should be treated as families and what benefits and freedoms should people receive as family members. Yet how should we make such choices? I think we first need to acknowledge that we cannot be neutral about them. I also advocate tolerance in making these choices—but tolerance itself is a substantive value that departs from neutrality. Tolerance can be chosen only as a tradeoff against other values. This is a slippery point, so let me elaborate and locate it in our constitutional tradition.

A Tradition of Tensions

Committed to equality and liberty, riven by legacies of differences and discrimination, our legal system reflects simultaneous devotion to neutrality toward—or better yet, tolerance of—private choices and devotion to officially articulated values. For example, the First Amendment stands as a protection of religious liberty and governmental neutrality toward religion, and yet in repeated decisions, it also expresses, through judicial interpretation, what the secular or dominant forces in the society will not accept, ranging from polygamous[30] to the use of peyote in religious ceremonies.[31] Similarly, both religious and family freedoms protect the autonomy of the Amish who resist a compulsory school law as an incursion on their way of life,[32] and yet neither religious nor family freedoms could shield a parent or guardian from a child labor law applied to forbid a child from distributing religious leaflets on the street[33] or from conviction for child endangerment for withholding medical treatment due to religious belief.[34] Commitment to subgroup autonomy justifies deference to an Indian tribunal with regard to questions of sex discrimination in the treatment of tribal inheritance laws,[35] but subgroup autonomy has not been accorded sufficient weight to justify excusing children from public school sessions involving texts that offend their parents' religious views.[36]

Yet the question remains of whether the legal system can respect the choices of private individuals and groups while also implementing specific values that limit those choices. Navigating between these two alternatives is especially tricky when courts deal with religious differences within families such as the custody and visitation cases previously discussed. "Neutrality" in some absolute sense is not an option; instead, there is the choice between deference to private freedom and the alternative of publicly imposed values.

Consider the problem faced by courts when one parent's religious beliefs call for shunning the other parent—what stance toward child custody and visitation could a court take and remain neutral? Either the court will favor the stringent religious belief or hinder it. No neutrality is possible even if the courts leave it to the parties to work things out privately, for then the court effectively perpetuates the child's role as a pawn in the parents' tug-of-war.

A similar problem arises beyond the context of religious divisions. How can the legal system defer to private freedoms in forming families and at the same time adopt policies to support families or to protect children? The very choice of a legal definition of family curbs private freedoms, especially when that definition is used to distinguish those who are eligible for a benefit—immigration, food stamps, social security, and the like—from those who are not. At the same time, deference to private freedoms itself is ambiguous: whose freedoms are to be protected in the context of family life—which adults, and which children?

We could work for legal rules that never recognize the "family" in distributing benefits and instead confer benefits solely on individuals regardless of family status. That, too, is a preference—a preference against preferring particular groupings of people. In practice, however, this may work out to be a preference for the conventional groups already privileged as family by social institutions. As long as "family," "spouse," and "parent" are used as legal and social terms in allocating benefits, legal, and thus political and social, decisions will articulate which groupings to value or prefer.

Some people call for a return to the "traditional" family and argue against expanding the definition of "family" to include gay and lesbian couples, extended families, and other groupings. Some may view the trends of increased single-parenthood, unmarried parents, divorce, and gay and lesbian families as eroding the basic values of the society. These people may find proposals for supporting these developments noxious and a threat to the order that sustains their liberty. Especially concerned with assuring economic self-sufficiency within families, people with this view may support contemporary proposals for reforming the welfare system such as proposals to promote marriage and deter child-bearing by poor people.

Perhaps the constraints on the freedom of poor people do not trouble proponents of such proposals, but efforts to recreate traditional families more generally would be quite coercive, draconian, and likely to fail. As Stephanie Coontz wrote in her piece called "Pro-Family but Divorced from the Facts":

> To establish the family wage system, in which married men supposedly support all mothers and children within self-sufficient families, would require either mandating abortion and birth control for our nation's unmarried women or equipping them with chastity belts, prohibiting divorce except among the rich, obliging unwed

mothers to give up their children for adoption, and forcing prospective adoptive couples to accept the black, racially mixed, older white, and disabled children who now cannot find homes.[37]

What one may call order, another may call bias; what one may call traditional values, another may call exclusion. The progressive reformers at the turn of this century worried that immigrants would maintain group loyalties that would interfere with assimilation and hold the society back.[38] During the very same period, the Catholic church promoted ethnic parishes that preserved distinctive cultural traditions of the new immigrants.[39] Pluralists throughout this century promoted inclusion even while implying a basic faith in shared ground rules for the society, however diverse its members. Some critics argue, however, that the pluralists failed to sustain those ground rules that permitted tolerance itself.[40] Others assert that the core shared value in America is commitment to constitutionalism which asserts respect for difference.[41] Also threatening the inclusionary impulse, nativist forces opposed to new waves of immigrants resurface almost every decade.[42]

Philosopher Joshua Halberstam may have put it best when he asserted that genuine tolerance is impossible, because anyone with truly held convictions believes they and not another set are correct, and yet only those with convictions can be tolerant.[43] At the same time, Halberstam notes that "we can limit intolerance by limiting our convictions; by restricting the 'extent' of our convictions as well as their sheer number, we can avoid unwarranted intolerance."[44] He urges efforts to distinguish what we really think is fundamental from what we care about but need not treat as convictions as incompatible with toleration for others. We thus can expand the sphere for freedom while defending its limits in terms that can be understood and argued over by many other people.

Because I favor an expansive sphere for private freedom, I defend a tolerant, and thus expansive, response to legal claims of family membership. I doubt the value of state standardization and social stigma directed towards groups of people who depart from the state-sanctioned model of the family. I think the values signaled by "family" are worthwhile and yet fragile; stability, nurturance, and care should promoted wherever possible, and people committed to taking on these tasks should be encouraged to do so.

Thus far, I chiefly have explored a paradox. I have argued that it is not possible for the government to be neutral about families, just as it is not possible for a school to be neutral about the values and cultural images it teaches. Yet I have also suggested that it is possible, and commendable, to restrict the kind of commitments that make tolerance for others difficult or impossible.

This approach may seem most difficult when it comes to thinking about families—as one observer put it: "One of the difficult things about the family as a topic is that everyone in the discussion feels obliged to defend a particular set of choices."[45] Perhaps, ironically, the intensity of debate over families reflects not just our diversity but also a national commonality. Arlene Skolnick recently commented:

> Since the nineteenth century, Americans have looked to the family as the source of individual and social salvation. Europeans, by contrast, have looked at the family as

a fragile institution in need of support from the wider society. . . . The emphasis on the home as the source of both personal happiness and social order has been responsible for the recurring sense of crisis concerning children and the family that has afflicted American culture since the 1820's.[46]

The great expectations we bring to our own families and to the idea of the family actually may reflect something missing beyond families—a realm of social life and social meaning beyond home and also beyond workplaces. Perhaps we can reduce our intolerance toward family groupings we do not recognize by working for sociability in more places beyond families.

As we each participate in constructing our own families, and in claiming benefits and privileges of family status, can we also contribute to a constructive public debate about how society should define family and family benefits and privileges? Can we acknowledge the impossibility of neutrality and the inevitability of choice? Can we refrain from characterizing our own preferences as natural, consensual, or obvious, given the extensive disagreements on these issues? Can we articulate a possibility of tolerance *and* commitment to particular values? I pursue and reconsider these questions now as I turn from "All in the Family" to "In All Families—Loving and Owing.

II. IN ALL FAMILIES—LOVING AND OWING

Introduction

What do you owe a member of your family—however you define "family"? Financial support? How about an organ? Bone marrow? What does a child owe a sibling? Can a parent approve the transplanting of one sibling's organ into another—or would this breach the parent's duty to preserve and protect each child's interests?

Tamas Bosze of Hoffman Estates, Illinois, brought these issues to public attention when he sought to test the bone marrow of two children he had fathered out-of-wedlock; Tamas hoped to find a donor match for an older son who was dying of leukemia. As one commentator put it,

> Would even the most loving family members want to be forced by the courts to donate a kidney or retina to an ailing child or sibling? The chemistry of love and courage often inspires one relative to donate organs to another. But to do so is an act of will, born of the impulses of a generous individual—not the mandate of the law.[47]

Tamas's lawyers argued that by participating in a transplant, the half-brothers would benefit: insofar as they would avoid the pain of knowing that they might have been able to save the life of their half-brother, but did not.[48] But the mother of the younger boys reasoned that, as a mother, she had to focus on protecting her children from potential complications from the procedures requested by the father of the children.

This is an unusual problem. Yet, in many ways, it resembles other problems of family obligation. For example, how much child support should a noncustodial father owe, especially after he fathers new children with another woman? Should he be able to reduce the support payments to children he fathered in an earlier marriage or relationship because of these new obligations, or should the initial obligations remain unchanged? These questions resemble those raised by the bone marrow transplant in that a parent may have obligations to more than one child as well as to himself or herself. Yet should these obligations be defined? Contemporary industrialized societies lack clear answers about the scope and definition of family duties.

By looking to family duties, I mean to include issues of moral as well as legal responsibility. While these are potentially distinct issues, they also mutually inform each other. Indeed, emphasizing distinctions at the cost of connections is a mistake when such emphasis disguises how mutual impact and influence work—a point I will return to several times in this discussion. It reminds me, though, of one definition of legal reasoning as thinking about two inextricably connected things as if they were detached.[49] Some of the difficulties in defining family obligations, I will argue, arise from just this kind of thinking.

My central argument here will urge a generous definition of family membership and a strict approach to family obligations. One way to defend this is by reference to notions of consent or acceptance. If someone claims family membership and the benefits that go along with it, this person may also be said to consent to and accept the obligations that attach to family roles. In other words, let us be welcoming toward those who are willing to take on family obligations, but serious in enforcing the expectation that those obligations will in fact be fulfilled.

You may well disagree with me on many points. You may think that "consent" is mythological. One does not consent to parenthood by engaging in sexual activities, you may say. Or one does not accept a duty to donate an organ or other body part simply because one is a parent. Surely one does not accept this duty as a sibling who never chose to be born much less to be a sibling (I say this as a middle child). You may think that preserving traditional narrow definitions of family would avoid any ambiguity about obligations. Or you may think that people should be able to negotiate their own terms of family relationships and not have obligations assigned simply because of the fact of family membership. (This is the "tailor-made" rather than "off-the-rack" theory of family ties.)

These potentially important points of disagreement actually dim in significance when compared with the three difficulties in defining family duties I will now explore. The first difficulty stems in part from the fact that people disagree not only about family duties but also about govern mental duties. The two disagreements are linked and therefore compounded.

In industrial societies since the nineteenth century, governmental support is the likely alternative to privately performed family obligations; refusal to support a member of one's family may well translate into requests for state subsidy. Thus, disagreement about the scope and enforceability of family obligations quickly collapses into disagreement about the proper boundary between the family and the government.

In the United States, one side in this debate views governmental aid as a dangerous tinge of socialism that undermines private initiative; another side criticizes the availability of governmental subsidies for the ventures of the rich but not for the needs of the poor or middle class. Whatever view one takes, it becomes difficult to articulate family obligations without engaging large and controverted political questions about the role of the government, the rate of taxes, and conceptions of public and private responsibility. Political debates over the scope of a "social safety net" will affect significantly the articulation of family duties even as articulation of family duties will affect the scope of governmental programs. Working on one problem requires work on the other, as if they were simultaneous equations. But politics is not as neat as math.

A second difficulty in articulating family obligations grows from the particularly painful disagreements that arise when family members no longer—if they ever did—love one another. Alimony payment after divorce is a classic example. Support for an elderly parent is another. Unfortunately, so is child support, though often here it is the lost love between the adults that undermines an obligation to children.

Noncompliance with legally-announced family duties can reflect many things, and certainly one is resentment or disaffection toward the recipient. Views about providing care or financial support for a relative may be colored by how that person feels about the relative. And those feelings, in turn, may be influenced in part by affection and personal compatibility, and in part by a sense of debt due to the benefits the person in need has offered the one in the past.

This issue of reciprocity points to the third difficulty: many family duties are difficult to define because the simple measure of reciprocity will not work. A parent cares for an infant, one hopes, out of love, but if there is a sense of obligation, it more likely derives from the parent's acknowledgment of responsibility for bringing the child into the world, or for attending to someone with special vulnerabilities and needs, than it does from an expected payback sometime in the future. Some philosophers argue explicitly that an adult child does not owe anything to an aging parent simply as a corollary of parental duty, because there is no necessary reciprocation of acts the parent initially performed due to the parent's own sense of duty.[50] Nor do we owe a return of favors done for us. But if a familial duty does not arise out of reciprocation, what is its source, and what should define its scope?

I will examine each of these difficulties in greater detail while searching for an appropriate pop song to accompany each one. It is not that I have run out of television shows, or judicial opinions, but I do believe that contemporary issues of family duty should become as familiar as pop songs. Then, they may run through our minds and enrich the rhythm of our lives. I will also consult a range of sources that might help in articulating family duties, especially where an individual potentially carries an obligation to more than one other family member. Finally, I will return briefly to defend my initial proposal of stringent attitudes toward family obligations to accompany expansive definitions of family membership. And I hope this provides a starting point, not the end point, for discussing the contemporary issues of family law.

Boundaries Between Public and Private Obligations to Family Members

You will quickly see why I want something more catchy to use to describe the first difficulty—"the contested boundaries between public and private obligations to family members" just is not going to hit the charts. Nor is "solving the simultaneous equations of family duties and governmental responsibilities." Unfortunately, not many pop songs, or popular discussions for that matter, address this issue directly. There are some candidates if we put the issue more generally, however: consider folk singer Nanci Griffith's song, "It's a Hard Life Wherever You Go,"[51] or blues artist Etta James's number, "Shakey Ground,"[52] or R.E.M.'s "Turn You Inside Out."[53] The basic idea is that the risk of dependency is real for each of us, and deciding whether anyone must help the dependents involves not just definitions of family duties but also definitions of governmental programs.

The Role of the Government

Roscoe Pound in 1916 alluded to this point when he noted that "[i]t is important to distinguish the *individual* interests in domestic relations from the *social* interest in the family and marriage as social institutions."[54] Lee Teitelbaum, Dean of the Utah Law School, put the point this way: "[T]he family is a member of a set of social systems which, in shifting configurations and alignments, participates and to some extent controls the distribution of opportunities, goods, and benefits in our society."[55] Student loan programs put it more bluntly: if the loan program can in any way characterize the student as a family dependent, it will look to the resources of other family members in calculating eligibility for and terms of the loan.

Clearly, then, such ambiguity about the scope of family duties allows governmental regulations to assume the existence and magnitude of such duties even if the people involved do not or cannot accept them, and the results are often perverse or unfair. A painful example arises for spouses who must themselves become poor if their spouses are to qualify for Medicaid when they need care in an institutional setting like a nursing home. The states vary in their specific regulations under Medicaid, but they are permitted to "deem" the resources of a non-institutionalized spouse as being available for paying the medical expenses of an institutionalized spouses[56] whether or not those resources are actually contributed. For many people this creates a dilemma: the spouse who remains at home can contribute the portion of income that the state determines he should contribute—and then live on a severely reduced amount of money, or he can refuse to contribute the money and potentially deny his spouse needed medical and nursing care. While a few states, more humanely, allow spouses to agree to divide their property, as long as the federal government allows the practice of "deeming" with no particular time restrictions, most people will be placed in very difficult situations.

Whether an individual feels a sense of responsibility to provide financially for family members is complicated by the high costs of institutional care and by the governmental determinations of the appropriate level of contribution. Yet the problem should not be viewed solely in terms of the hardship individuals may feel. The demographic shifts in the United States provide the larger social context: more and more people live longer, and more and more medical expenditures are devoted to caring for people in the last years of their lives. Large-scale public policies, not only public and private articulations of family duties, are at stake in the allocation of resources to the care of the elderly. Whether the government assumes private duties is simply part of a larger question about the allocation of social resources that is inevitably a public policy question.

The problem grows even more complex when the question of care of the elderly involves not their spouses, but their adult children. Because families across the United States tend to have fewer children than in the past, "[f]or the first time in history, the average couple has more parents living than it has children."[57] And because many more people live long enough to become not only elderly, but frail, and because they tend to have fewer adult children, the burden of caring for elderly parents has changed. Whatever intuitive ideas people may have about a duty to care for their elderly parents, these demographic patterns affect the shape of the need and people's abilities to cope with that need. In addition, the presence or absence of coherent social policies and institutions alters the landscape within which adult children define their own sense of duty to elderly parents. Thus, despite a legal and cultural tradition distinguishing sharply between public and private realms, public and private duties end up tied together and mutually defining, as people actually struggle to address the needs of members of their families.

Other demographic patterns affecting the relationship between public and private duties include the high rates of divorce and remarriage. Adult children with elderly parents may divorce and remarry and then develop changing notions of responsibility for those parents, or for the parents of their spouses and ex-spouses. Perhaps more profound is the changing role of women in the work force, since typically women provided the day-to-day care for dependents in the family. Many families may not be able accept that solution if it removes a woman from the wage-market. Many women will not choose this alternative; some may choose it if their employers make accommodations for dependent-care leave or otherwise protect the woman's job security. While these choices may be experienced as private dilemmas, they are social phenomena shaped at least in part by the practices of employers and governments. For women especially, the articulation of family duties spills over into public policies about the workplace, subsidized dependent care, respite care, and institutional options.

The status of women in the society in general also contributes to difficulties in articulating spousal duties following divorce, especially the terms of alimony. Professor Carl Schneider suggests that "[t]he riddle of alimony is why one former spouse should support the other when no-fault divorce seems to establish the principle that marriage need not be for life and when governmental regulation is conventionally condemned."[58]

The riddle is not difficult to understand, nor perhaps to answer, given the historical context of gender relations and divorce. Alimony originally was the duty owed by the husband to the wife following the breach of the marriage contract; it reflected the continuing duty to provide support that the husband undertook with the marriage itself. The reforms that brought no-fault divorce in turn expressed some of the erosion of these gendered ideas of marriage, but also revealed more profoundly that increasing numbers of people did not treat marriage as an agreement for life. At the same time, women's continuing disadvantages in the labor market consigned many women after divorce to sharp declines in economic welfare. Opportunities foregone during time spent at home attending to the marriage and childraising may not be recaptured by most women.

Some are prompted to ask why an ex-husband should bear through alimony payments the burdens of ongoing societal sex discrimination. Others, in contrast, call for continuing recognition after divorce of spousal obligations undertaken at marriage. A third, very long-run option would involve redressing sex discrimination in the labor market and thereby altering the need for alimony, but not entirely; women who enter marriages with an understanding that they will forgo careers and instead devote more of their time to managing the home and caring for family members would still face economic dependency if divorced. I do not mean to push a position on this debate here; I have done so elsewhere.[59] I only mean to point out that here, too, the articulation of private family duties necessarily implicates larger social issues and public policies.

In sum, the first difficulty is that we cannot articulate family duties in the absence of public policy discussions about work structures, gender roles, allocation of medical resources, and subsidies for caring for the elderly. Yet the deep controversies about each of these issues, and about the government's role in them, severely complicate this task.[60]

Lost Love

Finding a pop song for the second difficulty is no problem. Much of the airwaves and record grooves are filled with songs about love lost; a modest sampling includes Whitney Houston's "Where Do Broken Hearts Go";[61] Bonnie Raitt's "I Can't Make You Love Me";[62] Joan Baez's "Never Dreamed You'd Leave in Summer";[63] and The Pretenders' "Thin Line Between Love and Hate."[64] For a specialized genre of these songs expressing anxious anticipation about the end of love, Roberta Flack's "Will You Still Love Me Tomorrow"[65] provides a good example. The truth is, when love stops from one direction, it may not stop from the other. The difficulty all these songs suggest for family duties is whether obligations once formed by love should endure when the love ends.

Not surprisingly, philosophers as well as songsters have devoted much time to this issue. Philosophers pose the question: are family duties more like the duties of friendship or the duties of contractual agreements? If friendship is the proper analogy, then love rather than debt is the medium of exchange. This view implies that when the love ends, so do the obligations. Once again, issues about alimony following divorce come to mind.

Here, I would challenge the analogy between family roles and friendship, but I do so chiefly to expose the kind of difficulties loss of love poses for articulating family duties. Jane English, who advanced that analogy, maintains that "after a friendship ends, the duties of friendship end. The party that has sacrificed less owes the other nothing."[66] Similarly, she argues, an adult child owes parents nothing. She offered an example involving not organ donation, but blood donation:

> For instance, suppose Elmer donated a pint of blood that his wife Doris needed during an operation. Years after their divorce, Elmer is in an accident and needs one pint of blood. His new wife, Cora, is also of the same blood type. It seems that Doris not only does not "owe" Elmer blood, but that she should actually refrain from coming forward if Cora has volunteered to donate. To insist on donating not only interferes

with the newlyweds' friendship, but it belittles Doris and Elmer's former relationship by suggesting that Elmer gave blood in hopes of favors returned instead of simply out of love for Doris. It is one of the heart-rending features of divorce that it attends to quantity in a relationship previously characterized by mutuality. If Cora could not donate, Doris's obligation is the same as that for any former spouse in need of blood; it is not increased by the fact that Elmer similarly aided her. It is affected by the degree to which they are still friends, which in turn may (or may not) have been influenced by Elmer's donation.[67]

I am not troubled by the rejection here of a *quid pro quo* analysis; the world is simply not neat enough to present many issues of obligation that take the form of "a pint of my blood for yours." Many other things, however, trouble me about this example,[68] but I will focus here on only one. This presentation suggests that what one former spouse owes the other former partner depends on the current state of their feelings for one another. Missing altogether is the potential impact and power of the past—past friendship, past commitment, and past trust.

The fickle quality of present feeling is a problem not merely following divorce, but even in ongoing family relationships. If family membership implies no further obligations beyond the degree of friendship one member feels toward another, then I wonder what justifies preserving the family institution, with its privileges and opportunities. Moreover, tying family duties on feelings of friendship tethers those duties to emotions that can and will change rather than assuring stability and continuity.

Tying family duties to feelings most significantly precludes the chance that feelings can themselves be educated as someone learns about and carries out responsibilities. Professor Bruce Hafen has suggested that "[a] genuine personal willingness to assume affirmative duties and lasting commitments depends heavily upon the influence of normative models that have the innate power to produce altruistic attitudes regardless of legal enforceability."[69] As this point implies, difficulties in defining family duties arise not merely because people disagree about whether those duties should exist apart from feelings, but also because the specified content of family duties will itself influence and shape what people come to feel.

Duties and feelings interact in complicated ways. Many people know they have a family duty—even a legally enforceable one—and resent it rather than grow to accept it. Certainly the dismal rates of child support payments demonstrates this problem. Professor David Chambers' classic study of child support enforcement suggests the complex motives and feelings of those who do not pay.[70] Especially sad is the apparent spillover onto the children of negative feelings towards the ex-spouse.

The spillover renders especially difficult the task articulating parental duties for an individual who seeks to modify child support obligations after fathering additional children in a new marriage or relationship. As one observer of these kinds of families noted: "There is anger when money needed by the new family goes to one spousels children from the old family. There is hurt at the recurring evidence of a past history shared with the first family and forever closed from the new spouse."[71] Clearly, making family duties contingent on feelings is especially fraught with trouble in this context. But articulating sensible duties without taking account of shifting feelings may also be terribly mistaken simply as a practical matter.

Perhaps the problem arises with tying family duties to sentiments altogether. It is possible to articulate family duties that survive the flux of feelings; it is possible to frame family responsibilities through which one's own good depends on the welfare of another. Norms predicated on such a view could actually affect what people come to feel, and such norms could include a continuation of duty beyond sentiment that the past should matter when it comes to family obligations. But pursuing these ideas is hardly uncontroversial. Lost love animates so many songs because it is painful, and articulating family duties in the light of past or future painful feelings will be a troubled task indeed.

Inadequacy of Reciprocation Theory

On the flip side of love that ends is love that is not returned. Consider Joan Armatrading's "Can't Let Go";[72] or Tina Turner's "You Can't Stop Me Loving You";[73] or even the Indigo Girls' "You And Me of the 10,000 Wars."[74] It is funny that we do not hear many songs about "Thanks for All You Did But I Don't Owe You Anything."

Even more scarce, though, are song titles that capture the third difficulty in defining family obligation—that the notion of reciprocation is inadequate to capture the complexity of family bonds, and therefore the measure of family duties becomes difficult to define. For example, unlike an exchange of promises between two people, and even unlike a marriage in which two adults agree to provide and care for one another, relationships between parents and children are not obviously reciprocal. Of course, parents derive benefits from their children, but they differ from those the children derive from their parents. Parents may hope that the children, once grown, will provide comparable financial, emotional, and physical support in return, and indeed, many societies implement such assumptions.

Yet reciprocation implies a more exact one-for-one exchange than the dynamics of most parent-child relations exemplify. Of course, parents derive pleasure and gratification from children as they grow up, but not as *quid pro quo* for what the parents themselves provide the children. Moreover, intergenerational exchanges between adult children and their parents may be complicated by the death, disability, or mobility of one or both parties before completion.

Even this understates the complications, because often more than two parties are involved. Since families often involve more than one generation and more than two people, the notion of reciprocation that so often defines the scope of duties seems out of place. The adult child may have two parents, plus stepparents, who need help as older adults; the adult child may have siblings and stepsiblings with whom to negotiate about who will provide support for the older relatives. The adult child in turn may have children and feel conflicting pulls of duties in two generational directions. Moreover, some may actually understand their duty to their aging parents in terms of providing for their own children the way their parents provided for them.

What, though, are the duties of a parent who has more than one child, and one has a disability that calls for more time and attention than the other child? Given all the possible complications, it is difficult, if not impossible, to articulate family duties removed from the particularities of each complicated constellation of family membership; the notion of reciprocity does not help, at least if it implies simply tit-for-tat.

As an alternative to simple reciprocation, some people and some families operate complex network of exchange. African-American families often build patterns of sharing and exchange of favors across networks of siblings, aunts and uncles, and other family members, especially when it comes to caring for children. Today, middle-class blacks often find their economic security jeopardized because they reach out to help more impoverished relatives. A network of kin, including a variety of related and unrelated people, in many communities works cooperatively to meet the basic demands of cooking, cleaning, childcare, and making ends meet.

Some people worry that complicated family patterns may produce "thinner bonds" even while creating wider kinship patterns. The problem of defining duties within families seems complicated for everyone who has more than one other person who counts as family. Simple notions of reciprocation will not work.

Revisiting Duties

Let us revisit the definition of duty in the context of the bone marrow transplant sought by Tamas Bosze. Remember, he wanted to save one son and therefore asked a court to order tests on two other children he fathered with a woman other than his wife.[75] The mother of the two children declined the tests because she believed her duty was to ensure that the children suffered no harm. If she had been the mother of the child needing the bone marrow transplant, should her assessment have differed?[76] Should a parent consider exposing one child to harm in order to help another child?

What notion of duty could help here? Prevailing normative frameworks of analysis could help, despite the difficulties I have explored. Perhaps a parent should try to ensure the greatest good for the greatest number within the family. If so, the parent could weigh the risk to the donor child with the gain to the recipient child in order to fulfill the duty to the family as a whole. Yet even this formulation is inadequate to the multiple interests involved if it neglects long-run consequences. For example, this approach might seem quite wanting if it implied that the greatest good for the family could be achieved by selling one child's organs—or one child altogether—in order to improve the financial security of the remaining family members.

Condemning such a result depends upon a norm that differs from the greatest good for the greatest number. Instead, at work is a norm of respect for each individual person that demands that no one is to be used simply as a means. Accordingly, sacrificing one child altogether for the good of others would seem a violation. Yet short of complete sacrifice, this norm could still permit a parent to fulfill duties to more than one child by authorizing bone marrow transplant from one to another. The parent could conclude that the donor child would be devastated by the loss of the sibling or would later regret a failure to help save that sibling. Under this view, it is the duty between siblings that is salient; the parent's duty derives from the donor sibling's duty. By authorizing the bone marrow transplant, the parent may fulfill a duty to protect the donor's interests, not only a duty to the recipient child.

Articulating a parent's duties in this fashion is bound to be tentative and abstract. Besides revealing deeply conflicting normative frameworks for defining such duties, this discussion reveals once again the special problems posed by multiple relationships among family members. Again, reciprocity does not seem a useful concept to provide the measure of duty; at best, it could play a role as part of a process of hypothesizing what one would be willing to do for another if called upon to do so.

Perhaps obligations within families should be defined as correlates of the very definitions of families and of benefits accorded on the basis of family membership. Here the reciprocity would run between the family and the state rather than between family members. In exchange for the privileges of family status, each family would carry the same package of obligations. For example, if the state accorded lawful marital status to a gay or lesbian couple that so desired it, the argument would run, that couple should have the same obligations as would any other married couple with respect to that benefit. If that couple is entitled to benefits such as eligibility for inheriting a rent-controlled apartment, or spousal employee benefits, then that couple should be subject to the same income deeming rules applied to other married couples. Yet even this notion of reciprocity leaves the articulation of family duties undefined. Not only are the family duties applicable to "each family" still ambiguous, but the application of any articulated set of duties across the vast array of family types would yield enough problems to fill Family Law exams from here to eternity.

One response to the confusion about family duties is to use private ordering techniques such as antenuptial contracts, separation agreements, parent-child contracts, and domestic partnership agreements. Yet these private agreements, like all contracts, do not resolve or avoid publicly articulated duties. The question still remains, then, what duties should provide the background assumptions for such private agreements, and what duties should not be subject to private contractual alteration?

Modification of child support once again provides an example. The noncustodial parent may seek to modify child support payments despite a prior agreement or court order. As I have already mentioned, a typical reason for such a request is the appearance of children in a subsequent marriage or relationship. This problem implicates each of the difficulties already discussed. The state's AFDC [Aid to Families with Dependent Children] payments or other income supports may be implicated if the custodial parent is financially eligible; statutory guidelines for child support would govern in every case and these reflect assumptions about the requisite private investment to keep children off of public dependency programs. The custodial parent might also be inclined to accept a negotiated agreement to reduced child support payments in order to avoid unpleasantness or to avoid nonpayment altogether, especially if the noncustodial parent bears resentment for the loss of love.

The competing obligations owed to the older children and the younger children renders the entire question even more difficult. The support-owing parent may be willing to take on a second job or work overtime in order to meet those competing obligations, but may also decline such extra work if all or some of the added income is directed toward the children not in his household. Perhaps the duties should be evaluated on the imagined assumption that all the children are part of the same family. Hypothesizing that all the children lived in the same household—and the same two parents jointly produced the children and cared for them together—there is an argument for allowing reduced payments per child. The argument would look to economies of scale and also toward fairness within that group of children as a whole. But precisely that assumption of "one family" is absent here, where the noncustodial parent has produced children in a second household. Implicating all the difficulties in articulating family duties, this problem I hope will stir discussion among us.

This discussion suggests what should now be the predictable three difficulties in articulating family duties: they presuppose and yet also affect governmental duties; they reflect lost love and emotional flux; they lack a clear measure of reciprocity and bear the complications of relationships among many people. Prevailing value discussions that compare utilities or call for respecting persons have paid little attention to issues within families and prompt divergent suggestions when applied to families.

Yet I hope this discussion illuminates more than these difficulties. In particular, I think attention to the connections between matters too often separated enriches the analysis of family duties. Thus, recognizing the inter-dependence of family duties and state treatment of families can clarify how some apparent dilemmas could be resolved with a shift in governmental policies.

The government will not and cannot be neutral about family duties. Some duties will be enforced and others will not be. But the background governmental rules do have an important impact on the family duties that people accept and those they find too burdensome. Having a reliable safety net would help; having a coherent universal health policy would help. Here, I am reminded of a discussion with a Canadian friend whose father had suffered a heart attack. We discussed questions about how this would affect the family and who would care for him if he became disabled. Then she remarked that however difficult these matters were, she could not imagine the burdens people in comparable situations in the United States would feel if they simultaneously had to worry about the costs of the medical care.

Another useful insight about connections: predicating family duties on feelings may be hazardous, but so is disregarding the possibility that well-articulated family duties could influence positively the feelings people develop. This notion includes attending to the value of enduring commitments. Commitments can last even beyond the feelings, especially if we encourage them to last. Granted, reciprocation may fail as a measure of duty where families involve many people across generations. That very failure suggests alternative conceptions of duty that can operate within complex networks of care and exchange. Finally, conceptions of family duties must also be considered in relation to shifting notions of who is in the family and what benefits and duties should attach to family membership.

These insights would not solve, but would enrich, consideration of many controversies. These include contests over religious exposure during visits by noncustodial parents discussion in Part I. The courts tend to treat many cases as clashes between parental prerogatives and children's best interests. For example, courts tend to translate debates over religious exposure during visits with noncustodial parents as a question about the child's best interests. I think it is helpful to start by acknowledging that the government cannot remain neutral. The notion of the child's best interests, if secular, could depart from a religious view, and a decision to permit exposure to more than one religion is no more neutral than a decision to restrict exposure to only one religion, since both affect deeply the child's religious understandings and identity.

I suggest that we shift to the task of articulating more fully the parents' *duties* in this context, including duties to attend to the impact of their prerogatives on the child. Perhaps a different notion of simple reciprocity between the parents is present here, a basic respect for one another's religious views. Yet, once again, that notion is inadequate for this task. Clarifying who is the family for the purpose of respecting family privacy should involve attention to the privileges and duties the parents plan to exercise.

Let me offer one last case. Again, I do not claim to resolve it but instead offer considerations that could deepen our legal and moral understandings of it. A car driven by a drunk driver struck a school teacher named Sharon Kowalski and left her brain-damaged and otherwise considerably disabled.[77] Karen Thompson at that time informed Sharon's parents that the two women had been living together in a close and loving lesbian relationship; they had exchanged rings and were buying a house together.[78] Karen sought authority to serve as Sharon's guardian. The Kowalskis refused, sought and obtained guardianship, barred Karen from visiting Sharon, and tried to sever the connection between the two women. Recently, the parents, due to their own physical frailty, sought to have another person appointed guardian. The court initially approved this appointment of a third party, but then, finally, accepted Karen Thompson's request for guardianship. The case elicited public attention and involved long and complicated legal proceedings in local, state, and federal courts.

No doubt the Kowalskis believed they acted with concern for their daughter's best interests. At the same time, the case demonstrates the difficulties for people in nontraditional relationships lacking state recognition; without an official marriage or even a durable power of attorney, the law treated Karen Thompson as a stranger for much of the proceedings. The case implicates the contemporary, unresolved questions about who is in the family and who should be eligible for the benefits of family membership.

But receiving less discussion are the equally significant questions of family duty here. I began by asserting that family duties should be strict even as I assert that the definition of family should be generous. Karen Thompson clearly accepted the duties accompanying what she treated as a marriage; she pursued the kind of care she believed would be in Sharon's best interests. Sharon's parents also tried to perform a duty to their daughter.

Assuming that Sharon's parents owed a duty to care for their daughter—or wished to fulfill such a duty—how should that duty be described? That duty of parents of an adult child, I suggest, should include an obligation to recognize and try to respect the child's life choices, especially choices in defining her own family. A judicial appreciation of this element of parental duty could complicate some cases, but would help join the issues of loving and owing with the issues of family diversity that are bound to perplex us for some time to come.

Notes

An earlier version of this essay appeared with more extensive citations in 95 *West Virginia Law Review* 275 (1992-93) (Edward G. Donley Memorial Lectures).

1. Arlene Skolnick, *Embattled Paradise: The American Family in an Age of Uncertainty* 8 (1991).

2. "Only One U.S. Family in Four Is 'Traditional,'" *New York Times*, Jan. 30, 1991, at A19 (citing census data).

3. See Martha Minow, "Redefining Families—Who's In and Who's Out," 62 *University of Colorado Law Review* 269, 274 (1991).

4. Reep v. Commissioner of Dep't of Employment & Training, 593 N.E.2d 1297 (Mass. 1992). After this decision, the legislature overrode an executive veto and amended the governing statute to prohibit payment of unemployment benefits to anyone who (spouse or not) accompanies a person to a new locale. 1992 Mass. Legis. Serv. ch. 26. (Westlaw) (H.B. 2935, § 20).

5. Braschi v. Stahl Assocs. Co., 543 N.E.2d 49 (1989).

6. Tony Arjo, "'Family Fairness' Policy Helps Some Newly-Legalized Immigrant Families, Not Others," *Youth Law News*, May–June 1990, at 15; Carol Sanger, "Immigration Reform and Control of the Undocumented Family," 2 *Georgia Immigration Law Journal* 295, 295–96 (1987).

7. Sanger, supra, note 6, at 328–29.

8. Ibid., at 329–30 (footnotes omitted). See also INS v. Hector, 479 U.S. 85 (1986) (*per curiam*) (denying petition for suspension of deportation of teenage nieces living with an aunt because the extreme hardship exemption applies only spouses, parents, or children).

9. Lying v. Castillo, 477 U.S. 635 (1986).

10. National Commission on Children, *Beyond Rhetoric: A New American Agenda for Children and Families* 18 (1991).

11. Ibid., at 20. But note that "family disruption" due to divorce is comparable to disruption in the last century due to death of a parent. See Skolnick, supra note 1, at 144 (discussing research by Mary Jo Bane).

12. Michael J. Dale, "The Evolving Constitutional Rights of Nonmarital Children: Mixed Blessings," 5 *Georgia State Review* 523, 523 (1989.

13. See Paul Glick, "Remarried Families, Stepfamilies, and Stepchildren: A Brief Demographic Analysis," 38 *Family Relations* 24–27 (1989).

14. Compare Jimenez v. Weinberg, 417 U.S. 628 (1974) (disabled worker's nonmarital children born after onset of disability eligible for social security benefits), and Gomez v. Perez, 409 U.S. 535 (1973) (nonmarital children entitled to child support), with Mathews v. Lucas, 427 U.S. 495 (1976) (social security survivorship benefits unavailable to certain nonmarital children absent proof of dependency at time of the worker's death), and Califano v. Boles, 443 U.S. 282 (1979) (nonmarital children can be denied social security insurance benefits).

15. Judith Stacey, *Brave New Families* 38 (1990).

16. Pamela Painter, "New Family Car," in *The Graywolf Annual Eight: The New Family* 240, 244 (Scott Walker, ed., 1991).

17. Edward A. Slavin, Jr., "*What Makes a Marriage Legal?*" 16, 18 *Human Rights* 18 (1991).

18. Loving v. Virginia, 388 U.S. 1 (1967).

19. Elizabeth Bartholet, "Where Do Black Children Belong? The Politics of Race Matching in Adoption," 139 *University of Pennsylvania Law Review* 1163 (1991).

20. Palmore v. Sidoti, 466 U.S. 429 (1984).

21. Ibid., at 434.

22. The sobering footnote to reality here is that the child lived with the white father during the litigation—without court approval—and the father ultimately obtained an opportunity to claim lawful custody. Palmore v. Sidoti, 472 So. 2d 843 (Fla. Dist. Ct. App. 1985) (permitting proceeding in Texas to resolve the child's best interests).

23. Mentry v. Mentry, 190 Cal. Rptr. 843, 844 (Ct. App. 1983); *accord* Munoz v. Munoz, 489 P.2d 1133 (Wash. 1971). Other courts in contrast have relied on psychologist evidence that exposing a child to two different religious traditions would *per se* harm a child and therefore issued a restraint against the noncustodial parent. See, e.g., Morris v. Morris, 412 A.2d 139 (Pa. Super. Ct. 1979). Another enjoined the father from taking his children to Assembly of God meetings because the parents' dispute over religion would cause future harm to the children. Andros v. Andros, 396 N.W.2d 917 (Minn. Ct. App. 1986).

24. Brown v. Szakal, 514 A.2d 81 (N.J. Super. Ct. Ch. Div. 1986); see also *In re* Tisckos, 514 N.E.2d 523 (Ill. App. Ct. 1987) (allowing noncustodial parent to take child to his church rather than mother's church during visitation time); Kelly v. Kelly, 524 A.2d 1330 (N.Y. Super. Ch. 1986) (rejecting custodial parent's request, based on her assertion of the commands of her Catholic faith, for a restraint against the father to prohibit overnight visits of their children in his home in the presence of unrelated persons of the opposite sex because the psychological expert in the case testified that greater harm would come to the children by suggesting that the father is a bad man than by exposing them to his lifestyle).

25. Dick Johnson, "Struggle for Custody of Children's Faith Becomes Nightmare," *New York Times*, Dec. 11, 1988, at 1 (describing case of Jerold Simms and Dorothy Boeke).

26. Mentry v. Mentry, 190 Cal. Rptr. 847 (Ct. App. 1983).

27. Ibid. at 848.

28. Ibid., at 851 (Miller, J., dissenting).

29. Brown v. Szakal, supra noted 24, at 83 (emphasis added).

30. Reynolds v. United States, 98 U.S. 145 (1878).

31. Employment Div. v. Smith, 494 U.S. 872 (1990).

32. Wisconsin v. Yoder, 406 U.S. 205 (1972).

33. Prince v. Massachusetts, 321 U.S. 158 (1944).

34. People v. Rippberger, 283 Cal. Rptr. 111 (Ct. App. 1991).

35. Santa Clara Pueblo v. Martinez, 436 U.S. 49 (1978) (rejecting claim of a private right of action in federal court under the Indian Civil Rights Act in deference to tribal sovereignty).

36. Mozert v. Hawkins County Bd. of Educ., 827 F.2d 1058 (6th Cir. 1987).

37. Stephanie Coontz, "Pro-Family but Divorced from the Facts," *Wall Street Journal*, Aug. 9, 1989, at 10.

38. See William C. MacWilliams, "American Pluralism: The Old Order Passeth," in *The Americans*, 306–309 (Irving Kristol and Paul Weaver, eds., 1976); Robert H. Wiebe, *The Search for Order* (1967).

39. R. Laurence Moore, *Religious Outsiders and the Making of Americans*, 63–71 (1986).

40. See MacWilliams, supra note 38, at 318; Martin E. Marty, "Pluralists Take It on the Chin—Deservedly," *New York Times*, Apr. 2, 1988, at 23.

41. Kenneth L. Karst, "Paths of Belonging: The Constitution and Cultural Identity," 64 *North Carolina Law Review* 303 (1986).

42. Ibid.

43. Joshua Halberstam, "The Paradox of Tolerance," 14 *Philosophical Forum* 190 (1982–83).

44. Ibid., at 199.

45. Skolnick, supra note 1, at 200 (quoting Joseph Featherstone).

46. Ibid., at 200, 223.

47. Nancy Gibbs, "The Gift of Life—or Else," *Time*, Sept. 10, 1990, at 70.

48. Cf. Strunk v. Strunk, 445 S.W.2d 145 (Ky. 1969) (court approves donation of a kidney by a mentally impaired person to his ailing brother).

49. Attributed to Thomas Reed Powell, the quotation appears paraphrased by Lon Fuller: "Thomas Reed Powell used to say that if you can think about something that is related to something else without thinking about the thing to which it is related, then you have the legal mind." Lon Fuller, *The Morality of Law* 4 (1969).

50. Norman Daniels, *Am I My Parents' Keeper?: An Essay on Justice Between the Young and the Old* 39 (1988); see also Jane English, "What Do Grown Children Owe Their Parents?" in *Vice and Virtue in Everyday Life* 682 (Christina Sommers and Fred Sommers, eds., 1989).

51. Nanci Griffith, "It's a Hard Life Wherever You Go," on *Storms* (MCA Records 1989).

52. Etta James, "Shakey Ground," on *Save Your Itch* (Island Records 1988).

53. R.E.M., "Turn You Inside Out," on *R.E.M. Green* (Warner Bros. Records 1988).

54. Roscoe Pound, "Individual Interests in the Domestic Relations," 14 *Michigan Law Review* 177 (1916).

55. Lee E. Teitelbaum, "Placing the Family in Context," 22 *University of California at Davis Law Review* 801, 820–21 (1989).

56. See The Social Security Act, 42 U.S.C. § 1369a(a) (17) (Supp. II 1990); see also Schweiker v. Gray Panthers, 435 U.S. 34 (1981) (permitting states to treat spouses as a single economic unit for an indefinite time period in establishing Medicaid terms). The government also uses "deeming" in allowing states to attribute to the entire household child support received by one child in a household even if this could estrange the parent paying that child support or otherwise harm the recipient child. Bowen v. Guillard, 483 U.S. 587 (1987). See generally Lucy Billings, "The Choice Between Living with Family Members and Eligibility for Government Benefits Based on Need: A Constitutional Dilemma," 1966 *Utah Law Review* 695.

57. Skolnick, supra note 1, at 154.

58. Carl E. Schnieder, "Rethinking Alimony: Marital Decisions and Moral Discourse," 1991 *Brigham Young University Law Review* 197, 197.

59. See Martha Minow and Deborah Rhode, *Divorce Reform at the Crossroads* 201–204 (Steve Sugarman and Herma Hill Kay, eds., 1991).

60. Cf. Daniels, supra note 50, at 35 (the problem is how to produce principles of justice that yield a framework of institutions "within which people having different views about what is good and right in other regards can cooperate").

61. Whitney Houston, "Where Do Broken Hearts Go," on *Whitney* (Arista Records 1987).

62. Bonnie Raitt, "I Can't Make You Love Me," on *Luck of the Draw* (Capitol Records 1991).

63. Joan Baez, "Never Dreamed You'd Leave in Summer," *Classics Vol. 8* (A & M Records 1987).

64. The Pretenders, "Thin Line Between Love and Hate," on *The Singles* (Sire Records 1987).

65. Roberta Flack, "Will You Still Love Me Tomorrow," on *The Best of Roberta Flack* (Atlantic Records 1981).

66. English, supra note 50, at 685.

67. Ibid., at 685–86.

68. I am troubled by the initial effort to reframe the issue by introducing a potential conflict with the new wife who conveniently has the same blood type and would feel interfered with by an offer to help from the ex-wife. This seems both a dodge from the hard question—should the ex-spouse feel obliged to donate blood *when it is needed*—as well as an effort to accentuate

competitive and interchangeable dimensions of family relationships. I am even more troubled by the switch to a post-divorce example in an essay about ongoing family ties between adult children and their parents; the implication is that adult children and their parents are situated similarly to divorced spouses, perhaps because they too presumably no longer cohabit. The inattention to the differences between these relationships and their shifts over time allows the author to avoid difficult and important questions about what family duties should entail.

69. Bruce C. Hafen, "The Family as an Entity," 22 *University of California at Davis Law Review* 865, 914 (1989).

70. David L. Chambers, *Making Fathers Pay: The Enforcement of Child Support* 241–53 (1979).

71. Alex Shoumatoff, *The Mountain of Names* 169 (1985) (quoting Letty Cottin Pogrebin, *Family Politics: Love and Power on an Intimate Frontier* [1983]. Progrebin identifies further complications: "A father feels guilty about spending every day with his stepchildren while his own kids, in the custody of their mother, hunger for more time with him."

72. Joan Armatrading, "Can't Let Go," on *Hearts and Flowers* (A & M Records 1990).

73. Tina Turner, "You Can't Stop Me Loving You," on *Foreign Affairs* (Capitol Records 1989).

74. Indigo Girls, "You and Me of the 10,000 Wars," on *Nomads, Indians, Saints* (Epic Records 1990).

75. The Illinois Supreme Court rejected his request. Curran v. Bosze, 566, N.E.2d 1319 (Ill. 1990).

76. It is difficult to figure what role love past or lost may have played between the Tamas Bosze and the mother of these children.

77. See generally Karen Thompson, *Why Can't Sharon Kowalski Come Home?* (1988); Ruthann Robson and S.E. Valentine, "Lov(h)ers: Lesbians as Intimate Partners and Lesbian Legal Theory," 63 *Temple Law Review* 511, 514–21 (1990).

78. See Thompson, supra note 77, at 15; *In re* Guardianship of Kowalski, 382 N.W.2d 861, 863 (Minn. Ct. App.), *cert. denied* 475 U.S. 1085 (1986).

13

Beyond Lesbian and Gay "Families We Choose"

William N. Eskridge, Jr.

Modern family law in this century has been characterized by a shift in emphasis from status to choice, from the status-based roles imposed by communal tradition to the consensual duties created by contract. This shift reflects a progressive adoption in the family law context of the consequences of a "liberal" conception of self. The liberal self is an autonomous actor whose liberty is constrained only to the extent the actor agrees (contract) or harms others (tort and crimes). Hence, the liberal self is free to enter into, and exit from, family arrangements largely at will, uninhibited by social custom or old-fashioned status rules. Lesbians and gay men have been among the avant-garde of this shift, for we do not usually follow the traditional husband-wife-kids model of family formation. Instead, we have turned to "families we choose"[1]—circles of consent-based intimacy among friends, partners, former lovers, children, and others.

On the other hand, the law still retains many requirements founded on traditional status-based understandings about family. As a consequence, lesbian and gay families of choice lack many of the options and securities enjoyed by heterosexual families. For example, the status of being a married "spouse" entitles one to mutual emotional and financial support, priority as representative in the event of the other spouse's incapacity or death, and presumptive inheritance and property rights. Also, the status of being "parents" to children assures enormous control over those children, even if they are not biologically related to the parents. Adhering to traditional status ideas, no state (as of 1995) permits, lesbian or gay people to be spouses to one another, and most states offer barriers to their being parents. The gaylesbian response is that such limitations are outdated, in light of family law's embrace of the liberal self and its freedom to negotiate the terms of intimate relationships in so many other areas (such as no-fault divorce). Under a rigorously liberal jurisprudence, gaylesbian families we choose would not be discouraged, indeed, they would be accorded legal recognition.

This libertarian jurisprudence is an insufficient response to antihomosexual status-based rules, in part because status is resurgent in family law, and properly so. Liberalism's insistence upon an autonomous self is more appropriate for the market (where it has nonetheless been repeatedly compromised) than for the family. The liberal construct of the acontextual self is not only at war with antihomosexual limitations on family formation, but also with the prohomosexual need for human interconnection that impels people to form families in the first place. A risk of conceiving our interhuman relationships as nothing more than families we choose—a marketplace of intimacies—is to neglect or even sacrifice the advantages of relational features that are constitutive of self.

Libertarian arguments can and should be important for criticizing antihomosexual traditions, but status-based arguments ought not be ignored. By excluding us from the legal status of spouse and parent, law denies us possibilities for human interconnection routinely afforded other people and frustrates opportunities for lesbians, gay men, and bisexuals to foster their "relational selves." These exclusions constitute a denial of citizenship. The whole web of excluding practices is unjustified because sexual orientation is an irrational organizing principle for creating family statuses. I shall conclude by applying status-based arguments to argue that the gaylesbian movement should seek recognition of same-sex marriage, or its equivalent.

FAMILIES WE CHOOSE, FRACTURING OF SELF

American family law in the twentieth century has shown a general shift from status to contract, and this shift rests on the apparent acceptance of the liberal view of the self as autonomous and self-regarding, constructing patterns of intimacy on its own terms rather than the terms dictated by traditional institutions and the roles they impose.[2] Out of necessity, same-sex couples have been the shock troops of the liberated family. For example, "Boston marriages" between pairs of women and legal marriages between a woman and another woman "passing" as a man flourished during the Victorian era, the rhetorical apex of status-based intimacy.[3] Because homosexual relations have been illegal in most of the United States until recently, same-sex intimacy has been both closeted as well as socially constructed in modern American history. Today, such intimacy is no longer necessarily closeted, but it remains constructed: lesbians and gay men must rely on our own devices, instead of those off-the-rack rules offered by the state to heterosexuals, to form and cement families we choose.

When people started "coming out" in significant numbers after the Stonewall riots of June 1969, more gay people were able to form what can be called "families we choose." Professor Kath Weston, the anthropologist who coined the term, associates such families with the coming out process itself. Such an association reflects the fundamentally liberal assumptions of most gaylesbian thinking about families and relationships. Coming out has thus been conceptualized as a classic liberal move: the self asserts its acontextual identity as "gay"—in defiance, if need be, of disapproval by society, family, and friends. For the "out" gay person, family is much less likely to be defined by either blood or marriage than is the case for the closeted gay or the straight person because some members of the blood family will not accept the gay person's identity and the gay person does not have the formal option of getting married to the person she or he loves. Lacking the marriage option and often losing some ties of blood, the gay person is left to construct—to choose—her own family. Such families of choice both complement the traditional family and transcend it. Consider the following range of choices:

1. *The Functional Equivalent of the Victorian Family.* Although lesbian and gay couples cannot marry as a matter of law and cannot procreate with one another as a matter of biology, they can create the functional equivalent of the Victorian family or its recent exemplars, the Ward and June Cleavers and the Ozzie and Harriet Nelsons.[4] Some religions in America will conduct a marriage ceremony for same-sex couple if so desired, and most of the accoutrements of marriage (such as community property, joint obligations, and legal capacity to act for one another) can be created by contract, albeit at substantial trouble and expense. Same-sex couples can and often do have children: lesbian couples through artificial insemination from a male donor and (less often) male couples through surrogacy contracts with a female donor. Thus June and Harriet don't need Ward and Ozzie to have a family; like generations of Boston marriages, June and Harriett can construct their own relationship and, unlike such unions in the past, can come by children as well.

2. *A Web of Friendships.* Replicating the Victorian family is not Professor Weston's vision. Her families we choose are webs of friendships, with or without children and typically without formal commitments. Your family might consist of the partner with whom you live, as well as her child by a prior marriage; your former lover with whom you own and run a business; your best friend from college who was the first person you came out to (and whom you had a crush on); a person with AIDS whom you and your partner have agreed to help support; and your hang-out buddies on the local women's softball team, the same team where you met your current partner. The family might well consist of blood relatives (such as your child and your own mother who loves you even though she does not completely understand your sexuality) and even of legally imposed relationships (such as your former husband with whom you share custody of your child), but it often does not.

3. *Something of Each.* There are, of course, variations falling between the two patterns. For example, a gay man may marry a woman who is or becomes his best friend and the mother of his children, but still may have one or more men as his primary sexual lovers.[5] In most major cities today, same-sex couples can quasi-formalize their relationships by registering as "domestic partners," something of a rhetorical ways station between relationship and marriage. In an increasing number of states, same-sex couples can adopt one another's children through the process of a "cross-parent adoption."[6]

These developments are usually represented in gay-friendly accounts as positive one. Lesbians and gay men can have just as rich a personal life as straight people, and that life can and usually does include intimate relationships. Such positivity is all but dictated by the conventional liberal script: once a person discovers her "true" acontextual self and rationally pursues strategies that fulfill the needs and desires of that self, the person will do well. I subscribe to this script, as far as it goes, but the lesbian and gay experience suggests the cogency of Professor Milton Regan's argument that this conventional understanding of self is insufficiently rich.[7] For gays and lesbians more than for most straight people, the self is fractured by the variety of contexts into which it is tossed. The families we choose expose and perhaps even contribute to such a fractured self. Lesbian and gay experience with families we choose illustrates the way in which the technologically advanced global community plays on the liberal conception of personhood: the openness of the acontextual self to a variety of experiences undermines the possibility that there will be a stable self.

Consider the case of Sharon Lynne Bottoms.[8] Ms. Bottoms married Dennis Doustou in 1989 and became pregnant the next year. Being a wife was not a role that she desired for long. In 1991, before her child, Tyler Doustou, was born, Ms. Bottoms left Mr. Doustou and began dating women, initiating a dramatically different script for her life. Ms. Bottoms retained her role as a mother, but the need to support her family impelled her to rely on her own mother, Kay Bottoms, to care for Tyler most of the time. In 1992, Sharon Bottoms began living with April Wade, her partner with whom she shares a bed. In January 1993, Ms. Bottoms informed her mother that Tyler would spend less time at his grandmother's house because of the presence of Tommy Conley, whom Sharon Bottoms considered an undesirable influence on her son.

The foregoing account illustrates both the libertarian efflorescence of families we choose and the antilibertarian implications once self is turned loose. However much different the "liberated" Sharon Bottoms is from the married Sharon Bottoms, I doubt that the latter is the "final" or the "real" Sharon Bottoms, for she will continue to change as she continues to have new experiences and relationships. Thus, there is no assurance that she will be in a relationship with Ms. Wade ten years from now. Nor is it guaranteed that Ms. Bottoms will consider herself a lesbian ten years from now, even if she is still partnered with Ms. Wade. Examples could be multiplied for the following proposition: the liberal aspiration that the person be open to her desires and to new experiences assures that the person will change and, hence, that there will be no "core" or acontextual person the liberal can call "the real Sharon Bottoms."

Even at one point in time, there will be no acontextual Sharon Bottoms. Consider the following (plausible but hypothetical) scenario. In the morning, Ms. Bottoms may be warm and nurturing as she prepares lunches for her child and takes him to day care. At her job, she will act in a different context, where she must take orders and respond to problems that arise; she is delighted to be employed, after a period of unemployment and reliance on AFDC [Assistance to Families with Dependent Children] payments to support her family. Hence, Ms. Bottoms shows eagerness and gritty determination to do well in this job, and the nurturing mother becomes a serious nose-to-the-grindstone worker. During the day, she calls her mother and engages in a conversation about the bad influence Mr. Conley is on her son; Sharon Bottoms is passionately judgmental and curses Mr. Conley as she hangs up in picque at what she considers her mother's folly. When she returns home to cook dinner, she is creative and animated as she devotes herself to domestic chores, and she beams with parental approval when her son brings home fingerpainting from school (which Ms. Bottoms tapes to the refrigerator door). Ms. Wade receives a hug and a kiss when she returns home, and Ms. Bottoms discusses with her the AA meeting they plan to attend the next evening (Ms. Wade is a recovering alcoholic).

Who is the real Sharon Bottoms: the decisive decision maker, the chef, the cursing daughter, the devoted parent, the domestic partner, the former wife? The Ms. Bottoms I have hypothesized is all of these and a great deal more. While there are recurring themes in the various contextual Sharon Bottoms, her self is "protean," shifting from one situation to another.[9] This contextualized protean self is also a fractured self, never revealing more than a few of its potentialities or features in any one situation. Such fractures are particularly apparent in the current lesbian version of Sharon Bottoms. The lesbian Sharon Bottoms is more fluid than the housewife of old (or the employee of today) because her role is less well-defined and less secure. Notwithstanding the precedents of Boston marriages and an increasing number of open lesbian relationships, same-sex couples like Ms. Bottoms and Ms. Wade are making up the roles as they go along, which is both exciting and exhausting. The relative absence of traditions requires the exercise of choice constantly, but the constant need to exercise choice envelopes the self in a gyre of reaction and rebirth—a process by which the self evolves. The liberal paradigm of an acontextual self open to new experiences is undermined by its practice in a dynamic world.

Families we choose are also less than secure legal constructions. The next section will examine how this is so and the legal arguments for and against this insecurity. The final section will argue that this insecurity is not desirable. From that argument, I shall develop a status-based case for legal recognition of same-sex marriages that complements the libertarian case. I shall insist that, for reasons of personhood and identity, it is important for gays and lesbians to seek this controversial goal.

RESPONSES TO STATUS-BASED ARGUMENTS AGAINST LESBIAN AND GAY FAMILIES

The choice of same-sex couples to form relationships and to raise children is fraught with a great deal more uncertainty than different-sex couples face. That uncertainty is directly (albeit not exclusively) connected with the legal regime for same-sex relationships, which rejects the liberal perspective of choice and pervasively discriminates against same-sex couples by reason of status-based arguments.

For the leading example, consider the right to marry. Marriage is one of the least exclusive institutions in the United States, but it is a club that still excludes homosexuals in every state of the union.[10] The reasoning of these decisions has been status based. The following, from the Kentucky Supreme Court, is typical:

> Marriage has always been considered as the union of a man and a woman and we have been presented with no authority to the contrary.

> It appears to us that the [same-sex couple appealing the denial of their marriage license] are prevented from marrying, not by the statutes of Kentucky or the refusal of

the County Court Clerk of Jefferson County to issue them a license, but rather by
their own incapability of entering into a marriage as that term is defined.[11]

A few courts have gone one step further in reasoning from the status of gay men and
lesbians as "outlaws": [L]egislative authorization of homosexual, same-sex marriages would constitute tacit approval or endorsement of the sexual conduct, to wit,
sodomy, commonly associated with homosexual status—conduct deemed by society
to be so morally reprehensible as to be a criminal offense in the District of
Columbia."[12]

Similar status-grounded arguments have been raised to deny lesbian and gay
parents custody of their children. Some states permit denial of custody based on
nothing more than pure status. Florida's adoption law, for example, states that "[n]o
person eligible to adopt under this statute may adopt if that person is a homosexual."[13] Other states will permit homosexual activity to justify denial of custody if a
sufficient factual showing is made. In a particularly antihomosexual version of this
approach, Virginia presumes a parent involved in a same-sex relationship to be unfit
if there is a custody dispute with the other parent.[14] In the Sharon Bottoms case, a
Virginia trial judge extended this rule to deny custody to a lesbian mother, in favor of
the child's grandmother:

> Sharon Bottoms has . . . admitted . . . that she is living in an [sic] homosexual rela-
> tionship. . . . She is sharing . . . her bed with . . . her female lover. . . . Examples given
> were kissing, patting, all of this in the presence of the child. . . . I will tell you first
> that the mother's conduct is illegal. . . . I will tell you that it is the opinion of the
> court that her conduct is immoral. And it is the opinion of this court that the conduct
> of Sharon Bottoms renders her an unfit parent. However, I also must recognize, and
> do recognize, that there is a presumption in the law in favor of the custody being
> with the natural parent. And I ask myself are Sharon Bottoms' circumstances of un-
> fitness . . . of such an extraordinary nature as to rebut this presumption. My answer
> to this is yes . . . .[15]

Although this judge's explanation was unusually discriminatory even under Virginia
law (and has been reversed on intermediate appeal), judges throughout the country
accomplish surreptitiously what this Virginia judge did openly: deny child custody to
lesbian or gay parents essentially because of their status.

The liberal response to these arguments has been to emphasize their inconsistency with the libertarian view of the family as a construction of free choice by autonomous agents. Indeed, the United States Supreme Court has held that the due
process clauses in the Constitution assure individuals both a right to marry[16] and a
liberty interest in their biological children.[17] Under such a libertarian approach, the
state must allow people to do what they want, so long as they cause no harm to others. Resting on an incomplete understanding of personhood, this has been an incomplete response to the arguments just noted.

As an initial matter, there is the problem that arguments of status cannot easily
be separated from arguments of choice, for one's status and the status of those affected will influence the normative evaluation of one's choices. If two parents choose to
end their marriage, the existence of children—and their status as parents—will con-

strain their choices. Because of the children's status as vulnerable persons, their "best interests" will override parental preferences to the contrary, and each parent will be saddled with financial and other obligations by reason of their parental status. When the Virginia Supreme Court created a presumption against custody to lesbian and gay parents, it cited the "intolerable burden upon [the child] by reason of the social condemnation attached to [the gay parent], which will inevitably afflict her relationships with her peers and with the community at large."[18] The connection between status and choice is fainter but still discernible in the context of marriage. For many heterosexuals, to give state sanction to gay and lesbian marriages would be to diminish their own, which is a third-party effect of such recognition, and an effect that sometimes assumes hysterical proportions. The context in which one's choice is assessed is infinitely elastic, and there is not much a libertarian can say to impose one context (what I want) over another (the effect on my bigoted neighbor).

More importantly, status arguments have not disappeared from family law, nor should they disappear. Consider the issue of surrogacy contracts, in which a woman (usually one needing money) agrees to bear a stranger's child and to relinquish her parental rights to the child. Such contracts and other forms of "baby selling" are a logical consequence of one form of libertarian thinking,[19] subject to the just-noted objection that the third-party effects on the child must be explored and considered. Notwithstanding the libertarian appeal of surrogacy arrangements, they are explicitly prohibited in about a dozen states[20] and are heavily regulated in other jurisdictions.[21] Proponents of such laws reject a simple libertarian conception of family in this setting, either because the conditions for free choice are not present or (perhaps much the same idea) because status-based concerns are overriding. Thus, surrogacy laws serve either to prevent women from making decisions they will likely regret (the libertarian conception is inappropriate) or to express society's valorization of the parent-child connection as inalienable (a status-based idea).[22] Although I am sympathetic to the libertarian position generally, in this particular situation it does not unequivocally support a laissez-faire approach and is overshadowed by status-based concerns.

Indeed, the surrogacy issue suggests a status-based argument for overturning the family law presumptions and prohibitions based on sexual orientation. Why would moral thinkers consider the mother-child connection close to inalienable? It is inalienable for precisely the same reason that Sharon Bottoms ought not to lose her child, either to her own mother or to her former husband, and for much the same reason why Sharon Bottoms and April Wade ought to be able to get married on the same terms as Sharon Bottoms and Dennis Doustou. The parent-child and partner-partner connections receive and ought to receive special legal protection because they are critical to identity. They are critical to identity because the self is relational both in its formation and in its expressions.[23]

Recall the earlier argument that liberalism cannot maintain its conception of the acontextual self in the face of experience in an increasingly mobile world; one's identity is shaped and reshaped by the many different contexts in which one finds one self. I now maintain that individual identity is shaped and reshaped through relationships. It is inhumane to seize a newborn baby from the arms of a surrogate mother because even outside of the womb that baby remains a part of her, and she remains with him. Her personhood becomes tied up with his. The familiar willingness of a mother to sacrifice her life for her child is a rational response of one whose self is inextricably intertwined with the self of the child. A similar even if less intense phenomenon infuses committed partnerships, whereby the partner's aches are my aches, the partner's joy, mine as well.

Human selves are from birth relational. Our early identity is interconnected with (and for a while dominated by) our parent(s) and other caretakers.[24] If adolescence is a period where we declare emotional independence from our parents, it is also one where begins the deep emotional bonding with our peers. Becoming an adult— achieving a flourishing personhood—typically involves one or more intimate relationships. Sharon Bottoms's personhood cannot be understood without reference to her relationships with her mother, Kay Bottoms; her former husband, Dennis Doustou; her son, Tyler, and her lover, April Wade. By initially denying her custody of her son and by denying her the opportunity to marry Ms. Wade, the state of Virginia is trying to discourage Ms. Bottoms from pursuing a flourishing personhood. The security the state offers heterosexual partners and parents, and denies to homosexual ones, is an invidious discrimination, a denial of Ms. Bottoms's citizenship.[25]

Under any fair constitutional system, the discrimination posed by these state prohibitions requires a justification beyond mere prejudices.[26] Does the discrimination against lesbian and gay marriages and custody protect innocent children, for example? Every respectable study I have seen concludes that lesbian and gay parents are just as responsible, loving, and capable as heterosexual parents and that there is no basis to believe that children of gay households will be adversely affected by the experience.[27] Does the discrimination foster a healthy and thriving society? I strongly doubt it because it channels people's energies into unproductive quarrels about features of one's personhood that are not easily alterable and that have little if any bearing on other people or their own entitlement for citizenship.

STATUS-BASED REFLECTIONS ON FEMINIST AND LESBIAN ARGUMENTS ABOUT SURROGACY, INSEMINATION, AND MARRIAGE

Feminist critiques of family law have reintroduced status concerns but with a decidedly different twist from traditional status-based arguments. Liberal feminists have argued against status in family law: the wife should be treated just like the husband for purposes of alimony, custody, and the like. Reflecting developments within feminist thought and within family law as well, other feminist theorists have strongly differentiated women from men in matters of domestic relations. Such theorists have introduced new status-based arguments, and their arguments have relevance for thinking about gay and lesbian families. I shall focus on issues of surrogacy, insemination, and marriage.

Professor Robin West maintains that women have distinctive "selves" because they are, or potentially are, mothers who will bear and nurture children.[28] Their relational selves are particularly constituted by the connection with a child. West's theory is at least in part status based, for it maintains that being a mother—or even potentially being a mother—ought to have consequence because of the centrality of childbearing to a woman's self. A variety of interesting legal corollaries might follow from such a claim.

For example, West's theory provides a robust defense for state laws prohibiting or heavily regulating surrogacy contracts. To allow a woman to precontract to give up her child and her parental rights to the purchasing family in return for money is objectionable in part because the woman would "regret" this earlier contract once the child is born. Liberal theory would justify regulation on the ground that the regret is a predictable cognitive dysfunction: people often underestimate future costs (losing the baby) and overvalue present satisfactions (the friendship of the purchasing family, up-front gifts, and the promise of money). This is not a completely satisfying justification, as our polity routinely enforces such irrational behavior (extravagant credit arrangements, for example). West's theory offers a richer, and I think better, defense for surrogacy laws: what the woman is selling in a surrogacy contract is part of herself, and that relational feature of selfhood should be either inalienable (the child cannot be sold any more than the surrogate can sell a limb or an organ) or alienable only in the best interests of the child (the traditional family law approach).

I embrace this corollary of Professor West's theory but am skeptical of another possible corollary (neither of which is discussed by Professor West). While about half the states stringently regulate or prohibit a woman from giving up her parental rights before the birth of the child (surrogacy), almost all of the states freely allow a man to give up his parental rights before the birth of the child (insemination). Discrimination between women and men can be justified on status grounds: the surrogate mother is much more connected to or invested in the child than the sperm donor, who can easily be anonymous to the child. This rationale does, in my view, justify different treatment of surrogacy and insemination. Does it justify the drastically different way our polity treats surrogacy (heavily regulated) and insemination (unregulated)? I am more skeptical. What the sperm donor is giving up is an important relational opportunity, a fundamental part of his future self. The state that protects surrogate mothers ought also to provide some protection for sperm donors —surely informed-consent rules would be appropriate and perhaps also a short period after the child's birth in which the biological father can change his mind about giving up parental rights.[29]

A more celebrated venue for feminist status-based concerns has been the institution of marriage. Several generations of feminist theorists have criticized the institution as patriarchal, and lesbian feminist theorists have criticized gay and lesbian lawyers and litigants seeking recognition of same-sex marriages. The leading critic, lawyer Paula Ettelbrick maintains that lesbians, gay men, and bisexuals should reject marriage, and its patriarchy, and should instead seek to form their own families.[30] In other words, by rejecting the roles of "husband" and "wife," gays and lesbians can undermine an institution that contributes to preserving the underclass status of women generally, and lesbians in particular. Ms. Ettelbrick also argues that if gays and lesbians are able to marry, their rebel status will be ended, leaving nonmarried lesbians as a group of permanently subordinated outsiders.[31] Her ultimate position is consistent with liberalism for she is skeptical about marriage for anyone, and presumably she would support the same rights for homosexual couples as for heterosexual couples. Nevertheless, her arguments strike me as ultimately status- rather than choice-based arguments: we should refrain from expanding our range of choices because some of us outsiders would become insiders, leaving the rest out in the cold. This kind of argument is different in kind from those made by traditional moralists or by Professor West, but they are also status-based justifications for narrowing choice.

Not surprisingly, the primary response to Ms. Ettelbrick by promarriage gay and lesbian activists is unabashedly liberal and speaks in the argot of choice. Lawyer Thomas Stoddard and Professor Nan Hunter, for example, believe that there is no inherent patriarchal consequence arising from the status of being married and, indeed, that same-sex marriage would destabilize gender-based status arrangements in traditional marriages.[32] I am open to this argument, though the historical evidence does not much support Mr. Stoddard's and Professor Hunter's position.[33] A better argument is a status-based one that appeals to another feature of the institution of marriage: commitment.

A decision to marry is a decision to limit one's future choices, a commitment to consider the interests of another person (and often children as well) in the future. This is in part a consequence of law, which treats the partners as an interdependent legal team and makes it difficult and costly for the team to break up. The promise and the reasonable expectation of partnership and commitment are valuable for a variety of reasons, including the personal security that comes from knowing that one can depend on someone else, for better or for worse (with an emphasis on the latter). What I should like to emphasize, however, is the importance such partnership and commitment potentially have for a relational conception of identity.

Partnership is important because it provides an intense focal point for one to transcend one's "self" and to deepen one's identity through intimate interaction with another self. This is, of course, a status-based argument for families we choose—a series of open-ended partnerships more closely analogous to friendships than to marital relationships. I think this is good, but not complete, for there is an additional value to the partnership's being committed.

We are all products of our relationships with our parents, and I think the healthiest parent-child relationships are ones where the child feels secure about the parent's unconditional love, her unquestioning commitment to the child and the child's well-being. Although the mutual love between parent and child is complicated, involving biological as well as emotional connections, I would hypothesize that the love is as much a consequence as a cause of the mutual expectation that the relationship will be a lasting one. An analogous point can be made about partnership relations; they will be different, and in my view deeper, if they are conducted within a mutual understanding of lasting commitment.

As Professor Regan has indicated, status—including the status of spousehood—protects people's capacity for intimacy and thereby fosters a stable sense of self over time. The stable sense of self is at risk in a society of nothing but choice because such a world fractures self, as argued above. A stable sense of self is a worthwhile aspiration for both negative and positive reasons. As to the former, recall the parable of Buridan's ass. Finding itself equidistant from two equally attractive haystacks, the animal starved because it could not choose between them. Buridan's ass may be an early example of the fractured personality, torn apart by too many choices. Similarly, the protean individual of the late twentieth century risks being torn apart by too many roles.

While a world of nothing but choice risks the fracturing of self, a world of nothing but status risks the ossification or subordination of self. Hence, I am quite comfortable with the current plasticity of marriage as an institution where exit is merely hard and not impossible. Moreover, commitment may carry a precious tariff if one relational self exploits the other, as has too frequently been the case not only in marriages but also in families we choose. Nonetheless, I would insist on the value of commitment for many couples, and if commitment is valuable, it ought to be available to lesbian and gay couples on the same terms it is offered to heterosexual ones.

CONCLUSION

A thriving society is one that accommodates the needs of its productive citizens. A worthy polity is one that contributes to the personal flourishing of its citizens. In light of these goals, our country at the turn of a new century faces these important and complementary challenges: on the one hand, to construct flexible safe harbors for citizens to form lasting intimate relationships that minimize risks of interpersonal exploitation and, on the other hand, to reconcile the citizenry to opening up these constructions to previously excluded persons, particularly lesbians, bisexuals, and gay men.

Notes

1. Kathy Weston, *Families We Choose: Lesbians, Gays, Kinship* (1991).
2. See Milton C. Regan, Jr., *Family Law and the Pursuit of Intimacy* (1993); Marjorie M. Schultz, "Contractual Ordering of Marriage: A New Model for State Policy," 70 *California Law Review* 204 (1982); Jana B. Singer, "The Privatization of Family Law," 1992 *Wisconsin Law Review* 1443. See generally Mary Ann Glendon, *The Transformation of Family Law: State, Law, and Family in the United States and Western Europe* (1989).
3. See Lilian Faderman, *Surpassing the Love of Men: Romantic Friendship and Love Between Women from the Renaissance to the Present* (1981).
4. Surveys of do-it-yourself Victorian family formation can be found in Hayden Curry, Denis Clifford, and Robin Leonard, *A Legal Guide for Lesbian and Gay Couples* (8th ed., 1994); Barbara J. Cox, "Alternative Families: Obtaining Traditional Family Benefits Through Litigation, Legislation, and Collective Bargaining," 2 *Wisconsin Women's Law Journal* 1 (1986).
5. See Catherine Whitney, *Uncommon Lives: Gay Men and Straight Women* (1990).
6. For leading cases, see Adoption of Tammy, 619 N.E.2d 315 (Mass. 1993); Matter of Adoption of Child by J. M. G., 632 A.2d 550 (N.J. Ch. 1993); *In re* B. L. V. B., 628 A.2d 1271 (Vt. 1993); *In re* L. S., 119 WLR 2249 (D.C. Super. Ct. 1991). See generally Nancy D. Polikoff, "This Child Does Have Two Mothers: Redefining Parenthood to Meet the Needs of Children in Lesbian-Mother and Other Nontraditional Families," 78 *Georgetown Law Journal* 459 (1990).
7. See Regan, *Pursuit of Intimacy*, supra note 2, at ch. 3.
8. The facts in the account that follows are taken from Judge Coleman's opinion in Bottoms v. Bottoms, 444 S.E.2d 276 (Va. Ct. App. 1994), *revised*, 457 S.E.2d 102 (Va. 1993), and from a law review article by Sharon Bottoms's attorney in the case. See Stephen B. Pershing,

"'Entreat Me Not To Leave Thee': *Bottoms v. Bottoms* and the Custody Rights of Gay and Lesbian Parents," 3 *William and Mary Bill of Rights Journal* 289 (1994).

9. Robert Jay Lifton, *The Protean Self: Human Resilience in an Age of Fragmentation* (1993); see Kenneth J. Gergen, *The Saturated Self: Dilemmas of Identity in Contemporary Life* (1991); Anthony Giddens, *Modernity and Self-Identity: Self and Society in the Late Modern Age* (1991).

10. The main decisions rejecting same-sex marriage are Jones v. Hallahan, 501 S.W.2d 588 (Ky. 1973); Baker v. Nelson, 191 N.W.2d 185 (Minn. 1971); Singer v. Hara, 522 P.2d 1187 (Wash. Ct. App. 1974); Dean v. District of Columbia, Civ. No. 90-13892 (D.C. Super. Ct. Dec. 30, 1991), *affirmed*, 653 A.2d 307 (D.C. Ct. App. 1995); DeSanto v. Barnsley, 476 A.2d 952 (Pa. Super. Ct. 1984). As of 1995, there is a good chance that the Supreme Court of Hawaii will invalidate that state's prohibition of same-sex marriage. Its opinion in Baehr v. Lewin, 852 P.2d 44 (Haw. 1993), found the prohibition to be sex discrimination and remanded to the trial court for a hearing to determine whether the state has a compelling justification for the discrimination. See William N. Eskridge, Jr., *The Case for Same-Sex Marriage* (1996).

11. Hallahan, 501 S.W.2d at 589; see G. Sidney Buchanan, "Same-Sex Marriage: The Linchpin Issue," 10 *University of Dayton Law Review* 541 (1985).

12. Dean, Civ. No. 90-13892, Slip opinion, 9 (D.C. Super. Ct. Dec. 30, 1991). The district's sodomy law was repealed soon after this opinion was issued.

13. Fla. Stat. Ann. sec. 63.042 (West 1985). See also N.H. Rev. Stat. Ann. sec. 170-B:4 (Butterworth 1994) ("any individual not a minor and not a homosexual may adopt . . .").

14. Roe v. Roe, 324 S.E.2d 691 (Va. 1985).

15. Bottoms v. Bottoms, No. CH93JA0517-00 (Va. Cir. Ct. Henrico County, Sept. 7, 1993), *rev'd*, No. 1930-93-1 (Va. Ct. App. June 21, 1994). See Pershing, "Custody Rights," supra note 8.

16. See Turner v. Safley, 482 U.S. 78 (1987) (state cannot deny prisoners [!] the right to marry); Zablocki v. Redhail, 434 U.S. 374 (1978) (state cannot deny dead-beat dads the right to remarry); Loving v. Virginia, 388 U.S. 1 (1967) (state cannot deny different-race couples the right to marry).

17. See Lassiter v. Department of Social Services of Durham County, N.C., 449 U.S. 819 (1981). But see Michael H. v. Gerald D., 491 U.S. 110 (1989) (upholding statute establishing conclusive evidence of paternity in the husband of the woman who bears the child).

18. Roe v. Roe, 324 S.E.2d at 694.

19. See Lori B. Andrews, *Between Strangers: Surrogate Mothers, Expectant Fathers, and Brave New Babies* (1989); Richard A. Posner, *Sex and Reason*, 409–29 (1992).

20. As of 1995, statutes prohibit surrogacy contracts in Arizona, the District of Columbia, Indiana, Louisiana, Maryland, Michigan, Nebraska, New York, North Dakota, Oregon, Utah, and Washington. A court decision rendered them illegal in New Jersey.

21. As of 1995, statutes regulating permissible surrogacy contracts have been adopted in Florida, Illinois, Kentucky, Maryland, Nevada, New Hampshire, and Virginia.

22. Commentators supporting regulation of surrogacy include Martha A. Field, *Surrogate Motherhood* (1990) (libertarian-based arguments on the whole); Judith Areen, "Baby M Reconsidered," 76 *Georgia Law Journal* 1741 (1988) (criticizing libertarianism as a partial perspective and raising status-based arguments; Alexander M. Captron and Margaret J. Radin, "Choosing Family Law over Contract Law as a Paradigm for Surrogate Motherhood," in *Surrogate Motherhood: Politics and Privacy* 59 (Larry Gostin, ed., 1990) (status-based arguments); Lisa Sowle Cahill, "The Ethics of Surrogate Motherhood: Biology, Freedom, and Moral Obligation," in id. at 151 (status-based arguments).

23. This concept is associated with postmodernism, see Regan, *Pursuit of Intimacy*, supra note 2, at ch. 4, but I am using the term in ways consistent with, even if subversive of, liberal or

modernist premises. See Anthony Giddens, *The Consequences of Modernity* (1990). See also William N. Eskridge, Jr., and Brian Weimer, "The Economics Epidemic from an AIDS Perspective," 61 *University of Chicago Law Review* 733, 753–60 (1994), drawing the idea of "relational preferences" from Amartya Sen, "Behavior and the Concept of Preference," 40 *Economica* 241 (1973).

24. See Erik Erikson, *Childhood and Society* (1953).

25. For legal indictments of these discriminations, see William N. Eskridge, Jr., "A History of Same-Sex Marriage," 79 *Virginia Law Review* 1419 (1993); Pershing, "Custody Rights," supra note 8; "Note, Custody Denials to Parents in Same-Sex Relationships: An Equal Protection Analysis," 102 *Harvard Law Review* 617 (1989).

26. See Palmore v. Sidoti, 466 U.S. 429 (1984) (court making custody determination cannot consider race of either parent; "private biases and the possible injury they might inflict" are not "permissible considerations for removal of an infant child from the custody of its natural mother"); see also Robinson v. California, 370 U.S. 660 (1962) (state cannot punish status of being an addict). See generally Kenneth L. Karst, *Belonging to America: Equal Citizenship and the Constitution* (1989).

27. For examples of such studies, see Mary E. Hotvedt and Jane Barclay Mandel, "Children of Lesbian Mothers," in *Homosexuality: Social, Psychological, and Biological Issues* 275 (William Paul et al., eds., 1982); Sharon L. Huggins, "A Comparative Study of Self-Esteem of Adolescent Children of Divorced Lesbian Mothers and Divorced Heterosexual Mothers," in *Homosexuality and the Family* 123 (Frederick W. Bozett, ed., 1989); Charlotte J. Patterson, "Children of Lesbian and Gay Parents," 63 *Child Development* 1025 (1992) (surveying the social science literature). See also Gregory M. Herek, "Myths About Sexual Orientation: A Lawyer's Guide to Social Science Research," 1 *Law and Sexuality* 133, 156 (1991).

28. Robin West, "Jurisprudence and Gender," 55 *University of Chicago Law Review* 1 (1988).

29. If the latter proposal were adopted, it would necessitate modification of presumptive parenthood rules in many states. Most states conclusively presume that the husband of the biological mother—and therefore not the biological father—is the legal father of the child. I recognize that such modification raises important issues of status and do not maintain that the husband or the partner of the biological mother is without interest that should be protected. I am only questioning the one-sidedness of current law.

30. Paula L. Ettelbrick, "Since When Is Marriage a Path to Liberation?" in *Lesbian and Gay Marriage* 20 (Suzanne Sherman, ed., 1992).

31. Ibid., at 26; see Nancy D. Polikoff, "We Will Get What We Ask For: Why Legalizing Gay and Lesbian Marriage Will Not 'Dismantle the Legal Structure of Gender in Marriage,'" 79 *Virginia Law Review* 1535 (1993); Ruthan Robson and S. E. Valentine, "Lov(h)ers: Lesbians as Intimate Partners and Lesbian Legal Theory," 63 *Temple Law Review* 511 (1990).

32. See Nan Hunter, "Marriage, Law and Gender: A Feminist Inquiry," 1 *Law and Sexuality* 9, 18–19 (1991); Thomas B. Stoddard, "Why Gay People Should Seek the Right to Marry," in *Lesbian and Gay Marriage*, supra note 30, at 13.

33. See Polikoff, supra note 31.

14

Causes of Declining Well-Being Among U.S. Children

William A. Galston

INTRODUCTION

On July 7, 1992, the Children's Defense Fund (CDF) released a study documenting a significant increase in child poverty during the 1980s. CDF argued that this trend was primarily attributable to declining wages for younger workers and to federal budget cuts. Olivia Golden, CDF director of programs and policy, stated, "There's a range of evidence that suggests that what's happening is much more pervasive than a small group of parents who are making bad choices for their children." Gary Bauer, president of the Family Research Council and a key domestic policy advisor during the Reagan administration, vigorously disagreed: "We believe they've got it exactly backwards." Two-parent families are able to rise out of poverty, "but the poverty of single-parent families is persistent and trends up even when the economy is improving." Until the children's fund and others are "willing to address that behavior, we are not going to address child poverty."

This dispute represents the continuation of a long-running political debate between liberals and conservatives concerning the causes of (and by implication, remedies for) declining well-being among families with young children. The purpose of this article is to bring some reasonably reliable data to bear on this controversy. While I have well-advertised views on a number of family policy issues, in the following remarks I will steer away from policy per se and stick as close as is possible to the question of causation and what we know about it.

Two preliminary notes. The first concerns terminology. I shall use "well-being" to denote the multiple dimensions—economic, educational, and emotional, among others—along which a sound and healthy upbringing of children can occur. Within this context, poverty is a very important problem, but it is not the only problem. We cannot safely assume that poverty is always the exogenous or independent cause producing a range of undesired social effects; it is at least possible that in some circumstances the causal arrow points in the opposite direction, or in both directions simultaneously. For example, the familiar but by no means self-evidently true hypothesis that poverty causally contributes to crime must be tested against the less familiar but by no means self-evidently false counter-hypothesis that crime exacerbates poverty.

Second, it is important to distinguish between the absolute *levels* of key variables and *changes* in those variables. For example, many scholars believe that, setting to one side our deep racial differences, the lack of publicly funded child and family allowances in the United States has contributed to persistent differences in child poverty rates between this country and other comparable industrialized countries. For example, child poverty among U.S. *whites* is six percentage points higher than among Canadians. But clearly the absence of such allowances—a longstanding feature of our social policy—cannot account for the significant rise in U.S. child poverty over the past two decades.

WHAT IS HAPPENING TO CHILDREN AND THEIR FAMILIES?

By some measures, the well-being of America's infants and children has actually improved during the past generation. Both infant mortality and child death rates have fallen by more than 50 percent since 1960; the rate of high school completion has increased, as has the overall average of years of education; drug use among teens has plummeted during the past decade. On balance, however, scholarly and public opinion has converged on the conclusion that our children are in trouble and that their overall well-being has declined during the past generation. The major trends that reinforce this view appear in Table 14.1.

Table 14.1 Child Well-Being: Indices of Decline

	1960	1970	1980	Most recent
Average SAT scores (verbal)	477.0	466.0	424.0	423.0 (1994)
Average SAT scores (math)	498.0	488.0	466.0	479.0 (1994)
Suicide rate				
(ages 15–19, per 100,000)	3.6	5.9	8.5	11.3 (1990)
Homicide rate				
(perpetrators aged 15–19, per 100,000)	4.0	8.1	10.6	13.7 (1990)
Juvenile violent crime arrest rate				
(ages 10–17, per 100,000)	137.0	215.9	338.1	430.6 (1990)
Children in poverty (%)	26.9	15.1	18.3	19.9 (1990)

The breakdown of aggregate child poverty into subcategories helps pinpoint the areas of greatest distress. While among all children eighteen years and younger, one in five is poor, among children younger than six, the figure is almost one in four; among children headed by adults younger than thirty, one in three; among African-American children, almost one in two.

The surge in child poverty has occurred in the face of countervailing trends. In the U.S. population as a whole, poverty is no higher today than it was twenty years ago, and some groups have experienced very significant declines. While fully one quarter of those aged sixty-five or older had incomes below the poverty line in 1970, less than one-eighth of the elderly are poor today. For most of our history, elderly Americans were on average far worse off than children. It was not until 1974, in fact, that the two lines crossed, As far as we know, the current situation, in which Americans under eighteen are almost twice as likely to be poor as those over sixty-five is unprecedented.

It is also extraordinary by international standards. The U.S. poverty rate for the elderly is about average for advanced industrialized nations. By contrast, our poverty rate for children is the highest of any of the comparable countries included in a 1988 survey.

While incomes of families with children have declined in the aggregate during recent years, benefits and burdens have been unequally distributed among income groups. In fact, the best-off families have enjoyed significant improvements while the worst-off have endured major reductions as evidenced by Table 14.2. These adverse developments for the least well-off families are not the artifact of an arbitrarily selected time period. A glance farther back reveals that inflation-adjusted family income in the bottom fifth of the population was 11 percent lower in 1987 than in 1973. Single mothers fared the worst: the two lowest quintiles had incomes 21 and 15 percent lower than their counterparts fourteen years earlier.

Table 14.2 Change in Median Income of Families with Children, 1979–1990 (%)

Top Quintile	Second	Third	Fourth	Lowest	Total
+9.2	+4.8	+0.2	-1.5	-12.6	-4.9

To be sure, the situation is not quite as bad as these figures would seem to indicate. Family income statistics do not reveal, or correct for, the significant decline in the average number of children per family. By several measures, average income per child has actually gone up. In addition, the snapshot of poverty for any given year obscures the fact that many families will quickly move out of poverty. Still, about 10 percent of all children will experience persistent, as opposed to temporary, poverty, and the figure for African-American children is almost four times as high. The spatial distribution of poverty has shifted dramatically during the past generation. The incidence of poverty has dropped by one-third in the suburbs and by one-half in non-metropolitan areas but, as indicated in the figures in Table 14.3 has risen in central cities.

Table 14.3 Spatial Distribution of Households with Incomes Below the Poverty Line (%)

	1960	*1970*	*1980*	*1987*
Central cities	13.7	9.8	14.0	15.4
Suburbs	9.6	5.3	6.5	6.5
Non-metro areas	28.2	14.8	12.1	13.8

When analyzed by ethnic group, family income trends over the past decades reveal some surprises (Table 14.4). The large drop among Hispanics may well be the product of reporting changes as increasing numbers of previously overlooked non-citizens are brought into official statistics. The African-American figure represents two countervailing trends: improved economic prospects for married couples, especially families with two earners; and increased privation for female-headed households. While both two-earner and female-headed households increased as a percentage of the total African-American community, the latter increased more percentage points than three times as fast as the former ten percentage points versus three percentage points), yielding the reported aggregate decline.

Table 14.4 Change in Median Income of Families with Children, 1979–1990, by Ethnic Classification (%)

African-American	*Hispanic*	*White*
-2.7	-11.5	-3.5

U.S. PUBLIC OPINION CONCERNING CHILDREN AND FAMILIES

Public policy is, of course, influenced by expert analysis and prescription, but in a democracy it is circumscribed by public sentiment. This is certainly the case for domestic policy, where ordinary citizens have more direct experience and confident judgments than they do in many areas of defense and foreign policy. It is particularly true for policies affecting children and families, about which nearly every citizen has a wealth of strong views. That is why it is appropriate here to include a brief review of public attitudes toward children and families. The main points are captured in five general propositions, each summarizing a large body of survey data.

First: Most Americans see moral decay at the heart of our social problems, and the breakdown of the family at the epicenter moral decay. Family values are considered weaker than they used to be, and as a result children are thought to be worse off than they were a generation (or even a decade) ago. It is widely held that these negative trends will continue.

Second: The overwhelming majority of Americans (between 80 and 88 percent, according to recent polls) believes that being a parent is much more difficult than it used to be. The principal external forces pressuring parents include dangerous streets and schools, drugs, and mass media that are saturated with sex, violence, and commercialism.

Third: Most Americans believe that parents are contributing to the troubles of their children by failing to discipline them strictly enough and, even more important, by failing to spend enough time with them. While this belief is phrased in moral terms, it is linked to economic issues as well. More than half of those who acknowledge spending too little time with their own children say that they "have to spend time working in order to support myself and my family." An even greater majority agrees that "it is getting to be impossible to support a family on just one income." (As we shall see, the economic data support this belief.)

Fourth: Large majorities believe that both mothers and fathers should spend more time with children. In the case of fathers, this means taking on a larger share of the responsibility for running the home. In the case of mothers, it means altering the current balance between work inside and outside the home. Numerous polls taken during the past three years all point in the same direction: most women with young children are working outside the home for economic rather than psychic income, are spending more time away from their children than they want to, and would work fewer hours outside the home if economic circumstances permitted.

Fifth: Americans believe that in addition to changes in private parental behavior, the well-being of children and families will require greater assistance from community institutions and government as well as from private business. At the same time, many Americans are very skeptical about the capacity of these under-performing institutions to effectively deliver the needed help.

WHY IS WELL-BEING DECLINING AMONG U.S. CHILDREN?

I now turn directly to the causes of declining well-being among children in the United States. I shall explore a number of different proposed explanations. Some are sustained by the evidence, others contradicted. Defensible propositions are to be found within liberal and conservative as well as politically unclassifiable accounts. As some wise person once said, intelligence includes the ability to keep more than one thought in view simultaneously.

Demography

According to the Census Bureau, *family* poverty rates increased only slightly over the past decade, while, as noted, *child* poverty rates significantly increased. This suggests a shift in the distribution of children among families, that is, poor families contain a disproportionate and growing share of all children. In a recent exploration of this issue, David Eggebeen and Daniel Lichter calculated that the gap between the mean number of children in poor and nonpoor families has in fact grown during the past decade; both means declined, but among the nonpoor it declined more rapidly.

They calculated that about 22 percent of the increase in the child poverty rate over the past decade is attributable to the shifting balance of children as between poor and nonpoor families. Interestingly, this variable accounts for only about 10 percent of the increase among African-Americans, versus fully one-third for whites. (Eggebeen and Lichter suggest that this reflects the spread of zero- and one-child families within the white middle class.)

Obviously, this does not mean that the well-being of a single poor child would increase if the nonpoor suddenly began having more children. At most, it suggests a modest degree of caution in drawing inferences from raw percentages.

Economics

For some years, liberals have been arguing that families with children are being squeezed by declining wages for young workers. This argument is consistent with recent analyses. For example Frank Levy has shown that between the early 1970s and late 1980s, the mean annual earnings of young high-school-educated men working full-time declined by 16 percent. (Among those with less than a high school education, the decline was almost twice as steep.) Levy suggests that, coupled with declining unionization, increased international competition since 1973 reduced the availability of low-skill, high-wage jobs especially in the manufacturing sector, and forced many poorly educated younger men to accept lower paying jobs in the service sector. Income inequality widened, not because wages for college-educated men increased (they actually declined a bit), but because wages for high school graduates and dropouts declined so much faster.

For women, on the other hand, wages increased across the board regardless of age and education between the early 1970s and late 1980s. Gains were greatest for younger, higher-educated workers, but they were significant in every category.

As male earnings declined, young men became less able to sustain their families at a middle-class standard of living as sole breadwinners. In 1973, median annual earnings for young high school educated men amounted to about 90 percent of median family incomes. By 1986, their earnings were only 72 percent of median family incomes. Meanwhile, women became increasingly able to translate their skills into income. Taken together, these facts go a long way toward explaining the surge of women, especially younger women, into the work force during the past two decades. Setting aside questions of personal satisfaction, women's income earned outside the home became more significant in securing a middle-class way of life for their families.

I want to underscore the significance of these shifts. It is sometimes argued that the economic rationale for the two-parent family has eroded during the past generation. The truth is just the reverse: economically, the two-parent family is more rather than less necessary because, increasingly, families need two incomes to sustain even a modest middle-class existence. This truth, however, cuts both ways: not only do husbands need wives more, but wives need husbands more. The thesis that increased economic opportunity for women makes it more possible for women with minor children to go it alone is not supported by the evidence.

As women work in far greater numbers and for much longer hours outside the home, the contribution of men on average to homemaking and child rearing has increased only modestly—though there is some evidence that behavior is changing more among upper-middle-class men than elsewhere. The interaction of these two trends goes a long way toward explaining the dramatic drop in the amount of time that parents spend, on average, with their children. According to sociologist John Robinson, parents in the United States today devote about 40 percent less time to direct child rearing activities than did their own parents. In 1965, parents on average spent about 33 hours a week in contact with their children; by the mid-1980s this figure had declined to just seventeen hours. While Robinson's findings have not gone unchallenged, they are supported by field-level focus groups, interviews, and observations. Summarizing nearly a decade of such research, social historian Barbara Whitehead reports that, "Increasingly, family schedules are intricate applications of time-motion principles" in which more leisurely, free-form family time is all but squeezed out.

It is sometimes argued that these developments are less serious than they appear because the remaining hours of parental contact time are spent in "high quality" activities such as playing with children, going to the park, or reading. The evidence on this point is hardly unequivocal. While rising levels of education, are positively correlated with quality time, various studies conducted during the 1980s confirm what common sense suggests: a larger fraction of parental time not spent working outside the home is now spent doing errands and chores. I have not been able to locate any studies that hold other variables constant and directly examine the impact of varying parental time on key dimensions of child well-being. Still, in normal, that is, non-abusive, circumstances parental time could well be considered an intrinsic element of child well-being. In addition, a range of indirect evidence suggests that reduced parental time is correlated with negative trends such as increased television watching and diminished adult supervision (latchkey kids, "mall rats," and the like).

There is no clear evidence that children of women who work outside the home do worse than others. One conjecture is that the increased income from two-earner families creates additional opportunities for children that counterbalance the impact of reduced family time. There is evidence, however, that infants need the opportunity to bond with at least one loving adult who is present steadily and predictably during the earliest stages of life. The Family and Medical Leave Act, signed into law in 1993, represents a modest but significant response to this concern.

Inadequate Government Programs

The other element of the standard liberal explanation for declining child well-being revolves around cutbacks in government programs for poor and at-risk children. According to this thesis, the Reagan-Bush attack on discretionary domestic spending, coupled with fiscal squeezes at the state level, had a disproportionate impact on the worst-off children and their families.

There is some truth to this view: one recent study estimates that inflation-adjusted federal spending for children declined by 4 percent between 1978 and 1987. But a broader view of the data suggests a different conclusion. In an article published in *Science* in 1992, Stanford economist Victor Fuchs and his colleague Diane Reklis divided government (federal, state, and local) purchases of goods and services into three categories: those directed to children and their families, those directed to adults without reference to children, and unallocated purchases. Their findings are summarized in Table 14.5. This analysis, the most comprehensive known to me, lends no support to the proposition that overall government spending directed toward children declined, or even slowed its rate of increase, during the 1980s; if anything, the increase accelerated in the 1980s compared to the 1970s. It turns out, moreover, this aggregate pattern is mirrored in key individual components of children's programs such as education and medical care.

Table 14.5 Government Purchases of Goods and Services for Children and Adults, Inflation-Adjusted, 1960–1988 (in $ billion)

	1960	1970	1980	1988	Rate of change (%/year)
Children	83.1	141.6	154.3	188.1	2.92
Adults	34.0	102.8	160.2	228.7	6.81

Fuchs and Reklis do emphasize, however, that purchases for adults have increased at a much faster pace, primarily because of the introduction of Medicare and Medicaid in 1965, and adjustments to Social Security in the early 1970s. While the number of children remained roughly constant between 1960 and 1990, the number of adults aged eighteen to sixty-four increased by more than 50 percent, and the number of Americans sixty-five and older increased by more than 80 percent. The result was a significant increase in the percentage of American households without children, including a near-doubling among those headed by individuals in their prime child-rearing years (Table 14.6).

Table 14.6 Children and Their Families in the U.S. Population

	1970	1980	1990
Children's share of total population (%)	34.3	28.1	25.6
Families' (with children) share of all households (%)	45.0	38.0	35.0

Fuchs and Reklis acknowledge that their analysis does not completely undermine the core thesis of governmental failure: "Those who argue that children's problems result from insufficient government spending argue that the increase in purchases has not been sufficient to allow the schools and other publicly supported institutions to cope with the greater problems they now face." Two features of this claim are especially noteworthy, however. First, it can be advanced (and no doubt will be) that the well-being of children continues to deteriorate, regardless of the actual causal mechanisms at work. Second, it presupposes the existence of social processes other than government spending patterns that are producing negative outcomes for children.

Still, the fact that public spending for children has been rising rather than falling hardly undermines the possibility that even more spending would be justified. Indeed, evidence suggests that a range of programs directed toward young children and their families would yield between three and 10 dollars in savings and other benefits for each additional dollar invested. The Fuchs/Reklis analysis merely calls into question a specific causal hypothesis, not the policy implications frequently drawn from it.

Perverse Government Programs

Many conservatives argue that liberals have it exactly backwards: The problem is not the inadequacy of traditional government programs directed toward children and families, but rather their excessive generosity and the perverse incentives they generate. They specifically allege that welfare programs hurt children by diminishing the propensity of their parents to marry and work, and undermine the pride and independence so essential to a healthy child-rearing environment.

The latest round of this long-running debate was sparked by the publication of Charles Murray's *Losing Ground* in 1984. Murray's critics were quick to point out that while teen pregnancy and child poverty rates were rising through much of the 1970s and 1980s, cash payments to welfare recipients were actually diminishing in real terms. Moreover, comparisons among states with dramatically different levels of welfare support failed to sustain the thesis that high payment levels were correlated with undesirable outcomes. Murray responded that differences among states were less significant than the increased availability of welfare throughout the United States; that declines in AFDC [Aid to Families with Dependent Children] and other cash payments were more than offset by increases in in-kind assistance; and that the diminishing welfare stigma and rising utilization rates had created a new climate of overall incentives and effects.

By the late 1980s, this exchange of volleys had resulted in an analytical stand-off. Since then, however, additional evidence has helped crystallize a rough consensus. In an authoritative study of single women and their children, Irwin Garfinkel and Sara McLanahan estimate that rising government benefits were responsible for a 9 to 14 percent increase in the prevalence of single motherhood from 1960 to 1975—that is, between one-tenth and one-seventh of the 100-percent increase actually observed during that period. They further argue that this factor could account for as much as 30 percent of the growth within the bottom part of the income distribution. In a recently published comprehensive survey of literature on the incentive effects of the welfare system, Robert Moffit concludes that there is "unequivocal evidence" of undesirable consequences on work and family structure, particularly for female-headed families, but that these effects are too limited to explain more than a modest fraction of overall trends during the past two decades.

Others have examined individual cases rather than aggregate data. For example, in a *New York Times* article on July 8, 1992, Jason DeParle tells the story of Linda Baldwin, a former welfare recipient now working, who has about $170 per month less to meet regular living expenses than she did on welfare—not to mention limited health benefits rather than the far more comprehensive Medicaid for herself and her children. She works because she feels better about herself than she did on welfare, because she expects her current job to lead to higher-paying employment in the foreseeable future, because she wants to set a good example for her children, and because she can anticipate the time when all of them are grown and she will no longer be eligible for AFDC and related programs.

While Ms. Baldwin's choice is unusual, the options from which she was compelled to select are quite typical. They illustrate the critical importance of time-horizons, expectations, and hope. The choice between welfare and work revolves around a conflict between short-term and long-term self-interest. Individuals whose lives have given them few reasons to believe in a better future are asked to sacrifice their current well-being (and, even more poignantly, that of their children) in the name of that future. Common sense suggests that the current welfare/work comparison does discourage choices, such as Linda Baldwin's, that would over time promote the well-being of many children.

Family Structure

We come now to a portion of the "conservative" case that is gaining increased support among policy analysts of all persuasions—the negative impact of changes in family structure.

During the past thirty-five years, the percentage of children born outside of marriage has risen sixfold from 5 to 31 percent overall and now stands at 23.6 percent for whites and 68.7 percent for African-Americans. In this same period, the divorce rate has more than doubled, as has the percentage of children living with only one parent. Of white children born in the 1950s, 81 percent lived continuously with their two biological parents until the age of seventeen; projections of the rate for white children born in the early 1980s range from 30 to 58 percent. The corresponding rate for African-American children has fallen from 52 percent in the 1950s to a projected 6 to 16 percent today.

According to 1991 Census Bureau figures, 29 percent of the nation's families with children are classified as one-parent households, versus only 13 percent in 1970. For whites, the proportion rose from 10 to 23 percent; for African-Americans, from 36 to 63. While the percentage of children living in one-parent families because of divorce has nearly tripled during this period, the percentage attributable to births outside of marriage has risen by a factor of nearly 10. Today, 31 percent of the nation's one-parent families are now headed by never-married women, up from 6.5 percent in 1970.

The relation between family structure and family income is illustrated in Table 14.7. Not surprisingly, the poverty rate among female-headed families was nearly 45 percent in 1988, compared to just over 7 percent for married-couple families. The poverty rate among single-parent families with children under five years old is even worse—57 percent. And as David Ellwood shows in *Poor Support,* 73 percent of children from one-parent families will experience poverty at some point during their childhood, versus 20 percent for children from two-parent families; and 22 percent of children from one-parent families will experience persistent poverty (seven years or more), versus only 2 percent from two-parent families.

Table 14.7 Family Structure and Family Income (1988 $/year)

	Two-Parent	Female-Headed
All families (average)	40,067	11,989
White (mean)	40,833	13,754
African-American (mean)	31,423	8,929

Changes in family structure over the past generation are strongly correlated with rising rates of poverty among children. According to a comprehensive study recently published by Pennsylvania State University's David Eggebeen and Daniel Lichter, child poverty rates today would be one- third lower if family structure had not changed so dramatically since 1960. Fifty-one percent of the increase in child poverty observed during the 1980s is attributable to changes in family structure during that period; changes in African-American family structure during the 1980s accounted for fully 65 percent of the increase in African-American children living below the poverty line. In a similar vein, Fuchs and Reklis note that the percentage of children living in households without an adult male has nearly tripled since 1960. In 1960 only 7 percent of children lived in households without an adult male; in 1988, 19 percent. The median income per child in 1988 for households with an adult male present was $7,640; for households without an adult male, only $2,397. Fuchs and Reklis calculate that if the proportion of children without an adult male had stayed at 1960 levels, average income per child would have been 9 percent higher in 1988.

These data suggest that the best anti-poverty program for children is a stable, intact family. And this conclusion holds even for families with modest levels of educational attainment. For married high school graduates with children, the 1987 poverty rate was 9 percent, versus more than 47 percent for families headed by female high school graduates. Even for married high school dropouts with children, the poverty rate was 25 percent, versus more than 81. percent for families headed by female high school dropouts.

Divergence in family structure between whites and African-Americans, already notable a generation ago, has continued to widen as the figures in Table 14.8 indicate. Equally notable, but far less discussed, is the impact of family structure on inter-racial family income differences. The gap in child poverty rates between African-American and white married couples has shrunk dramatically over the past thirty years, while the corresponding gap among female-headed families has barely budged as noted in Table 14.9. During this same period, the poverty gap between African-American married couples and black female-headed couples has more than doubled. The figures show that the gap now stands at an astounding fifty percentage points. Overall, Frank Furstenberg, Jr., and Andrew Cherlin conclude in their authoritative study, *Divided Families,* the differences in family structure go "a long way toward accounting for the enormous racial disparity in poverty rates. Within family types, black families are still poorer than white families; but the racial gap in poverty shrinks considerably when the marital status of the household head is taken into account."

Table 14.8 Family Structure: Key Indicators

	Black (1988)	White (1988)
Married-couple families as percent of all households	51.3	83.2
Female-headed family households (percent)	43.0	9.0
Children not living with two parents (percent)	61.0	21.0
Children in poverty (percent)	44.0	15.0

To be sure, the causal arrow could point in the opposite direction: differences in family structure might be thought to reflect differences in economic status. William Julius Wilson offered an influential statement of this counter-thesis in *The Truly Disadvantaged:* reduced African-American marriage rates dramatically reflect higher rates of African-American male unemployment, which reduced the "male marriageable pool"—under the assumption that "to be marriageable a man needs to be employed." But the most recent research offers only modest support for this hypothesis. Robert Mare and Christopher Winship find that changes in employment rates among young African-American males account for only 20 percent of the decline in their marriage rates since 1960; they speculate that the various family disruptions of the past three decades may be self-reinforcing. Though Wilson continues to defend the validity of his thesis for the hardest-hit central cities of the Northeast and Midwest, he is now willing to say that "the decline in marriage among inner-city blacks is not simply a function of the proportion of jobless men . . . it is reasonable to consider [as well] the effects of weaker social strictures against out-of-wedlock births."

The economic disadvantages for children of unwed motherhood are matched by noneconomic problems. While not altogether straightforward (particularly with regard to causality), the data suggest that the daughters of teen mothers are more likely to become teen mothers themselves and are at higher risk of long-term welfare dependency. Equally suggestive is the anecdotal evidence of the difficulties many young single mothers experience in raising their sons. The absence of fathers as

Table 14.9 Child Poverty and Family Structure

	1960	1970	1980	1988
Children in poverty (white, %)	20.2	11.1	11.1	5.4
Children in poverty (black, %)	66.2	44.1	37.1	45.6
Children in poverty (married-couple families, %)	21.9	10.4	9.1	10.1
white	7.6	0.0	7.3	9.0
black	61.2	51.5	46.2	54.1
Children in poverty (female-headed families, %)	66.7	51.5	46.2	54.1
white	58.2	42.3	36.2	45.8
black	84.8	66.9	59.1	67.6

models and codisciplinarians is thought to contribute to the low self-esteem, anger, violence, and peer-bonding through gang membership that is characteristic of many fatherless boys.

While much attention has been focused on the impact of family nonformation and out-of-wedlock births (especially to teenage mothers), the breakup of previously intact families is another potent source of poverty and declining well-being among children. According to a Census Bureau study headed by Suzanne Bianchi that identified and tracked 20,000 households, it turns out that after parents separate or divorce, children are almost twice as likely to be living in poverty as they were before the split. The gross income of the children and their custodial parent (usually the mother) dropped by 37 percent immediately after the family breakup (26 percent after adjustment for the decline in family size) and recovered only slightly after sixteen months. These findings support the arguments of scholars who have long contended that divorce under current law spells economic hardship for most custodial parents and their minor children.

As Furstenberg and Cherlin show in their authoritative survey of current research on divorce, there are at least three sets of reasons for this hardship: many women bargain away support payments in return for sole custody of their children, or to eliminate the need to deal on a continuing basis with their former spouses; when awarded, child support payments are, on average, pitifully inadequate; and many fathers cough up only a portion (at best) of their required payments. A Census Bureau report from the mid-1980s showed that of mothers with court-ordered support payments, only half received all of what they were owed, a quarter received partial payments, and the remaining quarter got nothing at all. The evidence suggests that this pattern is persisting.

Furstenberg and Cherlin offer an ultimately troubling account of the noneconomic consequences of divorce for child well-being. For most children, it comes as an unwelcome shock, even when the parents are openly quarreling. In the short-term, boys seem to have a harder time coping than girls, in part because of an "escalating cycle of misbehavior and harsh response between mothers and sons." Girls more typically respond with internalized disruption rather than external behavior—with heightened levels of anxiety, withdrawal, inability to form lasting relationships, and depression that may become apparent only years later.

These differences reflect the fact that divorce almost always means disrupted relations with the father. It is difficult to overstate the extent of that disruption. Even in the period relatively soon after divorce, only one-sixth of all children will see their fathers as often as once a week, and close to one-half will not see them at all. After ten years, almost two-thirds will have no contact.

The problems produced by divorce extend well beyond vanishing male role models. Children need authoritative rules, stable schedules, and ample contact time, which harried single parents often find hard to supply. Along with economic pressures, family disintegration and nonformation are key sources of the decline in time parents spend with their children.

As Furstenberg and Cherlin point out, no straightforward inferences concerning the well-being of children can be drawn from these findings because they must be compared with the effects on children of intact but troubled families. On the one hand, various studies indicate that the children of divorce do no worse than children in families in which parents fight continuously and in which verbal and physical abuse are commonplace. On the other hand, a minority of divorces result from, and terminate, such clearly pathological situations. There are many more cases in which there is little open conflict, but one or both partners feels unfulfilled, constrained, or bored. Far from terminating conflict, the onset of divorce in these families can intensify it, particularly as experienced by children. As Nicholas Zill has observed, "Divorces tend to generate their own problems."

A substantial body of research suggests that family structure is an independent factor influencing the well-being of children. Even after correcting for variables such as family income, parental education, and prior family history, children from single-parent families tend on average to fare less well economically, educationally, and emotionally, and encounter more difficulties on the road to becoming self-sustaining adults.

Neighborhood and Community

Social theorists speak of "civil society"—the network of neighborhood, community, religious, and voluntary associations that stand between the individual or family and the institutions of the state. As observers of the United States ever since Tocqueville have noted, civil society plays an especially important role in this country as a counterweight both to our individualistic ethos and to the relative weakness of the public sector. In particular, nuclear families have been sustained and strengthened by the efforts of local associations. The fraying of the fabric of civil society would thus have serious negative consequences for the ability of families to raise children well.

While solid research in this area is hard to come by, there is considerable evidence that civil society in America has weakened over the past decade. Increased mobility on the part of both young families and the elderly has reduced the number of extended families living in the same or nearby communities. Growing differences among family schedules have reduced what Barbara Whitehead has called the "common rhythms" of neighborhood life, making it more difficult for parents to connect with each other, build friendships, and support each other as parents. As discussed earlier, the reduction in family time is also exerting pressure on organizations that depend heavily on volunteers. The fear of crime and the desecration of public spaces are impeding the development of neighborhood networks of mutual support. What Robert Reich has called the "secession of the successful"—the growing tendency among upper-middle-class families of all races to leave economically mixed urban neighborhoods for more homogeneous suburban enclaves—has removed important assets of leadership from many communities. Conversely, as William Julius Wilson has argued, the isolation of very poor neighborhoods from other communities and the concentration of social problems found within them serve as powerful counterweights to even the most strenuous parental efforts.

In short, families breathe the air generated by a broader social environment. When that environment deteriorates, an increase in the social equivalent of respiratory diseases, especially among children is all but inevitable.

Culture

At the core of the social environment lie the shared cultural and moral understandings that help define both the norms and the meaning of our lives. That significant cultural change has occurred in the past two generations is not open to serious doubt. In a recent study, Daniel Yankelovich has sought to catalogue and explain some of the key shifts. Among them: less value is now placed on what one owes others as a matter of moral obligation; on sacrifice as a moral good; on social conformity, respectability, and observing the rules; and on correctness and restraint in matters of physical pleasure and sexuality. Conversely, more value is now accorded to self-expression, individualism, self-realization, pluralism, and personal choice (as opposed to ascribed status and social roles).

As Yankelovich and others have documented, these broad value shifts are translated into specific changes in attitudes toward children and families. Compared to forty years ago, Americans today are much more accepting of (*inter alia*) sex before marriage, birth out of wedlock, and divorce. Far more Americans value marriage primarily as a means to personal happiness; far fewer say that parents in an unhappy marriage should stay together for the sake of the children. Not surprisingly, the conflict (frequently unacknowledged) between, on the one hand, self-actualization or career advancement and, on the other, responsibilities and commitments to spouses and children, appears to have intensified.

In cultural matters, establishing cause and effect relations is very difficult. Yankelovich argues that rising levels of affluence lead to a desire for increased personal choice and rising impatience with traditional bonds. William Julius Wilson suggests that cultural change is largely the consequence of economic changes, that (for example) attitudes toward work are affected by changes in the availability and quality of jobs. Isabel Sawhill has proposed a multicausal account with public policy, interest-group advocacy, demography, and behavior and its perceived consequences as some of key variables.

Although these and other analysts are inclined to understand cultural change as at least partly induced by noncultural forces, most of them are inclined to ascribe at least relative autonomy to culture: once set in motion, cultural transformation takes on a life of its own and becomes an independent source of further changes. So, for example, attitudes toward divorce and premarital sex may have shifted initially in response to socioeconomic factors—such as increased affluence, mobility, and employment opportunities for women—that induced significant changes in individual behavior. In turn, however, a more permissive cultural atmosphere added impetus to these behavioral shifts.

There is no good reason to believe that cultural change is linear or unidirectional; indeed, two lines of argument suggest just the reverse. First, to the extent that heightened individualism is indeed an "affluence effect," then economic hard times that interrupt the expectation of ever-rising prosperity should induce at least a partial return to traditionalism in matters of personal and family conduct as well as savings and consumption. Indeed, Yankelovich suggests that just such a shift is now under way and that the result is likely to be an uneasy synthesis of traditional (or communitarian) and progressive (or individualistic) values.

Second, individuals are capable of what I call "social learning." The consequences of certain patterns of belief and conduct may turn out to be different from (and worse than) early expectations. For example, optimistic predictions about the impact of less restrictive norms and laws of divorce have run up against the reality of economic privation and psychological distress for many custodial parents and their children. From this standpoint, it is hardly surprising that a wide-ranging reconsideration of divorce, including not only lawyers and policy analysts but also family therapists, is now well under way. Nor is it surprising that after three decades of rapid increase, the divorce rate appears to have stabilized a bit below its peak of the early 1980s.

No discussion of culture would be complete without at least a passing glance at the influence of television. Today, nearly every household has a television set, and the average child spends almost as much time watching television as with parents or in school. While much research on the impact of television yields murky results, it is fairly well established that educational programming accelerates early learning and that televised violence exacerbates aggressive behavior. Focus groups and survey research yield a bleaker view. In a 1991 survey, for example, only 2 percent of respondents thought that television should have the greatest influence on children's values, but fully 56 percent believed that it does in fact have the greatest influence—more than parents, teachers, and religious leaders combined. And in Barbara Whitehead's community-level research, television emerges in the eyes of parents as a prime vehicle for the transmission of hard-to-control consumer desires to their children.

CONCLUSION

I have tried to present the evidence on causal issues as impartially as I could, though no doubt certain biases have crept in. Let me conclude with the eminently contestable judgment that the two most important forces affecting children for the worse in the past generation have been declining economic prospects for young, poorly educated male workers and the accelerated movement toward single-parent households. Returning to a higher-wage, higher productivity growth track is not just an issue for the American economy, but for America's children and families as well. Reversing the trends of the past generation toward non-marriage and divorce poses even more complex challenges, but I am pessimistic that we can do more than scratch the surface of our social ills without real movement in that direction. No doubt direct cultural cues (e.g., the president's bully pulpit) have a role to play in this endeavor, but (as was the case for civil rights in the 1960s) legal changes may have to precede any jump-start of cultural transformations.

15

The Consequences of Single Motherhood

Sara McLanahan

In 1992, when Dan Quayle condemned the television character Murphy Brown for giving birth out of wedlock, he reopened an old debate that quickly became highly polarized. Some people claimed that growing up in a fatherless home was the major cause of child poverty, delinquency, and school failure, while others denied that single motherhood had any harmful effects. And some objected even to discussing the topic for fear of stigmatizing single mothers and their children.

Not talking about single motherhood is scarcely an option. More than half of the children born in 1994 will spend some or all of their childhood with only one parent, typically their mother. If current patterns hold, they will likely experience higher rates of poverty, school failure, and other problems as they grow up. The long-range consequences could have enormous implications.

But what exactly are the consequences—how large and concentrated among what groups? Do they depend on whether a single mother is widowed, divorced, or never married? Does public support for single mothers inadvertently increase the number of women who get divorced or choose to have a baby on their own?

Many people hold strong opinions about these issues. For example, conservatives such as former Education Secretary William Bennett and Charles Murray[1] the author of *Losing Ground*, believe that single motherhood is so harmful and public support is so significant an inducement for unwed women to have babies that it is time to get tough with the mothers. Murray has even proposed denying unwed mothers child support payments from nonresident fathers. In Murray's eyes, the mothers are fully responsible for any children they bear "in an age when contraceptives and abortion are freely available." Of the father, Murray says: "As far as I can tell, he has approximately the same causal responsibility as a slice of chocolate cake has in determining whether a woman gains weight."

Meanwhile, some liberal critics see "single mother" as a codeword for "black, welfare mother." They view the focus on out-of-wedlock births and family breakup as an effort to divert public attention and social policy from overcoming racism and lack of opportunity. And then there are the feminists who regard Quayle's attack on

Murphy Brown as a symbolic attack on the moral right of women to pursue careers and raise children on their own. So great are the passions aroused by the debate over the morality of single motherhood that a clear-eyed view of the consequences of single motherhood has been difficult. But to make any progress, we had best know what those are.

DOES SINGLE MOTHERHOOD HARM CHILDREN?

Children who grow up with only one of their biological parents (nearly always the mother) are disadvantaged across a broad array of outcomes. As shown in Figure 15.1, they are twice as likely to drop out of high school, 2.5 times as likely to become teen mothers, and 1.4 times as likely to be idle—out of school and out of work—as children who grow up with both parents.[2]

Children in one-parent families also have lower grade point averages, lower college aspirations, and poorer attendance records. As adults, they have higher rates of divorce. These patterns persist even after adjusting for differences in race, parents' education, number of siblings, and residential location.

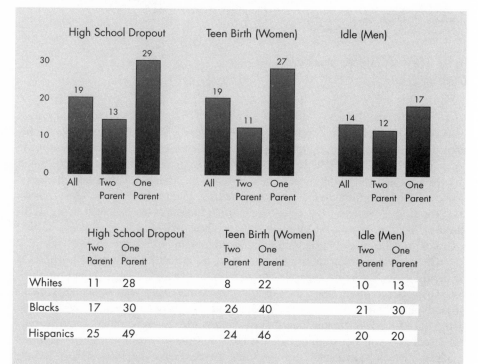

| | High School Dropout | | Teen Birth (Women) | | Idle (Men) | |
	Two Parent	One Parent	Two Parent	One Parent	Two Parent	One Parent
Whites	11	28	8	22	10	13
Blacks	17	30	26	40	21	30
Hispanics	25	49	24	46	20	20

Note: Estimates are adjusted for race, parent's education, number of siblings, and place of residence. Sample is too small to estimate effects for Hispanic children from advantaged backgrounds.
Source: National Longitudinal Survey of Youth

Fig. 15.1 The Risk of Dropping Out of School, Teen Birth, and Idleness by Family Structure

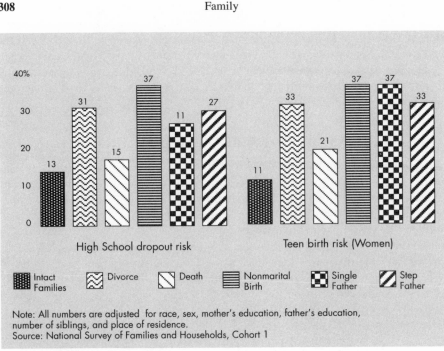

Note: All numbers are adjusted for race, sex, mother's education, father's education, number of siblings, and place of residence.
Source: National Survey of Families and Households, Cohort 1

Fig. 15.2 Is the Cause of Family Disruption Related to Child Well-Being?

The evidence, however, does not show that family disruption is the principal cause of high school failure, poverty, and delinquency. While 19 percent of all children drop out of high school, the dropout rate for children in two-parent families is 13 percent. Thus, the dropout rate would be only 33 percent lower if all families had two parents and the children currently living with a single parent had the same dropout rates as children living with two parents—a highly improbable assumption.

The story is basically the same for the other measures of child well-being. If all children lived in two-parent families, teen motherhood and idleness would be less common, but the bulk of these problems would remain (see Figure 15.2).

The consequences of family disruption are not necessarily the same in all kinds of families. Some might suppose family disruption to have a larger effect on black and Hispanic children since on average they come from less advantaged backgrounds and their underlying risk of dropping out, becoming a teen mother, and being out of work is greater than that of whites. Alternatively, others might expect the effect of family disruption to be smaller on minority children because single mothers in black and Hispanic communities are more common, more widely accepted, and therefore perhaps provided more support from neighbors and kin.

In our study, we found that family disruption has the most harmful effects among Hispanics and least among blacks. Family disruption increases the risk of school failure by 24 percentage points among Hispanics, 17 percentage points among whites, and 13 percentage points among blacks.

A striking result emerges from comparisons of the percentage increases in risk.

Family disruption raises the risk of dropping out 150 percent for the average white child, 100 percent for the average Hispanic child, and 76 percent for the average black child. Consequently, the dropout rate for the average white child in a single-parent family is substantially higher than the dropout rate of the average black child in a two-parent family and only two percentage points lower than the dropout rate of the average black child in a one-parent family. Thus, for the average white child, family disruption appears to eliminate much of the advantage associated with being white.

Children from white middle-class families are not immune from the effects of family disruption. Consider the children of families where one parent has at least some college education. If the parents live apart, the probability that their children will drop out of high school rises by 11 percentage points. And for every child who actually drops out of school, there are likely to be three or four more whose performance is affected even though they manage to graduate.

College performance may also suffer. The college graduation rate for white children from advantaged backgrounds is about 9 percentage points lower among children of disrupted families than among children of two-parent families (53 percent versus 62 percent). At the other end of the continuum, children from disadvantaged backgrounds (neither parent graduated from high school) have a bleak future, regardless of whether they live with one or both parents.

DOES MARRIAGE MATTER?

Some of the current debate presumes that being born to unmarried parents is more harmful than experiencing parents' divorce and that children of divorced parents do better if their mother remarries. Our evidence suggests otherwise.

Children born to unmarried parents are slightly more likely to drop out of school and become teen mothers than children born to married parents who divorce. But the difference is small compared to the difference between these two groups of children and children who grow up with both parents. What matters for children is not whether their parents are married when they are born, but whether their parents live together while the children are growing up.

Children who grow up with widowed mothers, in contrast, fare better than children in other types of single-parent families, especially on measures of educational achievement. Higher income (due in part to more generous social polices toward widows), lower parental conflict, and other differences might explain this apparent anomaly.

Remarriage is another instance where the conventional wisdom is wrong. Children of stepfamilies don't do better than children of mothers who never remarry. Despite significantly higher family income and the presence of two parents, the average child in a stepfamily has about the same chance of dropping out of high school as the average child in a one-parent family.

Some people believe that single fathers are better able to cope with family responsibilities because they have considerably more income, on average, than the mothers. However, our evidence shows that children in single-father homes do just as poorly as children living with a single mother.

WHAT ACCOUNTS FOR POOR OUTCOMES?

All of the numbers reported in the figures shown have been adjusted for differences in family background characteristics such as race, parents' education, family size, and place of residence. Thus the parents' socioeconomic status cannot explain why children from one-parent families are doing worse.

Unfortunately, we cannot rule out the possibility that the gap stems from some unmeasured difference between one- and two-parent families, such as alcoholism, child abuse, or parental indifference. Only a true experiment could prove that family disruption is really causing children to dropout of school—and no one is willing to assign kids randomly to families to answer these questions.

Nevertheless, it is clear that parental breakup reduces children's access to important economic, parental, and community resources. The loss of those resources affects cognitive development and future opportunities. Thus the evidence strongly suggests that family disruption plays a causal role in lowering children's well-being. When parents live apart, children have less income because the family loses economies of scale and many nonresident fathers fail to pay child support. The average drop in income for white children whose parents separate during the child's adolescence is about $22,000 (in 1992 dollars)—a loss of 40 percent. For black children, the decline is smaller—about $9,000, a loss of 32 percent. In contrast, when a parent dies, children do not generally experience a major change in their standard of living. Social Security and life insurance help to make up the difference.

Family disruption also reduces the time parents spend with children and the control they have over them. When parents live apart, children see their fathers a lot less. About 29 percent do not see them at all. Another 35 percent see them only on a weekly basis. Mothers often find their authority undermined by the separation and consequently have more difficulty controlling their children. One survey asked high school students whether their parents helped them with their school work and supervised their social activities. Students whose parents separated between the sophomore and senior years reported a loss of involvement and supervision compared to students whose parents stayed together.

Family disruption also undermines children's access to community resources or what sociologist James Coleman[3] calls social capital. Divorce and remarriage often precipitate moves out of a community, disrupting children's relationships with peers, teachers, and other adults. During middle childhood and early adolescence, a child in a stable family experiences, on average, 1.4 moves. The average child in a single-parent family experiences 2.7 moves; in a stepfamily, the average child experiences 3.4 moves.

Figure 15.3 ("Income and Divorce") shows how the loss of economic resources can account for differences between children in one- and two-parent families. The first bar shows the baseline difference between children whose parents divorced during adolescence and children whose parents remained married. The second and third bars show the difference, after adjusting for pre- and post-divorce income (income at age twelve and seventeen). Loss of economic resources accounts for about 50 percent of the disadvantages associated with single parenthood. Too little parental supervision and involvement and greater residential mobility account for most of the rest.

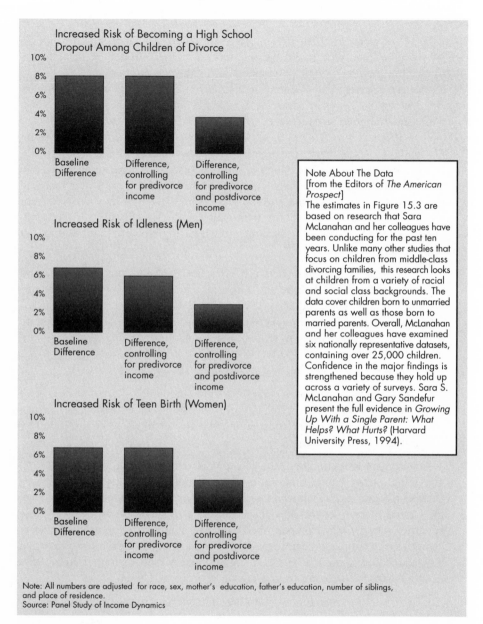

Note About The Data
[from the Editors of *The American Prospect*]
The estimates in Figure 15.3 are based on research that Sara McLanahan and her colleagues have been conducting for the past ten years. Unlike many other studies that focus on children from middle-class divorcing families, this research looks at children from a variety of racial and social class backgrounds. The data cover children born to unmarried parents as well as those born to married parents. Overall, McLanahan and her colleagues have examined six nationally representative datasets, containing over 25,000 children. Confidence in the major findings is strengthened because they hold up across a variety of surveys. Sara S. McLanahan and Gary Sandefur present the full evidence in *Growing Up With a Single Parent: What Helps? What Hurts?* (Harvard University Press, 1994).

Note: All numbers are adjusted for race, sex, mother's education, father's education, number of siblings, and place of residence.
Source: Panel Study of Income Dynamics

 Income and Divorce

WHY HAS SINGLE MOTHERHOOD INCREASED?

Changes in children's living arrangements result from long- standing trends in marriage, divorce, and fertility. Divorce rates in the United States have been going up since the turn of the century and have recently stabilized at very high levels. Out-of-wedlock birth rates have been going up gradually since at least the early 1940s. After

1960, the age of women at their first marriages began to rise, increasing the proportion of young women who might become unwed mothers. Together, these forces
have fueled the growth of single parenthood during the postwar period.

These trends exist in all Western, industrialized countries. Divorce rates more
than doubled in most countries between 1960 and 1990; in some they increased four-
fold.[4] Single parenthood also increased in nearly all Western countries between 1970
and the late 1980s. Yet the United States has the highest prevalence of single-parent
families, and it has experienced the largest increase between 1970 and 1990.

In the view of Murray and other conservatives, welfare benefits in the United
States have reduced the costs of single motherhood and discouraged young men and
women from marrying. In some parts of the country, welfare may provide poor
women with more economic security than marriage does. However, for three reasons, the argument that welfare caused the growth in single-parent families does not
withstand scrutiny.

The trend in welfare benefits between 1960 and 1990 does not match the trend
in single motherhood. Welfare and single motherhood both increased dramatically during the 1960s and early 1970s. After 1974, however, welfare benefits
declined, but single motherhood continued to rise. The real value of the welfare
benefit package (cash assistance plus food stamps) for a family of four with no
other income fell from $10,133 in 1972 to $8,374 in 1980 and to $7,657 in 1992,
a loss of 26 percent between 1972 and 1992 (in 1992 dollars).

Increases in welfare cannot explain why single motherhood grew among more
advantaged women. Since 1960, divorce and single parenthood have grown
among women with a college education, who are not likely to be motivated by
the promise of a welfare check.

Welfare payments cannot explain why single motherhood is more common in
the United States than in other industrialized countries. Nearly all the Western
European countries have much more generous payments for single mothers than
the United States, yet the prevalence of single motherhood is lower in these
countries. One way to compare the "costs" of single motherhood in different
countries is to compare the poverty rates of single mothers with those of married
mothers. While single mothers have higher poverty rates than married mothers
in all industrialized countries, they are worst off in the United States.

If welfare is not to blame, what is? Three factors seem to be primarily responsible.

The first is the growing economic independence of women. Women who can
support themselves outside marriage can be picky about when and whom they marry.
They can leave bad marriages, and they can afford to bear and raise children on their
own. Thus single mothers will be more common in a society where women are more
economically independent, all else being equal.

American women have moved steadily toward economic independence
throughout this century thanks to increased hourly wages, greater control over childbearing, and technological advances that reduce time required for housework. Since

the turn of the century, each new generation of young women has entered the labor force in greater proportions and stayed at work longer. By 1970, over half of all American women were employed or looking for work; by 1990, nearly three quarters were doing so. The rise in welfare benefits during the 1950s and 1960s may have made poor women less dependent on men by providing them with an alternative source of economic support. However, welfare was only a small part of a much larger change that was enabling all women, rich and poor alike, to live more easily without a husband.

A second factor in the growth of single motherhood is the decline in men's earning power relative to women's. After World War II and up through the early 1970s, both men and women benefitted from a strong economy. While women were becoming more self-sufficient during the 1950s and 1960s, men's wages and employment opportunities were increasing as well. Consequently, while more women could afford to live alone, the economic payoff from marriage continued to rise. After 1970, however, the gender gap in earnings (women's earnings divided by men's earnings) began to narrow. In 1970, female workers earned 59 percent as much as male workers; by 1980, they earned 65 percent as much and by 1990 74 percent.[5] (These numbers are based on full-time workers between the ages of twenty-five and thirty-four.) In just two short decades, the economic payoff from marriage had declined by 15 percentage points. Such reductions are likely to increases single motherhood.

The narrowing of the wage gap occurred among adults from all social strata, but the source of the narrowing varied. Among those with a college education, men were doing well, but women were doing even better. Between 1980 and 1990, the earnings of college-educated women grew by 17 percent, while the earnings of college-educated men grew by only 5 percent. (Again, I am referring to full-time workers, aged twenty-five to thirty-four. Thus, even though the benefits of marriage were declining, women still had much to gain from pooling resources with a man.

The story was much bleaker at the other end of the educational ladder. Between 1970 and 1990, women's earnings stagnated and men's earnings slumped. Between 1980 and 1990, women with a high school degree experienced a 2 percent decline in earnings, while men with similar education experienced a 13 percent decline. This absolute loss in earnings particularly discouraged marriage by some low-skilled men who were no longer able to fulfill their breadwinner role. During the Great Depression, fathers who could not find work sometimes deserted their families as a way of coping with their sense of failure. Again, welfare may have played a part in making single motherhood more attractive than marriage for women with the least skills and education, but only because low-skilled men were having such a hard time and received so little help from government.

The third factor in the growth of single motherhood was a shift in social norms and values during the 1960s that reduced the stigma associated with divorce and nonmarital childbearing. In the 1950s, if a young unmarried woman found herself pregnant, the father was expected to step forward and the couple was expected to marry. By the late 1980s, the revolution in sexual mores permitted young men and women to have intimate relationships and live together outside the bonds of legal marriage.

Attitudes toward individual freedom also changed during the 1960s. The new individualism encouraged people to put personal fulfillment above family responsibility, to expect more from their intimate relationships and marriages, and to leave "bad" marriages if their expectations were not fulfilled. In the early 1960s, over half of all women surveyed agreed that "when there are children in the family, parents should stay together even if they don't get along." By the 1980s, only 20 percent held this view.[6] Once sex and childbearing were "liberated" from marriage and women could support themselves, two of the most important incentives for marriage were gone. When the economic gains from marriage declined in the 1970s, it's not surprising that declines in marriage rates soon followed.

Today, changes in social norms continue to influence the formation of families by making new generations of young adults less trustful of the institution of marriage. Many of the young people who are now having trouble finding and keeping a mate were born during the 1960s when divorce rates were rising. Many grew up in single-parent families or stepfamilies. Given their own family history, these young people may find it easier to leave a bad relationship and to raise a child alone than to make and keep a long-term commitment.

Compared to the conservative argument that welfare causes single parenthood, these changes provide a more comprehensive and compelling explanation. They explain why single motherhood is more common in the United States than in other industrialized countries: American women are more economically independent than women in most other countries. For this reason alone, single-mother families should be more numerous in the United States. In addition, low-skilled men in the United States are worse off relative to women than low-skilled men in other countries. American workers were the first to experience the economic dislocations brought about by deindustrialization and economic restructuring. Throughout the 1970s, unemployment rates were higher in the United States than in most of Europe, and wage rates fell more sharply here than elsewhere. During the 1980s, unemployment spread to other countries but with less dire consequences for men since unemployment benefits are more generous and coverage is more extensive.

WHAT SHOULD WE DO?

Just as single motherhood has no single cause and no certain outcome, there is no simple solution or "quick fix" for the problems facing single mothers and their children. Strategies for helping these families, therefore, must include those aimed at preventing family breakup and sustaining family resources as well as those aimed at compensating children for the loss of parental time and income.

Preventing Family Breakup and Economic Insecurity

Parents contemplating divorce need to be informed about the risks to their children if their marriage breaks up. However, it is not clear we can prevent family breakups by making the divorce laws more restrictive, as William Galston, now deputy director of the White House Domestic Policy Council, advocates. Indeed, more restrictive divorce laws might have the opposite effect. Increasing numbers of young adults are living together and delaying marriage. Making divorce more difficult will only make marriage less attractive, relative to cohabitation.

A better way to encourage marriage is to make sure that parents—especially poor parents—are not penalized when they do get married. Our current system of income transfers and taxation does just that.[7]

Health care and child care are two areas in which poor two-parent families receive less government help than well-off two-parent families and impoverished single-parent families. Most middle- and upper-income families receive tax-subsidized health insurance through their employers, and all single-mother families receiving Aid to Families with Dependent Children (AFDC) are eligible for Medicaid. The most likely to be uninsured are the working poor. If some form of universal health insurance were adopted by Congress, this problem would be eliminated.

Similarly, middle-income and upper-income families can deduct child care expenses from their income taxes, while single mothers on welfare are eligible for government subsidized child care. Poor and near poor two-parent families receive virtually nothing in the way of government-subsidized help with child care because they pay no taxes. This problem could also be eliminated if the money going to upper-income families was redirected to subsidies for families below the median income.[8]

As a result of the 1994 budget, we now have a very good program, the Earned Income Tax Credit (EITC), for subsidizing the earnings of low-wage workers with children. Beginning in 1996, a two-parent family with two children and income below $28,000 will received an additional forty cents for every dollar earned up to a maximum of about $3,400 per year, which will reduce poverty and economic insecurity in two-parent families. Unfortunately, the EITC is currently under attack by the Congress, and it is unclear whether it will survive the next round of budget cuts. Moreover, the EITC does nothing for people without a job.

We are currently in the midst of a great experiment in which states are redesigning welfare programs to encourage single mothers to replace their welfare checks with paychecks. Some states are doing this by limiting the number of months or years a mother can receive welfare. Others are providing work and training programs to facilitate work. None of these initiatives, however, are addressing the employment problems of low-skilled men that underlie the decline in marriage for people at the bottom end of the income distribution. The only way to get around this problem is to guarantee a minimum-wage job to all parents who are willing to work, regardless of whether they live with their children.

Increasing Economic Security for Single-Parent Families

Until recently, we have relied on judicial discretion and parental goodwill to enforce child support obligations. For children the consequences have been devastating. Through the law and other means, we must send an unequivocal message to nonresident fathers (or mothers) that they are expected to share their income with their children, regardless of whether they live with them. This means making sure that all children have a child support award (including children born outside marriage) that awards are adequate and indexed to changes in the nonresident parents' income, and that obligations are paid promptly.

The Family Support Act of 1988 was a giant step toward redressing the failures of our child support system. It required states to increase efforts to establish paternity at birth, to develop standards for setting and updating awards, and to create mechanisms for withholding child support obligations from nonresident parents' earnings. Yet many states have been slow to carry out the Family Support Act. According to recent reports, the gap between what fathers could pay and actually do pay is about $34 billion.[9]

Enforcing child support will not only increase the income of single mothers but also sends a strong message to men that if they father a child they become responsible for supporting that child for at least eighteen years. This should make men more careful about engaging in unprotected sex and fathers more reluctant to divorce. My position is diametrically opposed to that of conservatives like Murray who argue that unwed mothers should get no support from the fathers of their children. Instead of getting tough on mothers, we should demand more of fathers. We have already tried tough love on the mothers: we cut welfare benefits by 26 percent between 1970 and 1990, and it didn't work.

Requiring men to bear as much responsibility as women for an "unwanted" pregnancy is not such a radical idea. In fact, it resembles the system that used to prevail in this country before the 1960s, when young men did share the "cost" of an unintended pregnancy: they were expected to marry. (The phrase "shotgun marriage" calls to mind a legendary threat the young woman's family might make.)

A stricter child support system has its risks. Some people argue that nonresident fathers often are abusive and that forcing these men to pay child support may endanger mothers and children. But most men do not fall into this category. A majority of children should not be deprived of child support because a minority of fathers threaten abuse. Rather, strong steps should be taken to protect single mothers and children from abusive fathers.

Other people object to enforcing child support for fear of overburdening poor fathers. While this problem has long been exaggerated—many fathers can afford to provide much more child support than they now pay—it is true that some fathers do not pay because they are unemployed or their wages are so low they can barely cover their own expenses. To help them support their children, nonresident parents—like resident parents—should be guaranteed a minimum-wage job. Those who find a private sector job (or a public non-guaranteed job) should be eligible for the earned income tax credit, even if they are not living with their child.

Making nonresident fathers eligible for the EITC would require restructuring the program. Under the current rules, the benefits go to the household with the dependent child. Under a reformed system, the benefits would go to individuals, and both parents in a two-parent family would be eligible for a subsidy if their earnings were very low. This approach avoids penalizing poor parents who live together.

Besides holding nonresident parents responsible for child support, resident parents should be responsible for raising their children and contributing to their economic support. Most single mothers are doing this already. Over 70 percent work at least part of the year, and over 25 percent work full-time, year round. These numbers are virtually identical to those for married mothers. Although most single mothers work outside the home, a substantial minority depend entirely on welfare for their economic support. And a small percentage remain on welfare for as long as eighteen or twenty years. The welfare reforms being carried out in various states require mothers on welfare to seek employment after their child is one year old (and sooner in some cases). I agree with the general thrust of these efforts, at least in principle. Most married mothers prefer to work outside the home, and single mothers on welfare are likely to have the same aspirations. Over the long run, employment should increase a mother's earning power and self-esteem and make her less dependent on government.

My major concern about the new initiatives is that they reduce the amount of time mothers spend with their children. The loss of parental time could mean less parental involvement and supervision. The result will depend on how many hours the mother works, whether children are placed in good day care and afterschool programs, and the net income of the family, after deducting for child care and other work expenses. If children have less time with their mothers and their families have no more income, they are likely to be worse off under the new system. If they have less time with their mothers but good child care and more income, they are likely to be better off.

The government should assure all children a minimum child support benefit, worth up to $2,000 per year for one child, to be paid by either the father or the government.[10] The benefit should be conditional on having a court-ordered child support award, so that single mothers have an incentive to obtain an award, and it should be implemented in conjunction with automatic wage withholding so that fathers cannot shirk their responsibility.

As yet, no state has carried out a guaranteed child support benefit. Such an experiment was nearly implemented in Wisconsin in the early 1980s but was aborted by a change in administration. New York State has been carrying out a version of the plan since 1989 with apparent success, but the program is limited to welfare-eligible mothers. The bipartisan National Commission on Children, headed by Senator Jay Rockefeller, recommended that the states experiment with a minimum child support benefit, and an early version of the Clinton welfare reform proposal contained a similar provision.

Local governments and community organizations could also be doing more. For example, they could extend the school day or use school facilities to house extracurricular activities that would offset the loss of parental time and supervision. Mentor programs could also be used to connect children to the adult world.

All these recommendations are driven by three underlying principles. The first is that something must be done immediately to reduce the economic insecurity of children in single-parent families. Low income is the single most important factor in accounting for the lower achievement of these children. Raising income, therefore, should be a major priority. The federal government has demonstrated considerable success in reducing the economic insecurity of the elderly. There is no reason why we cannot do the same for the young.

A second principle is shared responsibility. The costs of raising children must be distributed more equally between men and women and between parents and non-parents. At present mothers bear a disproportionate share of the costs of raising children. Fairness demands that fathers and society at large assume more responsibility.

Third, and most important, programs for child care, health care, and income security should be universal—available to all children and all parents. The problems facing single parents are not very different from the problems facing all parents. They are just more obvious and pressing. Universal programs avoid the dilemma of how to help children in one-parent families without creating economic incentives in favor of one-parent families. Universal programs also reenforce the idea that single motherhood is a risk shared by a majority of the population. Growing up with a single parent is not something that happens to other people and other people's children. It is something that can happen to us and our children's children.

Notes

1. Charles Murray. 1984. *Losing Ground*. New York: Basic Books.

2. Sara McLanahan and Gary Sandefur. 1994. *Growing Up With A Single Parent: What Helps? What Hurts?* Cambridge, Mass.: Harvard University Press.

3. James Coleman. 1988. "Social Capital and the Creation of Human Capital," *American Journal of Sociology* 94: S95–S120.

4. Sara McLanahan and Lynne Casper. 1995. "Growing Diversity and Inequality in the American Family." Pp. 1–46 in vol. II, *State of the Union*, ed. Farley New York: Russell Sage Foundation.

5. Suzanne Bianchi. 1995. "Changing Economic Roles of Women and Men." Pp. 107–54 in Vol. I, *State of the Nation*, ed. Farley. New York: Russell Sage Foundation.

6. Arland Thornton. 1989. "Changing Attitudes Toward Family Issues in the United States." *Journal of Marriage and the Family* 51: 873–95.

7. Irwin Garfinkel. 1996. "Economic Security for Children: From Means Testing and Bifurcation to Universality." Pp. 33–82 in *Social Policies for Children*, ed. Garfinkel, Hochschild, and McLanahan. Washington, D.C.: Brookings Institution.

8. Barbara Bergmann. 1996. "Child Care: The Key to Ending Child Poverty." Pp. 112–35 in *Social Policies for Children*, ed. Garfinkel, Hochschild, and McLanahan. Washington, D.C.: Brookings Institution.

9. Cynthia Miller, Irwin Garfinkel, and Sara McLanahan. 1966. "Child Support in the United States: Can Fathers Afford To Pay More?" *Journal of Income and Wealth*, forthcoming.

10. Irwin Garfinkel. 1992. *Assuring Child Support*. New York: Russell Sage Foundation.

Preference and Family:
Commentary on Parts III and IV

Martha C. Nussbaum

PREFERENCE

One of the most controversial areas in which law and public policy are confronted with ideas of "nature" and "social construction" is the area of same-sex sexual orientation and conduct. Same-sex relations are an especially obvious case of the ways in which laws and institutions shape the intimate personal lives of many Americans. The sexual conduct of gays and lesbians is limited by the sodomy laws that still exist in twenty-three states. Although only five states restrict the prohibition of oral and anal sex acts to same-sex actors, the constitutionality of sodomy laws has been upheld by the U.S. Supreme Court only insofar as they prohibit same-sex conduct, and "sodomy" is frequently understood to be definitive of same-sex conduct.[1] Lesbians and gays cannot serve in the military unless they conceal their sexual practices—although many nations, including Israel, Canada, Germany, Australia, France, and the Netherlands, and the police forces of several major U.S. cities, including New York, San Francisco, and Chicago, have all removed barriers to their full participation with no serious problems. Lesbians and gays cannot marry and cannot therefore enjoy the social privileges and benefits of marriage, including favorable tax, inheritance, and insurance status; immigration and custody rights; the right to the privileges of next kin in hospital visitations, decisions about burial, and so forth. Gays and lesbians frequently lose custody of children they have had in previous relationships and cannot adopt children should they wish to. Finally, gays and lesbians suffer discrimination of many types in the workplace, in housing, in social life generally. Although many localities and some states have enacted nondiscrimination statutes in the area of sexual orientation, many have not done so, and several statewide referenda have recently been proposed to make it impossible for local communities and groups within the state to enact such ordinances.[2]

These issues have been of intense concern in our recent political life and also in the many voluntary organizations that form the heart of American "civil society." Every major religious denomination, for example, is undergoing intense debate concerning the status of lesbians and gay people.[3] Such debates prompt the questions: What *is* a same-sex orientation? Is it an innate and/or immutable biological legacy? Is it a formation of the personality early in infancy? Is it a deliberate personal choice of a way of life? Is it a legacy of social forces and socially shaped categories? Is it some complex combination of more than one of these? To what extent is there an "it" at all, as opposed to a variety of overlapping forms of human behavior that have been differently organized and categorized by different societies at different times? The essays by Posner, Halley, and Sunstein all address these issues, diverging in their analyses.

It should be clear that the answer to these questions does not directly affect the answer to various policy questions concerning the status of homosexual orientation and conduct. The discovery that homosexuality is genetic, if it were clearly established, would in the view of some be a boon to gays rights. Such a conclusion, it is claimed, would make it easier to analogize sexual orientation to race as an "immutable" natural characteristic and, thus, easier to make legal arguments for the inclusion of sexual orientation alongside race, national origin, and (with some qualifications[4]) gender as a "suspect classification" in constitutional arguments interpreting the equal protection clause of the Fourteenth Amendment. (If a classification is admitted to be "suspect," the state must meet an unusual burden in justifying a proposed law based on it: it must demonstrate a "compelling state interest" rather than merely a "rational basis" for the legislation.) But it is in reality far from clear that the "immutability" of a characteristic is an essential, or even an important, feature of equal-protection argumentation. The fact that sex changes do exist and that corresponding racial changes may be possible does not make race and gender cease to be suspect classifications. On the other side, the fact that some forms of blindness may be hereditary does not entail that the laws saying blind people can't drive are subject to strict scrutiny (that the state must demonstrate a "compelling state interest" in order to enact such laws); if the predisposition to commit crimes were found to be genetic, this would not mean that the criminal law is subject to strict scrutiny. Immutability, in short, is neither necessary nor sufficient for strict scrutiny; it appears to be a rough way of getting at the idea of irrationally based prejudice. So it would appear that getting clear about what sexual orientation is does not by itself solve any legal problems. On the other hand, it may illuminate the arguments offered in legal contexts and make them more free from prejudice and ignorance;[5] it may also help us to understand the extent to which same-sex behavior and desire are themselves artifacts of laws and institutions. So such an inquiry still has a great deal to commend it in the public sphere.

The positions that have been advanced in this area differ over two questions: (1) What is the origin of sexual orientation? and (2) Is homosexuality a single thing, or are there many different forms of organization of human sexual conduct and desire in different times and places, exhibiting no fixed "essence"? The answers to the two

questions are connected in many complex ways. The person who ascribes to homosexuality a genetic origin is likely to be an "essentialist" on the second question since
human biology remains relatively stable across place and time, yet may readily concede that the behavior expressing same-sex desire will in many ways be shaped by
culture. The person who holds that sexual behavior and desire are shaped by social
forces even with respect to its most basic categories is likely to recognize a diversity
of forms of sexual orientation and desire with no single "essence," although this is
not strictly entailed since societies might for some reason all organize things in a
very similar way.[6]

We should also recall that there are several different levels on which claims of
biological and social origin may be made. At least five different areas of sexual life
call forth these competing explanations:

1. Customs and norms regarding the proper expression of sexual desire: what acts
   one chooses, what partners are acceptable.

2a. Norms regarding the nature and morality of sexual conduct and desire themselves: whether, for example, they are understood as intrinsically sinful and
   morally problematic.

2b. Norms regarding what is desirable in a sexual partner: body shape, features,
   dress, and so forth.

3. The basic sexual categories into which agents are divided: such as "the heterosexual," "the homosexual."

4. The membership of individuals in one sexual category rather than another. All
   writers in this section hold that social and moral judgments shape (1), although
   Posner would hold that there are biological factors predisposing people to prefer
   certain bodily acts rather than others. (He holds, for example, that a preference
   for vaginal intercourse is present in most heterosexuals as a result of biology.[7] It
   seems likely at again that all would accept that general normative positions on
   sexuality, such as the Christian doctrine of original sin, are cultural products
   that, once accepted in a given society, enter deeply into the ways in which agents
   experience their sexual lives. To accept that such a doctrine has a cultural rather
   than a biological origin does not rule out judging, as Weithman probably would,
   that it is in some sense objectively valid and "natural" in the sense that it represents a divinely ordained teleology; nor does it rule out judging, as Posner probably would, that they are ill-founded and inimical to human well-being. Nor
   does such a position rule out judging that a norm is objectively valid on the basis
   of some secular moral argument. This appears to be Posner's position on the
   norm he derives from J. S. Mill, that one should maximize liberty of choice except where there is harm to others, and there are many other sexual norms that
   one might attempt to justify in a similar, secular way.

Again, all our writers would presumably accept that societies eroticize certain
bodily shapes, certain styles of dress, and so forth, and that these styles (and desires
corresponding to them) vary greatly across place and time. Posner holds in other
writing (though not explicitly in this essay) that there is a biological basis to much of

what societies eroticize: for example, he holds that the preference for women with large breasts and hips has an evolutionary origin.[8] Halley and Sunstein would probably be more skeptical about such claims.

But the primary division among our authors is in two areas: the origin of the basic sexual categories, and the explanation of the placement of social actors in those categories. For Posner, the division between the homosexual and the heterosexual is an extrasocietal given, rooted either in a genetic or other organic difference or in some formative early experience of a uniform and rather ubiquitous character. In all places and all times, there have been these two categories of sexual actor, categories based on the gender of the partner a person prefers, and this category is of fundamental importance in the organization of sexual life. It has its basis in human biology and is not itself the product of cultural forces.[9] There is a determinate answer to the question, Is this person a homosexual? for any individual at any time, although (in keeping with his recognition of genuine bisexuality as defined by the Kinsey scale) the answer may be one that places the person between the two basic categories. Furthermore, the assignment of a person to one category or another is itself explained by biology. There is a fact of the matter about what a person really is, and sexual orientation is there in the person, awaiting discovery and expression. Notice that this view about origins also commits Posner to what is called "essentialism" in the area of basic sexual categories, though he may be a "social constructionist" about other areas of sexual life, such as sexual behavior.

Posner's thesis, put very generally, is that in all places and all times there have been a relatively small number of "true" homosexuals, who have an intense preference for a same-sex partner, and a much larger number of true heterosexuals. But, given that people are usually willing to substitute a less-desirable activity for the preferred one if need be, they will frequently be influenced by their social context and its norms and laws. The "true" homosexuals may choose heterosexual behavior or celibacy—the "true" heterosexuals, a pattern of same-sex conduct—in cases where the preferred alternative is either totally unavailable or very costly. Thus amounts of homosexual behavior will vary in a society, but the basic categories of persons, and the ultimate distribution of persons into those categories, will not.

It is important to note at the outset that Posner does not intend normative conclusions to be drawn from his economic analysis alone. This essay states even more explicitly than does his previous work Posner's view that a normative libertarian theory whose roots lie in Mill—individuals should be free to act as they choose provided their conduct does no harm—is not implied by his economic theory and is in some respects in tension with it. This is so because the Millean understanding of "harm" has a specific normative content that excludes mere offense to others, which an economic approach would typically count as a social cost. Posner recommends that public policy be guided on the whole by the libertarian theory, and his conclusions concerning the rights of gays and lesbians are informed by that theory, despite the use of economic analysis in setting up the issue. This twofold nature of Posner's theory seems insufficiently recognized by Janet Halley, who concentrates on the biological-economic theory alone and treats that as explaining Posner's policy recommendations.[10]

Posner's essay needs to be understood in the overall context of his attempt, throughout his career, to bring techniques of economic analysis to areas of nonmarket behavior that might at one time have seemed totally unlike market transactions.[11] Posner argues that this way of looking at sexual choices generates useful and on the whole correct predictions, whether or not it captures what is salient to the psychological experience of individual people. Thus it is not sufficient to criticize it simply by pointing to the ways in which people experience themselves and their lives; one needs not only to ask whether the assumptions Posner makes about preference and choice in sex are realistic but also, if they are not, whether they are in any case useful analytical tools.

Halley seems correct when she asserts that the assumption that people's preferences (in the sense of desired choices) in sexual matters are fixed independently of law and public policy is not realistic. She effectively demonstrates many ways in which not only the behavior of people (the acts they either will or will not perform) but also the basic categories they use to understand themselves and others will vary with shifts in laws and institutions. Halley is a social constructionist with respect to the most basic categories of sexual experience: she denies that the gender of a partner is always the basis for a salient distinction between two varieties of sexual actors. In the context of a person's entire life, her desire may be focused in some distinctive way on sex of object choice, but it also may not. Halley reminds us that sexual choices are shaped by a multitude of factors: aspirations to enact a particular role that we might have heard of, desires to live out a certain type of narrative. Even identical genital acts mean very different things to different people in different surroundings. Some people connect genital acts in complex ways with the rest of their lives, and some people do not. For some people, the choice of a same-sex partner may be a relatively derivative outcome of an overall choice of a certain style and mode of life; for another it might be *the* salient goal toward which desire orients itself. Thus Halley is not a biological determinist with regard to the placement of individuals in the basic categories. Is she a social constructionist here? Not really, since she stresses that individuals have great variety and a certain amount of freedom to choose their own "projects" from the menu of choices with which their historical context confronts them. To think of individuals simply as creations of their age is to underrate their capacity for creative personal use of their social possibilities.[12]

Halley makes it seem plausible that the human variety she describes, both in the formation of categories and in the choice of a life "project" from among the categories, has predictive significance, so that Posner's economic account may have not just interpretive but also predictive shortcomings.[13] Her conclusion is not that an economics of sexual choice is impossible, but rather that it will need to take account of the fluidity of people's preferences, their responsiveness to changes in laws and institutions. It will therefore be much more complicated than the theory Posner proposes.

Sunstein addresses legal issues, but his central contention is built on a variety of the social-constructionist claim, concerning the basic categories of human sexual experience. He alleges that policies discriminating against gays and lesbians are profoundly connected to the hierarchical structure of gender roles that prevails in many societies and to the closely related pressure on individuals to exhibit behavior that conforms to an antecedently given stereotype of the masculine or the feminine. What troubles many people about same-sex object choice, he argues, is the way in which it manifests deviance from expected patterns of male and female behavior. Lesbian women are women who have sexual pleasure without men and who define themselves and their pleasure independently of men. Gay men are men who do not assert their masculinity in the domination of women. They are threatening to men both because of what they are and because of what they desire to do: both because they (or some of them) represent their masculinity as available for penetration, and in this way show that men can be like women, and because they (or some of them) manifest the desire to penetrate other men, using them the way men characteristically treat women and in this way turning them into women. In this way, both gay male passivity and gay male penetrative desire evoke related fears, namely the fear that a man may be feminized. Sunstein plausibly suggests that this deep fear is at least one prominent cause of the fear and loathing with which lesbians and gay men are regarded in many societies. In other words, the way this category is understood is derivative from the articulation of male and female gender roles in society; and this articulation is understood by Sunstein to be, if prevalent, still mutable and something that, given its links with pervasive patterns of injustice to women, laws and institutions should seek to change.

In this way, Sunstein connects his analysis of homosexuality with an analysis of legal equality and of the interpretation of the equal protection clause of the Fourteenth Amendment. He analyzes parts of the tradition of equal-protection jurisprudence using the notion of "caste" or second-class citizenship. Looking first at the case that invalidated laws against interracial marriage, Sunstein finds that mere formal equality—the same prohibition applied to both whites and blacks—gives us an insufficiently deep understanding of the idea of equal protection. What was wrong with laws against interracial marriage was, he argues, their link with "White Supremacy." It was this idea of hierarchy and second-class citizenship, rather than mere formal equality, that was stressed by the U.S. Supreme Court in *Loving v. Virginia*. Sunstein sees racial hierarchy as closely related to gender hierarchy: both are instances of turning a morally irrelevant characteristic into a source of systematic social disadvantage. Laws perpetuating or creating such second-class citizenship are in most cases unconstitutional already, he points out. By linking discrimination against gays and lesbians with discrimination against women, he argues, we can judge discriminatory laws to be unconstitutional without addressing directly the question whether sexual orientation is itself a "suspect classification" within the meaning of equal-protection analysis (although Sunstein stresses that he believes it ought to be so regarded). Sunstein's strategy has obvious advantages in an era in which *Bowers v. Hardwick* has temporarily closed the door to some more direct approaches to the legal status of same-sex conduct. This analysis has been accepted by the Hawaii Supreme Court in its decision declaring a law against same-sex marriage to be unconstitutional.[14]

The notion of "caste" used by Sunstein in his argument[15] raises a number of questions. We need more clarification concerning the notion of a "morally irrelevant" characteristic. Many things that Sunstein considers morally irrelevant—for example, being female, or being Jewish or Hindu or Roman Catholic—have been treated as morally relevant, indeed as morally central, in many moral/religious world views. The type of liberal constitutional regime that is committed to treating these differences as morally irrelevant (or perhaps it is better to say politically irrelevant[16]) needs further articulation. "A difference is morally irrelevant," Sunstein continues, "if it has no relationship to individual entitlement or desert." It is not admitted by all his opponents that race and sex are morally irrelevant in this way (although at this stage in our political debate this might still be a good way to frame these issues). And it is also clear that many characteristics that do appear to be based on individual entitlement or desert—for example, academic and job performance—may themselves be the outgrowth of existing inequalities, so more clarification is needed, too, as to when we are entitled to trust that merit is merit and not caste masking itself as merit. Finally, it would appear that on many reasonable understandings of the proposal, differences of income, wealth, and social class must be considered (in many cases at least) to be morally irrelevant characteristics. But this will have far-reaching consequences for constitutional analysis that Sunstein nowhere addresses. For example, existing welfare and tax legislation, housing policies, and medical policies all would have to be evaluated in order to determine that they do not unequally disadvantage the poor. Some might favor such a development, but it is clear from his other writings that Sunstein does not.

Equally in need of clarification is Sunstein's notion that disadvantage in order to be a proper object of equal-protection argument, must be "systemic," that is, disadvantage "that operates along standard and predictable lines in multiple important spheres of life." It appears that Sunstein understands this to include, as a necessary condition, general economic disadvantage. For this reason, sexual orientation itself will not count as a caste-making category on the ground that gays and lesbians, as a group, do not suffer systemic disadvantage that includes pervasive second-class economic status. But if a disadvantage—let us say, the denial of a right to marry a partner of one's choice—is a serious source of second-class citizenship, why should we need to look for other sources of disadvantage? It would appear to be a serious difficulty for Sunstein that, to all appearances, Jews in late Weimar Republic and early Nazi Germany would not count as second-class citizens since they had many legally imposed disadvantages but, as yet, no second-class economic status. And, in general, many advocates of lesbian and gay rights may feel that it is odd for those rights to rest on the contingent and mutable social situation of women in such a way that sexual-orientation discrimination would cease to be unacceptable were women to enjoy a position of full equality in our society.

Sunstein clearly does not intend his anticaste reading of the equal protection clause to exhaust the meaning of the clause. So perhaps this objection is not a very grave one. But it seems important for Sunstein to spell out clearly what his full view is about the constitutional situation of such rights were the social contingencies that bring "caste" into play to be altered.

A final problem in Sunstein's argument is its heavy reliance on equality arguments to the exclusion of privacy arguments. One can agree that equal-protection arguments using ideas of hierarchy and second-class citizenship are extremely important legal tools in areas from abortion to same-sex conduct without granting that these arguments are the only ones we need. Sunstein seems too pessimistic about the history of substantive due process: through this admittedly controversial avenue, a number of important conclusions were reached that might have been more difficult to reach using equality arguments. In *Griswold v. Connecticut*, for example, the right of married couples to use contraception was defended using a due-process privacy argument.[17] Although conceivably an equal-protection argument might have been used, it is by no means clear that the contraception right is best understood as a right of women, or of any other traditional suspect class.[18] The problem with exclusive reliance on equal-protection argument is that it makes some very fundamental rights of personal choice contingent on a pervasive situation of social inequality. If the two races were ever equal in general socioeconomic terms, according to Sunstein's analysis, laws against miscegenation would not be unconstitutional. At the Brown conference, Michele Moody-Adams, a black woman married to a white man, made the point that her own marriage was vigorously opposed by many blacks and that she could envisage a situation in which blacks, equally empowered in society, would press for such laws. According to Sunstein's analysis, such a law would not be unconstitutional on the basis of "caste," any more than would a law right now restricting marriages between Presbyterians and Episcopalians.[19] In her view, this gives us strong reasons to hold on to privacy arguments, since in her view the free choices of individuals in a matter of such fundamental importance as the choice of a spouse should not be interfered with by law. Moody-Adams makes a strong argument, and one with a long history in the tradition of substantive due process. It is clear that a privacy-right argument is unavailable for the consensual sexual practices of same-sex partners, at least at the present time in the aftermath of *Bowers*. But that is no reason not to continue arguing (as Posner does in *Sex and Reason*) that *Bowers* was wrongly decided and that a due-process argument invoking the right to privacy should invalidate state sodomy laws.[20]

The arguments of Posner, Halley, and Sunstein all bypass the morality of homosexual conduct, whether because they believe, as does Posner, that the law has no business legislating sexual morality where there is no harm to others or because they believe that it is clear that there is no special moral problem about same-sex relations, as appears to be the view of Halley and Sunstein (and perhaps Posner as well). But, of course, a substantial number of people in our society do judge homosexual conduct to be immoral, and the basis for their judgments is often a religious teaching. None of the major religions has a simple view on this matter at the present time. In Judaism, Roman Catholicism, and various forms of Protestantism, there is intense debate.[21] But the conservative positions of a number of mainstream American religions have had widespread influence on public discussion. Many such positions are justified by appeal to scriptural authority; the proper role of such arguments in a liberal polity may be questioned.[22] But the arguments of the Roman Catholic natural law tradition purport to derive all their premises from secular reason, not revelation or authority; many of these arguments reach extremely conservative conclusions that coincide with the teachings of the Church. Such arguments, because of their alleged secular rational basis, would appear to have a special interest for public debate about sexual morality.

Weithman addresses the arguments of John Finnis, which are perhaps the most influential among the conservative Catholic arguments deriving from the natural law tradition. Finnis concludes that homosexual acts are morally wrong, "disintegrative" to the self, and a threat to genuine marriages and, thence, to the health of a political community. He believes that these properties of homosexual conduct give reasons for communities to discourage such conduct—for example, by passing referenda as the State of Colorado did, forbidding local communities from enacting nondiscrimination laws for sexual orientations.[23]

Through a careful analysis of the logical structure of Finnis's argument, Weithman concludes that Finnis relies on a notion of complementarity to derive his negative conclusion about same-sex conduct: sexual uniting, if it is to be a genuine partnership or union and not simply the simultaneous pursuit of personal pleasure (like simultaneous masturbation), requires that the partners be genuinely complementary, each bringing to the partnership something distinctive, something that the other lacks. Weithman argues plausibly that this goal of complementarity could be realized in many ways: it does not require difference of biological organs or reproductive functions. Two individuals might be complementary by bringing to their sexual relationship desires, emotions, and histories that contribute something distinctive to the sex and that interact in a morally valuable way. One could perhaps go even further: we could have two partners who bring very similar contributions to the relationship, but whose complementarity consists in their attentiveness and responsiveness to one another's needs and wishes. (We might think here of the analogy of a chamber ensemble: one valuable type of complementarity will involve differences of type of instrument, as when winds and strings play together; but another valuable sort may involve all string players, each playing a part that engages interactively and responsively with the others. A duet played by two violins, or sung by two soprano voices, may still contain valuable interaction and complementarity.) All this leads Weithman to the conclusion that Finnis's argument, though it makes a basically valuable moral point, fails to imply what Finnis thinks it implies: that is, it gives us no reason to view same-sex sexual conduct as inherently "disintegrative" or depraved or, indeed, morally problematic in any special way.

We should note that Weithman accepts an important premise of the Finnis argument that one might well question: that it is always wrong to use one's body simply as an instrument for one's own pleasure.[24] (Thus masturbation, for Weithman as well as for Finnis, would, presumably, always be morally bad.) Weithman gives us no reason to think this premise true. There are many ways in which people use their bodies for pleasure: going for a swim, running, hiking, smelling a rose, tasting delicious food (for its taste rather than its nutrition value), stroking a cat, feeling the morning breeze on one's face. Finnis has complicated ways of handling some of these apparent difficulties for his argument: in other writings he has introduced a category of basic human good called "skilled performance" and has included some uses of the body for pleasure under that category, holding that in this way they do fulfill a basic human good. It remains unclear why sexual activity, including masturbation, could not fulfill the good of "skilled performance," and it also remains unclear how Finnis would handle the items on my list (e.g., smelling a rose, feeling the morning breeze on one's face, or stroking one's cat) that do not appear to involve any particular skill. Even swimming, or tasting food, or hiking, which may be done in a cultivated way, do not seem to be valuable just on account of the cultivated skill they display—they may just be fun. In general, it seems to be morally unproblematic to derive pleasure from one's body, and it would only be some special view about sexual organs and capacities, which Weithman never makes explicit, that could show us what moral problem is actually worrying him.

All four writers in this section, despite their differences in starting point, theoretical orientation, and religious/secular affiliation, all conclude that there are no good reasons to treat homosexual orientation and conduct as morally or legally problematic in a special way.

FAMILY

The family has frequently been depicted as existing by "nature," and its allegedly natural structure has been cited in influential legal decisions concerning the proper role of women. In 1871, Myra Bradwell attempted to become the first woman in the state of Illinois to practice law. Since the state then had a law forbidding women to play this role, she took the state to court, and eventually the U.S. Supreme Court ruled against her, holding that the right to practice law was not a privilege or immunity of national citizenship and was therefore not protected by the Fourteenth Amendment. In a concurring opinion, Justice Bradley spoke about woman's place in the family:

> The natural and proper timidity and delicacy which belongs to the female sex evidently unfits it for many of the occupations of civil life. The constitution of the family organization, which is founded in the divine ordinance, as well as in the nature of things, indicates the domestic sphere as that which properly belongs to the domain and functions of womanhood. The harmony, not to say identity, of interests and views which belong or should belong to the family institution, is repugnant to the idea of a woman adopting a distinct and independent career from that of her husband. . . .
>
> It is true that many women are unmarried and not affected by any of the duties, complications, and incapacities arising out of the married state but these are exceptions to the general rule. The paramount destiny and mission of woman are to fulfill the noble and benign offices of wife and mother. This is the law of the Creator. And the rules of civil society must be adapted to the general constitution of things, and cannot be based upon exceptional cases.[25]

Nor is this an isolated instance. As late as 1961, the Court upheld as "rational" a Florida jury selection system excluding women who did not positively indicate a wish to serve. Justice Harlan wrote that "woman is still regarded as the center of home and family life. We cannot say that it is constitutionally impermissible for a State . . . to conclude that a woman should be relieved from the civic duty of jury service unless she herself determines that such service is consistent with her own special responsibilities."[26] This case was not identical to the Bradwell case since the law did not exclude women from jury service, it simply gave them a voluntary exemption. Nonetheless, jury duty is a symbol of civic competence and worth and a valuable civic education. Women, if given an easy out, would be pressured by their domestic duties (and perhaps their husbands) to bypass this valuable exercise. Harlan's argument, therefore, still seems to enshrine traditional sex roles as sacrosanct in a morally questionable way.

And although these legal arguments appear to have a vaguely religious basis, this same idea of the (nuclear Western-style) family as a harmonious body whose members' interests form a complementary (male-governed) unity can be found pervasively in our secular culture as well, even in the hardheaded science of economics. The most popular economic model of the family, that proposed by Nobel Prize-winning economist Gary Becker, maintains that the head of the household (imagined as typically male) is a beneficent altruist who looks after the interests of all family members. This assumption has many consequences, not least that we are prohibited from asking what conflicts of interest there might be between family members, or even how the separate members are doing with respect to basic indicators of a human being's quality of life.[27] In this respect, if not in many others, Becker and Justice Bradley see eye to eye.

As Mill long ago insisted,[28] the concept of nature—used explicitly in Justice Bradley's opinion and influential in forming the picture of the family that lies in the background of Becker's analysis—is a slippery one in such moral and political arguments. "Nature" can mean (1) the way things are without human intervention; (2) the way things always have been; (3) the way things are of necessity; and, finally, (4) the way it is right and proper for them to be. As Mill notes, users of the term all too rarely distinguish (1) from (2): they take the prevalence and longevity of certain male/female differences as evidence that this is the way people come into the world at birth. Moreover, although many aspects both of our innate equipment and of our heritage of custom and habit are regarded as changeable, recognizing "nature" in sense (1) or even (2), in the area of sex-role difference, is frequently taken, as here, to license the judgment that these roles are natural in sense (3), that is, that they are necessary and cannot be changed, they are our "destiny." Finally—and this is the most prominent difficulty in Justice Bradley's argument—a slippage all too easily occurs between "nature" in sense (1) or sense (2) and "nature" in sense (4), that is, the very fact that something is either customary or the way things are without intervention is taken to license the conclusion that this is the way they properly ought to be. In many areas of our life, we regard it as permissible and even good to strive to overcome both custom and innate heritage. Myopia, genetic diseases, customs of racial prejudice—all these are "natural" in either sense (1) or (2), but they are not regarded as "natural" in sense (4); we think that it is not fit and proper that things should be this way. We try to change innate equipment through medical science, custom and habit through moral education. Why, then, have so many people thought for so long that the customary structure of the family does show us a way things ought to be?[29]

A number of reasons for the sanctification of the habitual (nuclear Western) family structure in American legal history suggest themselves: the influence of JudaeoChristian scripture, the prevalence and longevity of gender-divided family roles, the self-interest of male politicians and judges. On the other hand, it should have been easy enough to look and see the many ways in which families have been constituted around the world. Even a cursory empirical inquiry would have shown that definitions of marriage and family membership, conceptions of child care and domestic labor, and configurations of daily living space vary enormously across cultures. This would not by itself show that the familiar structure to which Justice Bradley alludes is not the best and most fitting structure; but it would have prompted a genuine inquiry into the goals of family life and the different ways of fulfilling those goals. A simple empirical inquiry would also have quickly shown that the alleged "harmony, not to say identity, of interests and views" has not always characterized the family.[30] Family members frequently compete not only for power and respect, for money, for educational and employment opportunities, but also, at times, for necessary life-sustaining resources. Again, this would not show that law should not promote this harmony but it would at least have shown that the interests of family members are in principle distinct and that what serves the interests of one member may thwart the development of another.

For Justice Bradley, a family, as founded in "the divine ordinance," consisted of a breadwinning male head of household, a wife who performs the "noble and benign offices of wife and mother," and the children they have together. An unmarried woman was an anomaly in "the general constitution of things," and seems by definition not to be a part of any family unity—she is unaffected by its "duties, complications, and incapacities." Absent from Justice Bradley's portrait of the family are elderly parents and grandparents, aunts, uncles, and cousins, nonbiologically related friends who form part of an "extended family" group. Even more glaringly absent are the family relations that his imagined unmarried woman might possibly choose for herself: a nonmarital heterosexual relationship, a same-sex partnership, even ties of familial closeness between the woman and her nonspousal relatives and friends, as well as the children of her relatives and friends. All of these intimate connections were present in the United States at the time when Justice Bradley wrote; they are even more prominently present now.

The essays in this section reflect about the actual variety and complexity of family structures in American life and ask about the implications of this variety for law and public policy. They all start from empirical information that demonstrates the wide range of structures of closeness and commitment in which Americans actually live. As Martha Minow's essay shows, these structures are not only diverse but becoming more diverse as for example, by new reproductive technologies, new models of parenthood are created, and as care for elderly parents comes to occupy an ever larger amount of Americans' energies. Minow shows, furthermore, that the simple nuclear model enshrined in the *Bradwell* opinion never was the only family structure in American life. Legal judgments concerning such matters as immigration, citizenship, and child custody have been grappling for a long time with the status of the extended family and with tensions between biological and custodial parenthood. More recently, the claims of same-sex couples to various aspects of family status—the legal privileges of marriage, the custody of children they have had either by former marriages or by artificial insemination—makes the legal questions more complex still.

Minow's primary thesis is that the family is, in some very important respects, a legal artifact: that the groupings and commitments people form in a society are in many important ways shaped by laws and institutions—laws concerning marriage and next-of-kin status, laws concerning child custody, and so forth. This being the case, it is disingenuous to pretend that the law is neutral and simply reflects some preexisting natural structure. Law is an agent, involved in shaping what the family will and can be. Minow argues, plausibly, that facing up to this fact will promote a more adequate public debate about the proper role of the law in shaping the family.

Minow's own preference is for a liberal and tolerant norm. Given the diversity of the ethnic, religious, and personal ideas of family that can now be found in America, and given American traditions of tolerance and noninterference in matters of intimate personal choice, she would have the law adopt a very broad definition of what counts as "family." She favors something like the American Home Economics Association's definition: a family is "two or more persons who share resources, share responsibility for decisions, share values and goals, and have a commitment to one another over time . . . regardless of blood legal ties, adoption, or marriage." (A similarly broad definition was adopted by the United Nations in connection with the Year of the Family, 1994; Minow's analysis could easily be extended to the international arena.)

Minow seems to think that there is a paradox inherent in this sort of liberal toleration. Citing philosopher Joshua Halberstam, she writes that "genuine tolerance is impossible, because anyone with truly held convictions believes they and not another set are correct, and yet only those with convictions can be tolerant," (p. 260). We can have tolerance, she asserts, only by limiting the sphere in which we have deep-seated convictions. This seems wrong. Tolerance does not require moral skepticism; it requires only the view, fundamental to liberalism in both the Kantian and the Utilitarian traditions, that choice of a way of life is a fundamental human value and that there are some matters that are far too important to be decided any other way than by a person's own choice. There is a distinction between tolerance and respect: the decision to tolerate (not oppose or suppress) a practice stops short of respect for that practice. But it would appear that tolerance is connected with respect in another way: it is built on a prior respect for the choice capacities of one's fellow citizens, even when they choose what one disapproves—or even what one does not respect. None of this requires the suspension of moral judgment. The tolerant Roman Catholic in a liberal polity, for example, does not need to hold his or her views lightly, or to season them with skepticism; she need only judge that the faculty of choice in each of her fellow citizens is worthy of respect and acknowledgement and that political decisions should be based on this fact. As liberal Roman Catholic thinker Jacques Maritain observed,

> There is real and genuine tolerance only when a man is firmly and absolutely convinced truth, or of what he holds to be a truth, and when he at the same time recognizes the right of those who deny this truth to exist, and to contradict him, and to speak their mind, not because they are free from truth but because they seek truth in their own way, and because he respects in them human nature and human dignity and those very resources and living springs of the intellect and of conscience which make them potentially capable of attaining the truth he loves, if someday they happen to see it.[31]

On such a basis, Minow might have built a firmer foundation for her liberal jurisprudence in matters of the family. The neutrality proper to a court need not consist in skepticism: it can be based on a respect for the decision capacities of citizens in matters of intimate association vital to their well-being. There will remain hard questions about why liberal respect for agency should be given pride of place in a democratic regime. It would take a full theory of political justice, such as that of John Rawls, even to begin to answer those questions. Nonetheless, it appears plausible to think that a liberalism built on respect for choice can defend tolerance without skepticism.

Minow holds, however, plausibly enough, that courts must make some hard decisions and sometimes must use a normative conception of family in the process. Even if the conception is loose and elastic, it will have some boundaries and enshrine some norms at the expense of others. Here Minow's suggestions are promissory and speculative, but her basic idea is that government today should focus on the articulation of family duties in their relationship both to government duties and to the rights of individuals. Although less critical of the individualist focus on rights than are many communitarian thinkers of the present day, she seems to agree with them that we need to think more about our responsibilities and somewhat less about our rights, more about what we owe one another and less about what we are entitled to claim for ourselves. She argues plausibly that the duties owed by children to their parents are of an especially deep and lasting character and are unlike the obligations incurred in voluntary relationships such as personal friendship.

The contrast between responsibilities and rights, implicit throughout the last section of Minow's paper and by now ubiquitous in the political science and public policy literature, raises some conceptual problems. In the first place, the two categories appear to be conceptually intertwined: if I have a right to X, this entails (in most cases at any rate) that someone has a duty to give me X. And if law recognizes a duty as binding, this creates, without further ado, an individual right. If B has a legally binding duty to do something for A, then A has a right that this be done and a legal claim against B should B fail to perform. Furthermore, duties and rights are intertwined in other more indirect ways. Many duties require a supportive context of rights for their fulfillment. The moral duty to care for one's children or one's elderly parents may be difficult to carry out for a woman who cannot claim an equal right to well-paying employment or to child support from an ex-husband. The duty to care for one's partner in a terminal illness is impossible to fulfill for many same-sex domestic partners since, lacking a right to marry, they lack legal next-of-kin status in hospital visitations, decisions about care, and so forth. So it appears that it would be a mistake to focus on duties alone without thinking at the same time of associated rights. It is not clear that Minow makes this mistake, but at least the final section of the paper needs to be read with this warning in mind.

Eskridge's essay is a vivid reminder of the close connection in a tolerant liberal society between promoting love and care and protecting a sphere of individual choice. Like Minow, Eskridge believes that our society needs to think more about commitment and responsibility and that this aspect of traditional family relationships should be given strong public encouragement. He believes that it is both an empirical and an ethical mistake to think of individual selves as free and self-sufficient, cut off from all binding commitments. An empirical mistake because people usually do not live like that: they have interpersonal needs that are a deep part of who they are, and these needs are frequently best satisfied in relationships involving commitments that bind the parties over time in a way that requires them to give up many things they may want at this or that particular time. If we neglect this aspect of people, we end up with an impoverished picture of the self that does not reflect the way we really see ourselves. And this self-sufficient "self" is also ethically impoverished: it is better, Eskridge argues, to live in a way that makes both love and commitment central to one's projects and one's self-conception.

Eskridge seems to me to go wrong when he associates the impoverished picture of the self with the liberal tradition and its conception of personal autonomy. Liberalism does not deny the importance of sociality and responsibility. Liberal autonomy, as Kant, Mill, and a variety of other liberal thinkers depict it, is not the same thing as selfsufficiency and the absence of interpersonal commitment and love. Autonomy, as the Kantian liberal conceives it, is the power to make a plan for one's life, evaluating the various elements of a human life for oneself, and judging which ones are worth pursuing. It involves, then, reflection and choice about value; an autonomous person is envisaged as one whose way of life is validated through some personally undertaken process of deliberation, not by the mere reflex of habit or tradition.[32] But, of course, the procedures used by such a person need not be solitary: all major liberal theorists think public reasoning about value indispensable to the individual's own deliberations. Autonomy traditionally concerns the absence of constraint and authority, not the absence of advice or discussion. Nor need the *content* of the plan of life one chooses for oneself be especially solitary or detached; indeed, most liberal thinkers, including both Kant and Mill, argue that interpersonal friendships and commitments, including family commitments, are very important parts of what such an autonomous person ought to endorse. Nor need they deny that such commitments can enter so deeply into the person that they can be a part of the person's very identity. To see oneself as fundamentally constituted by ties and relations to loved ones and to fellow citizens is in no way incompatible with seeing oneself as a self-governing maker of one's own life choices; indeed, the liberal tradition argues that friendships, marital relationships, and other intimate ties flourish more fully when they do take place in a context of self-government.[33] Eskridge has good arguments against a tradition of thought about personal detachment and self-sufficiency that itself has deep roots in the Western philosophical tradition[34] and, in a different way, in some American popular traditions, which frequently equate manliness with independence of personal love and need. But these arguments seem to me to have little to do with political liberalism, and there seems to be no reason why Eskridge's insights cannot be fully accommodated in a liberal political regime.

Be this as it may, Eskridge, like Minow, combines his strong endorsement of care with an equally strong endorsement of diversity and toleration where the distinct conceptions of family life now prevalent in America are concerned. Like Minow, he points out the many ways in which law constructs possibilities for care and commitment and that these possibilities are not equally available to all citizens. He is not entirely happy calling gay and lesbian families by Kath Weston's by-now well-known name, "families we choose"—he worries that this depicts the family relationship as built on short-term, self-interested choices rather than on long-term commitments. But he is also insistent that the law make available to gay and lesbian people possibilities of committed relationship in forms that they do, in fact, choose for themselves. The legal unavailability of gay and lesbian marriage imposes a special burden on people who are frequently keenly desirous of long-term committed unions. Eskridge argues that there are no good reasons to deny marriage rights to such people: "if commitment is valuable, it ought to be available to lesbian and gay couples on the same terms it is offered to heterosexual ones" (p. 287).

Eskridge ends with a sternly worded challenge to current legal institutions and practices:"A thriving society is one that accommodates the needs of its productive citizens. A worthy polity is one that contributes to the personal flourishing of its citizens" (p. 287). Both Eskridge and Minow suggest that our society is neither thriving nor fully worthy to the extent that it fails to give its gay and lesbian members equal respect and equal treatment. Neither denies that relationships need to be morally assessed, to see whether they contain defects of exploitation, neglect, or inequality. They concede that many family relationships, some same-sex relationships among them, exhibit such defects. But, like all four writers in Part III, they see no good argument that such problems pertain especially and generally to same-sex relationships, and they hold that our polity will profit by expanding the legal understanding of family to include the new constructions of family that such unions will contribute.

William Galston and Sara McLanahan grapple with one of the most critical and urgent problems we face in America today as a nation of families: the increasing prevalence of family units headed by a single parent, usually a mother, and the mounting evidence that children in such families do badly in a number of ways. Both essays present empirical research rather than extensive theoretical discussion. Neither essay spends much time untangling the theoretical issue that concerned Minow and Eskridge, namely the variety of ways in which "family" may be defined. This is in a way unfortunate since this question has an obvious bearing on their empirical analysis. For a "single-parent family" may be many different things: it may be a woman caring for a child alone with no kin or intimate partner; it may be a woman and child living with her mother and grandmother and a variety of other relatives; it may be a woman in a committed lesbian relationship raising the child she has conceived in a previous marriage and so forth. It would seem to be a good thing to ask some further questions of the data in this area in order to find out, for example, whether the relatively poor school performance of single-parented children is more conspicuous when the mother is lacking in support from the extended family. (McLanahan's finding that "family disruption" has the least harmful effects on children among African-Americans than among whites and Hispanics prompts the question whether this is to some extent explained by the strong role played by the extended family in African-American culture; a divorced white mother may be more likely to be lacking in support.

Both Galston and McLanahan focus on the controversial claims about single-parent families made by Charles Murray in *Losing Ground*. Murray believes that single motherhood is encouraged by public support payments and that we ought to get tough with single mothers by denying support—including child-support payments from nonresident fathers. McLanahan rejects the argument that welfare caused the growth in single-parent families as inadequate in explaining both data within the United States and the relationship between the United States and other Western countries. She attributes the rise in single-parent families both to the changing status and opportunities of women and to a broader shift in social norms and values toward ideas of self-expression and self-realization. In her view, an important practical step in addressing our current problems is to get tough with fathers, not mothers, legally inculcating norms of responsibility and care. Here she agrees with both Minow and Eskridge concerning the important role for law in bolstering norms of interpersonal commitment. But she stresses also the need to make sure that our tax structure does not penalize people for getting married and the need to support poor two-parent families with adequate health care and other support systems. Here she echoes Eskridge's point that commitments cannot be undertaken in a vacuum: they require a supportive social context. Rather than blaming people for displaying a lack of commitment, we should address the defects in that context.

Galston also points to economic factors as central in the current difficulties faced by the family. Although many Americans believe that moral decay lies at the heart of our current problems, Galston emphasizes that matters are actually far more complex, and more mundane. Parents have less time to spend with their children than they did previously because it is now far more difficult than it was previously to raise a family on a single income. Increased economic opportunity for women does not make it possible for women with small children to prosper alone; the two-parent family is, if anything, more necessary for child well-being than it was formerly. Government support for children has not, in fact, declined, but government spending supporting adults has increased at a faster pace, largely owing to the increase in numbers of older Americans and their marked political influence.

While he does not support Murray's simple account of the role of welfare in encouraging single motherhood, Galston is concerned about the possible effects of welfare support on the long-term interests of women, as they may turn down work that increases their life prospects in order to maintain their current well-being. Turning to the relationship between poverty and family structure, he argues that the absence of father is indeed harmful to children and that in general divorce has bad consequences for child well-being. (Here again, one might have wished a richer consideration of different styles of family relationship and of the role of the extended family.)

Finally, Galston addresses cultural factors. He argues that a declining sense of commitment and of responsibility for child welfare is at least one factor behind the current decline in child well-being, and he supports using legal strategies to reshape the family in the desired direction, including, possibly, making divorces more difficult to obtain. He does not come to a definite conclusion about such strategies and he would need here to grapple with McLanahan's plausible point that making divorce more difficult would further reduce the number of marriages.

All four writers in this section hold, then, that the family is an institution resulting from a complex combination of individual choices and legal context and that laws and institutions have a powerful role in shaping the ways in which individuals give love and care to one another. All support long-term commitment to the well-being of a small number of intimate family members as an important moral goal, and all see ways in which government could promote this goal more effectively. Finally, all are concerned that government undertake this role with due respect for the diversity of structures within which individuals seek to care for one another. (McLanahan and Galston say less about this last issue than do Minow and Eskridge, and it seems likely that Galston would not support those two writers' very expansive account of the family since he strongly emphasizes the superior benefits of the nuclear two-parent form.)

Justice Bradley assumed that the shape of the family has always been and must always be the same and that sex roles within it are (apart from a few exceptional cases) determined by "nature." Law, in his view, could not alter these facts of nature, it could only either reflect them or fail to reflect them. It is clear, however, that the relationship between law and the family is, in fact, far more complex than this. The family has not always been the same in all times and places. Its shape, the roles of its members, and their access or lack of access to resources and opportunities—all are profoundly affected by laws and institutions. These facts make the questions faced by the law extremely complex. Recognizing their complexity is a necessary first step toward dealing with them well.

Notes

1. For further discussion of the laws, and an enumeration of cases, see Nussbaum, "Lesbian and Gay Rights," in *The Liberation Detente*, ed. M. Leahy, (London: Routledge, 1996). In the challenge to the Georgia sodomy law that led to the U.S. Supreme Court's decision in Bowers v. Hardwick (478 U.S. 186 (1986)) a heterosexual couple originally were involved, but their claim was dismissed for lack of standing on the grounds that they were in no danger of prosecution. More recently, Robin Shahar, an employee in the Georgia attorney general's office who had publicly announced a lesbian marriage, was fired from her job on the grounds that she could not plausibly enforce the state's sodomy law. It was simply assumed that she would be committing sodomy, defined as oral-genital or anal-genital conduct, although this is by no means obvious for a lesbian relationship; and the fact that many heterosexual employees no doubt commit such acts was ignored.

2. Colorado's Amendment 2 is the only statewide referendum of this sort to have been successful so far, and Amendment 2 has been declared unconstitutional by the U.S. Supreme Court.

3. See Nussbaum and Olyan, eds., *Homosexuality in the Major Religious Traditions*, forthcoming.

4. Gender is a "quasi-suspect" classification, giving rise to an intermediate level of scrutiny.

5. This is the case made by Posner for the study of sex as an important part of legal and judicial preparation; see *Sex and Reason* (Cambridge, Mass.: Harvard University Press, 1992).

6. Thus, many who hold that the male-dominated family is a social construct will also grant that it is relatively ubiquitous. This is not an inconsistency, although one then will wonder why the convergence exists.

7. *Sex and Reason*, 98 ff., explaining why, nonetheless, an interest in other sexual practices evolved.

8. *Sex and Reason*, p. 94.

9. In *Sex and Reason*, 101 ff., Posner adopts a genetic account of homosexuality. But the logic of his argument requires only that the forces producing it be university and invariant.

10. "Judge Posner proposes that regulation of sexuality should be maintained or adopted only if it is efficient, or rational in an economic sense" (p. 2). This seems an oversimplification of Posner's position. He says that the economic perspective is "helpful, but . . . not decisive."

This does not, however, much affect Halley's central points, which are directed at conclusions that Posner does derive from economic analysis.

11. This approach, strongly influenced by the work of Gary Becker, is evident in most of Posner's well-known books, including *The Economics of Justice* (Cambridge, Mass.: Harvard University Press, 1981), *Sex and Reason*, and *Private Choices and Public Health: The AIDS Epidemic in an Economic Perspective*, coauthored with Tomas J. Philipson (Cambridge, Mass." Harvard University Press, 1993).

12. Halley's work thus has affiliations with the work of sexuality scholars who have stressed the ways in which resourceful individuals can make something for themselves out of the constraints of their social roles; see, e.g., John J. Winkler, *The Constraints of Desire: The Anthropology of Sex and Gender in Greece* (New York: Routledge, 1990).

13. We might add to this the fact that some of Posner's empirical claims, even in the brief scope of this paper, appear dubious. The claim that lesbians would have been overrepresented in the number of girls sent into nunneries (p. 180), to cite just one example, runs up against a number of difficulties, not least being the difficulty of identifying a sexual orientation in a society in which women were secluded. But the fatal difficulty is that the evidence, though not unequivocal, indicates that selection for nunneries was made quite early in life—some major studies suggest as young as the age of six, see A. Molho and J. Kirchner, "The Dowry Fund and the Marriage Market," in the *Journal of Modern History* 50 (1978): 403–38. The criteria for selection are agreed by all major interpreters, including those, like Molho, who date the age of assignment relatively late—in the teens—to be primarily physical illness or deformity, mental retardation, and/or poverty in the family making the choice.

14. *Baehr v. Lewin*; and see A. Koppelman, "Why Discrimination Against Lesbians and Gay Men is Sex Discrimination," *New York University Law Review* 69 (1994): 197–287.

15. See also Sunstein, *The Partial Constitution* (Cambridge, Mass.: Harvard University Press, 1993).

16. The advantage of "morally irrelevant" is that it is a relatively clear notion about which there is at least some agreement. The notion of "politically irrelevant"—though potentially more precise in that it asks the right question, focusing on the traits that public policy may or may not consider, and allows that citizens may continue to make private moral distinctions in areas that are judged off-limits to public policy—nonetheless remains unclear without the backing of a well worked out political theory, such as the one developed by John Rawls in *Political Liberalism* (New York: Columbia University Press, 1993).

17. 381 U.S. 479 (1965).

18. In Eisenstadt v. Baird, 405 U.S. 438 (1972), an equal-protection argument was used, in connection with the denial of contraception to unmarried individuals, on the grounds that the law in question treated the married and the unmarried differently. Although the unmarried are obviously not a suspect class, this was not relevant since the Court purported to be applying rational basis review rather than strict scrutiny. This very unusual approach to the issue seems fragile, without independent privacy argumentation.

19. Would it be unconstitutional on some other equal-protection ground, according to Sunstein? This remains unclear.

20. Posner, *Sex and Reason*, 341–50.

21. See Nussbaum and Olyan, *Homosexuality*, forthcoming.

22. Consider, for example, the arguments of John Rauls in *Political Liberalism*, which, however, apply to all "comprehensive doctrines," both secular and religious; Rawls clarifies and modifies his view in "The Idea of Public Reason," forthcoming; on the other side, see Philip Quinn, "Political Liberalisms and Their Exclusions of the Religious," (1995): 35–56.

23. Finnis was an expert witness for the state in the Amendment Two case. For his account

of his position, see *Notre Dame Law Journal* (Spring 1995); for some criticisms of Finnis's argument, see Michael Perry, *Notre Dame Law Journal*; M. Nussbaum, "Platonic Love and Colorado Law," *Virginia Law Review* (1994): 1515–1651.

24. See Weithman (p. 237): "I am inclined to agree that there is something both alienating and morally bad about treating one's body as nothing more than an instrument for producing one's own or another's pleasure." Weithman doe snot pause to elaborate the "nothing more" condition, which might possibly suggest more latitude in his position on masturbation than in the position of Finnis.

25. *Bradwell v. Illinois* 83 U.S. (16 Wall.) 130 (1873).

26. *Hoyt v. Florida*, 368 U.S. 57 (1961). See discussion of this and related cases in *Constitutional Law*, ed. G. Stone, L. Seidman, C. Sunstein, and M. Tushnet (Boston: Little, Brown, 1991), 676 ff.

27. See the criticisms of Becker's approach in A. Sen, "Gender and Cooperative Conflicts," in *Persistent Inequalities*, ed. I. Tinker (New York: Oxford, 1991). And see Introduction in *Women, Culture, and Development*, ed. M. Nussbaum and J. Glover. I. Becker has recently modified his approach, conceding that his model assumes too much altruism; see his Nobel Prize address, "The Economic Way of Looking at Life," Novel Committee 1992.

28. J. S. Mill, *The Subjection of Women* (1869); see also "Nature."

29. For a valuable discussion of this history, see Susan Moller Okin, *Women in Western Political Thought* (Princeton: Princeton University Press, 1978); and for a critique, see Okin, *Justice, Gender, and the Family* (New York: Basic Books, 1989).

30. See Nussbaum and Glover, *Women, Culture, and Development*.

31. J. Maritain, "Truth and Human Fellowship," from *On the Use of Philosophy: Three Essays* (Princeton: Princeton University Press, 1961), 24.

32. For a powerful modern accounts of autonomy deriving from the Kantian tradition, see John Rawls, *A Theory of Justice* (Cambridge, Mass.: Harvard University Press, 1971), and Dewey Lectures 1980. A different type of liberal autonomy is the "Perfectionist liberalism" developed in Joseph Raz, *The Morality of Freedom* (Oxford: Clarendon Press, 1986).

33. See the helpful reflections on this point in Jean Hampton, "Feminism and Contractarianism," in *A Mind of One's Own: Feminist Essays on Reason and Objectivity*, ed. L. Antony and C. Witt (Boulder: Westview, 1993); see also Marcia Homiak's paper on Aristotle in the same volume.

34. Its antecedents include Plato, the Greek and Roman Stoics, Spinoza, and others.

Index

Contributors

William N. Eskridge Jr. is Professor of Law at Georgetown University.

David M. Estlund is Associate Professor of Philosophy at Brown University.

William A. Galston is Professor of Public Affairs, and Director of the Center for Ethics and Public Policy at the University of Maryland.

Janet E. Halley is Professor of Law at Stanford University.

Stephen Macedo is Associate Professor of Political Science at Syracuse University.

Catharine A. MacKinnon is Professor of Law at the University of Michigan.

Sara McLanahan is Professor of Sociology and Public Affairs at Princeton University.

Martha Minow is Professor of Law at Harvard University.

Susan Moller Okin is Professor of Political Science, and Director of the Program in Ethics and Society at Stanford University.

Michele M. Moody-Adams is Associate Professor of Philosophy at Indiana University.

Martha C. Nussbaum is Professor of Law and Ethics at the University of Chicago.

Richard A. Posner is Senior Lecturer at the University of Chicago Law School, and Honorable Judge of the U.S. Court of Appeals for the Seventh Circuit.

Nancy L. Rosenblum is Professor of Political Science at Brown University.

Cass R. Sunstein is Professor of Jurisprudence and Policial Science, and Co-Director of the Center for the Study of Constitutionalism in Eastern Europe, at the University of Chicago.

Paul J. Weithman is Assistant Professor of Philosophy at University of Notre Dame.